DICTIONARY OF ENVIRONMENTAL LAW

To
The Hon. James McClelland (1915–1999)
First Chief Judge of the
Land and Environment Court,
New South Wales, Australia

Dictionary of Environmental Law

Alan Gilpin

Honorary Visiting Fellow, University of New South Wales, Australia

Edward Elgar
Cheltenham, UK • Northampton, MA, USA

aog 7987

Published by
Edward Elgar Publishing Limited
Glensanda House
Montpellier Parade
Cheltenham
Glos GL50 1UA
UK

Edward Elgar Publishing, Inc.
136 West Street
Suite 202
Northampton
Massachusetts 01060
USA

A catalogue record for this book
is available from the British Library

Library of Congress Cataloguing in Publication Data
Gilpin, Alan.
    Dictionary of environmental law / Alan Gilpin.
        p.   cm.
    1. Environmental law—Dictionaries.   I. Title.

K3584.6.G55   2000
344'.046'03–dc21

00–021267

ISBN 1 84064 188 6

Typeset by Manton Typesetters, Louth, Lincolnshire, UK.
Printed and bound in the United Kingdom at the University Press, Cambridge

CONTENTS

BOXES

ABBREVIATIONS

APEC	Asia-Pacific Economic Cooperation Forum
ASEAN	Association of South-East Asian Nations
CFCs	Chlorofluorocarbons
DDT	Dichloro-diphenyl-trichloro-ethane
ECE	Economic Commission for Europe
EEZ	Exclusive economic zone
EIA	Environmental impact assessment
EIS	Environmental impact statement
EPA	Environmental Protection Agency (US)
ESCAP	Economic and Social Commission for Asia and the Pacific
EU	European Union
FAO	Food and Agriculture Organization
GDP	Gross domestic product
GEF	Global Environment Facility
ha	Hectare
ILO	International Labour Organization
IMO	International Maritime Organization
IPCC	Intergovernmental Panel on Climate Change
IUCN	International Union for the Conservation of Nature and Natural Resources (WCU)
MW	Megawatt
NAFTA	North American Free Trade Association
NATO	North Atlantic Treaty Organization
NGO	Non-government organization
NSW	New South Wales
OECD	Organization for Economic Cooperation and Development
ppbv	Parts per billion by volume
ppmv	Parts per million by volume
UNCED	United Nations Conference on Environment and Development
UNDP	United Nations Development Program
UNEP	United Nations Environment Program
UNESCO	United Nations Educational, Scientific and Cultural Organization
UNICEF	United Nations Children's Fund
USEPA	United States Environmental Protection Agency
WCU	World Conservation Union (IUCN)
WHO	World Health Organization
WMO	World Meterological Organization

WTO   World Trade Organization
WWF   World Wide Fund for Nature

PREFACE

Material in this dictionary has been used in undergraduate and postgraduate courses at several Australian and Asian universities, recently in the degree of Master of Environmental Engineering Science in the School of Civil and Environmental Engineering, University of New South Wales, Australia. The work reflects my experience as a Commissioner of Inquiry (Environment and Planning) conducting some 50 public inquiries in Australia over ten years. My experience as chairman of the Third Party Appeals Tribunal in Victoria was particularly valuable, embracing all aspects of environmental law. Earlier experience in Britain has also been most valuable, involving inquiries into major power stations, slum clearance and redevelopment schemes, including the first public inquiry in Britain into a smoke control order. My background in environmental law was also enriched by my experience as Chief Environmental Health Officer, County Borough of Wallasey, England; as Director of Air Pollution Control, Queensland, Australia; as Chairman of the Environment Protection Authority, Victoria, Australia; and as Advisor to the Australian House of Representatives Committee on Environment and Conservation, examining various branches of environmental and planning policies. My doctorate contributed also to the abandonment of Australian nuclear power plans.

Dr Alan Gilpin
Honorary Visiting Fellow
School of Civil and Environmental Engineering
University of New South Wales

A

Acid Rain

Rain or snow that contains significant amounts of sulfuric acid or nitric acid. Sulfuric or nitric acid is formed when sulfur dioxide (SO_2) or nitrogen oxide (NO_x) emitted by industry or transport undergo a chemical transformation in the atmosphere. The US National Commission on Air Quality, in its 1981 report, found that the process by which manmade pollutants were transformed into acid rain was now 'reasonably well known'. It described how SO_2 or NO_x gas released into the atmosphere is first oxidized to sulfate or nitrate particles. If water vapor is present, the particles are further transformed into sulfuric or nitric acid which contaminates rain, snow, or fog. Alternatively, sulfate or nitrate particulates may be deposited on the ground in dry form, later combining with surface water or groundwater to produce acid.

In the United States, rain that is ten to 40 times as acidic as normal rainfall has been occurring frequently in many parts of New England and New York. The average pH of rainfall over substantial portions of the Northeast is 4.3, approximately ten times normal acidity. Comparable levels of acidity are occurring in many parts of Canada. Highly acidic rainfall has also been observed in a number of southeastern states, particularly Florida, Virginia, Texas and North Carolina, in the Northern Plains states of Minnesota and Wisconsin, and in the Colorado Rockies.

In 1979, the US President established a ten-year comprehensive Federal Acid Rain Assessment Program to be planned and managed by a standing Acid Rain Co-ordination Committee. The assessment program includes applied and basic research on acid rain effects, monitoring, transport modes, and the study of control measures. Collaboration with the Canadian and Mexican governments, and with other nations and international organizations, was anticipated.

In August, 1984, New York became the first state to legislate on acid rain. By the end of that year, the areas of the state most at risk had to be identified, and tolerance levels for sulfur deposition determined. Rules governing emissions from the industrial burning of coal and oil were to be produced by 1986, and to come into force by 1988.

With respect to the acid rain issue, the debate in the US Congress has split along regional lines: members from the Northeast have pressed for a tough control program, while members from the Midwest fear a control program could hamper the region's economy. The West, neither a primary victim of nor contributor to acid rain, does not want to pay to control it.

The Swedish Fisheries Board has now done a national survey of Swedish lakes and has found that 18 000 out of a total of about 90 to 100 thousand are acid. These lakes, poor in calcium, magnesium and nutrients, are situated (mainly in the southwest of Sweden) in areas with coniferous forests and pre-Cambrian bedrock. The pH of the acid lakes varies between four and about 5.5. Lakes have a natural defense mechanism or buffering capacity caused by the presence of hydrogen carbonate. However, the majority of Scandinavian lakes and watercourses have low lime content, and thus a low content of hydrogen carbonate, and are therefore particularly vulnerable to acidification. While it was agreed that there were many factors involved in the acidification of lakes and soils in Sweden and other parts of Scandinavia, there was no doubt that sulfur and nitrogen compounds resulting from combustion of fossil fuels in Europe were transported over long distances and contributed to the acidification problem in vulnerable areas.

Acid precipitation over southern Norway has increased considerably in recent years. Measurements have shown that there is a marked decrease in the pH value in rivers and lakes after rain. In winter, grey snow has sometimes been observed. In the southernmost counties in particular the soil is poor with low calcium levels, so that acid precipitation is only partly neutralized by the soil and thus immediately affects the pH value of rivers and lakes. An observed decline in stocks of fish in a large number of lakes may be related to increased acidity. Acid also has a leaching effect on mineral substances in the soil with possible detrimental effects on forest growth. Norway takes considerable interest in the new OECD research project on the long-range movement of air pollutants.

An October 1983 report to the West German Bundestag (federal parliament) suggested that more than one-third of West German forests had been damaged by acid rain. In Bavaria and the Black Forest it was claimed that nearly half of the trees had been damaged. New limits on emissions from power stations were announced later in 1983 aiming to reduce SO_2 emissions by over 85 per cent.

In 1984, the Netherlands Environment Minister released a plan to reduce industrial SO_2 emissions by 70 per cent, NO_x emissions from motor vehicles by 30 per cent and ammonia released from agricultural fertilizers by 50 per cent, by the end of the century. During the same year, the French government announced its intentions to halve SO_2 emissions by 1990.

However, the United States and British governments continued to question the relationships between SO_2 emissions and acid deposition.

The US Clean Air Act of 1990 aimed at cutting SO_2 emissions virtually in half by the year 2000. This was Phase 1 of the US Acid Rain Program linked with the US Emission Trading Program. Phase 2 begins in 2000 with a further substantial reduction in sulfur emissions.

In 1998, Resources for the Future published the first integrated assessment of both the projected costs and benefits of Title IV of the 1990 amendments to the US Clean Air Act. The report concluded that the dollar value of reduced mortality risk alone measured several times the expected costs of compliance with the acid rain program.

Administrative Law

Law regulating the powers, procedures and actions of public administrators, departments and agencies. Administrative law embraces rule-making, or the power to make regulations having the force of law, the issuing of licences, with or without attached conditions (or the refusal or revocation of licences), affecting the operation of a range of businesses, powers of inspection and investigation, and powers of enforcement, including prosecution. All these features are common to pollution-control legislation in general and much environmental protection legislation. Such laws bestow considerable powers on ministers, public officials, departments and agencies; they also restrict what can be done by these bodies, often naming avenues of appeal.

See also:
Adversarial Procedure; Common Law; Environmental Law; Statutory Instrument.

Adversarial Procedure

A court procedure observed primarily in countries in which the Anglo-American legal system of common law prevails. The system requires the opposing sides to bring out pertinent facts and information, and to present and cross-examine witnesses, each side hoping to gain an advantage to its side of the case. The adversarial approach is used also in UK public inquiry procedures.

African Economic Community (AEC)

An economic community established by a treaty adopted in 1991. The treaty contains broad economic objectives promoting economic, social and cultural development and the integration of African economies. It promotes self-sustainable development. With respect to the environment, the treaty recommends the harmonization and coordination of environmental protection policies throughout the continent. The AEC functions as an integral part of the Organization of African Unity (OAU). It has several specialized committees including a committee on natural resources and environment.

An obligation is placed on member states to promote a healthy environment and to adopt appropriate national, regional and continental policies, strategies and programs for environmental development and protection. The dumping of hazardous wastes is to be banned where possible or subject to careful management and processing. Dispute resolution attracts special attention. Some forty states have ratified the treaty.

Agenda 21

Adopted by UNCED on 14 June 1992, a comprehensive document summing up the international consensus on actions, necessary to move humanity towards the goal of sustainable development during the twenty-first century. The objective is to alleviate poverty, hunger, sickness and illiteracy worldwide, while at the same time arresting the deterioration of the ecosystems on which humanity depends to sustain life. Agenda 21 is divided into four principal sections:

1. *Social and economic dimensions*   The seven chapters which comprise the first section address central issues such as poverty, health, consumption patterns, population, trade and resource transfers between countries, human settlement patterns, and integration of environment and development in decision-making.
2. *Conservation and management of resources for development*   The 14 chapters of this section deal with a very wide range of issues such as the atmosphere, land resources, deforestation, desertification, mountain development, agriculture, biological diversity, biotechnology, oceans, freshwater resources, toxic chemicals, hazardous wastes, solid wastes and radioactive wastes.
3. *Strengthening the role of major groups*   The nine chapters of this section deal with women's affairs, youth and children, indigenous peoples, NGOs, local authorities, trade unions, business and industry, science and technology, and farming.
4. *Means of implementation*   The eight chapters of this section deal with finance and the funding of Agenda 21 programs, technology transfer, science in sustainable development, education and training, capacity building, institutional arrangements, legal instruments, and information for decision-making.

See also:
Environmental Law; Framework Environmental Laws.

Air Pollution

The contamination of the atmosphere with undesirable solids, liquids and gases. In a strict sense, air may be considered polluted when there is added to it any substance foreign or additional to its normal composition. This definition of pollution is much too wide, however, for the purposes of practical air pollution control, and the term 'air pollution' is usually restricted to those conditions in which the general atmosphere contains substances in concentrations which are harmful, or likely to be harmful, to humans and their environment. A fuller definition, of American origin, is: 'substances present in the atmosphere in concentrations great enough to interfere directly or indirectly with man's comfort, safety or health, or with the full use or enjoyment of his property'. With respect to health, this reiterates the dictum that there are no such things as toxic substances, only toxic concentrations. The concept of concentration cannot be divorced, however, from time or duration of exposure; or from the acute or chronic effects likely to arise from high short-term or low long-term exposures, respectively.

The degree of air pollution varies according to population density, industrial development, geographical situation, meteorological characteristics, social and economic structure, and local customs. The contaminants arising from human activities (power production, the metallurgical and petrochemical industries, and transport) include sulfur oxides, nitrogen oxides, carbon monoxide, soot and other compounds; they have clearly defined effects on vegetation, property and local climate, and are also believed to have adverse effects on human health.

The history of air pollution has been characterized by a number of dramatic incidents, notably the Meuse Valley, 1930; Donora, Pennsylvania, 1948; London, England, 1952 and 1962; Poza Rico, Mexico, 1950; and Seveso, Italy, 1976. Yet some of the more spectacular long-term effects have received little publicity.

Air Quality Act, 1967, US

An act to amend the Clean Air Acts, 1963 and 1965, revamping the whole US clean air program. It provided procedures for the issuance of air quality criteria, the delineation of atmospheric areas and air quality control regions, the setting of standards, and the adoption of implementation plans by the states. The act also authorized planning grants to air pollution control agencies. If the states failed to act, provision was made for federal intervention.

The act also extended federal powers to control emissions from new motor vehicles, and promoted a national emission standard study for stationary sources; for the first time, national standards could be set for automotive emissions. In 1970, the National Air Pollution Control Administration established emission criteria for motor vehicle pollutants such as carbon monoxide, hydrocarbons and nitrogen oxides.

Following the designation of control regions, each state had to formulate ambient air quality standards (as opposed to emission standards) and an enforcement plan.

See also:
Clean Air Amendment Act, 1970, US.

Alaska National Interest Lands Conservation Act, 1980, US

An act which expanded the Alaska national parks system by 45 million acres* (18 million ha), and wildlife refuges under the US Fish and Wildlife Service by 54 million acres (22 million ha); the US Forest Service also gained about 3 million acres (1.2 million ha).

Alaskan National Parks

A range of national parks, wildlife refuges and wilderness areas established since the initial creation of Denali National Park and Preserve in 1917. Denali is an area of mountain peaks on the northern flank of the Alaska Range. A special feature is Mount McKinley, the highest peak in North America. Denali was followed by the establishment of the Katmai National Park and Preserve in 1918 (including the Valley of Ten Thousand Smokes), Glacier Bay National Park and Preserve in 1925 and the Sitka National Historic Park.

Among the notable features of Glacier Bay are great tidewater glaciers, a dramatic range of flora and an unusual variety of wildlife, including brown and black bears and mountain goats. The Tongass and Chugach national forests in the southeast and south-central regions, respectively, are also public land reserves. The national parks and wildlife sanctuary system was expanded by the US National Interest Land Conservation Act, 1980.

Amazonian Rain Forest

A massive tropical rain forest, occupying the drainage basin of the Amazon River and its tributaries covering an area of 7 000 000 sq km. It comprises 40 per cent of Brazil's total land area, bounded by the Guiana Highlands in the north, the Andes Mountains in the west, the Brazilian central plateau to the south, and the Atlantic Ocean to the east. The rain forest stretches from the swampy mangroves in the east near the Atlantic Ocean to the tree line of the Andes.

The Amazon Valley is rather like an immense canyon, opening into the Atlantic Ocean with a mouth more than 400 km wide. With 1000 tributaries, it is the largest basin area in the world. The Amazonian rain forest has a wide variety of trees including myrtle, acacia, rosewood, Brazil nut, rubber tree, mahogany, cedar and palm. Wildlife includes the jaguar, matee, tapir, red deer, capybara and several kinds of monkeys. The rich bird life of the forest includes parrots, toucans, haugnests, perdizes, cormorants and scarlet ibises. Fish include catfish, electric eels and piranhas.

The Amazon River is the greatest river in the world in its volume and the area of its drainage basin. The Amazon flows some 6400 km across northern Brazil to its mouth in the Atlantic Ocean. It has been estimated that from 20 to 25 per cent of all the water that runs off the surface of the Earth is carried by the Amazon. The average annual discharge is roughly ten times that of the Mississippi River and about four times that of the Congo River. Its length is second only to that of the Nile.

In 1978, a Treaty for Amazonian Cooperation was agreed by affected countries of the region to promote harmonious developments and permit equitable sharing of the benefits. Joint studies were to be promoted for the better use of the natural resources within the region. An Amazonian Cooperation Council was created, working under the ministers for Foreign Affairs.

The date of entry for the treaty was 1980, with the endorsements of Bolivia, Brazil, Colombia, Ecuador, Guyana, Peru, Surinam and Venezuela.

See also:
Brazil.

Argentina

The Argentine Republic is a federal republic with two legislative houses, the Senate and the Chamber of Deputies. Its capital is Buenos Aires and in 1997 it had a population of 35 million at a density of 12.7 per sq km. It is located in South America, adjacent to Chile, facing the Atlantic Ocean. See Box 1 for the evolution of environmental law.

Box I   Argentina: evolution of environmental law

1868   Cholera epidemic; industries ordered to destroy their wastes without polluting the River Riachuelo
1871   Yellow fever epidemic; certain polluting industries banned in Buenos Aires
1934   Nahuel Huapi National Park established; Argentina's first national park
1937   Los Glacieres National Park established
1964   First studies into air pollution in Buenos Aires
1970   National parks, natural reserves and natural monuments classified
1972   Creation of an Interministerial Commission for Environmental Conservation to advise the Ministry of Social Welfare
1973   A secretariat of Natural Resources and the Human Environment created
1976   National Law on Environmental Pollution Control
1977   National Law to Control Pollution from Industries
1979   National Law on Prevention of Sea Pollution
1980   National Law Relating to Pesticides; National Law Relating to International Trade in Endangered Species of Fauna and Flora
1981   National Law Relating to Conservation of Fauna; National Law Relating to Soil Conservation
1983   A secretariat of Housing and Environmental Order created within the Ministry of Health and Social Welfare
1995   Life expectancy: 69.6 years for males; 76.8 years for females

---

Asia-Pacific Economic Cooperation Forum (APEC)

An international forum established in 1989 to encourage free trade in the Pacific area and to consider security and development issues. APEC comprises 17 nations: Australia, Brunei, Canada, Chile, China, Indonesia, Japan, Malaysia, Mexico, New Zealand, Papua New Guinea, the Philippines, Singapore, South Korea, Taiwan, Thailand and the USA, with others such as Russia, India, Vietnam and Peru seeking to join. The existing membership (1998) has a combined population of over two billion.

In the Bogor Declaration of 1994, APEC stated that it would 'achieve free and open trade and investment in the region' by 2010 for the most industrialized APEC economies, and by 2020 for the less industrialized. At the 1995 meeting in Osaka, it was also decided to begin implementing individual action plans (IAPs) and collective action plans (CAPs) from 1997, to start the process.

In 1997, the Indonesian forest fires, which blanketed Malaysia, Singapore, the Philippines and Brunei with a smoky haze, together with the international differences on global warming, reminded APEC of environmental issues in the region. Studies suggest that environmental and pollution effects cost the APEC economies up to 8 per cent of annual GDP. The problems are aggravated by varying environmental standards throughout the region. APEC is ideally placed now to tackle the problems of fire, drought, Pacific fishing stocks, acid rain, poverty, safe drinking water, infant mortality, sanitation, primary and preventive health care, education and the promotion of sustainable development.

An APEC Environmental Vision Statement was issued at a meeting of the APEC Ministers for the Environment held in Vancouver, Canada, in 1994, prior to the Bogor Summit. The statement affirmed APEC's commitment to sustainable development in the spirit of the Rio Declaration on Environment and Development. The Ministers asserted that environmental protection and economic growth are inseparably linked, and supported the integration of environmental considerations into relevant policy development and economic decisions throughout the region.

Another document issued at the meeting was entitled 'The Framework of Principles for Integrating Economy and Environment in APEC'. The APEC approach is to promote the principles of sustainable growth, equitable development and national stability.

Association of South-East Asian Nations (ASEAN)

Formed initially in 1967, the association today comprises Brunei, Cambodia, Indonesia, Laos, Malaysia, Myanmar, the Philippines, Singapore, Thailand and Vietnam, with a combined population of over 500 million. ASEAN promotes trade and regional security, facilitating the settling of disputes between members and promoting joint ventures within the region. ASEAN has been working towards the establishment of a common market by 2003 by phasing in tariff reductions and promoting economic growth around the region.

In 1985, ASEAN reached an Agreement on the Conservation of Nature and Natural Resources. The aim was to promote joint and individual state action for the conservation and management of natural resources within the ASEAN region, promoting sustainable development, preserving genetic diversity, promoting soil conservation and environment protection, reversing environmental degradation, creating national parks and reserves, and promoting harmonious

Box 2 *Kuala Lumpur Accord on Environment and Development issued by the ASEAN Ministers for the Environment at the Fourth ASEAN Meeting of Ministers for the Environment in Kuala Lumpur, Malaysia, 19 June 1990*

Aware, that the management of the environment and the pursuit of sustainable development are imperative to secure the well-being of the people of ASEAN today and in the future,

Further aware, that the management of the environment and the pursuit of sustainable development require close co-operation between the member-countries of ASEAN in particular and global co-operation in general, and that ASEAN should endeavour to strengthen such co-operation,

Conscious, that the United Nations Conference on Environment and Development, to be held in 1992, provides a forum and an opportunity to further promote such co-operation and for ASEAN to assert its views on environmental management and sustainable development,

Recognizing, that the formulation of such views and practices would require preparatory steps and studies, jointly as well as separately,

Also recognizing that in such formulation, it would be beneficial to take note of:

the Manila Declaration of 1981

the Bangkok Declaration of 1984

the Jakarta Resolution of 1987

the Manila Summit Declaration of 1987 and

the Langkawi Declaration of 1989,

We the ASEAN Ministers for the Environment hereby agree

1. To initiate efforts leading towards concrete steps pertaining to environmental management, including:
   a. the formulation of an ASEAN strategy for sustainable development and a corresponding action programme,
   b. the harmonisation of environmental quality standards,
   c. the harmonisation of transboundary pollution prevention and abatement practices,
   d. the undertaking of research and development and the promotion of the use of clean technologies.
2. To initiate efforts leading towards concrete steps pertaining to natural resource management, including:
   a. the harmonisation of approaches in natural resource assessment,

Box 2 continued

    b.   the development of joint natural resource management pro-
        grammes,

    c.   the development and harmonisation of procedures aimed at
        obtaining a better reflection of the state of natural wealth in
        the context of the System of National Accounts.

3.   To initiate efforts enabling the inclusion of environmental factors
    into economic calculations and thus providing a better base for
    international economic co-operation.

4.   To develop and formulate a common ASEAN position to be pre-
    sented to the Ministerial Level Conference on the Environment
    for Asia and the Pacific and later to the United Nations Confer-
    ence on Environment and Development in 1992, including:

    a.   affirming ASEAN's commitment to the pursuit of sustainable
        development,

    b.   stressing the need to strengthen regional and international
        co-operation and proposing the principles upon which such
        co-operation should be based,

    c.   emphasizing the importance of a global environmental agenda
        which reflects the priorities and concerns of all countries,

    d.   calling attention to the patterns of international relations that
        inhibit the implementation of national environmental efforts in
        developing countries and their participation in global environ-
        mental efforts,

    e.   reiterating the urgency for a supportive and predictable inter-
        national economic environment which promotes economic
        growth and development of all countries,

    f.   stressing the need for equitable sharing of responsibilities and
        allocation of liabilities in global environmental efforts,

    g.   stressing that although global environmental efforts will benefit
        the common good, such benefits should be shared equitably,
        including the benefits of Research and Development,

    h.   underlining the need for substantial additional resources to
        assist developing countries to pursue their goals of sustainable
        development as well as access to, and transfer of, environmen-
        tally sound technologies at affordable costs and the
        establishment of appropriate funding mechanisms.

cooperation. The agreement was endorsed by Brunei, Indonesia, Malaysia, the Philippines, Singapore and Thailand.

In 1995, ASEAN agreed to declare the region a nuclear-free zone, banning the testing, storage and siting of nuclear weapons in the region. The treaty was part of a regional effort to stop France and China exploding devices.

Box 2 records the Kuala Lumpur Accord of 1990 reached by the ASEAN Ministers for the Environment. In 1997, ASEAN approved a Regional Haze Action Plan to address the problems of smoke haze in the region, caused by land and forest fires.

Australia

The Commonwealth of Australia is a federal parliamentary state with two legislative houses, the House of Representatives and the Senate. It had a population in 1997 of 18 million at a density of 2.4 persons per sq km. Australia comprises six states and two Territories, with Canberra as the capital. It is a member of the Australia and New Zealand Environment and Conservation Council (ANZECC). Located in Oceania, it has close working economic relations with New Zealand. See Box 3 for the evolution of federal and state environmental law.

Australia–China Migratory Birds Agreement

A bilateral agreement between Australia and the People's Republic of China for the protection of migratory birds and their environment. In 1986, the parties arrived at a mutually agreed text and list of species. The Towra Point Nature Reserve on the southern side of Botany Bay, Sydney, plays an important part in the agreement.

Australia–Japan Migratory Birds Agreement

An agreement between the Australian and Japanese governments for the protection of migratory birds and birds in danger of extinction. It was signed in Tokyo in 1974 and ratified in 1981. Towra Point Nature Reserve on the southern side of Botany Bay, Sydney, plays an important part in the agreement; management plans are required under the agreement. Towra Point is a major site for wading birds on the NSW coast.

Box 3   Australia: evolution of environmental law

1879	Royal National Park established, Sydney
1958–64	Australian states introduce clean air legislation
1964–79	Australian states introduce solid- and liquid-waste management and anti-litter legislation
1970	New South Wales (NSW) establishes the State Pollution Control Commission; Victoria (Vic) establishes the Environment Protection Authority and the Land Conservation Council
1970–71	Australian states introduce water pollution control legislation
1971	Australian Environment Council established; Western Australia (WA) establishes an Environment Protection Authority
1972	South Australia (SA) establishes an Environment Protection Council
1972–78	Australian states introduce noise control legislation
1973	Tasmania establishes a Department of the Environment
1974	Australian (federal) government introduces EIA legislation
1975	Australian government creates the Great Barrier Reef Marine Park Authority and the Australian Heritage Commission
1978	Victoria introduces EIA legislation
1979	NSW introduces EIA legislation and creates a Department of Environment and Planning
1980	Northern Territory establishes a Conservation Commission
1981	SA establishes a Department of Environment and Planning
1983	National conservation strategy adopted by most states; World Heritage Properties Conservation Act
1985	National unleaded petrol (gasoline) program adopted
1986	WA Environment Protection Act; Protection of Moveable Cultural Heritage Act
1987	Murray–Darling Basin Commission created; Ningaloo Marine Park created off WA coast; Queensland creates Department of Environment and Heritage; Environment Institute of Australia established
1992	Intergovernmental agreement on the environment; national strategy adopted for ecologically sustainable development; NSW creates Environment Protection Authority
1994	National strategy for the conservation of Australia's biological diversity

Box 3   continued

1996	National Environment Protection Council formed: adoption of the Australian Natural Heritage Charter
1997	NSW passes Native Vegetation Conservation Act; Contaminated Land Management Act; Protection of the Environment Operations Act; and the Environmental Planning and Assessment Amendment Act. Under the Kyoto Convention on Climate Change, Australia negotiated an increase in its carbon dioxide emissions of 8 per cent by 2010. No regrets measures being introduced
1999	Federal government introduces Environment Protection and Biodiversity Conservation Act; WA and NSW introduce new environmental laws; Great Australian Bight Marine Park proclaimed; Blue Mountains National Park created; Queensland Environment Protection Authority established; National Pollution Inventory Program introduced; Regional Forests Agreement Bill; Australian Radiation Protection and Nuclear Safety Acts; Victorian Environmental Science Centre created

B

Basel Convention

A global environmental treaty to strictly control the transboundary movements of hazardous wastes, obliging the participating parties to ensure the environmentally sound management of wastes and their disposal. The convention was adopted in 1989, coming into force in 1992. The first meeting of the Conference of the Parties to the Basel Convention took place in 1992 at which a draft protocol on liability and compensation for damage resulting from the transboundary movement of hazardous wastes and their disposal was prepared. At the Second Meeting held in Geneva, Switzerland, in 1994, the Conference of the Parties decided to establish an immediate prohibition of all transboundary movements of hazardous wastes which are destined for final disposal from OECD to non-OECD countries. The transboundary movement of hazardous wastes destined for recycling or recovery operations was phased out in 1997.

The Secretariat of the Convention has provided technical and legal advice for the elaboration of regional conventions and protocols for the control of transboundary movements of hazardous wastes in such regions as Africa, the Mediterranean, the Caribbean and the South Pacific. UNEP works closely with the Secretariat of the Convention. Assistance is also being provided to developing countries for the improvement of infrastructure and institutional capacities and appropriate legislative frameworks. Technical guidelines are being further developed for the sound management of hazardous wastes. Clean technologies are being encouraged. Enforcement mechanisms are being strengthened.

Bayer Public Inquiry, Australia

In 1987, a public inquiry conducted under the Environmental and Assessment Act, NSW, Australia, to assess the environmental implications of a proposal for a plant to produce agricultural and veterinary chemicals, to be located at Botany Bay, Sydney. The proposal attracted many objectors, mainly residents of the Kurnell Peninsula. After reviewing all the evidence, the commissioners failed to be satisfied that the proposal was environmentally acceptable. The development application was refused by the NSW Minister for Planning. Box 4 offers extracts from the final report.

Box 4   *Proposed Bayer Australia Ltd Facilities for the Formulation and
Storage of Agricultural and Veterinary Products at Kurnell Peninsula,
Sydney, Australia 1987: summary of the Commission of Inquiry
findings and recommendations to the NSW Minister for Planning*

This Commission of Inquiry concerns a highly controversial development application by Bayer Australia Limited to develop its land at
Kurnell and establish facilities for the formulation of agricultural and
veterinary products, the filling of aerosols for house and garden products and the storage of certain pharmaceuticals, imported chemicals
and finished products awaiting distribution to customers. Products
include insecticides, fungicides, herbicides, cattle dips and sprays, and
sheep drench, many of which contain toxic chemicals. It should be
noted that this proposal is for the formulation (mixing) of chemicals
and not for the manufacture of chemicals, although the prospects of
future manufacturing were foreshadowed by Bayer at the Inquiry. The
Bayer site has been unused for some time. It was formerly owned by
Phillips Australia Chemicals Pty Ltd, who produced carbon black and
synthetic rubber there.

The Commissioners have completed a review of all the submissions
presented to the Inquiry since conclusion of the public hearings together with subsequent written submissions from parties on conditions
that might be attached to consent should it be granted. These submissions on conditions included Bayer's submission setting out its strong
objections to a number of environmental controls proposed by the
Department of Environment and Planning as a result of the Department's environmental assessment of the project.

As a result of the review of submissions the Commissioners recommend to the Minister that consent to the proposed Bayer project at
Kurnell be refused.

In summary, the Commissioners find as follows:

1.   We are not satisfied on the evidence put to the Inquiry that the
     Bayer project would operate without harmful effect on the local
     environment of the Kurnell Peninsula, in particular, nature re-
     serves, oyster leases, fishing and prawn breeding grounds and
     wetlands of Botany Bay generally.
2.   On the evidence put to the Inquiry, considerable uncertainties in
     present knowledge exist about the impact of toxic chemicals on
     sensitive marine environments of the kind found at the Botany
     Bay wetlands.

Box 4   continued

3. The evidence does not establish with certainty that emissions of toxic chemicals even at low levels from all sources would not have a detrimental environmental impact on the Kurnell Peninsula, particularly the aquatic environment.

4. The proposals for the containment of surface water run-off and collection on-site do not establish with certainty that contaminated waters would not enter the aquatic environment.

5. Spillages of toxic chemicals are likely to occur on Captain Cook Drive through accidents. Captain Cook Drive is of substandard design and construction and in poor condition. It carries considerable traffic, residential, recreational and heavy trucks. Captain Cook Drive runs along the foreshore fringe of the wetlands. Toxic chemical spillages are incapable of containment on Captain Cook Drive and could have a disastrous long-term impact on the wetlands of Botany Bay. The Department of Environment and Planning's recommended road improvements for Bayer to undertake would not eliminate this risk on Captain Cook Drive. Bayer objected to undertaking these works. No means have been identified to adequately mitigate such damage, or to reverse the long-term harm to the environment that may occur.

6. Bayer in its submissions to the Inquiry objected strongly to a number of environmental controls on the project which the Department of Environment and Planning considered essential if the plant was to operate in a satisfactory environmental manner. The Commissioners are not confident the stringent controls proposed are capable of practical application and strict enforcement on the Bayer site, particularly in view of Bayer's strong objection and submissions by the State Pollution Control Commission on difficulties of adequate, independent and constant supervision of the proposed high-temperature incinerator.

7. Conservation of the wetlands should have priority at Kurnell Peninsula and those wetlands should be protected from environmental damage likely to be caused by location of new industries at Kurnell.

8. Alternative sites have not been adequately explored.

9. Our findings do not preclude other types of industry locating within the industrial zone at Kurnell provided it can be established, with certainty, on the merits of each case, that hazardous industry is likely to operate without damage to the environment of the Peninsula and the surrounding waterways. Some anomalies

Box 4   continued

> exist in present and proposed zonings and land use controls on the Peninsula in relation to industrial zoning, the lands of Besmaw Pty Ltd, proposed regional open space, marine and nature reserves.
>
> 10.   It is regrettable that Bayer Australia Limited have spent in the order of $4 million on acquisition and upgrading of buildings and facilities on the site prior to determination of their development application. The Commissioners find this surprising in view of the controversial nature of the Bayer pesticide and veterinary products plant and its potential for adverse impact on the local environment. However, should the project be refused consent, as we recommend, Bayer should be able to recoup, at least, a substantial amount of funds already spent on acquisition and improvement of the site through sale.
>
> For these reasons, which are commented upon in more detail in the Commissioners' report, we recommend that the Bayer Australia Limited application for Kurnell be refused.
>
> *Note:*   The decision of the NSW Minister for Planning was to immediately refuse the development application of Bayer Australia.

Beaver Committee on Air Pollution, 1954

In 1954, the Beaver Committee on Air Pollution reported to the Minister of Housing and Local Government on its findings into the London smog disaster of 1952, in which some 4000 additional deaths occurred. The report declared that air pollution on the scale familiar in Britain was a social and economic evil that should no longer be tolerated. The committee was confident that the carrying out of its proposals would secure happier and more healthy living conditions for millions of people. Also that, on all counts, the cost of the cure would be far less than the national loss in allowing the evil to continue.

The committee was satisfied that the most serious immediate problems to be tackled were smoke, grit and dust. An objective of the recommendations was to reduce smoke in the most heavily polluted areas by 80 per cent within ten to 15 years. This would mean relief from air pollution not known in many parts of the country for more than a century. It recommended a Clean Air Act with appropriate measures against industrial and domestic pollution, largely through the introduction of smoke control areas.

The committee examined the economic cost of air pollution referring to many earlier studies, assessing both direct and indirect costs. The findings were published in considerable detail in Appendix II of its report (*Committee on Air Pollution Report*, 1954). Sir Hugh Beaver subsequently reviewed these estimates and considered them too low.

Smoke control areas were introduced under the Clean Air Act, 1956, the concept being a geographical area proclaimed smoke free.

Beneficial Use

In the context of statutory and environmental planning, a use of the environment or any element or segment of the environment that is conducive to public benefit, welfare safety or health, and which requires protection from the effects of waste discharges, emissions, deposits and despoliation. Beneficial uses include: potable water supply for drinking, domestic and municipal purposes; agricultural and industrial water supply; habitats for the support and propagation of fish and other aquatic life; recreational activities such as bathing, fishing and boating; scenic and aesthetic enjoyment; navigation; and wildlife habitats. A residual use is a use other than a beneficial use such as the disposal of liquid effluents into water, after treatment. The term 'beneficial use' occurs frequently in planning and environmental law.

Benefit–Cost Analysis

A technique developed in the United States in response to a legal requirement imposed in 1936 on the water resource projects of the federal government; this requirement specified that projects be undertaken only 'if the benefits to whomsoever they may accrue are in excess of the estimated costs' (US Flood Control Act, 1936). Efforts to implement this requirement led to the preparation of a *Green Book* by a federal interagency committee composed of the representatives of the major water-resource agencies. This report embodied the general principles of economic analysis as they were to be applied in the formulation and evaluation of federal water-resource projects. The principles of benefit–cost analysis (known as cost–benefit analysis in the United Kingdom) have since been applied to a wide range of projects and to the design of public policies in various areas, including environmental planning. The principles have been applied, despite the inherent difficulties, to pollution control, transportation, urban development, electric power, health, education, welfare, and in social issues such as equity, income distribution and unemployment. Benefit–cost analyses proceed by adding up total money costs and benefits (reduced to present worth), generally disregarding who incurs the costs and receives the benefits. If the money aggregate is positive, this is taken to indicate that the gainers could compensate the losers and still be better off after the project is completed. If the net monetary gain is negative, the compensation test fails. The net monetary gains are generally held to measure the efficiency of government projects, or policy changes.

See also:
Regulatory Impact Analysts (RIA), US.

Best Practice Concepts

As in many areas of activity, several concepts of best practice have emerged in the environmental arena, being applied by practitioners, proponents, operators and government agencies. Six prescriptions for best practice are summarized in Box 5.

Betterment

Also called unearned increment. Profits likely to accrue to the owner of land as a result of an advantageous rezoning of the land, for example, from agricultural pursuits to housing. In Britain, the Town and Country Planning Act, 1947 laid down the basic principle that simply to own land in an area scheduled for a profitable change of use did not entitle the owner to anything more than the return that would have been obtained from its sale for the original use. If sale occurred, the profit or 'betterment' would go to the public authority.

The experiment ended in the early 1950s because of difficulties in administration, rather than a change of view regarding the principle itself. A central difficulty was determining the size of the gain, for the land in its original use may have undergone many improvements. Decisions, therefore, required a large skilled assessment staff. The costs of this, measured against the return, did not prove attractive. There were also the claims of those who had incurred a loss through disadvantageous rezonings. There was also the problem of the distribution of gains between the local and central government.

Bhopal Disaster, India, 1984

A catastrophic gas leak at a pesticide plant in Bhopal, India, in December 1984, as a result of which over 2000 people, mostly children and older

Box 5   *Pollution control: best practice concepts*

Best available control technology (BACT)
Emission controls or production methods, techniques, processes or practices that are capable of achieving a very high degree of reduction in the emission of wastes from a particular source. Financial and economic considerations are excluded from this concept.

Best available control technology not entailing excessive costs (BACTNEEC)
Essentially a refinement of BACT, allowing the level of costs to be taken into consideration. A concept incorporated into the British Environmental Protection Act.

Best practicable environmental option (BPEO)
A term introduced by the British Royal Commission on Environmental Pollution in its Fifth Report in order to take account of the total pollution from an enterprise or activity and the technical possibilities of dealing with it; possibly a successor to BPM. Apart from dealing with all pollutants, BPEO was to take into account the risk of pollutants transferring from one medium to another.

Best practicable means (BPM)
A commonly used approach to pollution control requirements from industrial and other premises. The word 'practicable' is taken to mean 'reasonably practicable having regard, among other things, to the state of technology, to local conditions and circumstances, and the financial implications of the measures'. The concept is much easier to apply than the ambient quality approach.

Good control practice (GCP)
The application of established pollution control methods, or practices, that a control agency considers capable of achieving an adequate degree of reduction and subsequent dispersion of wastes emitted from a particular source. GCP might be appropriate in a relatively isolated situation.

Maximum achievable control technology (MACT)
Emission control requirements that are more exacting than those imposed by BACT. This higher standard may involve the application of new, original, or innovative control technology to emission sources, almost regardless of cost.

people, died and some 50 000 suffered from various degrees of blindness, temporary and permanent. Methyl isocyanate, a gas used in the manufacture of the pesticide Sevin at a Union Carbide plant, leaked from an underground storage tank and flowed into neighboring slum areas.

It appeared that pressure had built up in the storage tank, rupturing a valve, and allowing the gas to escape through a scrubber system which failed. The poisonous gas appears to have diffused over some 65 sq. km of the town in an area populated largely by poor families. This air pollution incident was the world's worst industrial disaster. The disaster has promoted intensive reviews of industrial practices in the USA (resulting in a toxic air pollutant control bill in 1985), and in the EU and the OECD.

See also:
Disasters.

Biochemical Oxygen Demand (BOD)

An index of water pollution, which represents the content of biochemically degradable substances in a sample of water or effluent. A test sample is stored in darkness for five days at 20°C; the amount of oxygen taken up by the microorganisms present is measured in grams per cubic metre. However, when samples contain substances such as sulfites or sulfides, which are oxidized by a purely chemical process, the oxygen so absorbed may form part of the BOD result. For this reason, the BOD test is no longer considered an adequate criterion by itself for judging the presence or absence of organic pollution. Further, it cannot be used to assess the presence of many relatively new pollutants such as pesticides, industrial organic compounds, fertilizing nutrients, dissolved salts, soluble iron and heat. However, the test remains widely used, particularly in sewage treatment.

See also:
Water Pollution.

Biodiversity

Biodiversity, or biological diversity, is an umbrella term to describe collectively the variety and variability of nature. It encompasses three basic levels of organization in living systems: genetic, species and ecosystem. Plant and animal species are the most commonly recognized units of biological diversity, thus public concern has mainly been devoted to conserving species diversity. This has led to efforts and to legislation to conserve endangered species and to establish specifically protected areas. However, sustainable human economic activity depends upon understanding, protecting and maintaining the world's many interactive diverse ecosystems with their complex networks of species and their vast storehouses of genetic information. Most countries have now taken legal and physical measures to protect endangered species from extinction. Also the idea of protecting outstanding scenic and scientific resources, wildlife and vegetation has taken root in many countries and developed into national policies, embracing both terrestrial and marine parks. The World Heritage List, maintained by UNESCO, includes properties of great cultural significance and many geographic areas of outstanding universal value, augmenting the principle of biological diversity. Increasingly, wilderness areas are being identified and preserved, including some very substantial areas such as the Great Barrier Reef, Australia. However, major world resources such as the Amazon rain forest, covering about 40 per cent of the land area of Brazil, are still only partially protected and subject to progressive logging and clearing.

The Convention on Biological Diversity signed at UNCED in Rio de Janeiro in 1992, was the first international treaty on biodiversity and went further in addressing the issues involved. The convention began as a document drawn up by the World Conservation Union (IUCN). It was submitted to the UNEP Governing Council which recognized the need and value for an international biodiversity convention. UNEP redrafted it to broaden the proposed agreement. Formal negotiations involving some 75 countries began in November 1990. A final version was signed by 156 nations and the EU at the 1992 UN Conference. The convention aims to save species of animals and plants from extinction, and their habitats from destruction. It aims also at sustainable use of genetic resources and the fair and equitable sharing of the benefits. The parties are required to develop national strategies for the conservation and sustainable use of biological resources; establish protected areas, restore degraded ecosystems, control alien species, and establish conservation facilities; establish training and research programs; encourage technology and biotechnology transfer, particularly to developing countries; provide financial resources to developing countries in support of the convention; carry out EIAs prior to proposed projects that might reduce biodiversity; and undertake reviews of national biological resources. The studies will allow an assessment of the costs and benefits of implementing appropriate measures, and the additional funding required from the Global Environment Facility. The possible extra financial support required by developing countries has been estimated at US$20 billion a year.

Biosphere Reserves

An international network of reserves forming part of UNESCO's Man and Biosphere Program. The purpose of the reserves is to ensure the conservation of representative ecological areas and the genetic resources they contain, so as to implement in part the World Conservation Strategy, and to strengthen international cooperation in the field of ecological research and monitoring. In 1984, the International Coordinating Council for the Man and Biosphere Program adopted an Action Plan for Biosphere Reserves.

BOD

See:
Biochemical Oxygen Demand (BOD).

Botanical and Zoological Gardens

See:
Biosphere Reserves; Geneva City Conservatory and Botanical Gardens; Indonesia Botanical Gardens; Kavkazsky Nature Reserve; Kew Gardens; Laplandsky Nature Reserve; National Botanic Gardens of Belgium; National Botanic Gardens of South Africa; National Zoological Park; Selous Game Reserve.

Brasilia

The national capital of Brazil. The idea of a capital city located in the interior was first proposed in 1789, and was reiterated in 1822 when Brazil gained its independence from Portugal. The concept was embodied in the Constitution of 1891. The present site was selected in 1956. Construction work was sufficiently advanced by 1960 for the federal government to begin its move from Rio de Janeiro.

The entire city was to have been built according to the plan submitted by the Brazilian architect, Lucia Costa, but within ten years the plan had been significantly altered. Today an artificial lake surrounds much of the city. The cross-shaped plan of the central city is emphasized by the North–South Axis. The East–West or Monumental Axis is lined by federal and civic buildings. Around the Square of Three Powers stand the executive, judicial and legislative buildings, including the National Congress Building. Many of these major buildings were designed by the Brazilian architect Oscar Neimeyer, including the cathedral.

Brasilia may be considered a brilliant concept launched with political fervour, straining national resources to the limit. Some of the achievements are awesome in an architectural or structural sense. However, following the superblocks, the pace slackened and squatter settlements sprang up. The area is now a scenario of middle-class apartments and lower-class shacks. The city tends to mirror Brazilian society as a whole, reflecting splendour and poverty with corresponding attitudes of mind. In 1995 the population approached 1 750 000, covering 5800 sq km.

Brazil

The Federative Republic of Brazil is a multiparty federal republic with two legislative houses, the Senate and the Chamber of Deputies. The capital is Brazilia. The population in 1997 was 160 million, at an average density of 19 persons per sq km. Located in South America, facing the Atlantic Ocean, Brazil abuts to the west French Guiana, Surinam, Guyana, Venezuela, Colombia, Peru, Bolivia, Paraguay, Uruguay and Argentina. See Box 6 for the evolution of environmental law.

Brundtland Commission

See:
World Commission on Environment and Development (Brundtland Commission).

Buffer Zone

An area of land separating land uses which are incompatible with each other, which is (or should be) of sufficient width to prevent any conflict between them. Buffer zones may be established to separate industrial from residential areas; or to separate airports from all other developments. Buffer zones may be planted with various forms of suitable vegetation, shrubs and trees, and may be contoured to form noise bunds. Buffer zones may also form a part of an open space program.

Buffer zones are required, for example, around quarries to protect them from encroachment by land uses such as urban and small-scale rural residential development which, if permitted too close to quarries, can lead to their premature closure or to the imposition of severe restrictions (including restricted working hours) on their operations.

Box 6   Brazil: evolution of environmental law

1939   Iguaca, Parque Nacional do established
1966   Amazon Basin opened up for ranches
1973   Special Environment Agency (SEMA) established to identify environmental problems and suggest solutions, recommend standards in respect of pollution control, and protect fauna and flora
1974   Amazonia, Parque Nacional do established
1975   Limits set for mercury in water
1976   Standards set for bathing waters; classification of waters; water quality criteria; air quality standards, and a ban on non-biodegradable detergents
1977   Ecological monitoring stations introduced
1978   Policy on rational use of water resources; treatment of effluents
1979   Policy on treatment and disposal of solid wastes; Forest Policy Committee recommends reversal of policy on opening up the Amazon with the establishment of national parks and ecological reserves
1984   Cubato disaster, with the deaths of some 500 people following the explosion of a gasoline pipeline
1988   Creation of a National Environment Guard to deter further deforestation of the Amazon by ranchers, miners, and lumber and rubber companies; murder of internationally known ecologist, Francisco Mendes Filho
1992   Brazil hosts the UN Conference on Environment and Development, held in Rio de Janeiro with representatives from 167 countries, resulting in the Rio Declaration and Agenda 21
1993   Two Brazilian conservationists murdered; one opposed to the extraction of sand from beaches, dunes and salt marshes, and the other opposed to the logging of mahogany in tribal lands and ecological reserves
1994   The World Bank funds a water and sanitation program assisting some 800 000 people in 11 Brazilian towns and cities
1996   Life expectancy: 56.7 years for males; 66.8 years for females
1998   Brazilian President Fernando Henrique Cardoso introduces a law imposing strict penalties for environmental offences. Companies violating regulations would be forbidden to tender for government contracts for ten years and would also lose tax breaks. Their owners would be fined in proportion to company profits. Anyone caught illegally trading animals, burning trees,

> Box 6   *continued*
>
> extracting minerals without authority, or causing pollution, could
> be imprisoned for up to three years

The amount of land required for a buffer zone around a quarry will vary
from deposit to deposit, depending on such factors as size of the resource,
quarry design, method and scale of extraction, and topography. The buffer
zone has to be of a sufficient width to ensure that noise, vibration and dust
levels at the outer margin are compatible with existing or permissible land
uses in the surrounding area. Consideration may also need to be given in the
design of the buffer zone to the reduction of visual impact.

The restrictions on land use within buffer zones will, of course, no longer
be necessary once the deposit has been worked out and, depending on the
nature of the deposit and the manner in which mining is carried out, it may be
possible to reduce the size of the buffer zone during the life of the quarry.

Built Environment

A reference to buildings, dwellings, structures, utilities, roads and services
which enable people to live, work and play, circulate and communicate, and
fulfil a wide range of functions in whole or part. The quality, however, may
range from grandeur to blight. The built environment reveals the historical
and spatial development of a place, its past and its present, and something of
its social structure and conflicts. It is in many ways the outward, physical
expression of the degrees of power in society. While urban form and physical
structure is to some degree also a mirror of the social structure, it is nonetheless constantly undergoing change as the social structure changes. Political
power, ideologies and values may leave an indelible imprint on the built
environment. The built environment is a translation of a complex, kaleido-
scopic variety of social and economic values and ideologies.

Burley Griffin Plan for Canberra

In 1911, the Australian government launched a worldwide design competition for the layout of Canberra as the seat of government and national capital
of Australia. The competition was won by Walter Burley Griffin, an American architect and landscape designer. His plan for a city of 75 000 was
far-sighted, serving Canberra until the mid-1950s; the population today is

over 300 000. The Griffin Plan was concerned primarily with the formal layout of the central area as a setting for Parliament House and the location of the main functions of government. The plan also established a number of important principles relating to the pattern of urban development (the Y-plan) and its relationship with the topographic and landscape elements. The great artificial lake in the middle of Canberra is named Lake Burley Griffin. The essence of the Griffin Plan remains intact.

The site of the city is one of great natural beauty, augmented by a massive tree-planting program for individual streets and avenues. The quality of housing is generally of a high standard, while the average income is the highest in Australia. Canberra is the home of the Australian National University, the University of Canberra, the National Library, the High Court of Australia, the Australian National Gallery, the National Museum and the National Science and Technology Centre. The new Parliament House was opened in 1988. Important subcentres include Belconnen, Woden and Tuggeranong with numerous shopping centres, libraries and medical centres. Black Mountain incorporates a telecommunications tower and important botanic gardens.

C

Canada

Canada is a federal multiparty parliamentary state with two legislative houses, the Senate and the House of Commons. The capital is Ottawa. The population in 1997 was 30 million, at an average density of 3.3 persons per sq km. There are ten provinces and two Territories. Quebec is strongly French. See Box 7 for the evolution of environmental law.

Canadian Environmental Assessment Agency (CEAA)

Located in Ottawa, an agency responsible for the Canadian environmental assessment and review process (EARP). The process was established by Cabinet decision in December 1973, being later revised in 1977. It applies to federal departments and agencies and seeks to take environmental matters into account throughout the planning and implementation stages of new projects, programs and activities. It requires an EIA to be carried out for all projects which may have adverse effects on the environment before commitments and irrevocable decisions are made.

In addition to projects initiated by federal departments or agencies, the process applies also to projects requiring federal funds and those involving federal funds. The departments and agencies are responsible for assessing the environmental consequences of their own projects and activities or those for which they assume the role of initiator.

The Canadian provinces derive their authority to carry out an EIA from a variety of legal bases. Manitoba established an environmental assessment and review process by Cabinet directive in 1975; New Brunswick adopted a similar policy in the same year. Ontario passed specific environmental impact assessment legislation in 1975; Saskatchewan and Newfoundland followed suit in 1986. In 1978, Quebec amended its Environmental Quality Act to provide for EIA. British Columbia supplemented EIA procedures within existing statutes through the passage of the Environmental Management Act in 1981.

Capacity Building

The concept of capacity building arose during UNCED, 1992 and the adoption of Agenda 21. It recognized the inherent weakness of many nations,

Box 7   Canada: evolution of environmental law

1868   Fisheries Act
1885   Banff National Park established
1886   Glacier National Park established
1895   Waterton Lakes National Park established
1907   Jasper National Park established
1909   USA–Canada Boundary Waters Treaty
1914   Mount Revelstoke National Park established
1922   Wood Buffalo National Park established
1937   Gaspesian Provincial Park established
1941   Trail Smelter legal case
1946   Atomic Energy Control Act
1957   Fertilizers Act
1970   Canada Water Act; Canada Shipping Act; Fisheries Act; North-
        ern Inland Waters Act; National Parks Act
1971   Clean Air Act; Environment Canada established
1972   Great Lakes Water Quality Agreement (USA–Canada); Environ-
        ment Ontario established; Pest Control Products Act
1973   Federal Environmental Assessment Review Office established
1975   Environment Contaminants Act; Ocean Dumping Control Act;
        Environmental Assessment Act, Ontario
1980   Memorandum of Intent on Transboundary Air Pollution, USA–
        Canada
1985   Water Act Amendments; Clean Air Act; Canada Shipping Act;
        Fisheries Act; Northern Inland Waters Act; Pest Control Prod-
        ucts Act; Environmental Contaminants Act
1988   Toronto Conference on the Changing Climate
1989   Environmental Protection Act
1991   Accelerated program to reduce toxic emissions, with targets
        for the year 2000
1992   Canadian Environmental Assessment Act; creation of Canadian
        Environmental Assessment Agency
1993   Canadian round-tables on sustainable development; Pollutant
        Release Inventory
1994   Kilope Valley temperate rain forest wilderness preserved, with
        800-year-old trees; Wild Animal and Plant Protection Act;
        Canada–Ontario Agreement on the Great Lakes Basin; Cana-
        dian Biodiversity Strategy; Environment Canada Regulatory
        Review
1996   Life expectancy: 74.9 years for males; 81.2 years for females

Box 7   *continued*

1997   Kyoto target: 94
1998   Revision of the Canadian Environmental Protection Act; the Act
       included a Canada-wide Accord on Environmental Harmoniza-
       tion, dealing with EIA, the establishment of national environmental
       standards, and inspections under federal law; agreement with
       the Inuit to clean up 15 military radar sites, the sites being
       contaminated with polychlorinated biphenyls (PCBs), heavy met-
       als and other substances

mainly developing, to achieve competent environmental management and the
ultimate aim of sustainable development. See Box 8 for some of the ingredi-
ents of capacity building.

Box 8   *Capacity building for sustainable development*

- The establishment of environmental institutions and machinery.
- The development of policies and strategies.
- The preparation and enforcement of laws and regulations.
- The development and use of economic instruments and
  market-based incentives.
- Mechanisms for gathering, assimilating and dissemination of information.
- Training of human resources in relevant technical disciplines.
- The development of new analytical tools via national environmental profiles, environmental impact assessment, environmental
  accounting, environmental audits, environmental indicators, environmental education, community involvement, technology
  transfer and development, and national and international
  financing.

Catchment Management

A catchment is a drainage basin that collects all the rainwater that falls on it,
apart from that removed by evaporation, sending it into a river, stream, lake
or reservoir. The boundary of a catchment basin is defined by the ridge
beyond which the water flows in the opposite direction, that is, away from the

basin. Effective catchment management is central to maintaining water quality. It involves the control of any activities that contribute to specific or diffuse sources of pollution including human habitation, agriculture, industry, forestry and mining. The clearing of vegetation should be carefully controlled as this can result in soil erosion and increased water salinity.

Effective catchment management requires catchment management legislation enabling a catchment management body to coordinate policies, programs and activities within a catchment to promote the sustainable use of natural resources, stable and productive soil, high-quality water and productive vegetation cover. A high level of community participation is involved. It may be necessary to raise revenue to support catchment management activities and staff, and facilitate research.

Central Business District (CBD)

Consequent upon the scale and intensity of physical development, and the variety of its functions and activities, the center of a metropolitan area, city, or large town. It is often the preferred location for the head offices of major private and public sector organizations; a communications center; a cultural, educational and recreational center; a commercial and financial center; an entertainment, tourist and retail center; and contains residential components. Economically, the CBD serves people and companies within and beyond the metropolitan boundary.

In many cities, major suburban shopping and office complexes have developed, detracting from the importance of the CBD while easing strains on transport services and parking facilities. Nevertheless, the CBD is prominent and obvious in all cities; it has been likened to the hub of a wheel from which communication and transport 'spokes' radiate, or sometimes as a magnet towards which all things tend to gravitate. Its success depends on economic viability in the service as distinct from manufacturing sectors, though travelling to work in the CBD for a better salary can be a long and tedious process for many people.

The CBD always presents fairly intense land-use conflicts, for land values are high and the retention of land for parks and open space, or for the preservation of historic buildings, becomes correspondingly expensive. The provision of housing for lower-income workers who are needed in the CBD becomes a difficult problem.

Zoning and development control codes have been generally applied by city government to resolve land-use conflicts as far as possible. Environmental criteria which can be controlled through planning and building regulations include:

- bulk and height of buildings,
- overshadowing,
- wind tunnel effects,
- on-site parking,
- continuity of street façades,
- visual impact of scale of building,
- pedestrian resting areas,
- building setbacks and floor-space ratios,
- preservation of special vistas,
- proximity to historical features, and
- sidewalk protection and skyways.

In many North American and European cities the central business districts have undergone profound changes during the post-Second World War years as a result of massive investments in new business developments, dwarfing prewar structures, coupled with the redesign of freeways and expressways to accommodate the domination of the private car as a means of transport. Large areas of derelict and blighted properties have been cleared.

In Britain and Europe, many city centers had to be reconstructed following devastating damage sustained during the war years; many took the opportunity to restore the historic character of their city centers in meticulous detail. Warsaw is an outstanding example; a cultural victory for the Poles over a barbarous enemy.

In Britain, central London, especially around St. Paul's Cathedral, was extensively reconstructed. Coventry also reconstructed its battered city center in a modern manner; however, the ruins of the bombed Cathedral were retained as a fitting historical approach to the new Cathedral. Other city centers have undergone extensive reconstruction through collaboration between the public and private sectors including Birmingham, Leicester, Liverpool and Newcastle-upon-Tyne.

Central Park, Manhattan

Officially opened in 1876, Central Park, Manhattan, New York represents one of the greatest achievements in landscape architecture. Most of the park's present land was acquired as early as 1856. The clearing of the site then entailed the removal of a bone-boiling works, many hovels and squalid farms, and several open drains and sewers. A plan for the site was devised by the architects Frederick Law Olmsted and Calvert Vaux to preserve and enhance the natural features of the site and provide a pastoral park for city use. The plan was chosen from 33 submissions. During the park's ensuing development, millions of tons of earth were moved and over 5 million trees planted and many bridges, arches and roads constructed. The Metropolitan Museum of Art is located in the park, facing Fifth Avenue.

Central Place Theory

A body of theory relating to towns and cities, the foundation of which was laid by Walter Christaller in his study of south German towns. Christaller described central place theory as 'general deductive theory' designed to 'explain the size, number and distribution of towns' in the belief that 'some ordering principles govern the distribution'.

Christaller regarded the basic function of a city to be a central place providing goods and services to the surrounding tributary area. To perform such a function efficiently, it was argued, a city is found at the center of minimum aggregate travel for its tributary area, that is, central to the maximum profit area it can command. The greater the centrality of a place, the higher is its order. Higher-order places offer more goods, have more establishments and business types, larger populations, tributary areas and tributary populations, do greater volumes of business, and are more widely spaced than lower-order places.

Low-order goods are generally necessities requiring frequent purchasing but little consumer travel, while high-order goods are goods for which the consumer is willing to travel longer distances, although less frequently. Because higher-order places offer more shopping opportunities, their trading areas for low-order goods are likely to be larger than those of low-order places.

Centers of each higher-order group perform all the functions of lower-order centers plus a group of central functions that differentiate them from, and set them above, the lower order. Central place theory remains one of the most widely applicable of theories relating to systems of cities, particularly in relation to the location of tertiary activity.

It is, however, a simplification of reality, holding many factors constant; the theory assumes an even plain and a uniform distribution of natural resources and people. In reality, resource localization distorts the hierarchy. It is best to regard central place theory as providing a valuable partial framework for the understanding of regional structures.

Chernobyl Nuclear Disaster

Occurring in April 1986, the worst accident in nuclear power station history. Located 104 km north of Kiev in the Ukraine (then part of the Soviet Union), the Chernobyl nuclear power station consisted of four reactors, each of 1000 MW capacity. The station was commissioned during 1977–83. During 25–26 April 1986, a test was being run on the No. 4 reactor involving a breach of several safety precautions. These errors were compounded by others and a chain reaction in the reactor core went out of control. Several explosions and a large fireball followed, blowing the steel and concrete lid off the reactor. The result of these events and the subsequent fire in the graphite core released large amounts of radioactive material into the atmosphere, where it was carried great distances over Europe by air currents. The radioactive fallout reached as far as Norway and Scotland, but most people affected were in the Ukraine and the then Soviet Republic of Belarus, immediately to the north. About 5 million people are believed to have been exposed to the radioactivity. On 27 April, the residents of Pripyat, the nearest town, began to be evacuated; more than half-a-million people were eventually displaced from towns in the Ukraine, Belarus and Russia. Thousands of square kilometres of land were heavily contaminated, as well as water supplies. Chernobyl caused the deaths of more than thirty people and many more were afflicted by radiation sickness. The incidence of thyroid cancer rose markedly in adults and children. Several thousand extra cancer deaths were expected over the years from the radioactivity. The event strengthened opposition throughout the world to nuclear power plants.

In 1996, work began on the decommissioning of units 1, 2 and 3; waste management on site and in the exclusion zone; the storage of spent fuel and high-level waste; and the enclosure of unit 4. The aim was to close Chernobyl completely by 2000. At a meeting of the Group-of-Seven nations (the top industrial nations) in 1996 in Moscow, just over $3 billion worth of international assistance was offered to the Ukraine to close the station permanently by the end of the century and to complete reactors under construction at the Khmelnytsky and South Ukraine nuclear power station sites.

In 1998, official reports revealed that some 12 000 people had died since the Chernobyl incident, including some three-quarters of the rescue workforce.

See also:
Disasters.

China

The People's Republic of China is a single party republic with one legislative house, the National People's Congress. The capital is Beijing. The population in 1997 was 1228 million, at an average density of 128 persons per sq km. A communist society, modifying, China entered the UN in 1971. China abuts

---

Box 9   China: evolution of environmental law

1956	Drinking-water quality standards; hygiene standards for industrial enterprises promulgated
1958	Yujiang of Jiangxi Province becomes first county in China to have eliminated schistosomiasis (bilharzia)
1972	China represented at the UN Conference on the Human Environment, Stockholm, Sweden
1973	Office of the Environmental Protection Leading Group of the State Council established, issuing a wide range of environmental standards relating to water quality, industrial emissions, and agricultural herbicides and pesticides
1972–78	Preparatory stage for the introduction of EIA
1978	EIA regulations introduced; amendment of the Constitution of the People's Republic of China by the Fifth National People's Congress:'The State protects the environment and natural resources and prevents and eliminates pollution and other hazards to the public' (Article 11)
1979	Environmental Protection Law passed and promulgated by the National People's Congress based on Article 11 of the Constitution; Law provides for rational use of the natural environment, the control of pollution, the prevention of damage to ecological systems, and establishes a legal basis for EIA; Forestry Law introduced, permitting the planting of a 'Green Great Wall' across Northern China to reduce wind and sand
1981	EIA applied to the petrochemical industry, large water conservancy projects, coal mining, light industry, steel industry and the construction industry
1986	EIA administrative and technical regulations issued, including management measures for construction projects
1988	Three-Gorges hydroelectric and irrigation project endorsed by a feasibility study prepared by the CIPM Yangtze Joint Venture, a consortium led by Canadian International Project Managers Ltd and sponsored by the Canadian International Development Agency
1989	National Environmental Protection Agency (NEPA) created, reporting directly to the State Council; EIA requirements made more specific
1990	Environmental Protection Law adopted and promulgated by the National People's Congress, authorizing NEPA to su-

Box 9   *continued*

	pervise and implement environmental protection management measures throughout the country; technical guidance issued by NEPA for construction projects, industry, railways, highways, ports and airports, natural resources and agricultural developments
1991	A 10-year programme for economic and social development of China 1991–2000 approved; includes the controversial Three-Gorges water conservation and hydro-electric project
1992	The Three-Gorges project reaffirmed at the Fifth Plenary Session of the Seventh National People's Congress; a strategy of sustainable development adopted and the principles of Agenda 21.
1995	The strategy of sustainable development adopted by the National People's Congress adjusting the National Five-Year Plan for Social and Economic Development.
1996	Total Quality Control Plan for Industrial Pollutants adopted; Laws on Prevention and Control of Water Pollution, Air Pollution, Solid Waste Pollution and Noise Pollution introduced; Forest Law; Mineral Resources Law; and Water Resources Law.
1997	New Criminal Law specifies environmental crimes, imposing criminal punishments for crimes related to radioactive wastes, toxic substances, hazardous wastes, aquatic resources, endangered wild animals, land management, mineral resources and forest management. State of the Environment Report released. Mr William Ping Chen sentenced to 10 years imprisonment for smuggling into China prohibited wastes; Chen was deported to the US.
1998	NEPA now known as State Environment Protection Administration (SEPA)

Mongolia, Russia, India, Nepal, Burma, Laos, Vietnam, North Korea and Bhutan. China incorporated Hong Kong in 1997. See Box 9 for the evolution of environmental law.

Chlorofluorocarbons (CFCs) Phase-out

The Montreal Protocol on Substances that Deplete the Ozone Layer was an international agreement reached in 1988 by over 30 countries aimed at protecting the ozone layer by controlling the emission of chlorofluorocarbons (CFCs) and halons. Under the agreement, initiated by UNEP, CFC consumption was to be progressively reduced worldwide, being phased out completely by 1996. The consumption of halons was not to be allowed to increase above the levels of 1988. This protocol implemented the Convention for the Protection of the Ozone Layer (the Vienna Convention) of 1985. The CFCs and halons had been found to be harmful in the upper atmosphere as ozone-depleting agents. Such impairment of the ozone layer would allow more ultraviolet light to reach the Earth with detrimental effects such as increasing incidence of skin cancer.

CFCs had been widely used in a range of products and industrial processes, such as refrigerators, polystyrene packaging, in the electronics industry and as aerosol propellants. The US, among others, banned production of CFCs by 1996. US measures also included: a tradable permit regime covering CFC manufacturers and importers, an excise tax on ozone-depleting chemicals, the development of alternatives, and changes to defence procurement rules.

Alternatives to CFCs were found more readily than had been anticipated, and the changeover proved much cheaper than expected. Consumption of CFCs fell rapidly; reductions occurred ahead of the legally-mandated timetable. The two main market instruments in the package of measures, the tradable permits scheme and the ozone-depleting chemical tax, stimulated the progress made, with low administrative costs.

The marketable permit system allocated CFC allowances to existing importers and producers of CFCs and halons, based on each firm's market share in 1986; the initial allocation of allowances involved fewer that 30 firms. Firms could trade permits among themselves, while the system capped and progressively reduced the aggregate use of CFCs. The system was operated by a staff of four at the US EPA. As the market for CFCs declined, the system allowed firms to rationalize production between different production facilities according to the least-cost pattern of supply. The ozone-tax was progressively increased, and the scope of the tax was broadened to include additional compounds; this added substantially to the prices of CFCs, and was thus another reason for the rapid fall in CFC demand.

Civic Amenities Act, 1967, UK

An act 'to make further provision for the protection and improvement of buildings of historic interest and of the character of areas of such interest; for the preservation and planting of trees; and for the orderly disposal of disused vehicles and equipment and other rubbish'. The act enabled local authorities, for the first time, to seek the protection of areas of cities, towns and villages, as distinct from the protection of individual buildings. Tree preservation orders became more effective and provided means for planting more trees with new development. The act made it an offense to abandon vehicles on the highway and required local authorities to provide proper facilities for the collection of old cars and other similar unwanted articles. The Civic Amenities Act was later incorporated in the Town and Country Planning Act, 1971.

Class Action

A lawsuit instituted by one or more parties on behalf not only of themselves but also of many other parties, when common issues of law, fact and circumstance are involved. This procedural device, when permitted, enables large numbers of people to gain access to the courts seeking equitable rights. Often shareholders may bring actions against corporations using the principle of a class action; consumers may bring class actions against manufacturers; while class actions may be initiated against polluters, where many have a potential grievance but only a few could initiate action. The outcomes of class actions are, however, binding on many.

See also:
Environmental Law; Framework Environmental Laws.

Clean Air Acts, 1963 and 1965, US

US clean air legislation which made available federal technical and financial assistance to state air pollution control agencies, and generally sought to encourage cooperative action by the states and local authorities. The control of air pollution from new motor vehicles was inaugurated.

The Clean Air Act, 1963, designated three specific research areas for special attention: control of motor vehicle exhausts, removal of sulfur from fuels, and the development of air quality criteria for major pollutants. The act provided an abatement procedure in respect of interstate pollution.

The Clean Air Act, 1965, provided specifically for federal regulation of motor vehicle emissions, authorizing an expanded research program, creating a federal laboratory, and initiating an investigation of new sources of pollution.

See also:
Air Quality Act, 1967, US.

Clean Air Amendment Act, 1970, US

An amendment to the US Clean Air Acts, 1963 and 1965. Under the 1970 act, the EPA was enabled to set national ambient air quality standards for six major pollutants: sulfur dioxide, particulate matter, carbon monoxide, photochemical oxidants (for example, ozone), oxides of nitrogen and hydrocarbons. Allowable emission limitations for different kinds of stationary sources of pollution could also be established; motor vehicle pollution was also to be substantially reduced. The act requires that 1981 and later model cars conform to an emission limit of 1.0 grain per mile (gpm) of nitrogen oxide, and 3.4 gpm of carbon monoxide. The emission of lead has been restrained by restrictions on the lead content of gasoline.

The main administrative mechanism used by state governments to define strategies to achieve national standards has been the State Implementation Plan (SIP). Since 1970, there has been a significant reduction in the emission of some pollutants: particulates by 58 per cent, sulfur oxides by 25 per cent, and carbon monoxide by 27 per cent. The Clean Air Amendment Act, 1970, expired in 1981; it was then extended indefinitely by the US Congress without change pending a thorough review which continued through 1985.

See also:
National Ambient Air Quality Standards (NAAQS), US.

Clean Air Amendment Act, 1977, US

A further amendment to the US Clean Air Acts, 1963 and 1965. The 1977 act required the 'best available control technology' (BACT) to be installed in new stationary plants. The act also required the EPA to establish national emission standards for hazardous air pollutants – pollutants to which national ambient air standards are not applicable because they do not occur on a sufficiently widespread basis. By the end of 1985, standards had been issued in respect of asbestos, beryllium, mercury, vinyl chloride, benzene, arsenic, radionuclides and coke oven emissions. The act also paved the way for stricter air quality standards for 'clean air areas'.

Clean Air Amendment Act, 1990, US

A further amendment to the US Clean Air Acts to set national ambient air quality standards and state implementation plans; set new source performance standards and hazardous air pollutants standards; provide for federal enforcement procedures; create an allowance program to reduce national utility SO_2 emissions, reduce other hazardous air pollutants from industrial sources, further reduce pollutants from automobiles and other contributors to urban smog, and phase out the production and use of ozone-depleting substances.

Clean Water Act, 1977, US

US clean water legislation which amended earlier 1972 legislation. Its aim was to attain and maintain the quality of water necessary for a variety of uses, including public water supplies, propagation of fish and wildlife, recreation, agriculture, industry and navigation. It imposed more stringent controls on toxic pollutants.

Industries discharging to publicly-owned sewage treatment facilities are subject to a separate set of requirements; these stipulate pre-treatment standards for the discharges, prohibit certain discharges, and establish a system of user charges to support the operation and maintenance of publicly-owned facilities.

Stricter requirements in respect of new discharges aim at the adoption of the 'best demonstrated control technology, processes, operating methods, or other alternatives, including, where practicable, standards permitting no discharge of pollutants'.

The principal enforcement mechanism under the act is the 'national pollutant discharge elimination system'. A permit is required within the context of this system for every point source discharge into US waters; the use of permits ensures compliance with effluent limitations and other requirements under the act. For example, new power plants must have a permit; such a permit incorporates all applicable effluent and water quality standards promulgated under the Clean Water Act, and the applicant must demonstrate to the permitting agency that these limitations and standards can and will be met. Permits are for five years, and must then be renewed; a case has been put forward for ten-year permits to simplify administration and reduce the uncertainties for industry.

By 1985, effluent guidelines for the control of toxic discharges had been issued for such industries as coal mining, coil coating, inorganic chemicals, iron and steel, leather tanning and finishing, ore mining, petroleum refining, porcelain enameling, pulp and paper, steam-electric generation, textile mills, aluminum smelting, battery manufacturing, electrical and electronic components, foundries, metal finishing, pesticides and pharmaceuticals.

See also:
Insecticide, Fungicide and Rodenticide Act, US; Water Pollution Control Amendment Act, 1972, US.

Clean Water Amendment Act, 1981, US

A US federal measure to modify the programs under the Water Pollution Control Amendment Act, 1972 to reduce the economic burden on federal taxpayers. The maximum federal share to be paid for the construction of a water pollution control project was reduced from 75 per cent to 55 per cent.

The act also introduced greater flexibility to establish priorities at state and local level; and more 'reasonable' treatment requirements were introduced. By 1985, the states were managing over three-quarters of the US construction grants program.

However, between 1972 and 1985, the US federal government had spent over $40 billion to construct wastewater treatment facilities in communities large and small across America. In May, 1985, the Senate Environment and Public Works Committee approved a renewal bill to continue a construction grants program through 1994 at a total cost of $18 billion.

Clean Water Restoration Act, 1966, US

US clean water legislation which authorized an appropriation of $3.9 billion for construction grants to state water pollution control programs. In addition, the act, without setting a fixed dollar figure, authorized the appropriation of such additional funds as might be necessary for enforcement, comprehensive planning and other functions.

Cleaner Production

Production processes which minimize waste and effluents, maximizing economic efficiency, reducing risks to humans and the environment. It is a principle applicable to the whole production process beginning with the natural resources utilized and ending with the final disposal of all unavoidable wastes and the discarded product. Cleaner production moves away from end-of-pipe solutions towards the minimization of waste streams. Cleaner production often improves technical efficiency and enhances profitability. Inspectors and authorized officers under planning and environmental legislation may negotiate with companies to promote cleaner production.

Coastal Barrier Improvement Act, 1990, US

An act amending the Coastal Barrier Resources Act, 1986, which established the Coastal Barrier Resources System consisting of undeveloped coastal barriers and other areas located on the coast of the USA.

Coastal Protection

Measures to prevent coastal erosion including the stabilization of beaches and dunes by mechanical means in the lower parts of the beaches, and by both mechanical and vegetational means on the upper beaches and dunes. Heavy sea walls and revetments may also be used in appropriate cases.

Groynes are used extensively to slow beach erosion and to build beaches. Made of wood or other material, and designed to take advantage of the long-shore currents that carry the sediments along the beach, groynes are usually developed in a series so that their spacing, length and height form a tapering system.

Natural vegetation has been the most effective measure in stabilizing dunes and upper beaches; the vegetation may consist of herbs, shrubs and trees. Wattles, fences and stakes may be used in conjunction with plantings to inhibit the movement of sand. The planting arrangements are related to the topography, wind, and drift-character of the sands. The problem of dune management is complex.

Coastal Wetlands Planning, Protection and Restoration Act, 1990, US

An act which authorizes wetlands restoration activities for Louisiana, a national coastal grants program, and increased funding for coastal wetlands conservation projects authorized by the North American Wetlands Conservation Act, 1989.

Code of Ethics on International Trade in Chemicals

To fully achieve the objectives set out in the Amended London Guidelines of 1989, UNEP provided an international forum for industry, NGOs and others, to prepare a code of ethics on international trade in chemicals The preparation of such a code was envisaged in Agenda 21. In 1994, UNEP issued a code of ethics to guide the private sector in enhancing safety in the international trade in chemicals. The code was initially distributed to 185 industry associations and 77 NGOs. It was also sent to all governments and relevant intergovernmental organizations. It is complementary to, though broader in scope than, the Amended London Guidelines for the Exchange of Information on Chemicals in International Trade. The code takes into account the entire life cycle of chemical production, transport, use and disposal. It was developed to reduce health and environmental risks. Wide application of the code was recommended by the International Conference on Chemical Safety, which met in 1994.

Codex Alimentarius Commission

A body created within the joint UN Food and Agriculture–World Health Organization foods standards program to reach agreement between member countries on standards for foods, to provide adequate protection for the health of consumers. A subsidiary of the commission is the Codex Committee on Pesticide Residues which seeks to establish international maximum limits for pesticide residues in specific foods. The recommendations of the commission in respect of substances and residues find their way into national legislation.

Command-and-control or Direct Regulation

Environmental legislation in all countries was initially fragmentary and limited in scope. It was not until after the Second World War that more far-reaching measures were adopted in many countries in respect of air and water pollution, noise, insecticides, town planning, EIA, catchments and endangered species. The postwar period, particularly after the first UN Conference on the Human Environment in 1972, witnessed the setting up of many national environmental agencies and a proliferation of legislation. At the same time, training in the environmental sciences, environmental planning and environmental law came into being in many universities throughout the world. Media attention on oil spills, greenhouse gases, nuclear incidents, woodchipping, smogs, threats to natural resources, population growth, threatened wildlife,

Box 10   *Characteristics of a direct control (command-and-control) system within government*

- The passing of environmental laws and regulations by government at national, state and local level.
- The creation of an Environmental Protection Agency to implement the legislation.
- The distribution of various duties among other branches of government.
- The drafting and introduction of codes and regulations relating to pollution control.
- The drafting and introduction of codes relating to environmental planning.
- The drafting and introduction of codes implementing international conventions.
- The formulation of procedures for environmental impact assessment at policy, program and project levels.
- Procedures for the establishment and maintenance of national and marine parks, nature reserves and public open space.
- The protection of rare and endangered species.
- The identification and preservation of places, buildings and assets of heritage value.
- The establishment of procedures for the conduct of public inquiries in appropriate instances.
- The enforcement of laws and regulations relating to pollution of air, water and land; excessive noise; environmentally hazardous chemicals; contaminated sites; nuisances; noxious accumulations; and odours.
- The creation of systems for the prior approval of proposed developments, and the licensing of discharges.
- The creation and maintenance of adequate monitoring and recording systems.
- The creation of environmental plans at national or state, regional and local levels to promote good town and regional planning and contribute to the strategic control of pollution.
- The promotion of the aims of natural resource conservation, recycling, cleaner production, efficient waste disposal, litter reduction and beautification.
- The establishment of policies and plans to integrate economic, social and environmental progress and further the objectives of sustainable development.

Box 11   Categories and subcategories of environmental regulatory instruments in OECD countries

1. *Command-and-control instruments*   These directly regulate behaviour affecting the environment, typically through permit and authorization procedures relating to the following:
   a. the products produced and distributed;
   b. the materials used in production and distribution;
   c. the technologies by which goods and materials are produced;
   d. the residuals which are released into the environment;
   e. the locations at which production and other economic activities take place.
2. *Economic instruments*   These modify behaviour, using financial incentives and disincentives, to improve environmental performance through:
   a. charges and taxes;
   b. grants and subsidies;
   c. fines etc. for non-compliance;
   d. market creation mechanisms, such as emission permit trading schemes.
3. *Other instruments*   These, often containing a non-mandatory element, aim to improve environmental performance by (i) improving the supply of information relating to environmental problems and the ways of reducing them, and (ii) raising the level of voluntary commitment, both at an individual organization and collective level, to modify practices to reduce these problems. Elements of this approach are to be found in the following examples (although they also often contain elements of the other approaches):
   a. environmental planning, EIA, life-cycle assessment and related extended producer responsibility procedures;
   b. voluntary individual and association agreements to promote environmental policy objectives through industry covenants, negotiated agreements, self-regulation, codes of conduct and eco-audits;
   c. information disclosure schemes (voluntary or compulsory);
   d. environmental management systems and environmental audit procedures to improve cost-effective compliance with agreed environmental quality targets.

Box 12   *Environmental regulatory reform in the USA: some examples*

President Bill Clinton issued a report *Reinventing Environmental Regulation* in March 1995. EPA's response, summarized in the slogan 'cleaner, cheaper, smarter', encompasses a number of initiatives such as:

- *Reducing paperwork and cutting red tape* 1400 pages of obsolete environmental rules are to be eliminated; 10 million hours of paperwork and red tape for large and small businesses seeking to comply with environmental laws have been eliminated; a further 10 million hours of paperwork were due to be eliminated by the end of 1996.
- *Making it easier for businesses to comply with environmental laws* through commonsense compliance incentives, for small businesses on the Environmental Leadership Programme, to enhance businesses' ability to meet environmental requirements through innovative approaches; funding of Small Business Compliance Centers for the metal finishing, printing, automotive repair and farming industries.
- *Using innovation and flexibility to achieve better environmental results* Providing flexibility and cutting red tape to find the cheapest and most efficient ways to achieve higher environmental performance standards.
- Basing environmental regulations on *environmental performance goals*, whilst providing maximum flexibility in the means of achieving these.
- *Increasing community participation and partnerships* through expanding public access to agency information, establishing Performance Partnerships to combine federal funds to meet environmental needs and partnerships between EPA, industry and other groups to improve drinking water safety.
- Enact *simpler regulations*, understandable to those affected.
- Promote '*environmental justice*', that is, an equitable distribution of costs and benefits.
- Encourage *self-policing* by companies and voluntary systems.
- Implement 'place-based programmes', that is, taking an ecosystem as the basis for designing a management strategy (rather than an approach based on administrative boundaries).

Source: *Reinventing Environmental Regulation*, 1996, US Environmental Protection Agency, Environment Directorate Survey and OECD (1996).

coastal erosion, marine pollution, transboundary pollution and environmental economics, intensified.

Box 10 describes the characteristics of a command-and-control system; Box 11 summarizes the categories of environmental regulatory instruments; while Box 12 lists some of the regulatory reforms undertaken in the USA.

See also:
Environmental Law; Framework Environmental Law.

Committee on Air Pollution

See:
Beaver Committee on Air Pollution, 1954.

Common Law

Common law or Anglo-American law is customary law based upon judicial decisions, and embodied in precedents and traditions, which has been administered by the old common law courts of England since the Norman Conquest. It is opposed to equity, concerned primarily with fairness and natural justice; to statute law, that is law laid down in Acts of Parliament and regulations, and to special laws, such as ecclesiastical law. Common law continues to prevail, though undergoing considerable modification over time. This body of customary law is to be found in the USA and most of the member states of the Commonwealth of Nations. However, while common law still prevails in appropriate cases, most environmental matters tend to fall within the scope of statute law, the task of judges being to interpret the law, and not make the law.

Common law is thus the law that was developed in England after the Norman Conquest by judges who ruled in individual cases in the light of precedent or custom. This body of law continued to develop through to the end of the eighteenth century, superseding Anglo-Saxon law, the power of the Church being restricted to the ecclesiastical courts. English statutory law took root with Henry III and particularly Edward I. Trial by jury was introduced in appropriate cases, the professions of judge and barrister were established as full-time occupations and separate courts were established to handle equity cases. Famous legal works appeared, including Jeremy Bentham's *An Introduction to the Principles of Morals and Legislation* (1789). He believed that legislators, not judges, should make the law. In the USA, English common law developed differently, rejecting a number of specific English practices. In the long term also, statute law began to prevail.

Zoning and planning legislation, with detailed land-use controls, has tended to dominate the scene, along with eminent domain. Special planning appeal courts and tribunals have also emerged. The role of common law has continued to diminish. The concepts of public and private nuisances became embraced in public health and housing legislation. Historical property rights became increasingly circumscribed, and the concept of liability widened. The growth of international law is now felt universally, while directives from Brussels acquire legal standing throughout the EU. Some conventions and agreements embrace the entire world. International organizations have increasing influence along with the UN. The International Law Commission has initiated codification and developments in a number of areas of international law.

England and the USA now have very diverse systems: while the USA has the Constitution, England continues to have no written constitution, at least not in a single document. In all other respects, legal interpretations and procedures differ. Indeed, the USA and England have been described as two countries separated by a common law.

Commonwealth of Nations

A free association of sovereign states comprising Britain and a number of former dependencies and colonies, together with the Dominions of Canada, Australia and New Zealand. The ties that bind the Commonwealth are highly diverse, but the main object is to maintain ties of friendship and practical cooperation. At a meeting of the Commonwealth Heads of Government at Langkawi, Malaysia, in October 1989 a declaration on the environment was issued. See Box 13.

Company Law Review Act, 1998 (Commonwealth)

An Australian act requiring companies to disclose how they comply with significant environmental regulations. The new provision applies to all companies other than small proprietary companies. The reporting relates to the implications of all environmental legislation: federal, state and territorial. This reporting requirement encourages the use of independent environmental auditing. It should improve the quality of annual reports.

Box 13   *Langkawi Declaration on Environment, issued by the Commonwealth Heads of Government at Langkawi, Malaysia, 21 October, 1989*

1. We, the Heads of Government of the Commonwealth, representing a quarter of the world's population and a broad cross-section of global interests, are deeply concerned at the serious deterioration in the environment and the threat this poses to the well-being of present and future generations. Any delay in taking action to halt this progressive deterioration will result in permanent and irreversible damage.
2. The current threat to the environment, which is a common concern of all mankind, stems essentially from past neglect in managing the natural environment and resources. The environment has been degraded by decades of industrial and other forms of pollution, including unsafe disposal of toxic wastes, the burning of fossil fuels, nuclear testing and non-sustainable practices in agriculture, fishery and forestry.
3. The main environmental problems facing the world are the 'greenhouse effect' (which may lead to severe climatic changes that could induce floods, droughts and rising sea levels), the depletion of the ozone layer, acid rain, marine pollution, land degradation and the extinction of numerous animal and plant species. Some developing countries also face distinct environmental problems arising from poverty and population pressure. In addition, some islands and low-lying areas of other countries, are threatened by the prospect of rising sea level.
4. Many environmental problems transcend national boundaries and interests, necessitating a co-ordinated global effort. This is particularly true in areas outside national jurisdiction, and where there is transboundary pollution on land and in the oceans, atmosphere and outer space.
5. The need to protect the environment should be viewed in a balanced perspective and due emphasis be accorded to promoting economic growth and sustainable development, including eradication of poverty, meeting basic needs, and enhancing the quality of life. The responsibility for ensuring a better environment should be equitably shared and the ability of developing countries to respond be taken into account.
6. To achieve sustainable development, economic growth is a compelling necessity. Sustainable development implies the incorporation

Box 13   continued

of environmental concerns into economic planning and policies. Environmental concerns should not be used to introduce a new form of conditionality in aid and development financing, nor as a pretext for creating unjustified barriers to trade.

7. The success of global and national environmental programmes requires mutually reinforcing strategies and the participation and commitment of all levels of society – government, individuals and organisations, industry and the scientific community.

8. Recognising that our shared environment binds all countries to a common future, we, the Heads of Government of the Commonwealth, resolved to act collectively and individually, commit ourselves to the following programme of action:

- advance policies and programmes which help achieve sustainable development, including the development of new and better techniques in integrating the environmental dimension in economic decision-making;

- strengthen and support the development of international funding mechanisms and appropriate decision-making procedures to respond to environmental protection needs which will include assisting developing countries to obtain access to and transfer of needed environmental technologies and which should take account of proposals for an international environment fund/Planet Protection Fund;

- support the work of the UNEP/WMO Inter-governmental Panel on Climate Change (IPCC);

- call for the early conclusion of an international convention to protect and conserve the global climate and, in this context, applaud the efforts of member governments to advance the negotiation of a framework convention under US auspices;

- support the findings and recommendations of the Commonwealth Expert Group's Report on Climate Change as a basis for achievable action to develop strategies for adapting to climate change and for reducing greenhouse gas emissions, as well as making an important contribution to the work of the IPCC;

- support measures to improve energy conservation and energy efficiency;

- promote the reduction and eventual phase-out of substances depleting the ozone layer;

Box 13   continued

- promote afforestation and agricultural practices in developed and developing countries to arrest the increase in atmospheric carbon dioxide and halt the deterioration of land and water resources;
- strengthen efforts by developing countries in sustainable forest management and their manufacture and export of higher value-added forest products and, in this regard, support the activities of the International Tropical Timber Organisation and the Food and Agriculture Organisation's Tropical Forestry Action Plan, as well as take note of the recommendations of the 13th Commonwealth Forestry Conference;
- support activities related to the conservation of biological diversity and genetic resources, including the conservation of significant areas of virgin forest and other protected natural habitats; support low-lying and island countries in their efforts to protect themselves and their vulnerable natural marine ecosystems from the effects of sea level rise;
- discourage and restrict non-sustainable fishing practices and seek to ban tangle net and pelagic drift net fishing;
- support efforts to prevent marine pollution including curbing ocean dumping of toxic wastes;
- strengthen international action to ensure the safe management and disposal of hazardous wastes and to reduce transboundary movements, particularly to prevent dumping in developing countries;
- participate in relevant international agreements relating to the environment and promote new and innovative instruments which will attract widespread support for protecting the global environment; and
- strengthen national, regional and international institutions responsible for environmental protection as well as the promotion of active programmes on environmental education to heighten public awareness and support.

9. We, the Heads of Government of the Commonwealth, resolve to take immediate and positive actions on the basis of the above programme. In this regard, we pledge our full support for the convening of the 1992 UN Conference on Environment and Development.

10. We call on the international community to join us in the endeavour.

Comprehensive Environmental Response, Compensation, and Liability Act, 1980 (CERCLA), US

Known also as 'Superfund', a measure introduced by the US Congress to meet the costs of the clean-up of abandoned hazardous waste sites. The goal of this legislation was to eliminate the most serious threats to public health and the environment posed by hazardous substance spills and uncontrolled hazardous waste sites, and to respond to such hazards in a cost-effective manner. The act imposed certain 'environmental taxes' on the petroleum and chemical industries, re-authorized in 1985, and set up the Hazardous Substance Response Trust Fund. Taxes were also imposed on the owners and operators of hazardous waste disposal facilities in order to establish a second fund, known as the Post-Closure Liability Trust Fund. In the event of the release of a hazardous substance, the procedures and methods to be followed are set forth in the National Contingency Plan. To deal with the immediate problems, the act required the preparation of a national priorities list.

See also:
Resource Conservation and Recovery Act, 1976, US.

Compulsory Purchase

The acquisition of private property and land without the owner's consent for an approved public purpose such as public housing, redevelopment, or new town construction. The power of compulsory purchase is embodied in British planning and housing legislation. The procedure for arriving at the purchase price is also laid down. In the USA, through the exercise of eminent domain, private property may be acquired for the public advantage, compensation being made to the owner. For example, a city may acquire land for a needed highway.

Concentration

The amount of a particular substance or gas contained in a given amount of a solution, gas, or mixture; for example, the concentration of salt in seawater. In environmental science and engineering, many concentrations are expressed as parts per million (ppm), parts per hundred million (pphm), or parts per billion (ppb), being proportional parts by volume. The International System of Units (SI) uses micrograms per cubic metre ($\mu g/m$) for air pollution, being weight per unit volume and milligrams per litre (mg/1) or grams per cubic metre (g/m³) for water pollution. For water, parts per million by volume is identical with grams per cubic metre, as one gram (1 g) of water occupies one cubic centimetre (1 cm³). One billion in this text is one thousand million.

Conservation

Defined by the World Conservation Strategy in 1980 as the 'management of human use of the biosphere so that it may yield the greatest sustainable benefit to present generations while maintaining its potential to meet the needs and aspirations of future generations'. Conservation is thus something positive, embracing preservation, maintenance, sustainable utilization, restoration and enhancement of the natural environment. Living-resource conservation is specifically concerned with plants, animals and microorganisms, and with those non-living elements of the environment on which they depend. Living resources are renewable if conserved, with the preservation of genetic diversity and the sustained utilization of species and ecosystems. Non-renewable resources are natural resources which, once consumed, cannot be replaced in that form. Mineral resources generally are regarded as wasting assets, though substitutes are often found.

Contaminated Sites

Sites that present a concentration of chemical substances that are likely to pose 'an immediate or long-term hazard to human health or the environment. A site may be unsafe or unfit for occupation or habitation by people or animals, or degraded in its capacity to support plant life. Historically, contaminated or degraded land has been recognized in public health and related legislation, such as sites used for refuse disposal which should not be built on for many years. In more recent times, the problem has taken on more widespread proportions due to the greater diversity of toxic substances that may be deposited and due to well-publicized incidents such as the Love Canal crisis in the USA, and other incidents of schools built on lead-contaminated sites or houses constructed on radioactive soil. Further, potential purchasers of land do not wish to acquire unwittingly an environmental problem that may require subsequent remediation. In the US, the Comprehensive Environmental Response, Compensation, and Liability Act, 1980 (CERCLA) (known also as Superfund) was introduced to meet the costs of the clean-up of abandoned hazardous waste sites, and to eliminate the most serious threats to public health and the environment. Special taxes were introduced to finance this program.

See also:
Environmental Audit.

Contingent Liability

A liability that may occur but not with certainty; something possibly involving obligations. For example, a guarantee given for another company's borrowings to be invoked in the event of a default by that company; or a risk that current legal proceedings may result in a judgment against the company. The remediation costs that may arise under the US Superfund provisions for the clean-up of contaminated sites is a liability that affects every industry, from chemical and manufacturing companies to banks and insurers. Under Superfund, a company may be held responsible for the entire cost of cleaning up a site even if it contributed only a small fraction of the waste so that a liability is difficult to identify and even more difficult to quantify.

Control of Pollution Act, 1974, UK

An act passed by the British Parliament which significantly extended the powers of local authorities to deal with noise problems, and was concerned also with the control of the deposit and disposal of waste on land; the prevention of water pollution, including controls over underground water; and the control of pollution of the atmosphere, notably from motor vehicles.

The act substituted a licensing system for the deposit of waste for the notification system of the Deposit of Poisonous Waste Act, 1972. Powers were given to collection and disposal authorities to recycle waste, and to purchase waste for this purpose; and to produce heat and electricity from waste.

The water pollution control provisions replaced almost all the provisions of the Rivers (Prevention of Pollution) Acts, 1951 and 1961, the whole of the Clean Rivers (Estuaries and Tidal Waters) Act, 1960, and some sections of the Water Resources Act, 1963. The approach has been to strengthen existing law, rather than to provide new methods of control. The defenses available to persons causing pollution remained restricted. Furthermore, the controls now apply to virtually all inland and coastal waters. Charges can now be made in respect to pre- and post-1973 discharges of trade effluent to sewers, and also in respect to discharges to rivers and streams.

Convention

A multilateral treaty or other international agreement which voluntarily binds a group of nations together to achieve some common purpose in, say, the environment. Early conventions in the environment date back to before the Second World War, becoming much more numerous in recent decades. A convention or multilateral treaty comprises a text, usually emerging from a long process of negotiation. A convention will be directed to one particular issue of regional or international importance. Examples include marine pollution, air pollution, dangerous chemicals, climate change, biodiversity, desertification, nature conservation, heritage conservation, oil pollution, fisheries, the protection of birds, ionizing radiation, nuclear weapons tests, wetlands, civil liability, whaling, seals, polar bears, regional seas, wild fauna and flora, protection of rivers, occupational health and safety, asbestos, the ozone layer, law of the sea and EIA.

Discussion at, say, UN level results in a document which meets broad agreement. Apart from a statement of aims, the draft convention creates a secretariat and a Conference of the Parties, a procedure for management and steps to be taken. A convention will be opened for signature by members of the UN and its specialized agencies and provide for ratification of the treaty, acceptance, approval, accession and entry into force. The convention will stipulate when it comes into force after a specific number of instruments of ratification have been accepted. The convention must also provide for the financial arrangements. Box 14 summarizes a range of conventions relating to the environment and resources, while Box 15 provides greater detail in some more prominent cases.

See also:
Environmental Law; Framework Environmental Law.

Costa Rica

The republic of Costa Rica is a unitary multiparty republic with one legislative house, the Legislative Assembly. The capital is San José. The population in 1997 was 3.5 million, at an average density of 68 persons per sq km. Costa Rica, in central America, is bordered to the north by Nicaragua, to the south by Panama, with the Caribbean to the east and the Pacific Ocean to the west. See Box 16 for the evolution of environmental law.

Box 14   *Summary of conventions and other agreements in the field of the environment*

- Convention Concerning the Use of White Lead in Painting, Geneva, 1921
- Convention Relative to the Preservation of Fauna and Flora in Their Natural State, London, 1933
- Convention on Nature Protection and Wildlife Preservation in the Western Hemisphere, Washington, 1940
- International Convention for the Regulation of Whaling (as amended), Washington, 1946
- Convention for the Establishment of an Inter-American Tropical Tuna Commission, Washington, 1949
- Agreement for the Establishment of a General Fisheries Council for the Mediterranean (as amended), Rome, 1949
- International Convention for the Protection of Birds, Paris, 1950
- Convention for the Establishment of the European and Mediterranean Plant Protection Organization (as amended), Paris, 1951
- International Plant Protection Convention, Rome, 1951
- Agreement Concerning Measures for Protection of the Stocks of Deep-sea Prawns (Pandalus borealis), European Lobsters (Homarus vulgaris), Norway Lobsters (Nephrops norvegicus) and Crabs (Cancer pagurus) (as amended), Oslo, 1952
- International Convention for the High Seas Fisheries of the North Pacific Ocean (as amended), Tokyo, 1952
- Protocol Amending the International Convention for the High Seas Fisheries of the North Pacific Ocean, Tokyo, 1978
- International Convention for the Prevention of Pollution of the Sea by Oil, London, 1954 (as amended on 11 April 1962 and 21 October 1969)
- Amendments to the International Convention for the Prevention of Pollution of the Sea by Oil, 1954, Concerning Tank Arrangements and Limitation of Tank Size, London, 1971
- Amendments to the International Convention for the Prevention of Pollution of the Sea by Oil, 1954, Concerning the Protection of the Great Barrier Reef, London, 1971
- Plant Protection Agreement for the South-East Asia and Pacific Region (as amended), Rome, 1956
- Interim Convention on Conservation of North Pacific Fur Seals (as amended), Washington, 1957

Box 14   continued

- Convention Concerning Fishing in the Waters of the Danube, Bucharest, 1958
- Convention on the Continental Shelf, Geneva, 1958
- Convention on Fishing and Conservation of the Living Resources of the High Seas, Geneva, 1958
- Convention on the High Seas, Geneva, 1958
- North-East Atlantic Fisheries Convention, London, 1959
- Convention Concerning Fishing in the Black Sea (as amended), Varna, 1959
- The Antarctic Treaty, Washington, 1959
- Protocol to the Antarctic Treaty on Environmental Protection, Madrid, 1991
- Agreement Concerning Cooperation in the Quarantine of Plants and Their Protection against Pests and Diseases, Sofia, 1959
- Convention Concerning the Protection of Workers against Ionizing Radiations, Geneva, 1960
- Convention on Third Party Liability in the Field of Nuclear Energy (as amended), Paris, 1960
- Convention Supplementary to the Paris Convention on Third Party Liability in the Field of Nuclear Energy (as amended), Brussels, 1963
- Protocol Concerning the Constitution of an International Commission for the Protection of the Mosel against Pollution, Paris, 1961
- International Convention for the Protection of New Varieties of Plants, Paris, 1961
- Convention on the African Migratory Locust, Kano, 1962
- Agreement Concerning Cooperation in Marine Fishing, Warsaw, 1962
- Agreement Concerning the International Commission for the Protection of the Rhine against Pollution (as amended), Berne, 1963
- Vienna Convention of Civil Liability for Nuclear Damage, Vienna, 1963
- Optional Protocol Concerning the Compulsory Settlement of Disputes, Vienna, 1963
- Treaty Banning Nuclear Weapon Tests in the Atmosphere, in Outer Space and Under Water, Moscow, 1963
- Agreement for the Establishment of a Commission for Control-

Box 14   continued

ling the Desert Locust in the Eastern Region of its Distribution Area in South-West Asia (as amended), Rome, 1963

- Convention and Statute Relating to the Development of the Chad Basin (as amended), Fort-Lamy (N'Djamena), 1964
- Convention for the International Council for the Exploration of the Sea (as amended), Copenhagen, 1964
- Agreement for the Establishment of a Commission for Controlling the Desert Locust in the Near East (as amended), Rome, 1965
- International Convention for the Conservation of Atlantic Tunas, Rio de Janeiro, 1966
- Protocol Amending the International Convention for the Conservation of Atlantic Tunas, Rome, 1984
- Treaty on Principles Governing the Activities of States in the Exploration and Use of Outer Space Including the Moon and Other Celestial Bodies, London, Moscow, Washington, 1967
- Phyto-Sanitary Convention for Africa, Kinshasa, 1967
- African Convention on the Conservation of Nature and Natural Resources, Algiers, 1968
- European Agreement on the Restriction of the Use of Certain Detergents in Washing and Cleaning Products, Strasbourg, 1968
- European Convention for the Protection of Animals During International Transport, Paris, 1968
- Additional Protocol; the European Convention for the Protection of Animals During International Transport, Strasbourg, 1979
- European Convention on the Protection of the Archeological Heritage, London, 1969
- Agreement for Cooperation in dealing with Pollution of the North Sea by Oil, Bonn, 1969
- Convention on the Conservation of the Living Resources of the South-East Atlantic, Rome, 1969
- International Convention on Civil Liability for Oil Pollution Damage (as amended), Brussels, 1969
- International Convention Relating to Intervention on the High Seas in Cases of Oil Pollution Casualties, Brussels, 1969
- Protocol Relating to Intervention on the High Seas in Cases of Marine Pollution by Substances Other than Oil, London, 1973
- Benelux Convention on the Hunting and Protection of Birds (as amended), Brussels, 1970

Box 14   continued

- Agreement for the Establishment of a Commission for Controlling the Desert Locust in North-West Africa (as amended), Rome, 1970
- Convention on Wetlands of International Importance Especially as Waterfowl Habitat, Ramsar, 1971
- Protocol to Amend the Convention on Wetlands of International Importance Especially as Waterfowl Habitat, Paris, 1982
- Treaty on the Prohibition of the Emplacement of Nuclear Weapons and Other Weapons of Mass Destruction on the Sea Bed and the Ocean Floor and in the Subsoil thereof, London, Moscow, Washington, 1971
- Convention Relating to Civil Liability in the Field of Maritime Carriage of Nuclear Material, Brussels, 1971
- International Convention on the Establishment of an International Fund for Compensation for Oil Pollution Damage (as amended), Brussels, 1971
- Convention Concerning Protection against Hazards of Poisoning Arising from Benzene, Geneva, 1971
- Convention for the Prevention of Marine Pollution by Dumping from Ships and Aircraft (as amended), Oslo, 1972
- Convention Concerning the Status of the Senegal River, and Convention Establishing the Senegal River Development Organization (as amended), Nouakchott, 1972
- Convention for the Conservation of Antarctic Seals, London, 1972
- Convention on the Prohibition of the Development, Production and Stockpiling of Bacteriological (Biological) and Toxin Weapons, and on Their Destruction, London, Moscow, Washington, 1972
- Convention Concerning the Protection of the World Cultural and Natural Heritage, Paris, 1972
- Convention on the Prevention of Marine Pollution by Dumping of Wastes and Other Matter (as amended), London, Mexico City, Moscow, [Washington], 1972
- Convention on International Trade in Endangered Species of Wild Fauna and Flora, Washington, 1973
- Convention Establishing a Permanent Inter-State Drought Control Committee for the Sahel, Ouagadougou, 1973
- Convention on Fishing and Conservation of the Living Resources in the Baltic Sea and Belts, Gdansk, 1973

Box 14   continued

- International Convention for the Prevention of Pollution from Ships, London, 1973
- Protocol of 1978 Relating to the International Convention for the Prevention of Pollution from Ships, London, 1973
- Agreement on Conservation of Polar Bears, Oslo, 1973
- Convention on the Protection of the Environment between Denmark, Finland, Norway and Sweden, Stockholm, 1974
- Convention on the Protection of the Marine Environment of the Baltic Sea Area, Helsinki, 1974
- Convention for the Prevention of Marine Pollution from Land-based Sources, Paris, 1974
- Convention Concerning Prevention and Control of Occupational Hazards Caused by Carcinogenic Substances and Agents, Geneva, 1974
- Agreement on an International Energy Programme, Paris, 1974
- Convention for the Protection of the Mediterranean Sea against Pollution, Barcelona, 1976
- Protocol for the Prevention of Pollution of the Mediterranean Sea by Dumping from Ships and Aircraft, Barcelona, 1976
- Protocol Concerning Cooperation in Combating Pollution of the Mediterranean Sea by Oil and Other Harmful Substances in Cases of Emergency, Barcelona, 1976
- Protocol for the Protection of the Mediterranean Sea against Pollution from Land-based Sources, Athens, 1980
- Protocol Concerning Mediterranean Specially Protected Areas, Geneva, 1982
- Protocol for the Protection of the Mediterranean Sea against Pollution resulting from Exploration and Exploitation of the Continental Shelf and the Sea Bed and its Subsoil, Madrid, 1994
- European Convention for the Protection of Animals Kept for Farming Purposes, Strasbourg, 1976
- Protocol of Amendment to the European Convention for the Protection of Animals Kept for Farming Purposes, Strasbourg, 1992
- Agreement Concerning the Protection of the Waters of the Mediterranean Shores, Monaco, 1976
- Convention on Conservation of Nature in the South Pacific, Apia, 1976
- Convention on the Protection of the Archeological, Historical,

Box 14   continued

and Artistic Heritage of the American Nations (Convention of
San Salvador), Santiago, 1976
- Convention on the Protection of the Rhine against Chemical
Pollution, Bonn, 1976
- Convention Concerning the Protection of the Rhine against
Pollution by Chlorides, Bonn, 1976
- Convention on the Prohibition of Military or Any Other Hostile
Use of Environmental Modification Techniques, Geneva, 1976
- Convention on Civil Liability for Oil Pollution Damage Resulting
from Exploration for and Exploitation of Sea Bed Mineral Re-
sources, London, 1977
- Convention Concerning the Protection of Workers against Oc-
cupational Hazards in the Working Environment Due to Air
Pollution, Noise and Vibration, Geneva, 1977
- Kuwait Regional Convention for Cooperation on the Protection
of the Marine Environment from Pollution, Kuwait, 1978
- Protocol Concerning Regional Cooperation in Combating Pollu-
tion by Oil and Other Harmful Substances in Cases of Emergency,
Kuwait, 1978
- Protocol Concerning Marine Pollution resulting from Explora-
tion and Exploitation of the Continental Shelf, Kuwait, 1989
- Protocol for the Protection of the Marine Environment against
Pollution from Land-based Sources, Kuwait, 1990
- Treaty for Amazonian Cooperation, Brasilia, 1978
- Convention on Future Multilateral Cooperation in the
North-West Atlantic Fisheries, Ottawa, 1978
- Convention on the Conservation of Migratory Species of Wild
Animals, Bonn, 1979
- European Convention for the Protection of Animals for Slaugh-
ter, Strasbourg, 1979
- Convention on the Conservation of European Wildlife and Natural
Habitats, Berne, 1979
- Convention on the Physical Protection of Nuclear Material, Vi-
enna, 1979
- Convention on Long-range Transboundary Air Pollution, Geneva,
1979
- Protocol to the 1979 Convention on Long-range Transboundary
Air Pollution on Long-term Financing of the Co-operative Pro-
gramme for Monitoring and Evaluation of the Long-range
Transmission of Air Pollutants in Europe (EMEP), Geneva, 1984

Box 14   continued

- Protocol to the 1979 Convention on Long-range Transboundary Air Pollution on the Reduction of Sulphur Emissions or Their Transboundary Fluxes by at least 30 per cent, Helsinki, 1985
- Protocol to the 1979 Convention on Long-range Transboundary Air Pollution Concerning the Control of Emissions of Nitrogen or Their Transboundary Fluxes, Sofia, 1988
- Protocol to the 1979 Convention on Long-range Transboundary Air Pollution Concerning the Control of Emissions of Volatile Organic Compounds or their Transboundary Fluxes, Geneva, 1991
- Convention for the Conservation and Management of the Vicuna, Lima, 1979
- Convention on the Conservation of Antarctic Marine Living Resources, Canberra, 1980
- European Outline Convention on Transfrontier Cooperation between Territorial Communities or Authorities, Madrid, 1980
- Convention on Future Multilateral Cooperation in North-East Atlantic Fisheries, London, 1980
- Convention Creating the Niger Basin Authority and Protocol Relating to the Development Fund of the Niger Basin, Faranah, 1980
- Convention for Cooperation in the Protection and Development of the Marine and Coastal Environment of the West and Central African Region, Abidjan, 1981
- Protocol Concerning Cooperation in Combating Pollution in Cases of Emergency, Abidjan, 1981
- Convention for the Protection of the Marine Environment and Coastal Area of the South-East Pacific, Lima, 1981
- Agreement on Regional Cooperation in Combating Pollution of the South-East Pacific by Hydrocarbons and Other Harmful Substances in Cases of Emergency, Lima, 1981
- Supplementary Protocol to the Agreement on Regional Cooperation in Combating Pollution of the South-East Pacific by Hydrocarbons and Other Harmful Substances in Cases of Emergency, Quito, 1983
- Protocol for the Protection of the South-East Pacific against Pollution from Land-based Sources, Quito, 1983
- Protocol for the Conservation and Management of the Protected Marine and Coastal Areas of the South-East Pacific, Paipa, 1989

Box 14   continued

- Protocol for the Protection of the South-East Pacific against Radioactive Contamination, Paipa, 1989
- Convention Concerning Occupational Safety and Health and the Working Environment, Geneva, 1981
- Regional Convention for the conservation of the Red Sea and Gulf of Aden Environment, Jeddah, 1982
- Protocol Concerning Regional Cooperation in Combating Pollution by Oil and Other Harmful Substances in Cases of Emergency, Jeddah, 1982
- Convention for the Conservation of Salmon in the North Atlantic Ocean, Reykjavik, 1982
- Benelux Convention on Nature Conservation and Landscape Protection, Brussels, 1982
- United Nations Convention on the Law of the Sea, Montego Bay, 1982
- Convention for the Protection and Development of the Marine Environment of the Wider Caribbean Region, Cartagena de Indias, 1983
- Protocol Concerning Cooperation in Combating Oil Spills in the Wider Caribbean Region, Cartagena de Indias, 1983
- Protocol Concerning Specially Protected Areas and Wildlife to the Convention for the Protection and Development of the Marine Environment of the Wider Caribbean Region, Kingston, 1990
- Agreement for Cooperation in Dealing with Pollution of the North Sea by Oil and Other Harmful Substances, Bonn, 1983
- International Tropical Timber Agreement, Geneva, 1983
- Vienna Convention for the Protection of the Ozone Layer, Vienna, 1985
- Montreal Protocol on Substances that Deplete the Ozone Layer, Montreal, 1987
- London Amendment to the Montreal Protocol on Substances that Deplete the Ozone Layer, London, 1990
- Copenhagen Amendment to the Montreal Protocol on Substances that Deplete the Ozone Layer, Copenhagen, 1992
- Convention for the Protection, Management and Development of the Marine and Coastal Environment of the Eastern African Region, Nairobi, 1985
- Protocol Concerning Protected Areas and Wild Fauna and Flora in the Eastern African Region, Nairobi, 1985

Box 14 continued

- Protocol Concerning Cooperation in Combating Marine Pollution in Cases of Emergency in the Eastern African Region, Nairobi, 1985
- Convention Concerning Occupational Health Services, Geneva, 1985
- South Pacific Nuclear Free Zone Treaty, Raratonga, 1985
- ASEAN Agreement on the Conservation of Nature and Natural Resources, Kuala Lumpur, 1985
- Convention Concerning Safety in the Use of Asbestos, Geneva, 1986
- Convention on Early Notification of a Nuclear Accident, Vienna, 1986
- Convention on Assistance in the Case of a Nuclear Accident or Radiological Emergency, Vienna, 1986
- United Nations Convention on Conditions for the Registration of Ships, Geneva, 1986
- Agreement on the Preservation of Confidentiality of Data Concerning Deep Sea Bed Areas, Moscow, 1986
- Convention for the Protection of the Natural Resources and Environment of the South Pacific Region, Noumea, 1986
- Protocol for the Prevention of Pollution of the South Pacific Region by Dumping, Noumea, 1986
- Protocol Concerning Cooperation in Combating Pollution Emergencies in the South Pacific Region, Noumea, 1986
- The European Convention for the Protection of Vertebrate Animals used for Experimental and other Scientific Purposes, Strasbourg, 1986
- Agreement on the Action Plan for the Environmentally Sound Management of the Common Zambezi River System, Harare, 1987
- European Convention for the Protection of Pet Animals, Strasbourg, 1987
- Convention on the Regulation of Antarctic Mineral Resource Activities, Wellington, 1988
- Joint Protocol Relating to the Application of the Vienna Convention and the Paris Convention, Vienna, 1988
- Agreement on the Network of Aquaculture Centres in Asia and the Pacific, Bangkok, 1988
- Basel Convention on the Control of Transboundary Movements of Hazardous Wastes and Their Disposal, Basel, 1989

Box 14   continued

- Convention on the Prohibition of Fishing with Long Drift Nets in the South Pacific, Wellington, 1989
- Protocol I to Convention on the Prohibition of Fishing with Long Drift Nets in the South Pacific, Noumea, 1990
- Protocol II to Convention on the Prohibition of Fishing with Long Drift Nets in the South Pacific, Noumea, 1990
- International Convention on Salvage, London, 1989
- Convention on Civil Liability for Damage Caused During Carriage of Dangerous Goods by Road, Rail and Inland Navigation Vessels, Geneva, 1989
- Fourth ACP–EEC Convention, Lomé, 1989
- Convention Concerning Safety in the Use of Chemicals at Work, Geneva, 1990
- Agreement on the Conservation of Seals in the Wadden Sea, Bonn, 1990
- International Convention on Oil Pollution Preparedness, Response and Cooperation, London, 1990
- Bamako Convention on the Ban of the Import into Africa and the Control of Transboundary Movement and Management of Hazardous Wastes within Africa, Bamako, 1991
- Convention on Environmental Impact Assessment in a Transboundary Context, Espoo, 1991
- Convention Concerning the Protection of the Alps, Salzburg, 1991
- Treaty Establishing the African Economic Community, Abuja, 1991
- Agreement on the Conservation of Bats in Europe, London, 1991
- European Convention on the Protection of the Archaeological Heritage (Revised), Valletta, 1992
- Convention for the Conservation of Anadromous Stocks, Moscow, 1992
- Agreement on the Conservation of Small Cetaceans of the Baltic and North Seas, New York, 1992
- Convention on the Transboundary Effects of Industrial Accidents, Helsinki, 1992
- Convention on the Protection and Use of Transboundary Watercourses and International Lakes, Helsinki, 1992
- Convention on the Protection of the Marine Environment of the Baltic Sea Area, Helsinki, 1992
- Convention on the Protection of the Black Sea against Pollution, Bucharest, 1992

Box 14 continued

- Protocol on Protection of the Black Sea Marine Environment against Pollution from Land-based Sources, Bucharest, 1992
- Protocol on Cooperation in Combating Pollution of the Black Sea Marine Environment by Oil and Other Harmful Substances in Emergency Situations, Bucharest, 1992
- Protocol on Protection of the Black Sea Marine Environment against Pollution by Dumping, Bucharest, 1992
- United Nations Framework Convention on Climate Change, New York, 1992
- Convention on Biological Diversity, Rio de Janeiro, 1992
- Convention Concerning the Conservation of the Biodiversity and the Protection of Priority Forestry Areas of Central America, Managua, 1992
- Agreement establishing the Fund for the Development of the Indigenous Peoples of Latin America and the Caribbean, Madrid, 1992
- Convention for the Protection of the Marine Environment for the North-East Atlantic, Paris, 1992
- North American Free Trade Agreement, 1992 (the Agreement contains provisions on, *inter alia*, relation to environmental agreements, sanitary and phyto-sanitary measures and technical barriers to trade, including standards-related measures)
- Convention on the Prohibition of the Development, Production, Stockpiling and Use of Chemical Weapons and Their Destruction, Paris, 1993
- Agreement for the Establishment of the Near East Plant Protection Organization, Rabat, 1993
- Agreement Establishing the South Pacific Regional Environment Programme, Apia, 1993
- Convention for the Conservation of Southern Bluefin Tuna, Canberra, 1993
- Convention on Civil Liability for Damage Resulting from Activities Dangerous to the Environment, Lugano, 1993
- North American Agreement on Environmental Cooperation, 1993
- Agreement to Promote Compliance with International Conservation and Management Measures by Fishing Vessels on the High Seas, Rome, 1993
- Agreement for the Establishment of the Indian Ocean Tuna Commission, Rome, 1993
- Convention on Nuclear Safety, Vienna, 1994

Box 14   continued

- Convention to Combat Desertification in Countries Experiencing Serious Drought and/or Desertification, Particularly in Africa, Paris, 1994
- Convention for the Establishment of the Lake Victoria Fisheries Organization, Kisumu, 1994
- Agreement Relating to the Implementation of Part XI of the United Nations Convention on the Law of the Sea of 10 December 1982, New York, 1994
- Agreement on the Preparation of a Tripartite Environmental Management Programme for Lake Victoria, Arusha, 1994
- Lusaka Agreement on Co-operative Enforcement Operations Directed at Illegal Trade in Wild Fauna and Flora, Lusaka, 1994

Box 15   Some international conventions relating to resources and the environment in greater detail

Convention for the Regulation of Whaling

A convention, signed in 1946, creating the International Whaling Commission with responsibility for the conservation and optimal utilization of whale resources. The management of whale stocks remained, however, unsatisfactory for many years with some species being hunted to virtual extinction. In 1982, the commission voted to ban commercial whaling worldwide, beginning in 1986. A few countries have defied the ban, at least in part.

Convention on International Liability for Damage Caused by Space Objects, 1972

A UN convention which stipulates that a state that launches a space object will be absolutely liable to pay compensation for damage caused by its space object on the surface of the Earth or to aircraft in flight.

Convention for the Prevention of Marine Pollution by Dumping from Ships and Aircraft (Oslo Convention)

A convention signed in Oslo in 1972 by 12 European nations pledging to take all possible steps to prevent the pollution of the northeast Atlantic. The signatory nations were Belgium, Britain, Denmark, Finland, France, Germany, Iceland, the Netherlands, Norway, Portugal, Spain and Sweden. A commission was created to administer the convention.

Box 15   continued

In 1996, a protocol was adopted, representing a major change in approach to regulating sea dumping. The protocol incorporates the precautionary principle and the polluter-pays principle. It also extends the definition of dumping to include storage of wastes in the seabed and the toppling or abandonment of humanmade structures at sea. Some materials previously permitted to be dumped were prohibited. In any event, dumping is only permitted where alternative options are exhausted. Parties must undertake waste prevention audits, consider waste management options, assess potential impacts and carry out monitoring programs. There is a complete prohibition on waste-incineration at sea and encouragement of reuse, recycling, or destroying materials to avoid dumping altogether.

Convention on Wetlands of International Importance, Especially as Waterfowl Habitat (Ramsar Convention)

Adopted in 1971 and coming into force in 1975, an agreement by the parties to take action to create reserves and otherwise protect wetlands that are internationally important for reasons including their habitat value for rare or migratory birds. Japan, for example, has concluded agreements for migratory bird protection with the USA, Russia and Australia to protect migratory birds facing extinction. Australia has designated three areas in the Northern Territory, including Kakadu National Park, as wetlands of international significance. A protocol, adopted in 1982, strengthened the convention.

Convention for the Protection of the World Cultural and Natural Heritage (Paris Convention)

A convention initiated by UNESCO and adopted in 1972; it established a World Heritage Committee and a World Heritage Fund to allow financing of conservation projects. A World Heritage List was also created.

Convention for the Prevention of Pollution from Ships (Marpol Convention)

A convention concluded in London in 1973 at the end of a conference convened by the International Maritime Organization. The convention effectively superseded a previous convention for the prevention of the pollution of the sea by oil, but does not deal with dumping from ships and aircraft covered by the Oslo Convention. The Marpol Convention aims at eliminating pollution of the sea by both oil and noxious substances, from ships of any type.

Box 15   continued

Convention on International Trade in Endangered Species of Wild Fauna and Flora (CITES) (Washington Convention)

A convention adopted in 1973 providing for the regulation of trade in plants and animals, dead or alive, and their parts and derivatives. It has been recognized that excessive international trade has contributed directly to the decline of many wild populations of rare and endangered species. The convention states that a listed protected species may not be the subject of international trade without a permit granted under the CITES procedures. The convention became effective in 1975; by 1997 it had 128 participating member countries. Timber species were not listed under CITES until 1992, when trade in Brazilian rosewood was banned; trade in other timbers is now banned or restricted. A Timber Working Group continually examines the relationship between CITES and the international timber trade.

Convention on the Law of the Sea (Montego Bay Convention)

A UN convention adopted in 1982, coming into operation in 1984; the outcome of international discussions which began in the early 1970s aimed at establishing a new legal regime for the oceans and their vast resources. The convention created the 200-mile EEZ and an International Seabed Authority to administer the new regime, conserving minerals and food supplies.

Convention for the Protection of the Ozone Layer (Vienna Convention)

A convention adopted by 21 countries together with the whole of the EU in 1985 as a first step in protecting human health and the environment from the adverse effects of activities likely to modify the ozone layer. The convention was reinforced by the Montreal Protocol of 1988 aimed at protecting the ozone layer by controlling the emission of CFCs and halons, with a specific program. Countries have kept to the timetable, with 163 nations participating and the USA leading the way. CFCs are being replaced by greener alternatives

Convention for the Protection of the Natural Resources and the Environment of the South Pacific Region (Noumea Convention)

Adopted in 1986, an agreement to take appropriate measures to prevent, reduce and control pollution in the South Pacific region,

Box 15   continued

including the Australian east coast. In the same year, two protocols were adopted relating to cooperation in pollution emergencies, and the prevention of dumping.

Convention for the Regulation of Antarctic Mineral Resource Activity (CRAMRA)

Concluded initially in 1988 by the parties to the Antarctic Treaty, an agreement to manage the potential development of the Antarctic continent, with the creation of a Mineral Resource Commission. Australia opposed the convention, objecting to all mineral exploitation in Antarctica. In 1991, a protocol (Madrid Protocol) on the protection of Antarctica was adopted; under this protocol mining was banned for a period of fifty years.

Convention on the Prohibition of Fishing with Long Drift Nets in the South Pacific (Wellington Convention)

Adopted in 1989, a convention emerging from the Tarawa Declaration of the 20th South Pacific Forum aimed at banning the practice of ecologically damaging drift-net fishing in the South Pacific.

Convention on the Control of Transboundary Movement of Hazardous Wastes and Their Disposal (Basel Convention)

A convention finalized in 1992. Its aim is to encourage countries to minimize the generation of hazardous wastes and the transboundary movement of such wastes. The convention was negotiated following concern about the dumping by industrialized nations of hazardous wastes on to African and other developing nations. In 1994, it was decided to prohibit immediately the export of hazardous wastes for final disposal from OECD to non-OECD countries, and to phase out by 1997 all exports of hazardous wastes destined for recycling operations from OECD to non-OECD countries.

Convention on Biological Diversity

Or, more fully, the Convention on Protecting Species and Habitats, a convention endorsed by UNCED in 1992 to conserve world biological diversity, or variability among living organisms. Initially treated with reserve by the USA, it was subsequently endorsed in 1993, the US establishing a National Biodiversity Center. The convention requires nations to develop and implement strategies for the sustainable use and protection of biodiversity, and provides for annual Conferences of

Box 15   continued

the Parties. The 1995 meeting dealt with marine biodiversity issues. The third conference in 1996 discussed such issues as access to genetic materials, and the impact of intellectual property rights on the conservation and sustainable use of biological diversity and equitable sharing of benefits derived from its use.

The fourth meeting of the Conference of the Parties to the Convention was held in Bratislava, Slovakia, in 1998. The agenda was broad including such topics as marine and coastal biodiversity, inland water, agricultural and forest biodiversity, the clearing-house mechanisms, biosafety, access and benefit sharing and national reports. The involvement of the private sector was also discussed. The COP-4 faced numerous administrative and organizational difficulties, though progress was discernible. COP-5 will focus on dryland, arid, semi-arid, grassland and savanna ecosystems and sustainable use; COP-6 will focus on forest ecosystems, alien species and benefit sharing; and COP-7 will focus on mountain ecosystems and protected areas and technology transfer.

Convention on Climate Change
A framework convention endorsed by UNCED in 1992, to protect the world's climate system, most notably against the effects of greenhouse gases and their warming influence. Developed nations are required to reduce their emissions of carbon dioxide and other greenhouse gases to 1990 levels or below. A succession of international conferences have followed in Berlin, Geneva, Bonn, Kyoto and Buenos Aires. The IPCC remains the principal advisory body.

Convention for the Conservation of Southern Bluefin Tuna (Canberra Convention)
A convention adopted in 1993 to ensure, through appropriate management, the conservation and optimal utilization of southern bluefin tuna. It established the Commission for the Conservation of the Southern Bluefin Tuna to implement the convention and to introduce regulatory measures. The convention came into force in 1984. The signatories included Australia, Japan and New Zealand.

Convention on Cooperation for the Protection and Sustainable Use of the Danube River (Sofia Convention)
Adopted in 1994, a convention to ensure the sustainable and equitable water management of the Danube River, including the rational use of

Box 15   continued

the catchment area; to control the hazards arising from accidents; and to contribute to the reduction of the pollution loads to the Black Sea. The polluter-pays principle and the precautionary principle apply to the convention. The convention established the International Commission for the Protection of the Danube River with all parties cooperating.

It was signed by Austria, Bulgaria, Croatia, Germany, Hungary, Moldova, Romania, Slovenia and Ukraine.

Convention to Combat Desertification
A UN treaty signed in Paris in 1994 and ratified later by individual countries aimed at tackling the spread of deserts globally; it involves the voluntary implementation of a national action plan to deal with the deterioration of farmland into desert. About one-fifth of the world's farmlands suffer from the effects of desertification.

The Second Conference of the Parties to the Convention was held in Dakar, Senegal, in 1999.

Convention on Straddling Stocks and Highly Migratory Fish Stocks
An accord signed in 1995 regulating the catch of deep-water and migratory species, including tuna, swordfish and cod stocks. The convention requires that special efforts be made by participating countries to monitor fish stocks, while strengthening inspection and reporting requirements for vessels. Regulations under the agreement apply both to international waters and to national EEZs.

Convention for the Creation of a Joint Arctic Council (Ottawa Convention)
Signed in Ottawa in September 1996, an agreement to create a joint council for the Arctic, with the aim of protecting the environment while providing for the long-term development of the region. The signatories were Canada, Denmark (on behalf of Greenland), Finland, Iceland, Norway, Russia, Sweden and the USA.

Convention on the Prior Informed Consent (PIC) Procedure for Certain Hazardous Chemicals and Pesticides in International Trade (Rotterdam Convention)
A convention finalized by 95 governments in 1998 in accordance with Agenda 21, Chapter 19, adopted at UNCED 1992. Later in 1998, the Conference of Plenipotentiaries adopted the Rotterdam Convention,

Box 15   *continued*

which was open for signature at the UN headquarters in New York, was ratified by more than fifty companies and came into force.

The Rotterdam Convention aims to monitor and control trade in dangerous chemicals that have been banned or severely restricted for health or environmental reasons. The PIC procedure is a formal mechanism for obtaining and disseminating the decisions of importing countries and for ensuring compliance with these decisions by exporting countries. Implementation of the Convention is guided by Conferences of the Parties. Another convention was being negotiated in 2000 in respect of persistent organic pollutants (POPs)

Note: *The chemicals covered by the Rotterdam Convention are: pesticides: 2,4,5-T, aldrin, captafol, chlorobenzilate, chlordane, chlordimeform, DDT, dieldrin, dinoseb, 1,2-dibromoethane (EDB), fluoroacetamide, HCH, heptachlor, hexachlorobenzene, lindane, mercury compounds, pentachlorophenol and certain formulations of methyl-parathion, methamidophos, monocrotophos, parthion, phosphamidon. Industrial chemicals: crocidolite, polybrominated biphenyls (PBB), polychlorinated biphenyls (PCB), polychlorinated terphenyls (PCT), tri (2,3 dibromopropyl) phosphate. These chemicals have been carried over from the current voluntary PIC procedure. Chemicals that are excluded from the PIC process include narcotic drugs, psychotropic substances, radioactive materials, wastes, chemical weapons, pharmaceuticals, food and food additives and chemicals imported for research or analysis in such quantities that are not likely to affect human health or the environment.

Council of Europe

A Council created in 1949 comprising a Consultative Assembly and a Committee of Ministers to make decisions and formulate recommendations to governments. The Assembly consists of 140 persons appointed by the national governments. Membership of the Council is limited to European countries; in 1979, there were 21 members.

It has been the task of the Assembly to propose actions to bring European countries close together, to keep under constant review the progress made, and to voice the views of European public opinion on the main political and economic questions of the day. The role of the Committee of Ministers is to translate the Assembly's recommendations into action. The recommendations may relate to the lowering of barriers, harmonizing of legislation, or the undertaking of tasks on a joint European basis. Projects have related to economic, legal, social, public health, environmental, education and scientific matters.

Over 70 conventions have been concluded among members of the Council as a result of its deliberations. These include the following nature conserva-

---

Box 16   Costa Rica: evolution of environmental law

1942   Water pollution legislation
1953   Drinking water legislation
1961   Sewerage legislation; wildlife legislation
1969   Forestry legislation
1970   Forestry and National Parks Service Act establishing an excellent national parks system
1972   Costa Rica represented at the UN Conference on the Human Environment, Stockholm
1973   National Council for Research in Science and Technology established, attracting interest in environmental problems. Public health legislation. Underground water legislation
1974   Chapter of 'UNESCO Man and Biosphere Program' established in Costa Rica
1976   Pollution the main cause of water-borne diseases. Industrial effluents identified causing soil contamination. Copper toxicity identified. Acid rain detected
1977   Urban planning legislation
1981   Insecticide poisoning detected, including DDT in human milk; many fruit and vegetables have traces of fungicides and insecticides. National System of Environmental Protection and Improvement introduced with a Board of Directors, to coordinate activities
1982   Noise problems identified
1985   Studies undertaken by the University of Costa Rica, the National University, the Costa Rican Institute of Technology, with environmental education promoted by the National Open University.
1992   EIA legislation

---

tion conventions: Convention on the Conservation of European Wildlife and Natural Habitats; Convention on Underwater Cultural Heritage; Convention on the Protection of International Freshwaters; Convention on the Conservation of Migratory Species of Wild Fauna; Convention on the Conservation of Antarctic Marine Living Resources.

In 1980, the Council organized the European Campaign for Urban Renaissance. Under the slogan 'A Better Life in Towns', the campaign had five main themes: the improvement of urban environmental quality; the rehabilitation of existing and older buildings, housing and areas; the provision of social, cultural and economic opportunities; the achievement of community development and participation; and a developing role for local authorities. Using a similar approach to the European Architectural Heritage Year in 1977, a campaign was organized through national committees, conferences and a program of demonstration projects.

The Council established over the years a number of special bodies and expert committees such as the European Committee on Crime Problems, the European Commission of Human Rights, the European Court of Human Rights, the European Conference of Local Councils, the Council for Cultural Cooperation, the European Committee on Legal Cooperation, the European Pharmacopeia Commission, and the Council of Europe Resettlement Funds. The judgments of the Court of Human Rights have acquired the force of law in most European countries and in the EU's Court of Justice. Since 1990, Russia and 17 other ex-communist countries have been admitted to the Council of Europe, bringing the number of members to forty. All have ratified the European conventions. The Council's remit extends now from Lisbon to Vladivostok.

Council on Environmental Quality, US

A Council created by the National Environmental Policy Act, 1969; the Council comprises three persons appointed by the President of the United States. The responsibilities of the Council include formulating policy recommendations on environmental matters for the President, advice concerning the environmental impact statement procedures and the publication of an annual report on the state of the environment in the United States. The Council functions in a manner convenient to the President. In respect to significant issues, it is normal for the Council to prepare a Presidential Review Memorandum which seeks to shape and influence administration policy. The President's Environmental Message for 1977 broadened the functions of the Council; by an Executive Order of 24 May 1977, President Carter directed the Council to issue regulations for the preparation of impact statements. The precise relationship of the Chairman of the Council to the President and the White House generally varies, understandably with each administration, from the cordial to the distant.

The Council has groups employed on various tasks. The energy group seeks to ensure that federal energy policy will evolve with full recognition of national environmental goals; and to identify emerging technologies which hold out the promise of the best results in environmental, social and economic terms. The environmental health group is concerned with a strategy for toxic substances, and the formulation of a program. It has convened a Toxic Substances Committee comprising representatives from all the federal agencies that have responsibilities for monitoring or scientific expertise. Another group is concerned with environmental economics, and the alleviation of any adverse economic effects arising from environmental decisions in specific cases. Another group is interested in recycling, inner-city environment, and land use.

The Czech Republic

The Czech Republic is a unitary multiparty republic with two legislative houses, the Senate and the Chamber of Deputies. The population in 1997 was 10.3 million at a density of 131 persons per sq km. The capital is Prague. See Box 17 for the evolution of environmental law.

Box 17   Czech Republic: evolution of environmental law

1869   Water Rights Act
1923   Effects of air pollution detected, due to increased domestic and industrial use of brown coal
1952   Air Pollution Control Act
1958   First program for construction of sewage plant
1966   Public Health Act; Act to Protect the Living Environment
1967   Environment Protection Act; Ministry of Health sets standards; charges and fines for polluting
1973   Water Pollution Act
1974   Water Resources Act addressing water management. Ministry of Management of Forests and Water
1975   Public Health Act; control of motor vehicle exhausts
1976   Brontosaurus Movement popular among young scientists
1977   Management of Forests Act
1981   Environment protection becomes a political issue
1986   Seventeenth Congress reviews environment protection and ecological problems
1992   EIA legislation; Decree on professional qualifications in EIA; Act on the Environment
1998   45 000 salmon spawn released into tributaries of the Elbe River, with the intention that the fish would migrate to the North Sea and return later. The release celebrated the reduction of pollution in the Elbe and its tributaries since the last salmon were caught in the Czech portion of the river in 1950

D

Debt-for-nature Swaps

The promotion of nature conservation projects out of the vast indebtedness incurred by many Third-World countries during the 1980s. International debt became a global problem during that period, as many lenders and investors found that they would never be repaid. It then became possible to buy fairly worthless debt from banks and institutions at prices much below face value. Lenders were glad to receive something, rather than lose all. Conservation organizations found that it was possible to acquire some of this debt cheaply, with subscribed money. These bodies then negotiated a settlement of the debt with the debtor country, again well below face value, on the understanding that the funds received to settle the debt would be invested in the country concerned on conservation projects. The indebted country thus shed debt at a substantial discount, while the proceeds did not leave the country and boosted the local economy. Depending on the costs of the transaction, conservation organizations have been able to achieve significant increases in the resources available for conservation in the debtor countries. Increasingly, swaps involve sustainable development projects. Creditor banks gain by converting their non-performing loans, though at substantial discounts, Debtor countries benefit from the reduction of their foreign currency debt, and add to their expenditure invested at home. The conservation investor receives a premium on its investment, through favourable rates of exchange.

Department of the Environment, UK

In Britain, a department formed in 1970 bringing into a single unit the three former ministries of Transport; Housing and Local Government; and Public Building and Works. For the first time, responsibility for planning and land use, for pollution control, for transport, public building and construction were brought together under a single Secretary of State. However, it was neither sensible nor possible to bring together in one department everything to do with a subject so all-embracing as the environment. Hence other departments retained some special functions. The Ministry of Agriculture, Fisheries and Food remained responsible for farming and fishing and for the control of pesticides used on the land, the disposal of farm wastes, and the monitoring of contaminants in foodstuffs. The Department of Trade and

Industry, responsible for shipping and aircraft, continued to look after oil pollution at sea and noise and pollution around airports. The Department of Employment sought to ensure that factories were safe places in which to work. The Department of Health and Social Security provided medical advice to government as a whole. The Department of Education and Science ensured that the research councils under its care provided a basis of scientific knowledge. In Scotland, Wales and Northern Ireland, environmental matters remained the responsibility of the respective departments and offices. The Foreign and Commonwealth Office remained concerned with the international and foreign policy aspects of environmental issues. However, the Secretary of State for the Environment became responsible for coordinating all the pollution control activities in all departments. Since then, the aim has been to develop a strategic approach to environmental planning and protection, to replace the fragmented approach which previously handicapped the effort.

In November 1976, the Department of the Environment was split into two departments by hiving off those parts concerned with transport. The reason for the split appeared to be purely political, being related to the balance of powers within the Cabinet. The Secretary of State for the Environment remained responsible for the Department of the Environment, encompassing such matters as regional affairs, inner urban and inner-city areas, new towns and devolution issues. Through other ministers assisting the department, the portfolio extended to housing, construction, planning, development control and land, water and sewerage, pollution, minerals, countryside affairs and sports. However, close collaboration between the Department of Environment and the Department of Transport was established with joint arrangements on urban transport and planning matters.

While the Department of the Environment tends to dominate the scene, individual regulations and policies are implemented in the UK by over 30 national and territorial departments headed by ministers, boards or appointed officials, over 70 free-standing executive agencies accountable to ministries, 375 public bodies such as single-industry regulators, 56 counties and regional councils, and about 450 district councils. To this team must be added the European Community which issues many directives applicable to the UK. Privatization tends to complicate environmental management and control. Pollution control is exercised by Her Majesty's Pollution Directorate in Whitehall and environmental health officers at the local council level. A body of commissioners conduct public inquiries throughout the UK into controversial planning and environmental issues.

Deposit-refund Schemes

Systems in which a surcharge is imposed on the price of potentially polluting products; when these products are returned to approved collection points, the surcharge is refunded. The surcharge is intended to avoid pollution and promote recycling. Deposit refunds have been applied to beverage containers, car batteries, tyres, car bodies and paint cans. Beverage containers include glass and plastic bottles and cans. Mandatory or voluntary deposit-refund systems are to be found in parts of the USA such as Michigan and Oregon, and in Sweden, Norway, Denmark, Germany, Belgium, Finland, Hungary, Poland, Austria, Canada, the Netherlands and South Australia.

South Australia is the only state in Australia that has introduced specific legislation for deposit refunds. A High Court challenge by a major brewery indicated that the system had arguably created market impediments for beer producers in South Australia compared with producers in other states. The South Australian scheme has nevertheless enjoyed wide public acceptance since its introduction in 1975, with high return rates for beverage containers.

Derelict Land Reclamation Programs, UK

Programs for the rehabilitation of land, previously utilized but abandoned and usually disfigured with industrial waste-heaps and ponds, discarded rusting machinery, crumbling buildings, discarded auto bodies and garbage. Derelict land may be reclaimed for a variety of uses. In urban areas it may be restored, where practicable, for housing or industrial use but in practice more of the derelict land in these areas is used to provide public open space for amenity or recreation, since there is a greater need for planned open space in such areas. In other areas the emphasis tends to be on restoration for agricultural uses, mainly rough grazing or woodland; substantial areas of land damaged by mineral working, for example, colliery spoil heaps, have been successfully reclaimed for such uses. Other examples of after-use are the reclamation of disused gravel pits for use as water recreation areas and as nature reserves, and the treatment of disused railroads to provide public walkways and bridleways in the countryside.

A particular problem, and one to which increasing attention is being paid, is the reclamation of contaminated land in urban areas – for example, the sites of former gas-works, sewage farms and scrap yards, or sites used previously for tipping toxic wastes (for example, cadmium, lead, phenols, cyanides and tars). A large number of contaminated sites are now being considered for redevelopment for a variety of uses involving various remedial measures to minimize the potential environmental problems. One example of current reclamation projects is the comprehensive development at Thamesmead, on the site of the former Woolwich Arsenal, where there is extensive pollution by a wide range of substances including toxic metals, pyrotechnic wastes and gas-works wastes. A national survey of derelict land conducted in 1984 revealed that Britain still had over 45 000 ha of such land.

Development

The application of human, financial and physical resources to satisfy human needs; inevitably, development involves modification of the biosphere and some aspects of development detract from the quality of life locally, regionally, nationally or globally. The breadth of development is not always appreciated as the term applies not only to the growth of industry, commerce and infrastructure but to sanitation, education, medicine, health, housing, national parks, tourist and recreational facilities.

Development Application

A formal application to a council, government, statutory body, or department seeking approval for the construction or development of a project. A development application may need to be accompanied by an EIS or a review of environmental factors. A report on an application will be prepared by professional planning officers for the approval authority. A controversial project or one of considerable difficulty may be subjected to a public inquiry by independent commissioners. Box 18 reviews the contents of a development application.

Development Control

Considered broadly, all those statutory and regulatory elements which provide a framework for development, including all environmental planning instruments, including EIS and EIA procedures, and pollution-control approvals and licences. However, the term may extend to much more detailed requirements stipulating, say, restrictions on the heights of buildings, facilities for car parking, landscaping and streetscape requirements, density and plot ratios, heritage conservation measures, facilities for disabled persons, design and location of signs, arrangements for refuse removal and recycling, pedestrian shelter and access, protection of trees, prohibited features, provi-

Box 18   Development application

Matters taken into account by consent authorities include:
- The nature and purpose of the proposal.
- The relationship between the proposal and any existing or intended statutory planning instrument or development control plan.
- The likely impact on the environment and the possible need for an EIS.
- The means proposed for the mitigation of adverse environmental effects.
- The possible or certain effects on the landscape.
- The social and economic effects of the proposal in the locality.
- The character, scale, density and height of the development.
- The size and shape of the land in question and the area of the site to be covered.
- The location of the development and the proximity of other developments.
- The entrances and exits to the site.
- The arrangements for the movement, loading and unloading of vehicles.
- The parking of vehicles.
- Traffic generation and its effects on the road system and road safety.
- The availability of public transport.
- The availability of utility services.
- The provision for landscaping and tree preservation.
- The possible effects on the amenities of the area.
- Access for the disabled, where necessary.
- Likely hazardous or offensive processes.
- The adequacy of water, drainage and sewerage services.
- The adequacy of emergency services.
- The effect on conservation areas and heritage items.
- The public interest.
- Representations by public and private bodies and the general public.
- Recommendations by council officers.
- The prospective financial contribution by the proponents towards improved infrastructure and community amenities.
- The housing of the workforce during the construction period and after.

sion of public spaces, pedestrian arcades, aesthetics, shadow and wind-tunnel effects, and procedures for future changes and alterations.

Development Rights

Traditional legal rights associated with the ownership of property, including (but not limited to) the rights to exclude trespassers and poachers, cut timber, mine or quarry, grow crops or keep animals, or to build structures for private use or for profit. These traditional rights have been progressively modified by planning legislation including planning schemes, zoning, development application, and development control requirements, the outcome of public inquiries and appeals to the courts. No one can any longer do what they like with their own property.

Direct Regulation

See:
Command-and-control or Direct Regulation.

Disasters

See:
Bhopal Disaster, India, 1984; Chernobyl Nuclear Disaster; *Exxon Valdez* Disaster; Flixborough Disaster; Mexico City Industrial Disaster, 1984; Times Beach, US.

Disputes Avoidance

A concept first examined at a meeting of experts convened by the Rockefeller Foundation at Belagio, Italy, in 1974. At that meeting, disputes avoidance was carefully distinguished from disputes settlement. The view that emerged from Belagio was unanimous: efforts should be made towards establishing feasible procedures whereby states might avoid disputes that may arise between them, in addition to traditional procedures such as the International Court of Justice or the European Court of Justice for the peaceful settlement of disputes once they have arisen.

The theme of disputes avoidance was further extended at the Third UN Conference on the Law of the Sea. It was suggested that states should seek to minimize the occurrence of disputes generally by setting out from the beginning all relevant facts and considerations of law. This helps to avoid the festering of disputes through lack of awareness. Emphasis was also drawn to the constant need for negotiation. In 1989, the issue was raised again at the Sixth (Legal) Committee of the General Assembly of the UN, particularly in relation to environmental issues and threats to the global commons. At the 1992 UNCED, Principle 19 of the Rio Declaration read: 'States shall provide prior and timely notification and relevant information to potentially affected States on activities that may have a significant adverse transboundary environmental effect and shall consult with those States at an early stage and in good faith.' This was a limited but vital contribution to the avoidance of disputes. Box 19 summarizes some of the basic elements of dispute-avoidance mechanisms.

Box 19   Disputes avoidance: basic elements

- Prior consultation, exchange of views and information, timely recognition of potential areas of dispute, smoothing the way to the avoidance of future disagreements.
- Clarification of facts and exploration of potential arguments.
- The appointment of a commissioner of inquiry, mediator or arbitrator to explore possible amicable solutions to potential problems, avoiding formal legal proceedings.
- Avoidance at a political level of issues that might provoke sharp disagreement. Such treaties as the 1987 Montreal Protocol on Substances that Deplete the Ozone Layer and the 1992 Framework Convention on Climate Change provide for the resolution of potential disputes via conciliation.
- The 1991 ECE Convention on Environmental Impact Assessment in a Transboundary Context creates a commission of inquiry which will, if necessary, reach agreement on unresolved points. This avoids submissions to the European Court of Justice.

Dobry Report, UK

The Report of the Dobry Committee on the British development control system, published in 1975, which supported the idea of EIA for selected major developments, with regard to six aspects (namely traffic, roads and public transportation; ground and surface water drainage; publicly provided services; appearance of the surrounding area; employment; and noise and air pollution). Partly in response to this report, the Secretary of State directed a study through the Department of the Environment into the need for EIA procedures and how best these could be incorporated within the existing development control system. The study recommended that EIA procedures should be undertaken as an experiment, without any amendment of the planning system in the first place. It also included some substantial qualifications about the type of EIA process that it was recommending.

See also:
Environmental Impact Assessment; Environmental Impact Statement.

Due Diligence

A defence permitted in some branches of environmental law, that the breach or offence occurred despite all due diligence to prevent the commission of an offence, that is that all reasonable measures had been taken and an appropriate level of responsibility exercised. In other words, that the commission of the offence was due to causes over which the accused had no control. For example, the offence might have been due to the failure of an employee to carry out reasonable instructions, or due to a technical failure or explosion that could not have been reasonably foreseen.

See also:
Strict Liability.

Duncan Classification, US

A classification, created by the American sociologist Otis Dudley Duncan and his colleagues, of the interrelations of metropolitan areas and regions of the United States. The classification constitutes an analysis of different levels of regional integration; it distinguishes:
- national metropolises;
- urban places with diversified manufacturing and metropolitan functions;
- regional metropolises;
- regional capitals;
- urban places with diversified manufacturing and few metropolitan functions;
- urban places with specialized manufacturing; and
- special cases.

This classification contains elements of hierarchy while suggesting a conclusion that the potential size of individual cities or metropolitan areas depends on the size and integration of the region of which they are a part.

E

Earth Charter

The environmental equivalent of the Universal Declaration of Human Rights, a fundamental statement of principles that presents an ethical framework for guiding individuals, organizations and nations towards an improved quality of life and sustainable development. The idea of an Earth Charter was first proposed at the UN Conference on the Human Environment, Stockholm, 1972, when it was recognized that global security and human development could not be divorced from national and global environmental concerns. In the early 1980s, the UN General Assembly adopted the World Charter for Nature, in itself a major advance in the articulation of fundamental principles. However, this charter did not deal adequately with social and economic concerns as embraced in the concept of sustainable development.

The Brundtland Commission report, *Our Common Future* (1987), reaffirmed the need for an integrated Earth Charter in which ecological objectives could be fully integrated with social and economic goals. Instead of a charter, however, at UNCED, 1992, the nations adopted the Rio Declaration on Environment and Development, again a major advance but still falling short of a comprehensive Earth Charter.

Following the Rio Conference, two NGOs, the Earth Council and the Green Cross International, with the support of the Netherlands government, joined forces with others to pursue the development of an Earth Charter. In 1997, an Earth Charter Commission, composed of 23 distinguished individuals from every continent, was created to oversee the development of a charter. It is anticipated that a final draft will be available in 2000 to be tabled in the UN General Assembly in 2002, being the review year for the Rio Summit.

Economic Instruments

A current trend in environmental legislation is to promote the use of economic instruments to augment or replace command-and-control (statutory regulation) measures. Economic instruments provide incentives to improve environmental performance through taxes, subsidies, deposit-refund systems, road-pricing schemes, emission charges, user charges, transfer of rights, and substantial fines, penalties and the award of damages. The adoption of economic instruments is making slow progress, much preference being given by enforcement authorities to command-and-control measures. See Box 20.

Box 20   Examples of economic instruments

Fines, penalties, and damages
- The imposition of substantial fines, penalties such as imprisonment, and the award of damages to victims as a restraining influence on the activities of polluters.

Charges and taxes
- Emission charges paid on discharges into the environment based on load or concentration.
- User charges for the public treatment of effluents or wastes.
- Product charges/taxes to discourage specific uses.

Subsidies
- Grants, being non-repayable forms of financial aid.
- Soft loans, that is loans with rates of interest below market rates.
- Tax allowances, exemptions, rebates and accelerated depreciation.

Tradable emission permits
- While discharges are permitted within an overall emission limit, trading is permitted on the open market within that limit.

Deposit-refund systems
- Deposit refunds on short-cycle goods.
- Deposit refunds on durables.
- Refunds of surcharges on potentially polluting goods, when goods are returned to an approved collection station.
- Refunds of deposits under performance bonds.

Other schemes
- Pay-by-the-bag systems.
- Debt-for-nature swaps.
- Road-pricing schemes.
- Noise fees.
- Transfer of development rights.
- Transfer of water rights.
- Oil pollution compensation schemes.
- Transferable quotas in fisheries management.

Edwards Dam, Maine, USA

The Edwards Dam, constructed in 1837, is located on the Kennebec River, Maine, near the state capital Augusta. Not a major dam, being only 300 metres wide and six metres high, it has nonetheless, for 160 years, prevented sturgeon, salmon and seven other species of migratory fish from reaching their original spawning grounds. In 1996, the Federal Energy Regulatory Commission (FERC), in a preliminary study, concluded that the dam could stay if the company added fish-lifts to help millions of spawning fish over the obstacle; however, later studies revealed that the cost of this would be double the cost of removing the dam and purchasing replacement electric power. The agency also concluded that Maine's economy would not be harmed by losing the dam.

In November 1997, the FERC gave the private owners of the Edwards Dam a year to develop a plan for the demolition of the dam at their own expense. This was an upset for the owners, Edwards Manufacturing, who had been seeking a renewed operating license from FERC; such a licence being needed because the company sold power to the Central Maine Power Company.

The decision was a victory for environmentalists. This was the first time that an operating dam was to be refused a licence; since 1920, the FERC had ordered the demolition of only seven out of 1600 private electricity-producing dams, all for safety reasons after the owners had abandoned them. Applications for the removal of other dams will follow.

EEZ

See:
Exclusive Economic Zone (EEZ).

Egypt

The Arab Republic of Egypt is a republic with one legislative house, the People's Assembly. The capital is Cairo. The population in 1997 was 62 million, at an average density of 62 persons per sq km. Egypt overlooks the Mediterranean, with Libya to the West, the Sudan to the south, and Israel to the east. Egypt is dominated by the Nile, which creates a fertile area. Much of the remainder is desert. See Box 21 for the evolution of environmental law.

Box 21   Egypt: evolution of environmental law

1348	The Black Death
1798	Cairo population 300 000
1863–79	Ismail orders construction of European-style city, influenced by the redevelopment of Paris
1945	Population of Cairo, two million
1952	Introduction of planned suburbs such as Nasser City, Muqattam City and Engineers' City; construction of satellite towns; flood-control permits riverfront development
1970	Completion of the Aswan High Dam, impounding the reservoir of Lake Nasser. Lake Nasser extends for 320 km within Egypt and 160 km further upstream into the Sudan. Although there are immense benefits to the Egyptian economy, the dam spreads the disease, schistosomiasis, through snails that live in the irrigation channels
1970–85	Sewerage substantially extended in Cairo
1986	Metropolitan rail system completed; reconstruction of opera house
1990	Over 400 registered historic monuments
1994	National Law Concerning the Environment, including EIA
1996	Cairo population reaches ten million; infant mortality 71 per thousand
1997	Inauguration of the Toshka Canal, to carry water from Lake Nasser to irrigate areas in the deep south and west, supplemented with water from aquifers
1998	Establishment of St Katharine Protectorate National Park, near Mount Sinai
2000	Construction of the Al-Salam Canal, feeding Nile water into the Sinai Peninsula, developing a vast agro-industrial irrigation scheme

---

EIS

See:
Environmental Impact Statement.

Emergency Planning and Community Right-to-Know Act, 1986, US

In response to the Bhopal and Chernobyl disasters, the US Congress enacted emergency legislation. The act requires states to create emergency response commissions and local emergency planning committees. Comprehensive emergency response plans were to be developed, with precise procedures for dealing with releases of extremely hazardous substances. The owners and operators of facilities are obliged to provide information on their stocks of hazardous materials. It established the rights of citizens, and state and local government agencies, to sue for enforcement and damages.

See also:
Comprehensive Environmental Response, Compensation, and Liability Act, 1980 (CERCLA), US; Superfund.

Eminent Domain

The superiority of the sovereign power over all property in the nation, whereby it is entitled to appropriate any part required for the public advantage, compensation being made to the owner. Certain public bodies in the United States are authorized by law to condemn (acquire) property when it is in the public interest, giving fair monetary compensation to the owner. For example, a city may condemn land for a needed highway; or a redevelopment agency may condemn land for an urban renewal project.

See also:
Compulsory Purchase; Taking Issue, US.

Emission Standard

The amount of pollutant permitted to be discharged from a source. Emission standards are commonly described in one or more of the following ways: weight of pollutants per unit volume of discharged gas, for example, micrograms per cubic metre; volume of pollutants per unit volume of discharged gas, for example, parts per million; weight of pollutants per weight of material processed, for example, ten kilograms per tonne; weight of pollutants over a certain time, for example, kilograms per hour, or tonnes per day. Test conditions may be prescribed. Limits for noise are set in the Decibel A-scale or dB(A).

See also:
Environmental Quality Standards; National Ambient Air Quality Standards (NAAQS), US; National Environment Protection Council (NEPC), Australia; US Emission Trading Program.

Endangered Species Act, 1973, US

Amended in 1978, 1982 and 1985, an act to protect endangered species in the United States; it requires the maintenance of a list of endangered species and empowers the US Fish and Wildlife Service to approve and review state and agency plans for the recovery of endangered species. It authorizes the prosecution of violators of the wildlife trafficking regulations, attempting to combat the black market in thousands of protected reptiles and birds. A current issue is whether Native Americans should continue to have a right to kill endangered species, such as bald eagles, for religious purposes. The US Lacey Act makes the violation of foreign wildlife laws a violation of US law.

Environment

The physical surroundings or circumstances in which humanity struggles to survive and thrive; it includes the planet Earth and outer space as well as the immediate province of living organisms, the biosphere. The environment of the individual includes the abiotic factors of land, water, atmosphere, climate, sound, odors and tastes; and the biotic factors of other humans, animals, plants, bacteria and viruses. The European Commission has defined the environment as 'the combination of elements whose complex interrelationships make up the settings, the surroundings and the conditions of life of the individual and of society, as they are or as they are felt'. The concept has emerged of the environment as a parcel of things which render a stream of beneficial services and some disservices to people, though largely unpriced, and which take their place alongside the stream of services rendered by real income, commodities, houses, infrastructure, transport and other people. The idea of a beneficial environment, in these terms, which we may enjoy, seems to relate at least in part to that other concept, the quality of life.

Environmental legislation generally defines the term 'environment' broadly. For example, the Environmental Assessment Act, 1980, of Ontario, Canada, defines the term as follows:

(i)   air, land or water;
(ii)   plant and animal life, including man;
(iii) the social, economic and cultural conditions that influence the life of man or a community;

(iv)   any building, structure, machine or other device or thing made by man;
(v)   any solid, liquid, gas, odor, heat, sound, vibration or radiation resulting directly or indirectly from the activities of man; or
(vi)   any part or combination of the foregoing in the interrelationship between any two or more of them, in or of Ontario.

Thus, Ontario legislation goes far beyond the limits of the natural environment and permits an assessment of almost any aspect of a proposed undertaking including its impact on people and society as a whole.

See also:
Environmental Law; Framework Environmental Law.

Environment Protection Act, 1997, ACT

An act relating to the Australian Capital Territory (ACT) which came into force in June 1998 replacing five pieces of existing legislation: the Air Pollution Act 1984; the Water Pollution Act 1984; the Noise Control Act 1988; the Pesticides Act 1989; and the Ozone Protection Act 1991. The new act was introduced by the ACT government to reform environmental management in Canberra and the Territory, recognizing the importance of sustainable development and the need for joint community responsibility.

See also:
Burley Griffin Plan for Canberra.

Environment Protection and Biodiversity Conservation Act, 2000 (Australia)

An Australian government act repealing and superseding a range of previous federal legislation, including: the Environmental Protection (Impact of Proposals) Act 1974; the National Parks and Wildlife Conservation Acts 1975; the Whale Protection Act 1980; the Wildlife Protection (Regulation of Exports and Imports) Act 1982; the Endangered Species Protection Act 1992; and the World Heritage Properties Conservation Act 1983. The new act revises and updates the whole procedure for EIA at the national level. It revises the procedures for World Heritage properties and for places of national heritage significance; endangered or vulnerable species and communities; nuclear activities; marine waters; ozone protection; hazardous wastes; Ramsar wetlands; and biodiversity conservation.

Environmental Audit

An assessment of the nature and extent of any harm or detriment, or any possible harm or detriment, that may be inflicted on any aspect of the environment by any activity, process, development, program, or any product, chemical or waste substance. Audits may be designed to: verify, or otherwise, compliance with environmental requirements; evaluate the effectiveness of existing environmental management systems; protect the organization against external criticism; assess risks generally; or assist in planning for future improvements in environment protection and pollution control. An audit may be conducted in-house, though an independent audit may sometimes be required by the authorities. Occasionally, an audit or post-project analysis may be conducted by an enforcement agency, or it may be undertaken when a transfer of ownership or control of land is taking place and it is necessary to declare the degree of contamination of the land.

Environmental Change Network (ECN)

A network for monitoring the changes which may be taking place in British ecosystems, distinguishing natural variations from humanmade changes and giving early warning of undesirable effects. ECN was launched in 1992; the operation of the network depends on the voluntary collaboration of the sponsoring agencies in providing sites and staff. Twenty-four sites in the system represent a broad range of climate, soil, habitat and land management in Britain. The project is managed by the National Environmental Research Council.

Environmental Health Impact Assessment (EHIA)

Environmental health impact assessment is a subset of EIA; it is concerned with the potential adverse health effects of development, in the immediate, short and long term, in the locality and further afield. Working conditions are generally considered under separate legislation. Health effects are sometimes sufficiently significant as to justify a separate chapter in an EIS. Many projects contribute to an improved quality of life, offering benefits in health terms. Some projects will present a threat to health under exceptional circumstances only. See Box 22.

See also:
Environmental Impact Assessment.

Box 22   *Environmental health impact assessment: economic, social and environmental matters for consideration*

In determining a development application, a consent authority should take into consideration such of the following matters as are of relevance to the proposed development:

1. Within the framework of environmental impact assessment (EIA), those aspects of the proposed development which might present adverse risks to the health and well-being of the community, either near or far, in the short or long term, either directly or indirectly; or any particularly vulnerable section of the community (the young, the old, the disadvantaged, the sick, or aborigines).

2. Emissions from the proposed development that may have a detrimental effect on the quality of air or water to the detriment of human beings either directly, or indirectly through the food chain; an inventory of pollutants with details of the handling or dispersal of these.

3. The risks of contamination of land from leachates or the dumping or storage of toxic materials; risk of contamination of aquifers.

4. Solid wastes from the development and their management; possible dust and grit from wastepiles, disposal areas and vehicles, roads, and tipping operations.

5. The levels of noise, blast and vibration that may occur, during the day, night or weekend.

6. Odors likely to be emanated at various times from various processes and disposal practices.

7. The volume of traffic likely to be generated by the development, particularly heavy vehicles; the implications for community noise, and for the safety of drivers and pedestrians, particularly children.

8. The risks and hazards of the activity: fire, explosion, sudden harmful fumes, major spills of toxic materials within the plant or on the roads, radiation, failures of safety systems, effects of sustained temperature inversions in the atmosphere, failure of flares, unexpected discharges of toxic materials such as dioxins, chain reactions, failure of treatment plant, asbestos risks, sewage discharge, floods and failure of emergency procedures.

9. Possible synergistic effects of several pollutants reacting together.

10. Possible promotion of vector breeding such as flies or mosquitoes; the effects of water resource development.

11. Cumulative effects of other developments in the region or locality, for example, effects on drinking water safety.

Box 22   continued

12. Other effects likely to have a negative effect on physical or mental well-being such as split communities, ecological damage, loss of access to recreational facilities, bright night lighting, loss of amenity, overhead transmission lines, surface pipelines, increased closure of railway crossing gates; nighttime noise from, say, aircraft or power plant, generators and transformers; increased stress; deterioration of the visual environment or amenities; anxiety about the future; isolation; adverse effects on local businesses in some cases; absence of facilities for the mediation of disputes or ventilation of opinion.

13. The effect on workers at home who are exposed to detrimental conditions at both work and home, such as air pollution and odors.

14. The existing environment, land uses, and current levels of pollution and risk; characteristics of the population and its current health status; other environmental degradation; existing standard of living of the population; aboriginal issues.

15. Mitigation measures proposed for the adverse effects of the development; proposals for monitoring and post-project analysis in respect of health effects.

16. Contributions by the proponent to improving the health, social and recreational facilities of the immediate locality.

17. Public perception of the risks and hazards; interaction with the media.

18. The incorporation of environmental health standards in development consent conditions; together with annual reporting requirements to the environmental, planning and public health agencies.

Sources: Derived from World Health Organization (1989), *Environmental Impact Assessment: An Assessment of Methodological and Substantive Issues Affecting Human Health Considerations,* WHO report No. 41, University of London, and other related literature.

Environmental Impact Assessment (EIA)

EIA is the critical appraisal of the likely effects of a policy, plan, program, project or activity, on the environment. To assist the decision-making authority, assessments are carried out independently of the proponent, who may have prepared an EIS. The decision-making authority may be a level of government (local, state or federal) or a government agency (at local, state or federal level). Assessments take account of any adverse environmental effects on the community; any environmental impact on the ecosystems of the locality; any diminution of the aesthetic, recreational, aesthetic, scientific, or other environmental values of a locality; the endangering of any species of fauna or flora; any adverse effects on any place or building having aesthetic, anthropological, archaeological, cultural, historical, scientific or social significance; any long-term or cumulative effects on the environment; any curtailing of the range of beneficial uses; any environmental problems associated with the disposal of wastes; any implications for natural resources; and the implications for the concept of sustainable development. EIA extends to the entire process from the inception of a proposal to environmental auditing and post-project analysis.

The outcome of an EIA is a recommendation to the decision-maker to either: (1) approve the project in its entirety, subject to a range of recommended statutory conditions or requirements; or (2) reject the proposal, outright and completely. Outright rejection is rare, but it does occur; while some proponents withdraw their applications in the face of growing public objection.

The general effect of EIA procedures has been to improve the quality of proposals, rather than to prohibit development. To those committed to zero-economic growth this has been a profound disappointment. EIA is presented as the servant of economic growth and the avenue to resource degradation.

Box 23 summarizes the principles of environmental impact assessment as outlined by UNEP; Box 24 records the introduction of statutory EIA requirements by countries; while Box 25 outlines typical matters dealt with in conditions of consent, binding on the developer.

See also:
Environmental Law; Framework Environmental Law.

Environmental Impact Assessment and Foreign Aid

The requirement of the US National Environmental Policy Act (NEPA) 1969 that all federal agencies prepare an EIS on 'major actions significantly affecting the quality of the human environment' immediately raised the question as to whether this applied to the action of providing foreign aid to countries outside US legal jurisdiction.

In 1975, the US Agency for International Development was sued by a public interest group to enforce the preparation of EISs on its loans and

Box 23   UNEP: principles of environmental impact assessment

1. States (countries, including their competent authorities) should not undertake or authorize activities without prior consideration, at an early stage, of their environmental effects. Where the extent, nature or location of a proposed activity is such that it is likely to significantly affect the environment, a comprehensive EIA should be undertaken in accordance with the following principles.

2. The criteria and procedures for determining whether an activity is likely to significantly affect the environment and is therefore subject to an EIA should be defined clearly by legislation, regulation, or other means, so that subject activities can be quickly and surely identified, and EIA can be applied to the activity as it is being planned.

3. In the EIA process, the relevant significant environmental issues should be identified and studied. Where appropriate, all efforts should be made to identify these issues at an early stage in the process.

4. An EIA should include, at a minimum:
   a. a description of the proposed activity;
   b. a description of the potentially affected environment, including specific information necessary for identifying and assessing the environmental effects of the proposed activity;
   c. a description of practical alternatives, as appropriate;
   d. an assessment of the likely or potential environmental impacts of the proposed activity and alternatives, including the direct, indirect, cumulative, short-term and long-term effects;
   e. an identification and description of measures available to mitigate adverse environmental impacts of the proposed activity and alternatives, and an assessment of those measures;
   f. an indication of the gaps in knowledge and uncertainties which may be encountered in compiling the required information;
   g. an indication of whether the environment of any other state or areas beyond national jurisdiction is likely to be affected by the proposed activity or alternatives;
   h. a brief, non-technical summary of the information provided under the above headings.

5. The environmental effects in an EIA should be assessed with a degree of detail commensurate with their likely environmental significance.

Box 23 continued

6. The information provided as part of an EIA should be examined impartially prior to the decision.

7. Before a decision is made on an activity, government agencies, members of the public, experts in relevant disciplines and interested groups should be allowed appropriate opportunity to comment on the EIA.

8. A decision as to whether a proposed activity should be authorized or undertaken should not be taken until an appropriate period has elapsed to consider comments pursuant to principles seven and twelve.

9. The decision on any proposed activity subject to an EIA should be in writing, state the reasons therefore, and include the provisions, if any, to prevent, reduce or mitigate damage to the environment. This decision should be made available to interested persons and groups.

10. Where it is justified, following a decision on an activity which has been subject to an EIA, the activity and its effects on the environment or the provisions (pursuant to principle nine) of the decision on this activity should be subject to appropriate supervision.

11. States should endeavour to conclude bilateral, regional or multilateral arrangements, as appropriate, so as to provide, on the basis of reciprocity, notification, exchange of information, and agreed-upon consultation on the potential environmental effects of activities under their control or jurisdiction which are likely to significantly affect other states or areas beyond national jurisdiction.

12. When information provided as part of an EIA indicates that the environment within another state is likely to be significantly affected by a proposed activity, the state in which the activity is being planned should, to the extent possible:
    a. notify the potentially affected state of the proposed activity;
    b. transmit to the potentially affected state any relevant information from the EIA, the transmission of which is not prohibited by national laws or regulations; and
    c. when it is agreed between the states concerned, enter into timely consultations.

13. Appropriate measures should be established to ensure implementation of EIA procedures.

Source: From *Goals and Principles of Environmental Impact Assessment* endorsed by decision 14/25 of the Governing Council of UNEP of 17 June 1987.

Box 24   *Introduction of statutory EIA requirements by country*

Albania	1993	Iraq	1986
Algeria	1983	Ireland	1988
Australia	1974	Italy	1988
Austria	1993	Jamaica	1991
Bahrain	1980	Japan	1972
Bangladesh	1995	Kazakhstan	1991
Belgium	1985	Korea, North	1991
Belize	1992	Korea, South	1981
Bolivia	1992	Kuwait	1980
Brazil	1981	Kyrgyzstan	1991
Bulgaria	1991	Latvia	1991
Burkina Faso	1994	Libya	1992
Canada	1973	Lithuania	1992
Cape Verde	1993	Luxembourg	1990
Chile	1994	Madagascar	1990
China	1979	Malaysia	1974
Columbia	1974	Mali	1991
Comoros	1994	Malta	1991
Congo	1991	Mauritius	1991
Costa Rica	1992	Mexico	1988
Cuba	1981	Moldova	1993
Czech Republic	1992	Mongolia	1994
Denmark	1989	Namibia	1994
Ecuador	1976	Nepal	1993
Egypt	1994	Netherlands	1986
Estonia	1995	New Zealand	1991
Finland	1994	Nigeria	1988
France	1976	Norway	1989
Gabon	1993	Oman	1979
Gambia	1994	Pakistan	1983
Germany	1975	Palau	1981
Ghana	1994	Papua New Guinea	1978
Greece	1986	Peru	1990
Guatemala	1986	Philippines	1977
Guinea	1987	Poland	1989
Honduras	1993	Portugal	1987
India	1986	Qatar	1994
Indonesia	1982	Russian Federation	1991
Iran	1986	Saudi Arabia	1982

Box 24 continued

Senegal	1983	Thailand	1992
Seychelles	1994	Togo	1988
Singapore	1972	Tunisia	1988
Slovak Republic	1994	Turkey	1983
Slovenia	1994	Ukraine	1991
South Africa	1989	United Arab Emirates	1981
Spain	1986	United Kingdom	1988
Sri Lanka	1980	United States of America	1969
St. Kitts and Nevis	1987	Uruguay	1994
Sweden	1987	Uzbekistan	1992
Switzerland	1983	Venezuela	1976
Taiwan	1979	Vietnam	1994
Tajikistan	1993	Zambia	1990

Box 25 EIA: typical matters dealt with in conditions of consent, binding on the developer

- Approvals, licences and permits to be obtained from statutory authorities, boards, departments and local councils.
- Conformity with certain specifications contained in the environmental impact statement (EIS).
- Compatibility with all applicable planning instruments.
- Control of air, water and noise pollution including discharges to catchments, protection of aquifers, control of leachates, blasting controls, incineration, waste disposal, oil contamination, sewage treatment, drainage, stormwater and runoff management, and dust suppression.
- Life of project.
- Location of buildings and individual items of equipment.
- Sequence of mining, quarrying and extractive operations.
- Working hours.
- Buffer zones.
- Access roads, junctions, traffic, rail, pipeline and transmission routes.
- Risks and hazards.
- Emergency procedures: fire-fighting, evacuation.
- Water supplies and storage.
- Heritage items.

Box 25   *continued*

- Visual amenity, trees, vegetation, screening.
- Rehabilitation.
- Social and economic effects of proposal.
- Housing of workforce.
- Monitoring and recording of results.
- Environmentally hazardous chemicals.
- Heights of buildings and stacks.
- Acquisition of properties.
- Protection of wetlands, parks and reserves, oyster leases, mangroves, rainforest and other natural resources.
- Subsidence.
- Closure of existing plant and replacement of less-efficient plant.
- Effects on residents, schools and hospitals, industries.
- Lodging of guarantee funds in respect of performance, payment of levies towards future management of the site, contributions towards infrastructure costs and road improvements.
- Appointment of environmental management officers by proponent.
- Independent auditing of risks and hazards.
- Annual reports to the Department of Planning.
- Arrangements for continuous liaison with the public, local councils, conservation bodies and resident action groups.
- Matters relating to sustainable development, sustainable yield, or cross-frontier or global environmental protection.
- Compliance with international conventions.

grants to other countries. As a consequence of this court case, the agency introduced in 1976 a process of EIA on many of the projects with which it has been involved. Subsequently, the US Export–Import Bank and the State Department were sued on similar issues.

Early in 1978, the Council on Environmental Quality (CEQ), reporting directly to the President, circulated draft regulations on the extension of NEPA to foreign aid; these were not well-received by all federal agencies. The President's Counsel then asked CEQ and the State Department to deliberate on an acceptable approach for consideration by the President. These deliberations resulted in 1979 in a President's executive order (an order with the force of law) entitled 'Environmental effects abroad of major federal actions'.

The order required that EISs, multilateral studies, or concise reviews of environmental issues be prepared and taken into consideration in making decisions for actions significantly affecting: (1) the environment of the global commons; (2) the environment of a foreign nation not participating with the US and not otherwise involved in the action; (3) the environment of a foreign nation when the activity involves radioactive substances or an emission of effluent prohibited or strictly regulated by US law; or (4) natural or ecological resources in the participating nation that are designated to be of global importance by the President of the United States or by international agreement. For category (1) an EIS is a standard requirement. All communications between federal agencies and foreign governments under this order are coordinated by the State Department.

Certain activities concerning largely national security and arms transfers are exempted from this order. This is, however, consistent with the statement of objective of the order which is 'to further environmental objectives consistent with the foreign policy and national security policy of the United States'. Actions not having a significant effect on the environment, as determined by the involved agency, are also exempt.

Environmental Impact Statement (EIS)

A document commonly required under EIA legislation setting out the merits and demerits of a proposed development, program or policy, in environmental terms. This document is intended to aid the decision-maker in respect of development consent or refusal, other parties and members of the public. The publication of an EIS may precede a public inquiry at which additional evidence from other parties and members of the public may be heard before an independent commissioner of inquiry. An EIS will often prove to be only one input into a process leading to a development decision by some level of government. See Box 26 for the characteristics of a good EIS.

See also:
Environmental Impact Assessment.

Environmental Improvement Plan (EIP)

A comprehensive strategy to improve the environmental performance of a company, industrial complex, municipality, catchment, region or state, involving all stakeholders in its formulation and implementation with continuous consultation processes. The idea of progressing beyond compliance with bare statutory requirements has gathered strength in recent years, resulting in the progressive improvement of the environment in all its dimensions, with both

Box 26   *Characteristics of a good environmental impact statement (EIS)*

1. A summary of the EIS, intelligible to non-specialists and the public, should precede the main text.
2. Acronyms and initials should be defined; a glossary of technical terms can be relegated to an appendix.
3. The list of contents should permit quick identification of the main issues.
4. The authors of the EIS should be clearly identified.
5. A brief outline of the history of the proposed development should be given, including details of early consultations.
6. A full description of the proposed project or activity, its objectives and geographical boundaries; its inputs and outputs and the movement of these; also the inputs and outputs specifically during the construction phase. Diagrams, plans, and maps will be necessary to illustrate these features, with a clear presentation of the likely appearance of the finished project.
7. A full description of the existing environment likely to be affected by the proposal; the baseline conditions; deficiencies in information; data sources; the proximity of people, other enterprises, and characteristics of the area of ecological or cultural importance.
8. The alternative locations considered, or alternative processes, resulting in the preferred choice of site; evidence of credible studies will be needed here.
9. The justification of the proposal in terms of economic, social, and environmental considerations; the consequences of not carrying out the proposal for the proponent, the locality, the region, and the nation.
10. The planning framework, relevant statutory planning instruments, zoning, planning, and environmental objectives.
11. The identification and analysis of the likely environmental interactions between the proposed activity and the environment.
12. The measures to be taken with the proposal for the protection of the environment and an assessment of their likely effectiveness, particularly about pollution control, land management, erosion, aesthetics, rehabilitation, ecological protection measures, and decommissioning. Measures to achieve clean production and recycling; the management of residuals.
13. The effect on the transport system of carrying people, goods, services, and raw materials, to and from the project.

Box 26 continued

14. The duration of the construction phase, operational phase, and decommissioning phase; housing the workforce, both construction and permanent.

15. The implications for public infrastructure such as housing, schools, hospitals, water supply, garbage removal, sewerage, electricity, roads, recreational facilities, fire, police, emergency services, parks, gardens and nature reserves; the implications for endangered species and threatened ecological features and ecosystems; the prospective financial contributions of the proponent.

16. Any transboundary or transborder implications of the proposal.

17. Any cumulative effects from similar enterprises should be considered, being either short term or long term, permanent or temporary, direct or indirect.

18. Proposals for annual reporting to the decision-making body on the implementation of the conditions of consent; post-project analysis (PPA) and environmental auditing.

19. Arrangements for consultation with the relevant government agencies, planners, the public and interested bodies during the concept, preliminary, screening, scoping phases, the preparation of the EIS, the EIA stage, the construction, operational and decommissioning stages; the communication of results.

20. Any unique features of the proposal of national or community importance such as technology, employment characteristics, training, contributions to exports or import replacement, defence, landscaping, recreational facilities; foreign investment, or marked multiplier effects.

21. The contribution to sustainable development, and the containment of global environmental problems.

Source: A. Gilpin (1995), *Environmental Impact Assessment: Cutting Edge for the Twenty-first Century,* Cambridge University Press, Cambridge.

public and corporate benefit. Targets may be achieved that have no legal specification, yet represent desirable environmental outcomes. EIPs may help to underpin wider local environmental plans, regional environmental plans, and state environment protection policies.

Environmental Law

A body of law dealing with the relationship between people and their environment, and the regulation of those relationships. Environmental law incorporates matters such as land use, water, water pollution, waste disposal, air pollution, mining, national parks, forestry, fauna and flora, soil, hazardous chemicals and noise, environmental planning and environmental economics. It draws on all branches of the law for its conceptual framework, including contract, property rights, administration, dispute resolution, criminal and constitutional law. It provides a system enabling environmental and planning decisions to be made by parliaments, councils, the public and private sectors, and provides guidance for decisions by individuals and households. It provides procedures for the handling of development applications, environmental appeals and public enquiries. It enables planning schemes, structural plans and statutory instruments to be put in place and to be varied or changed according to political circumstances.

Despite many successes and an increasing expectation of life in all countries, environmental problems have tended to intensify. This has led in more recent years to a whole series of UN conferences relating specifically to the condition of the human environment and the quality of life. The explosion in world population; the massive movement of people from country to town; increasing industrialization; the burgeoning of the automobile; the increasing widespread use of chemicals and fertilizers; noise problems; hazardous wastes, including radioactive wastes; the contamination of air, water, land and food; major industrial and marine mishaps; soil erosion; the destruction of forests; overfishing; a general overexploitation of natural resources; and evidence of global climate change with progressive loss of biodiversity, have all led to a worldwide recognition that development cannot be sustained in the longer term, in its present form, without a significant depletion of the resource base upon which all development ultimately depends. Industry itself, as well as government and its agencies, have become aware of new responsibilities that go beyond traditional concerns: a duty of care for the planet itself.

See Box 27 for a list of environmental laws that have been introduced in developing countries and countries with economies in transition. Numerous boxes throughout this book outline the evolution of environmental law in more economically advanced countries.

Box 27   *Environmental laws in developing countries and countries in transition*

Albania	1993	Law on Environmental Protection
Algeria	1983	Environmental Protection Law
Bahrain	1980	Decree for Establishment of Environmental Protection Committee
Bangladesh	1995	Environment Protection Act
Belize	1992	Environmental Protection Act
Bolivia	1992	Framework Law of the Environment
Botswana	1961	Fauna Conservation Act
Brazil	1981	National Law of Environmental Policy
Bulgaria	1991	Environmental Protection Act
Burkino Faso	1994	Code of the Environment
Cape Verde	1993	Basis for Environmental Policy
Chile	1994	Law on the Environment
China	1989	Environmental Protection Law of the People's Republic of China
Columbia	1974	National Code on Renewable Natural Resources and Environmental Protection
Comoros	1994	Law Relative to the Environment
Congo	1991	Law on the Protection of the Environment
Cuba	1981	Law on Environmental Protection and the Rational Use of Natural Resources
Czech Republic	1992	Act on the Environment
Ecuador	1976	Law for the Protection and Monitoring of Environmental Protection, Decree 374
Egypt	1994	Law Concerning the Environment
Estonia	1995	Act on Sustainable Development
Gabon	1993	Law on the Protection and Improvement of the Environment
Gambia	1994	National Environment Management Act
Ghana	1994	Environmental Protection Agency Act
Guatemala	1986	Law for the Protection and Improvement of the Environment
Guinea	1987	Environmental Code of the Republic of Guinea
Honduras	1993	General Environmental Law
India	1986	Environmental Protection Act
Iran	1986	Environmental Protection and Enhancement Act

Box 27   continued

Iraq	1986	Environment Protection and Improvement Act
Jamaica	1991	National Resources Conservation Authority Act
Kazakhstan	1991	Law on Protection of the Natural Environment
Kenya	1976	Wildlife Conservation and Management Act
Korea, South	1990	Basic Environmental Policy Act
Korea, North	1986	Law on the Protection of the Environment
Kuwait	1980	Law Protecting the Environment
Kyrgyzstan	1991	Law on Environmental Protection
Latvia	1991	Law on Environmental Protection
Libya	1982	Act Concerning the Protection of the Environment
Lithuania	1992	Law on Environmental Protection
Madagascar	1990	Environmental Charter and Annex
Malaysia	1974	Environmental Quality Act
Mali	1991	Law Related to the Environment
Malta	1991	Environment Protection Act
Mauritius	1991	Environment Protection Act
Mexico	1988	General Law of Ecological Equilibrium and Environmental Protection
Moldova	1993	Law on Protection of the Environment
Mongolia	1994	Environmental Law of Mongolia
Nigeria	1988	Federal Environmental Protection Agency Decree
Oman	1979	Act for Environmental Protection and Pollution Control
Pakistan	1983	Pakistan Environmental Protection Ordinance
Palau	1981	Environmental Quality Protection Act
Papua New Guinea	1978	Environmental Contaminants Act
Peru	1990	Code of the Environment and Natural Resources
Philippines	1977	Philippines Environment Code, Presidential Decree 1152
Qatar	1994	Law on Establishment of a Standing Committee for Protection of the Environment
Russian Federation	1991	Law on Protecting the Natural Environment

Box 27 continued

Saudi Arabia	1982	Environmental Protection Standards
Senegal	1983	Environmental Code
Seychelles	1994	Environment Protection Act
Slovenia	1993	Environmental Protection Act
South Africa	1989	Environment Conservation Act
Sri Lanka	1980	National Environmental Act
St Kitts and Nevis	1987	The National Conservation and Environment Protection Act
Tajikistan	1993	Law on the Protection of Nature
Tanzania	1974	Wildlife Conservation Act
Thailand	1992	Enhancement and Conservation of National Environmental Quality Act
Togo	1988	Environmental Code
Tunisia	1988	Law creating the National Environmental Protection Agency
Turkey	1983	Environmental Law
Ukraine	1991	Law on the Protection of the Natural Environment
United Arab Emirates	1981	Decree Concerning the Establishment of a Supreme Committee for the Environment
Uzbekistan	1992	Law on the Protection of Nature
Venezuela	1976	Organic Law on the Environment
Vietnam	1994	Law on Environment Protection
Zambia	1990	Environmental Protection and Pollution Control Act
Zimbabwe	1975	Parks and Wildlife Act

Environmental Law Information Base, Computerized (CELIB)

Established by UNEP in 1995, a computerized information base which provides worldwide access to updated information on environmental law through the Internet. CELIB contains a Register of International Treaties and other Agreements in the field of the environment and over 200 full texts of the international conventions in the field of the environment.

Detailed information is also available in respect of major global and regional conventions, including:

- Convention on International Trade in Endangered Species of Wild Fauna and Flora, 1973;
- Lusaka Agreement on Cooperative Enforcement Operations Directed at Illegal Trade in Wild Fauna and Flora, 1994;
- Convention on the Conservation of Migratory Species of Wild Animals, 1979;
- Vienna Convention for the Protection of the Ozone Layer, 1985;
- Montreal Protocol on Substances that Deplete the Ozone Layer, 1987;
- Basel Convention on the Control of Transboundary Movements of Hazardous Wastes and their Disposal, 1989;
- Convention on Biological Diversity, 1992; and
- UN Framework Convention on Climate Change, 1992.

Regarding national legislation and institutions, CELIB provides a list of national environmental legislation of developing countries and countries with economies in transition. Other publications, including the UNEP Environmental Law Handbook, are also available.

Environmental Planning, Objectives of

The aims of environmental planning as they have evolved during the twentieth century. They may be defined as follows:
- The pursuit of social improvement through the medium of ambient physical change maximizing opportunities for individual choice and protecting the individual from the adverse effects of the actions of others.
- The orderly arrangement of various parts of the city and region (residential, commercial, industrial, recreational) to enable each part to perform its functions at least cost and with minimum conflict.
- The provision of an efficient system of transportation and communication within the city and to other centers.
- The achievement of optimal standards in respect of infrastructure, lot sizes, building spacing, sunlight, open space, parking facilities and aesthetics.
- The provision of comfortable housing in a variety of types to meet the needs of all families and other categories.
- The provision of schools and colleges, recreational and other community services of a high standard in terms of location, size and quality with regard to special needs.
- The provision of a safe and adequate water supply, sewerage system, energy system and other public services,

- The achievement of desirable objectives in respect to the control of air pollution, water pollution, noise and vibration control, and the transport and disposal of hazardous wastes.
- The progressive development of landscaping, tree planting, anti-litter measures, bicycle paths, nature walks, national parks, community access to natural features, and recreational schemes.
- Where relevant, the adoption of special measures to protect the coast and beaches and ensure easy access by the public.
- The identification, preservation and restoration of items of the environmental heritage, either individually or as parts of conservation areas.
- The identification and clearance of substandard dwellings incapable of repair or improvement at reasonable expense, and the rehabilitation of blighted areas.
- The coordination of the proposals of single-purpose agencies concerned with the provision of services such as water, sewerage, and electricity; and the provision of transport by road, rail, sea and air.
- The identification of natural resources and the prospective future demands for those resources with a view to reasonable precautions against the sterilization and alienation of the most valuable of them, so that at some future time those resources are accessible for mining, fishing, extraction, harvesting, or felling.
- Consistency between local environmental plans and any regional, provincial, state, federal or national plans and policies, and relevant international conventions.
- The provision of ample opportunities for public participation at all stages of the planning process, including public hearings and inquiries into 'policy and need' as well as individual projects.
- The retention of flexibility within the planning system to cope readily with changing economic and social circumstances.
- The promotion of a balance of population and industry throughout the region, having regard to employment prospects and characteristics, and economic viability.
- The achievement of a fair and reasonable distribution of infrastructure and site development costs between the public and the developer.
- Where appropriate, the adoption of special measures for the protection of wildlife and wilderness.

Box 28 sets out the criteria for the choice and adoption of environmental policy instruments.

Box 28   Criteria for the choice and adoption of environmental policy
          instruments

- *The political climate*   That is, whether the climate is pro-development at any cost with an anti-regulatory bias; or whether development is welcomed but in a socially acceptable context after competent environmental impact assessment.
- *Factional support for certain projects and enterprises*   Projects being supported by particular segments of the government and the establishment, to the exclusion of proper planning and environmental considerations. Such projects, when approved, usually enjoy separate legislation, with exemptions from the planning system.
- *Sound environmental and planning measures*   The preparation of operational conditions with which the enterprise would need to conform to minimize community impacts. Conformity with national, regional and local environmental plans; and consistency with international conventions. Measures for the measurement of environmental performance.
- *Economic efficiency*   The measures proposed should minimize the costs to society overall and promote maximum environmental effectiveness.
- *Provision for public participation*   The public broadly should be consulted in respect of major enterprises by the proponents, government agencies and local government. If appropriate, public inquiries should be conducted by commissioners of inquiry.
- *Direct controls and economic instruments*   While direct controls may predominate, appropriate provision should be for incentives to innovate and reduce pollution, and promote cleaner production, through emission and other charges.
- *Conformity with best practice guidelines*   A regard to best practice international guidelines and any standards laid down by, say, the EU, through the European Eco-management and Audit Regulation; or through the British and Australian Standards Institutions.

Environmental Planning Instrument

A statutory document or regulation implementing, for example, a state environmental planning policy, a regional environmental or structure plan, or a local environmental plan.

Environmental Planning System

An organizational and legislative structure within which the environmental decision-making process takes place. In a generalized way, the system's objective is to provide the best framework for making planning decisions. Specifically, the following features are desirable in a planning system:
- It should be based on social, economic and environmental aims.
- It should avoid an overcentralized decision-making process, separating as far as possible state-wide, regional and local issues.
- It should provide for public involvement.
- It should be easily understood, contained in as few acts and regulations as possible and allow for speedy plan preparation and development decisions.
- It should encourage the guiding rather than the restrictive aspect of planning.

The overall planning body, agency, commission, or department, should be responsible for:
- coordinating the state's policies for environmental planning and land resource management in the state and regional context;
- coordinating information and activities of other government departments at the state and regional levels;
- integrating land-use planning with population distribution and policies on transport and other services;
- preparing regional environmental plans and subregional structure plans in cooperation with the regional development councils (if they have planning functions);
- exercising all regional environmental planning responsibilities (if the regional development council does not have planning functions);
- contributing, with others, to research, resource assessment, technical and administrative advice;
- ensuring that local plans are amended by the council concerned where any inconsistency with state and regional environmental plans is evident;
- certifying that local plans comply with state, regional or subregional plans.

Environmental Precincts

Or environmental areas, being convenient parts of a local government jurisdiction which either have a uniform character or are identified by some outstanding feature. The boundaries of such precincts may be natural (such as parks, rivers, cliffs or ridge lines) or artificial (roads, expressways, shopping centers and large institutions). Social characteristics and links, important community facilities such as schools, parks or hotels, may also be reflected in the division of the larger area into parts. The division of a local government jurisdiction (or municipality) into environmental precincts or areas may then form a convenient basis for planning.

The nature of environmental areas will vary. The task of the planning authority is to use judgement, based on local knowledge and experience, in deciding which areas should retain their existing character, which should change slightly, which substantially and which completely. In new areas, where any development means change, the question becomes not so much the extent of change as the intensity and kind of development appropriate to the area. Certain planning criteria will help in this judgement. The local government area's location within the wider region and its proper role in the region's growth will determine the extent of pressures to change. There is little point in making large areas available for high-density residential development in places where there is no demand for this housing form. Conversely, in areas in which strong pressures for redevelopment exist, plans should make some attempt to accommodate them in the most suitable areas; for if this is not done, the pressures will persist and may in time become so strong as to force accommodation in less suitable areas than would have been the case had the plan acknowledged their existence.

Environmental Protection Law, 1979, China

A measure passed and promulgated in September 1979, by the Standing Committee of the National People's Congress; the law is based on Article 11 of the Constitution of the People's Republic of China.

The law uses the term 'environment' to encompass the air, water, land, mineral resources, forests, grasslands, wild plants and animals, aquatic life, places of historical interest, scenic spots, hot springs, resorts and natural areas under special protection as well as inhabited areas of the country.

More efforts, the law stresses, must be made to control and prevent pollution from liquid and gaseous wastes, slag, dust, sewage, radioactive material and other harmful matter as well as pollution from noise, vibration and toxic odors.

The law stipulates that no enterprise or institution which might pollute the environment can be built near residential areas in cities and towns or beside protected water areas, places of historical interest, scenic spots, hot springs, resorts or natural areas under protection. Those already existing should adopt measures to control their pollution or be moved to other places within a specified period.

As pollutants from industrial enterprises are the main cause of public hazards, it is therefore necessary strictly to keep this source of pollution under control. The law requires the adoption of a series of measures to control and prevent pollution, including developing new technology and methods of processing as well as new products which will be totally or practically pollution free. It calls for multipurpose use of gaseous wastes, liquid and slag. Effective measures are to be taken to deal with smoke and dust, devices are to be installed to reduce noise and vibration. Cleaner energy sources such as coal gas, liquefied petroleum gas, natural gas, methane gas and solar energy are to be developed; the dumping of rubbish and slag into rivers, lakes or the sea will be strictly forbidden; more highly effective insecticides with low residual toxicity are to be produced and industrial dust and toxic gases in working areas are to be reduced to standards set by the nation.

Since China has suffered serious ecological damage, the law provides that land must be used rationally according to local conditions, soil erosion prevented and land kept from being turned into deserts. It also stipulates that rivers, lakes, seas and reservoirs must be protected and a good quality of water maintained. Forest and grassland resources and certain wild animals and plants are to be protected and developed, and great care is to be taken in exploring and utilizing mineral resources.

Article 6 of the Environmental Protection Law addresses the necessity of environmental impact reports. Specifically:

Article 6 All enterprises and institutions shall pay adequate attention to the prevention of pollution and damage to the environment when selecting their sites, designing, constructing and planning production. In planning new construction, reconstruction and extension projects, a report on the potential environmental effects shall be submitted to the environmental protection department and other relevant departments for examination and approval before designing can be started. The installations for the prevention of pollution and other hazards to the public should be designed, built and put into operation at the same time as the main project. Discharge of all kinds of harmful substances shall be in compliance with the criteria set down by the State.

The units which have caused pollution and other hazards to the environment shall, according to the principle of 'whoever causes pollution shall be responsible for its elimination', make plans to actively eliminate such, or alternatively submit an application to the competent authorities for approval to transfer the property or move to some other place.

Article 7 also addresses environmental impact studies, as follows:

Article 7 In rebuilding old cities or building new ones, assessments shall be made of the potential environmental effects in industrial and residential areas, public utility facilities, and green belts by reference to the meteorological, geographical, hydrological and ecological conditions, and overall planning and rational layout be made to prevent pollution and other hazards to the public so as to build a clean modern city in a planned way.

Environmental Protection Policies

Policies developed at a national, state, regional or local level by governments, agencies, associations, communities, groups, corporations and companies, relating to the protection of the natural environment, the control of wastes, the improvement of the human environment, the protection of heritage values, the declaration of national parks and reserves, the protection of flora and fauna, the conservation of forests and landscapes, the protection of wilderness, the promotion of environmental planning, the implementation of international conventions and agreements, and the promotion of sustainable development. Specific policies may relate to wetlands, rainforest, ambient air quality, potable water, ecosystems, airsheds, catchments, marine waters, endangered species, fisheries, oysters, urban development, regional development, cumulative effects, swamps, river estuaries, floodplains, residential development, highways, communications, airports, noise, central business district (CBD) parking, wildlife, timber and woodchips, hazards, buffer zones, town plans, marshland, peatland, trade wastes, indigenous peoples, soil conservation, lead-in-petrol, sewage treatment, ocean disposal, landfills, streetscapes, the picturesque, EIA, waste recycling, littering, stormwater, public inquiries, pollution charges, road pricing, plantations, fertilizers, hazardous wastes, packaging, open space, oil pollution, national monuments, heavy metals, specific habitats, green belts, flood mitigation works, emission trading, development standards, decentralization, habitat conservation plans, botanic gardens and redevelopment.

See also:
Local Environmental Plan; Regional Environmental Plan.

Environmental Quality Standards

Levels of exposure to pollutants which should not be exceeded; standards may be statutory or presumptive. Two levels have been adopted by the US EPA:
1. *Primary*   Levels judged necessary to protect health with an adequate margin of safety.
2. *Secondary*   Levels judged necessary to protect public welfare from any known or anticipated adverse effects.

These are essentially ambient environmental quality standards. Standards may also prescribe the contents of products, for example, the amount of phosphates in detergents or of pesticide residues in foodstuffs. They may also prescribe emission standards, for example, the upper limits of what may be emitted from the exhausts of motor vehicles or from the chimneys of industrial plants.

European Eco-management and Audit Regulation (EMAR)

Adopted by the EU in March 1993, a voluntary scheme encouraging companies to set up environmental targets, with external auditors verifying compliance. Companies fulfilling the requirements are entitled to a Statement of Participation. A list of participating companies is published once a year in the official EU journal. By the end of 1998, some 2000 companies had registered under EMAR.

European Union (EU)

An economic and political alliance formed initially by six European nations through the Treaty of Rome in 1957; by 1995, the EU (formerly the European Community) comprised Austria, Belgium, Britain, Denmark, Finland, France, Germany, Greece, Ireland, Italy, Luxembourg, the Netherlands, Portugal, Spain and Sweden (15 nations in all) with the prospects of future expansion under the Single European Act 1987 and the Maastricht Treaty 1993. The EU is committed to further steps in economic and monetary integration. The combined population now exceeds 370 million. The purpose of the EU is to avoid military conflicts between the members, as characterized by the past, and to provide a large common market for the free movement of goods and services. It would permit manufacturers to invest on the scale that modern technology makes possible and necessary; and enable workpeople to move wherever wages and conditions are best for them. Progress initially was rapid. By July 1968, virtually all remaining customs duties between members were abolished and a common external tariff completed. A considerable degree of mobility of labour and capital among members has been achieved. Progress in abolishing internal tariffs on agricultural products has been less rapid. Britain, Ireland and Denmark did not join the European Community until 1972, signing a Treaty of Accession. The nine-nation common market accounted then for over 40 per cent of world trade. Greece became the tenth member in 1981; while Spain and Portugal joined in 1985. The accession of Austria, Finland and Sweden in 1995 brought the total to 15 nations. Norway, once in favour of seeking membership, remained outside, together with Switzerland, at least for the time being. Other nations from Eastern Europe now seek membership.

The EU has come to adopt a broad approach to environmental policy formulation being accompanied by environmental directives, decisions and regulations intended to be adopted by member countries and embodied in national legislation. Any member country failing to implement EU directives may be brought before the European Court of Justice. Directives have related to motor vehicle exhausts, intractable wastes, drinking water standards, recreational water standards, marine pollution, dangerous substances, packaging, air quality standards, EIA, birds, habitats, and special conservation areas.

In 1993, the EU introduced an Eco-management and Audit Regulation (EMAR); this involves the appointment of independent verifiers to check environmental statements and their compliance with EMAR. In 1993, Copenhagen was chosen as the location for a new European Environment Agency. See Box 29.

Box 29   Environmental directives issued by the European Union

1970   Directive against air pollution by exhaust fumes from motor vehicle engines; Directive on motor vehicle noise standards

1973   Directive on polychlorinated biphenyls (PCBs), polychlorinated terphenyls (PCTs) and vinyl chloride monomer; Directive on detergents; Directive on the testing of the biodegradability of anionic surfactants

1975   Directive on drinking-water standards; Directive on bathing-water quality standards; Directive on the sulphur content of gas oils; Directive relating to the preparation of inventories of harmful wastes and residues

1976   Directive on the discharge of dangerous substances

1977   Directive on biological standards for lead and on screening of the population for lead

1978   Directive on the discharge of titanium dioxide; Directive on measures to combat oil pollution; Directives controlling pollution from the wood and pulp mill and other industries; Directive setting the maximum permitted lead compound in petrol (0.4 g/l)

1979   Directive on the classification of packaging and labelling of dangerous substances (sixth modification to 1967 Directive)

1980   Draft Directive on environmental impact assessments; Directive on air quality limit values and guideline values for sulphur dioxide and suspended particulates. Directive on the protec-

Box 29   continued

tion of ground water against pollution; Directive on drinking-water standards

1981 Directive on an air quality standard for lead; Directive following the conclusion of the Convention on the Conservation of Antarctic Marine Living Resources

1982 Draft directive on the environmental effects of proposed development projects, Directive on the conclusion of the Convention on the Conservation of European Wildlife and Natural Habitats; Directive on the conclusion of the Convention on the Conservation of Migratory Species of Wild Animals. Directive on the implementation of the Convention on International Trade in Endangered Species of Wild Fauna and Flora (CITES)

1983 Directive on establishing a Community system for the conservation and management of fishery resources

1984 Directive in respect of emissions from industrial plant; Directive in respect of lead in petrol (gasoline)

1985 Directive on Environmental Impact Assessment (EIA); Draft directive in respect of motor vehicle exhausts

1988 Directive on emissions from large combustion plants

1989 Directives on emissions from new municipal plants and the reduction of air pollution from existing plants

1990 Directive establishing the European Protection Agency; Directive on the freedom of access to information on the environment

1991 Directive on substances that deplete the Ozone Layer; Directive on hazardous waste

1992 Directive on the conservation of natural habitats and of wild flora and fauna; Directive on air pollution by ground-level ozone; Directive on a Community system for fisheries; Directive on a Community eco-label award scheme

1993 Declaration on the protection of animals (Maastricht Treaty), Eco-management, and audit regulation

1994 Packaging and Packaging Waste Directive

1996 Integrated Pollution Prevention and Control Directive; Review of EU environmental legislation

1997 Council Directive 97/11/EC of 3 March 1997 amending Directive 85/337/EEC on the assessment of the effects of certain public and private projects on the environment (*Official Journal of the European Communities* L73, 5–15, 14 March 1997); draft directive on strategic environmental assessment (SEA)

Examination

The questioning or interrogation of a person on oath before a court of law. In court, the evidence of a witness is normally obtained by oral examination, called the examination-in-chief. The witness is then examined on behalf of the opposite party, called the cross-examination. The effect may be to reduce the impact of the initial evidence, and perhaps to discredit the witness. The witness is then re-examined by the original party to allow an opportunity to remove false impressions left by the cross-examination and provide additional explanations. The re-examination is confined to matters arising out of the cross-examination. Under planning and environmental legislation, procedures are at the discretion of the presiding officer or commissioner; in such circumstances evidence may or may not be required on oath, and cross-examination may be allowed or disallowed, or allowed only in certain circumstances. This variation of the rules of evidence is allowed so that individual citizens will not be intimidated by formal proceedings. However, these variations in procedure have led to debate about the rules ensuring natural justice.

Exclusive Economic Zone (EEZ)

A concept introduced at the UN Conference on the Law of the Sea aimed at establishing a revised legal regime for the oceans and their resources; under the EEZ ruling, coastal nations would assume jurisdiction over the exploration and exploitation of marine resources including fish and seabed minerals in their adjacent sections of continental shelf. An EEZ is defined arbitrarily to be a band extending 320 km (200 miles) from the shore, with median lines agreed between nations separated by seas of lesser distance. The introduction of EEZs in 1983 resulted in the exclusion from many areas of high-performance long-distance foreign fleets. The British fleet of 168 distant-water trawlers gradually disappeared, to be replaced by a fleet of compact, coastal-type vessels.

Exxon Valdez Disaster

A major incident when the tanker *Exxon Valdez* ran aground in March 1989 in Prince William Sound, Alaska, on the Bligh Reef; 250 000 barrels of oil poured into the Sound. Some 2400 km of beach were fouled by the spill. A jury decided that the owners and the captain were reckless. Plaintiffs in the US Federal Court case included more than 34 000 commercial fishermen, native Alaskans, and property owners, who claimed they had suffered harm from the spill. The jury, in one of the largest awards in legal history, ordered Exxon to pay $5 billion in punitive damages to the plaintiffs. The captain was ordered to pay $5000 in damages.

See also:
Disasters.

F

Federal Land Policy Management Act, 1976, US

Part of US federal law clearly establishing a policy that public lands shall generally be retained in federal ownership, and managed for all Americans under the principles of multiple use and sustained yield. The Bureau of Land Management (BLM) has developed and implemented a planning and management system aiming to efficiently, effectively and fairly resolve many of the conflicting demands placed upon public lands. It aims also at the development of needed resources, while protecting other resources, including the environment, from inadvertent damage or destruction. The act requires that decisions on public land use shall be based on full resource inventories and an analysis of alternative possible uses; such decisions are to be made with the full participation of the public, with a careful balance of competing uses. The act also directs that lands administered by the Bureau of Land Management be inventoried for wilderness characteristics. The BLM's *Wilderness Management Policy* was published in 1981.

Federal Water Pollution Control Act, 1956, US

The basic US law relating to water pollution control, subsequently amended in 1961, 1965, 1966 and 1972. The act provided for pollution abatement procedures and water quality standard enforcement procedures. Action could now be taken in respect to pollution of interstate and navigable waters which endangered health and welfare. The act provided for conferences between federal and state agencies, in respect to interstate pollution; the federal government could in the ultimate bring an enforcement suit. The act also authorized, for the first time, the making of construction grants to municipalities for sewage treatment plant construction.

An earlier measure, the Water Pollution Control Act 1948, had restricted the US federal role to investigation, research, and surveys, with primary responsibility for water pollution control being left entirely with the states.

See also:
Water Pollution Control Amendment Act, 1972, US.

Fines, Penalties and Damages

The enforcement of pollution control legislation and other environmental control measures often results in the imposition of fines and penalties by the courts, or even the award of damages to victims. When the tanker *Exxon Valdez* ran aground in Prince William Sound, Alaska, in 1989, causing extensive damage to 2400 km of beach, a jury decided that the owners and the captain were reckless. Plaintiffs in the US Federal Court case included more than 34 000 commercial fishermen, native Alaskans and property owners, who claimed they had suffered harm from the spill.

In New South Wales, Australia, the most serious offences under the pollution control legislation, subject to proof of wilfulness or negligence and harm to the environment, may result in a maximum penalty of $1 000 000 for corporations, with fines of up to $250 000 for individuals and/or the possibility of imprisonment for up to seven years. By 1998, in Australia, two company directors had served sentences for pollution offences. Other offences, attracting lower fines, are generally categorized as strict liability offences, that is, the prosecution does not have to prove intent. Penalties for littering remain low at $300. Apart from fines and terms of imprisonment, the courts may impose a wide variety of orders to mitigate pollution, award damages to victims, and restrain possible offenders.

If an environmental control authority wishes to avoid entanglement with other economic instruments, it may choose to rely on enforcement and penalties for breaches of prescribed standards and procedures, such penalties having a similar effect to a Pigovian tax. Strict liability tends to internalize, in a similar way to an appropriate tax. Legal liability may also provide compensation to the victim, unlike a Pigovian tax. Either way, pressure is imposed on the potential polluter. However, it must be recognized that most writers do not include fines and penalties as an economic instrument, largely because no doubt it belongs to the subject of direct control. This is often described in US literature, in a somewhat derogatory way, as the command-and-control system.

Experience in several OECD countries, including Britain, over the past half-century suggests a generally high level of compliance with regulations and policies; visible pollution is now a rarity, when once commonplace. Experience shows that companies do not like adverse publicity, this being damaging to often expensive programs stressing a good neighbor image.

Finland

The Republic of Finland, bounded by Sweden and Russia, is a multiparty republic with one legislative chamber, the Parliament. Finland has a population of six million, with a density of 16.3 persons per sq km. The capital is Helsinki. Box 30 shows the historical evolution of environmental law.

Box 30   Finland: evolution of environmental law

1923	Nature Protection Act
1961	Water Act
1962	Decree on Precautionary Measures for the Protection of Water
1973	Outdoor Recreation Act
1974	Combating Oil Pollution on Land Act
1978	Waste Management Act
1979	Rules Concerning Hazardous Waste Liability for Oil Pollution from Ships Act
1981	Prevention of Marine Pollution Act
1982	Air Pollution Control Act and Decree
1984	Air Quality Guidelines
1986	Waste Oil Discharge Act; Municipal Environment Administration
1987	Council of State decisions on particulate emissions, sulphur concentrations in light fuel oil and diesel oil, emission of sulphur from oil refineries, sulphur concentration in coal, sulphur emissions from Kraft pulp mills, incineration of waste oil, lead and benzene in petrol, and general guidelines to restrict nitrogen oxide emissions from boilers and gas turbines
1989	Prevention of Pollution from Ships Act; Restrictions on the use of polychlorinated biphenyls (PCBs); Decree on Solid Waste Management; Chemicals Act
1990	Decree on Dangerous Chemicals
1991	Bans and restrictions on certain chemicals; Environmental Permit Procedures Act
1992	Implementation of the Basel Convention
1995	Life expectancy: 72.8 years for males; 80.2 years for females

---

Flixborough Disaster

A major explosion at the Flixborough plant of Nypro Ltd in 1974, killing 28 of the plant personnel. The plant was situated in a bend of the river Humber in northeast England. A temporary dogleg pipe connection with stainless steel bellows at each end failed between two reactors containing mainly cyclohexane at elevated temperature and pressure. The flashing liquid jets from the reactor openings formed a vapour cloud containing some fifty tonnes of flammable hydrocarbon. This finally ignited at a nearby furnace and exploded, devastating the site. In response to public pressure and concern, the British government created a single authority, the Health and Safety Commission.

See also:
Disasters.

Fluoridation

The addition of fluoride to public water supplies in appropriate cases as an additional precaution against dental decay. Water containing the optimal amount of fluoride appears to increase resistance to tooth decay, while waters containing too much fluoride are capable of producing dental fluorosis, a mottling of the tooth enamel associated with brittleness and general deterioration.

Fluoride occurs naturally in water and, in some cases, in adequate amounts. In a cool climate, any potable water supply containing less than 0.8 gram per cubic metre of fluoride is considered deficient; the optimal quantity usually recommended is 1.0 gram per cubic metre (equivalent to 1.0 milligram per litre, or 1 part per million parts, by weight). In warmer climates, such as Australia, a smaller amount may be satisfactory. The WHO regards fluoridation as a landmark in the history of public health. Investigation appears to affirm that wherever fluoridation has been introduced, dental decay in the teeth of children has been reduced by 65 to 75 per cent. It is claimed that this has been demonstrated in the United Kingdom, the United States of America, Canada, Germany, and in various parts of Australia.

Food, Drug and Cosmetic Act (FDCA), 1938, US

US federal legislation, with subsequent amendments, under which the US EPA has authority to establish tolerance levels for pesticide residues in or on food or feed crops in the United States. A 'tolerance level' is the pesticide residue legally permitted on food or feed and represents the maximum residue allowable in the harvested commodity. Such tolerances have been established in the United States since 1954 (from 1970, by the EPA).

A 'tolerance' must be established before a pesticide can be applied to a food or feed crop that is intended for sale, distribution, or consumption in the United States. A tolerance is derived from an evaluation of laboratory toxicity tests and crop residue data. Tolerances are set at levels considered adequate to protect the public health and which are consistent with good agricultural practice.

See also:
Insecticide, Fungicide and Rodenticide Act, US.

Forest and Rangeland Renewable Resources Planning Act, 1974, US

An act, subsequently amended, directing the US Secretary of Agriculture to prepare a comprehensive long-range assessment of the nation's renewable forest and rangeland resources, and develop a program for forest service activities. The assessment must embrace timber, range, water, fish, wildlife, outdoor recreation and wilderness resources. The future supply and demand for each of these resources must be projected together with the potential opportunities to meet the nation's future needs. The act requires a full assessment every ten years, with a program review and update every five years. The 1985 review and assessment was transmitted to the Congress, accompanied by a statement of policy from the President.

Framework Environmental Laws

Umbrella or framework environmental laws have been very popular with developing countries. Such legislation lays down basic legal principles without attempting to codify all relevant statutory requirements. A framework act contains a declaratory statement of national environmental goals, creates institutions for environmental control and management, and provides for decision-making procedures, licensing and enforcement, planning and coordination, and dispute resolution procedures, along with other environmental management mechanisms.

Framework laws are less specific, and perhaps less useful, than specific environment protection and pollution-prevention laws, but present a beginning. They may be supported by new pronouncements in the country's constitution. However, framework legislation soon calls for specific legislation addressing air and water pollution, noise, hazardous substances and environmental planning.

Examples of framework acts include: the Act for the Prevention and Control of Environmental Pollution in Ecuador (1976); and the Pollution Control Ordinance of Bangladesh (1977).

France

The French Republic has two legislative houses, the Senate and the National Assembly. The population in 1997 was 59 million, at an average density of 108 persons per sq km. The capital is Paris. France abuts Spain, Germany, Switzerland, Italy and Belgium. See Box 31 for the evolution of environmental law.

Box 31   France: evolution of environmental law

1913	Historic Monuments Act
1921	Cultural Heritage Act
1930	Act for the Protection of National Monuments and Sites of Artistic, Historical, Scientific, Traditional or Picturesque Interest
1942	Toxin and Hazardous Substances Act
1948–49	Noise and Air Pollution Control Acts
1957	Parks and Nature Reserves Act
1958	Fauna and Flora Act
1960	National Parks Act
1961	Air Pollution and Wastes Act
1962	Town and Country Planning Act; Urban Renewal Act
1963	First national parks established
1964	Water Supply and River Management Act
1970	Cevennes National Park established
1971	Ministry for the Environment established
1972	Protection of Mountain Regions directive
1973	Ecrins National Park established; Pollution Control and Water Acts
1974	Amendments to Environment Protection Acts
1975	Waste Acts
1976	National Conservation Act; Marine Pollution Act; Environmental Impact Assessment Act
1977	Chemical Products Act; *Amoco Cadiz* disaster
1980	Air Quality Agency
1983	Environment Protection Zone Act; Oil Pollution Act; Amendments to Environmental Impact Assessment Act
1986	Coastal Protection Act
1988	Jacques Cousteau reveals that the coral structure at Mururoa Atoll nuclear test site is deeply cracked
1990	Talloires Declaration

Box 31   continued

1991	Review of pollution control and environment protection legislation
1992	Akasuki Maru arrives to load reactor-grade plutonium for Japan
1993	Contaminated Land Act
1994	Life expectancy: 73.7 years for males, 81.8 years for females
1996	Commission Nationale created to encourage consultation about major projects, and to develop a framework for public consultation
1997	Kyoto target: 92
1998	French government announced the demolition and closure of the Mururoa nuclear testing site, leaving only basic infrastructure facilities. France had conducted 193 nuclear tests in Polynesia during 1966–96, mostly on Mururoa. Monitoring of the health of those living around the former test zone would continue

Franchise Agreements

Agreements reached directly between developers and governments, often endorsed by an Act of Parliament at state, federal, or national level. The effect usually is to exempt a developer from meeting normal planning and environmental requirements and procedures, while making the basic decision immune from review by the courts. Such agreements are sometimes referred to as 'indenture agreements'. The agreement may make some reference to pollution control or environment protection measures, but it exempts the developer from surveillance by the appropriate environment protection agencies. Indeed, in the making of such agreements, the state environment protection agencies are often not even consulted.

G

Garden-City Movement, UK

A movement in England developed from the writings of Ebenezer Howard in the 1890s which proposed pre-planned new cities, to be constructed on land held by the community and limited to a population of some 30 000, complete with business services and employment centers, and surrounded by permanent green belts of rural land. The initial experimental cities were constructed on private initiative in a spirit of reform; Letchworth was commenced in the early 1900s, and Welwyn Garden City in the 1920s. The movement was a great and continuing influence on efforts elsewhere to improve the urban environment.

General Plan, Los Angeles, US

A comprehensive plan adopted by the Los Angeles City Council, California, as the official guide to the intended future development of the City of Los Angeles. This comprehensive declaration of purposes, policies and programs for the development of the city includes a land-use element, a circulation element, a service-system element, and an environmental element. The General Plan now serves as a basic and continuous reference in planning, coordinating and regulating public and private development in the city. The objectives of the General Plan are:

- Preserve the low-density residential character of Los Angeles, except where higher-density centers are encouraged; protect stable single-family residential neighborhoods from encroachment by other types of uses; rehabilitate and/or rebuild deteriorated single-family residential areas for the same use; help make single-family housing available to families of all social and ethnic categories.
- Provide maximum convenience for the occupants of high- and medium-density housing (apartments); locate the bulk of such housing within, or near to, concentrations of urban facilities and employment opportunities; help make high- and medium-density housing available to persons of all social and ethnic categories.
- Provide employment opportunities and commercial services at locations convenient to residents throughout the city; reserve suitable and adequate lands for industrial and commercial uses; help make Los Angeles a desirable location for industry and business.

- Provide adequate transportation facilities for the movement of people and goods; provide a choice of transportation modes; alleviate traffic congestion; optimize the speed and convenience of all transportation modes; achieve economy and efficiency in the movement of goods.
- Provide needed public services to all persons and businesses; achieve economy, flexibility and efficiency in the provision of services, both those furnished by the City of Los Angeles and those furnished to Los Angeles citizens by other governmental jurisdictions; provide suitable sites for public facilities at locations convenient to their users.
- Provide facilities for leisure-time activities at locations readily accessible to all persons; furnish local recreational services; develop specialized recreational facilities; preserve the ocean shoreline and other comparable recreational resources for public use.
- Conserve the city's natural resources and amenities; preserve open space; protect outstanding geographical features; minimize all forms of environmental pollution including air pollution, water pollution, noise and visual pollution.
- Enhance the quality of the city's physical environment; integrate all aspects of the city's development through the application of urban design principles; establish the identity of the various communities of the city; preserve historical and cultural features; control the placement of commercial signs; provide landscaping where it serves or enhances the physical environment.
- Balance population growth with available facilities, services and amenities for a productive, healthy and desirable environment.

Geneva City Conservatory and Botanical Gardens

Founded in 1817, a major botanical research centre in Geneva, Switzerland, specializing in floristics, biosystematics and morphology. It has important collections of alpine plants and orchids, an arboretum, and collections to show characteristic species of different geographic regions of the world. It has a range of greenhouses and a herbarium with about five million reference specimens. The garden also has an extensive library.

Germany

The Federal Republic of Germany is a federal multiparty republic with two legislative houses, the Federal Council and the Federal Diet. The capital is Berlin. The population in 1997 was 82.2 million, at an average density of 230

Box 32   Germany: evolution of environmental law

1869   Regulations restraining air pollution and noise
1935   Nature Conservation Act
1957   Federal Water Act
1969   Federal government policy statement on the environment
1970   Environment Policy Act; Bavarian Forest National Park established
1971   Urban and rural renewal legislation
1972   Disposal of Wastes Act; DDT restricted; East Germany bans UN Conference on the Human Environment
1974   Federal Environmental Agency established
1975   EIA procedures adopted; Federal Forest Act; Federal Game Act; Plant Protection Act; Detergents Act
1976   Federal Nature Conservation Act; Conventions for the Protection of the Rhine against Pollution
1977   Waste Water Act
1980   Amendment of Federal Nature Conservation Act; Brandt Commission
1981   Federal Emissions Control Act
1983   Statutory restrictions on sulphur dioxide emissions
1986   Waste Avoidance and Waste Management Act; gradual introduction of EIA
1988   Endorsement of Vienna Convention for the protection of the ozone layer; also endorsement of the Montreal Protocol
1989   Amendment of Federal Nature Conservation Act
1990   Environmental Impact Assessment Act; Federal Emissions Control Act; carbon dioxide reduction program; Radiological Protection Act
1991   EIA Act extended to infrastructure projects; ordinances on the avoidance of packaging wastes and the problem of discarded automobiles
1992   EIA Act applied to industrial projects and adoption of environmental improvement programs for eastern Germany
1993   National waste recycling system
1994   National plan to halve emissions of methane, nitrous oxide, volatile hydrocarbons and carbon monoxide by the year 2005
1995   Life expectancy: 73.0 years for males; 79.5 years for females; Green Dot system for packaging; Topfer Law for recycling targets; Volklingen ironworks included in the World Heritage List; Berlin Climate Conference
1997   Kyoto target: 92

persons per sq km. Located in Central Europe, Germany borders France, Austria, Switzerland, the Czech Republic, Poland, Belgium, Holland and Denmark. See Box 32 for the evolution of environmental law.

Ghana

The Republic of Ghana is a unitary multiparty republic with one legislative house, the House of Parliament. The population in 1997 was 18.1 million, at an average density of 76 persons per sq km. Located in the Gulf of Guinea, Ghana borders the Ivory Coast, Burkina Faso and Togo. The capital is Accra. See Box 33 for the evolution of environmental law.

Global Diversity Assessment

Published in 1995, UNEP's *Global Diversity Assessment* was the world's first comprehensive review of biodiversity. It was presented to the second meeting of the Parties to the Convention on Biological Diversity. It examined the current state of knowledge, ways to approach the problem, and possible solutions. Some 1500 scientists participated in the preparation of the report, which had been sponsored by the Global Environment Facility. Although the total number of species remains unknown, the report considered that a reasonable estimate is close to 14 million, of which about 1.7 million have been scientifically described. The working estimates for insects was about eight million, though the actual figure could be much higher. The report saw grave threats to many species, at a profound cost to society; it concluded that between 5 and 20 per cent of some groups of animals and plants could be threatened with extinction in the foreseeable future.

Apart from its statistical assessment, the report reviewed strategies to protect biodiversity. The traditional approach had emphasized the separation of ecosystems, species and genetic resources from human activity through the creation of protected areas, prohibitions on the harvesting of endangered species, and the preservation of germ plasm in seed banks or cryogenic storage facilities. Instead, it was now thought that preservation efforts must embrace a blend of strategies, including programs to save species by creating controlled environments and developing policies to manage natural environments in ways that minimize adverse impacts. There is also a recognition of the need for more integrated approaches to conservation, including a consideration of entire ecosystems rather than just some protected areas within those ecosystems. Many existing international conventions relate in whole or part to the protection of biodiversity.

Box 33   *Ghana: evolution of environmental law*

1973   Environment Protection Council created by the government of Ghana, bringing together for the first time all activities and efforts aimed at protecting and improving the quality of the environment; and to 'ensure the observance of proper standards in the planning and execution of all development projects'

1978   EIA procedures introduced for industries, but supporting legislation not passed

1985   Ghana Investment Code passed, under which the Ghana Investment Centre must have regard to any effect an enterprise is likely to have on the environment and the measures proposed for the prevention and control of any such harmful effects

1986   Environment Protection Council sets up an EIA committee to examine ways in which EIA can be put into operation as a management tool in Ghana; guidelines issued on EIA

1988   Government of Ghana gives environmental issues a priority on the development agenda

1989   Environmental Action Plan (EAP) introduced by government for the 10 years 1991–2000; attempts to make developments more environmentally sustainable; the EAP states that the aim of the plan is to ensure sound management of resources and the environment, avoiding exploitation of resources that will cause irreparable environmental damage; the EAP refers to the need for EIA

1990   Environmental concerns given prominence in the national budget for the first time; directive to all agencies that the Environment Protection Council was to be consulted formally on all development proposals, with an EIA to follow

1991   Environment Protection Council produces EIA guidelines; no development to proceed without an environmental impact certificate; EISs subject to review

1992   Ghana Environmental Resource Management Project (GERMP) developed with the participation of the World Bank, the Danish international Development Agency and the British Overseas Development Administration; the aim is to have an effective national environmental management system for Ghana

1993   Life expectancy: 53.3 years for males, 57.2 years for females

1998   Drought grips the country, reducing output from hydroelectric plants; poverty prevails

The 1996 Red List of Threatened Animals issued by the World Conservation Union identified 5205 species in danger of extinction. In tropical forests alone, it was estimated by biologists that three species were being eliminated every hour. Much of the decline, it was claimed, was caused by habitat destruction, especially by logging. Only 6 per cent of the world's forests were formally protected, leaving 33.6 million sq km vulnerable to exploitation.

In 1992, at the Seventh International Coral Reef Symposium held in Guam, scientists estimated that some 10 per cent of the world's coral reefs were effectively lost, and a further 30 per cent were under immediate threat. To draw attention to this problem, 1997 was recognized as the International Year of the Reef.

Global Environment Facility (GEF)

In 1990, the World Bank, the UN Development Program and the UN Environment Program, established the Global Environment Facility (GEF) to provide concessional financial assistance to the developing world for investments that would: (1) protect the ozone layer; (2) protect international water resources; (3) protect biological diversity; and (4) reduce greenhouse gas emissions.

Measures to protect the ozone layer relate to steps required by the Montreal Protocol; that protocol was an agreement reached in 1988 by over thirty countries to control the emission of CFCs and halons to the atmosphere, thought to damage the ozone layer. By the mid-1990s, the developing countries continued to provide substantial markets for ozone-damaging chemicals made, but not sold, elsewhere.

International waters would clearly benefit from investments to prevent oil spills and toxic waste pollution. To protect biological diversity, the GEF may encourage debt-for-nature and debt-for-environment swaps and the conservation of tropical forest areas. To reduce greenhouse gas emissions, the emphasis is on investments in cleaner fuels and technologies in the energy sectors. An increase in the use of natural gas would qualify for assistance, as would investment in forests to create sinks for carbon dioxide.

Nations that have contributed financially to the GEF are known as 'participants'; at each of their regular meetings, the participants review and endorse the proposed work program. The GEF participants are supported by a Scientific and Technical Advisory Panel composed of 16 independent members. The GEF represents a highly innovative approach to environmental protection, though problems have arisen over the recurrent financing of GEF projects. A lack of agreement emerged between industrialized and less-developed countries on the purpose and strategy of the GEF, and the linking of projects to development schemes run by dominant institutions, groups and companies. At a meeting in Cartagena, Colombia, at the end of 1993, these differences were debated; negotiations were completed in March 1994, when GEF funds were replenished with US$2 billion.

Global International Waters Assessment (GIWA)

A global assessment of water-related environmental problems in transboundary waters, their societal root causes, and possible future trends. The implementing agent for this assessment is UNEP, on behalf of the UN. The program began in 1999. It is a project of GEF. The project is co-financed by a number of governments, with a core team located in the University of Kalmar, Sweden.

Gordon-Below-Franklin Dam, Australia

A hydroelectric project proposed for the South-West Tasmania Wilderness area; the campaign to stop the dam made conservation history. On a world scale, South-west Tasmania is a wilderness area of major importance; it is one of only three major remaining southern temperate wildernesses and one of the most important archaeological sites. Tasmania generates most of its electricity from its hydro resources. Prior to the Gordon-Below-Franklin proposal, a major conservation battle had been waged and lost over the flooding of Lake Pedder. The next proposal by the Hydro-Electric Commission of Tasmania was a further utilization of the resources of the River Gordon which would have involved a flooding of part of the Franklin River, an area of outstanding natural beauty.

The issue wracked Tasmanian Politics for over two years, bringing down a premier and later the state government; however, after the May, 1982, election the Tasmanian Parliament voted in favor of the scheme. The battle then switched to the federal scene, for the federal government has sought the inclusion of south-west Tasmania in the UN World Heritage List. The federal government introduced the World Heritage Properties Conservation Act 1983 with appropriate regulations, and launched High Court proceedings for an injunction to stop construction of the dam. The High Court of Australia ruled on 1 July 1983 that the federal act was constitutionally valid and that work on the dam must stop immediately. The decision was important also in establishing the principle that the federal government could intervene in what would normally be a state matter if an international convention, such as the World Heritage Convention, was involved.

Compensation was paid to Tasmania to cover the possibly higher cost of obtaining electricity from other sources, and to sustain employment. The battle over the Gordon-Below-Franklin Dam galvanized opinion throughout Australia; it became a truly national issue involving a national alliance of conservation groups. It was characterized by meetings and street marches, while the 'No Dams' triangle was to be seen from Perth to Cairns.

Great Barrier Reef Marine Park

A marine park established in 1975 by the Australian government embracing substantial areas of the Great Barrier Reef which runs in an extended system along practically the whole east coast of Queensland. It is the largest assemblage of living corals and associated organisms in the world, covering an area of 350 000 km^2. It has evolved over the last 8000 years. The park is managed by the Great Barrier Reef Marine Park Authority, which has prepared management plans for various sections of the reef. The reef was included in the World Heritage List in 1991 and is now fully protected against inappropriate activity, including oil exploration.

Great Lakes, North America

A chain of lakes forming a natural barrier between the United States and Canada comprising Lakes Superior, Michigan, Huron, Erie and Ontario. They cover an area of 245 000 sq km, constituting the largest area of freshwater in the world, outside the polar icecaps. The drainage basin is 754 000 sq km extending some 1400 km from Lake Superior in the west to Lake Ontario in the east. The lakes drain from west to east, emptying into the Atlantic Ocean via Niagara Falls.

The industry of the lakes area is highly diversified. Large quantities of coal, iron ore, grain and manufactured goods are moved annually between the ports or exported through the St. Lawrence Seaway. Large steel mills are located in Illinois, Indiana, Ohio and Ontario, while the automobile industry is located in Detroit, Michigan. The lakes supply water not only for these industries but also for about 240 regional municipalities. The lakes also serve a wide spectrum of recreational activities. Thirty million people live within the drainage basin.

However, vast industrial and residential developments have modified the environment. Huge tracts of forest were cleared, fisheries were devastated, and water-borne diseases such as typhoid and cholera became a major cause of death in lakeside communities. The destruction of the natural ecosystem was aggravated by human and agricultural wastes, and toxic pollutants such as mercury and petroleum products. By the mid-1960s Lake Erie was considered dead, a casualty of eutrophication. The Cuyahoga River caught fire from heavy pollution by oil and other flammable wastes. DDT and other pesticides decimated wildlife populations. Wetlands that originally covered one-fifth of the Great Lakes Basin were reduced by about half.

The Great Lakes Water Quality Agreement, signed by the USA and Canada in 1972 (and amended in 1978 and 1987) was a comprehensive accord that addressed the need of both countries for long-term environment protection measures. Measures were adopted at federal, provincial, state and local levels. Progress was made through Remedial Action Plans.

Lakeside management plans to control critical pollutants were developed for each of the Great Lakes. Coordinated strategies to protect and restore existing natural habitats, as well as to increase the size of habitats, were developed. A North American Waterfowl Management Plan was adopted to achieve a suitable and stable mix of wildlife population. All nuisance species were to be controlled. Measures to reduce emissions from industries and residences were vigorously adopted, with an integrated approach to pollution control.

Significant progress has been made in the last 25 years in restoring the ecological integrity of the Great Lakes. A massive public works program for the construction of municipal sewage treatment works (with federal grants) has much reduced pollutant loadings throughout the Great Lakes Basin. Fires no longer occur along Great Lakes waterways. Populations of predatory birds can once again be found throughout the Basin. However, significant problems still remain, including continued loss of habitat and the presence of persistent bioaccumulative toxic chemicals. A new program to combat acid rain has recently been introduced.

Greece

The Hellenic Republic of Greece is a unitary multiparty republic with one legislative house, the Greek Chamber of Deputies. The capital is Athens. The population in 1997 was 10.6 million, at an average density of 80 persons per sq km. Greece borders Albania, the former Yugoslavia, Bulgaria and Turkey. See Box 34 for the evolution of environmental law.

Box 34   Greece: evolution of environmental law

1938   Olympus National Park established
1972   Law 947 about Residential Areas
1976   Law 360 about Regional Planning and the Environment; Crea-
        tion of the National Council for Physical Planning and the
        Environment
1977   Law 743 about Protection of the Marine Environment and
        Other Topics
1979   Law 998 about the Protection of the Forests and Forest Ex-
        panses
1980   Law 1032 Creating the Ministry of Regional Planning, Urban
        Development and the Environment (now called the Ministry of
        the Environment, Regional Planning and Public Works)
1981   Law 1180 about Various Subjects Relative to the Establishment
        and Function of Industries
1983   Law 1327 about Measures Relating to Acute Pollution Episodes
1985   Law 1515 Regulative Plan and Program for the Protection of
        the Athens Environment
1986   Law 1650 about Environment Protection
1997   Kyoto target: 92

Greenpeace

Founded in 1971, the world's largest voluntary environmental organization
with some five million supporters in 150 countries and observer status on 25
international bodies. Greenpeace seeks to protect biodiversity through the
protection of rain forests and the protection of the marine environment from
drift netting, overfishing and commercial whaling. It also seeks to promote
the production of goods and services without involving toxic substances,
such as chlorine; to halt the international trade in toxic wastes; to protect the
atmosphere from the burning of fossil fuels and threats to the ozone layer;
and to oppose uranium mining, reprocessing and waste disposal. In 1985, the
Greenpeace flagship *Rainbow Warrior* was sunk in Auckland Harbour, New
Zealand, by French terrorists acting on behalf of the French government.
Greenpeace was protesting against France's program of nuclear testing at
Mururoa Atoll in French Polynesia.

H

Habitat Conservation Plan (HCP)

An important administrative tool available within the US Endangered Species Act for preserving wildlife and fragile ecosystems. Between 1993 and 1999, some 200 HCPs have been negotiated and signed by the White House. A typical HCP involves an exchange of land for money or other property and protects a company's exposure to lawsuits filed under the Endangered Species Act.

Hazard and Risk Impact Assessment

An important aspect of environmental impact assessment, it is a critical analysis of the risks and hazards presented by a project; that is the potential for human injury, damage to property, harm to the environment or some combination of these as a result of fire, explosion, toxic or corrosive effects, or radiation. Matters to be taken into consideration are outlined in Box 35.

Box 35   Hazard and risk impact assessment: economic, social and
        environmental matters for consideration

In determining a development application, a consent authority should take into consideration such of the following matters as are of relevance to the proposed development:
1. The choice of the location for the project, in particular the proximity of dwellings, other centres of employment, other vulnerable facilities such as schools and hospitals, and storage areas for inflammable and explosive materials.
2. Any proposed buffer zones, and any other planning restrictions.
3. The routeing of vehicles and trucks into and out of the proposed installation; the risk to life and limb of moving heavy trucks and road tankers through towns.
4. The nature of each process, identifying inputs, outputs, instrumentation and controls.
5. The location of chemical and hazardous waste storage areas, process areas where hazardous materials are used, equipment

---

Box 35   continued

fuelling areas, routes of pipelines carrying dangerous materials, electrical equipment and transmission lines.

6. The location and nature of wastewater treatment plant and air pollution control equipment; the disposal of their sludges and solids.

7. The risks of component, vessel, or system failure through material failure, leakage, corrosion, stress, explosion, breakdown, excessive pressure, fire, uncontrolled reactions, vibration, shock, collision, incorrect operation, inadequate design, lack of back-up and duplication of controls, inadequate monitoring; the risks of a boiling liquid expanding vapour explosion (BLEVE) or unconfined vapour cloud explosion (UVCE).

8. The proposed use of techniques to minimize hazards and risks, for example the use of bunds, sand-covered storage tanks, drip trays, or barriers; indicators and alarms; leak detection systems; groundwater monitoring; soil testing; automatic diversion systems; stormwater controls; secondary containment arrangements; clear identification of chemicals.

9. Compliance with all standards relating to the storage, movement and use of dangerous goods; poisons and environmentally hazardous chemicals legislation; occupational health criteria; and probable licence conditions.

10. The history of similar plant at other locations in respect of safety and the lessons learnt.

11. The disposal of all wastes, with clear identification; recycling.

12. Emergency measures, plans and procedures.

13. Periodic review of safety measures and monitoring results; arrangements for independent audits.

14. Laboratory facilities; sampling and testing.

15. Management and operational controls; hazards procedures manual; fines and penalties.

16. Training of staff and allocation of duties.

Hazardous Materials Transportation Act, 1975, US

An act which regulates the handling and transportation in commerce of hazardous materials. The act requires that shippers, transporters and persons who manufacture, sell or perform services relating to packages or containers of hazardous, radioactive or explosive materials in excess of specified quantities must file a registration with the US Department of Transportation. Regulations have created a comprehensive system for the safe transportation of hazardous materials by rail, air, vessel and public highway. Inspections are carried out to ensure compliance with the many requirements of the regulations. Labelling and placarding of containers is prescribed, with a whole range of standard procedures and technical requirements. In 1990, the US Congress enacted the Hazardous Materials Transportation Uniform Safety Act which limited the authority of the states to introduce legislation inconsistent with federal law. In 1994, the acts were reauthorized.

Headwater Forest Agreement

A 1999 agreement between the US Federal government, the State of California and the Pacific Lumber Company to protect the Headwater Forest, the world's last groves of privately-owned old-growth redwood trees. The agreement involves the use of federal funds to purchase the headwaters property from Pacific Lumber. Some of the trees that will be saved are more than 2000 years old and taller than 90 metres (300 feet). They are the remnants of what was once a vast redwood forest. The cost of the purchase has been shared between Washington and California. The agreement also bans logging in some lesser areas in order to protect the habitat of the marbled murrelect, an endangered waterfowl, and also to maintain buffer zones for the protection of the stream habitats of endangered coho salmon and steelhead trout. The agreement allows for some logging in the buffer zones also. Some parties such as the Sierra Club are unhappy with the agreement. The agreement forms part of a Habitat Conservation Plan.

Health and Safety at Work Act, 1974, UK

An act which created a Health and Safety Executive for Britain, and placed a general duty on those concerned to ensure that their workplaces were made and kept safe and healthy. Apart from supervising workplaces, the Executive was given an additional role in the assessment of public safety from potentially hazardous industrial development. For the first time, risk assessment was introduced to the main line of planning debate. The Executive and the planning authorities became responsible for ensuring that the public was properly protected from the external effects of works activities.

One of the key roles of the Executive is to provide information and guidance to planning authorities in cases where proposed development could prejudice community safety. Where plans and policies are being prepared to guide development, indicative standards are provided only. However, where specific proposals classed as hazardous developments are proposed, a compulsory notification system allows the Executive to consider each case and provide the planning authority with the detailed physical separation and safeguarding distances that should be observed. The standards adopted are kept under review by the Hazardous Substances Policy Group of the Executive. The Major Hazards Branch of the Executive carries out risk appraisal work on large-scale hazards and provides detailed advice to the authorities.

See also:
Department of the Environment, UK.

Heritage Coast, UK

In Britain, areas of coast identified as of outstanding beauty and merit. The Countryside Commission has identified over 40 stretches of the coastline of England and Wales, totaling over 1260 km, as 'heritage coast'. These stretches, representing some 30 per cent of the total length of the coastline, comprise undeveloped and outstanding national coastal scenery. The Commission has, in cooperation with the concerned maritime local authorities, defined many of these heritage coasts in detail as a first step towards the preparation of comprehensive long-term planning and management programs for these areas. The programs are prepared by the local authorities while the Commission provides a coordinating role coupled with technical and financial assistance. A full range of coastal planning and management methods is being explored.

Heritage Conservation

Measures adopted to restore, preserve and maintain buildings and townscapes of heritage value. In simple terms, conservation of buildings and townscape involves:

- Retaining the existing fabric and setting of the building including detailing, finishes, verandas, joinery, roofs, chimneys and so on.
- Reinstating missing components of the building's fabric including detailing, chimneys, color schemes, verandas, finishes and so on.
- Blending in new alterations and extensions to relate sympathetically with the existing building and townscape.
- Reuse of existing heritage buildings by strata titling or recycling in preference to demolition and redevelopment. Additional floor space

may be achieved with new extensions consistent with the design of the building.

- Sympathetically designed new 'infill' houses or development in terms of siting, massing, scale, character and materials to relate harmoniously with surrounding buildings.

Demolition is not the only way of destroying historic or architecturally valuable buildings. This loss frequently occurs in a more gradual and less dramatic process through lack of maintenance. This results in deterioration of detailing and the building fabric generally; mediocre additions, substitution of materials, veranda enclosures, inappropriate color schemes and subdivision; unsympathetically designed carports, garages, fences, walls and swimming pools; plus poorly sited and designed new development.

Heritage Criteria

Criteria which are used to identify significant buildings in heritage terms. These include:

- Association with an historic event, person, phenomenon, or institution.
- Being a good example of an architect's work.
- Being a good example of a particular style, which includes regional variations and vernacular buildings.
- Being a landmark or focal point in a townscape or stretch of countryside.
- Forming part of a group of buildings of townscape or rural value.
- Displaying technical or planning evolution such as the early use of concrete.

Holmepierrepoint, England

In 1961, in the face of severe electricity shortages, the Central Electricity Generating Board (CEGB) for England and Wales had selected a site at Holmepierrepoint, on the east side of the City of Nottingham, in the East Midlands, for a major power station, the first of ten such installations. The plant was to be the latest design, comprising four 500 MW units. The coal-fired plant would be connected to a single multi-flue stack some 200 metres in height, ensuring adequate dispersal of the flue gases during all meteorological conditions. Some 600 tonnes of sulphur dioxide would be dispersed daily from the daily consumption of 20 000 tonnes of coal. Dust-arresting equipment would remove over 99.3 per cent of the fly ash carried forward to the stack. High efflux velocities would be maintained. The development application was placed before the Minister for Power who ordered a public inquiry, which was held in Nottingham, attended by many objectors and representatives of the CEGB. The procedures allowed full legal representation by all parties, with extensive cross-examination of witnesses, a normal British procedure.

Witnesses for the CEGB argued that this excellent plant would have minimal adverse environmental impacts. However searching questions remained unanswered. What would be the ultimate fate of the 600 tonnes of sulphur dioxide released each day? Of the 40 tonnes of dust emitted per day, how much would be in the respirable range reaching the lungs of residents? What would be the effect of 20 trains a day bringing coal to the power station, using the level crossings in the city? How would 4000 tonnes of ash produced per day be adequately handled? How could the CEGB disguise the presence of huge steam generators and eight immense cooling towers, on a flat site open to the city? Witnesses stumbled on some of these questions.

The decision of the Minister of Power stunned the CEGB. The development application was rejected in its entirety, leaving a 2000 MW hole in the programme of an industry beset with electricity shortages, black-outs and brown-outs. The reasons for the rejection were entirely environmental.

The report of the Commission of Inquiry stressed the openness of the site in relation to the city, the wind directions for most of the year, the uncertainties regarding plume dispersal, the untested claims in respect of dust-arresting equipment, the absence of knowledge regarding the fate of large amounts of sulphur dioxide, the possible effects of warmed water on the river, and the poor record of the CEGB in respect of pollution control generally. All these factors mitigated against this development application, notwithstanding the technical merits of the station, being the first power station in Britain to have a high single stack with high-efficiency electrostatic precipitators for dust removal. A dramatic revision of site selection procedures was undertaken. It became essential to select sites more carefully with regard to possible resident reactions, and to research some of the more pressing questions, not yet fully answered. In the end it was concluded that much of Britain's sulphur pollution was reaching Scandinavia.

The CEGB returned to the Nottingham area quite quickly, with the proposal of a site at Ratcliffe-on-Soar, to the south of the city, further away, and screened by hills. Being less intrusive, it attracted less opposition. The sulphur in the fuel was restricted to one per cent, and the coal trains would no longer run through the city of Nottingham. Notwithstanding a long and exhausting public inquiry, the development application was successful without modification. This was followed by a successful application at Fiddlers Ferry, Didcot, and a chain of others.

Human Rights

Fundamental rights accorded to human beings, in varying degrees, and sometimes denied in whole or part. In 1948, the United Nations passed the Universal Declaration of Human Rights, a first attempt to catalogue what members considered to be fundamental rights and freedoms. Containing thirty articles, it was adopted by the General Assembly in 1948. It asserted *inter alia* that all human beings are born free and equal in dignity and rights. In 1976, the General Assembly adopted the International Covenant on Civil and Political Rights, establishing legal obligations in the ratifying states. The issue of human rights remains controversial: the crushing of political opposition in many countries inevitably involves a denial of rights; ethnic groups attempt to deny rights to others; religions in a variety of ways deny rights; dictatorships thrive on a denial of rights; regimes and creeds oppress women and oppose their advancement. In 1993, the UN held a World Conference on Human Rights. Its purpose was to review the protection and promotion of human rights since the Universal Declaration. The conference identified the obstacles to further progress; examined the relationship between development and the enjoyment of economic, social, cultural and environmental rights; and evaluated the effectiveness of various measures. It emphasized the need to promote the active participation of indigenous peoples in the management of the environment and underlying resources. Box 36 summarizes some of the human rights agreements and conventions.

Hungary

The Republic of Hungary is a unitary multiparty republic with one legislative house, the National Assembly. Its neighbors include the Czech Republic, the Slovak Republic, Austria and Romania. The population in 1997 was 10 million, at an average density of 110 persons per sq km. See Box 37 for the evolution of environmental law.

Box 36   Selected list of human rights agreements

June 1945	Charter of the United Nations
June 1946	UN Commission on Human Rights
December 1948	Genocide Convention/Universal Declaration of Human Rights
August 1949	Four Geneva Conventions governing treatment in war of the wounded, prisoners of war and civilians
November 1950	European Convention on Human Rights
July 1951	Convention Relating to the Status of Refugees
December 1952	Convention on the Political Rights of Women
September 1954	Convention on the Status of Stateless Persons
September 1956	Convention Abolishing Slavery
June 1957	ILO's Convention on the Abolition of Forced Labour
November 1962	Convention on Consent to Marriage
December 1965	Convention on the Elimination of Racial Discrimination
December 1966	International Covenants on Economic, Social and Cultural Rights/Civil and Political Rights
November 1973	Convention on the Suppression of Apartheid
June 1977	Two additional protocols to the Geneva Conventions
December 1979	Convention on the Elimination of All Forms of Discrimination against Women
December 1984	Convention Against Torture
November 1989	Convention on the Rights of the Child
May 1993	International Criminal Tribunal for Ex-Yugoslavia
November 1994	International Criminal Tribunal for Rwanda
July 1998	UN conference agrees treaty for a permanent International Criminal Court

Box 37   *Hungary: evolution of environmental law*

1790	Act to prevent the pollution of waters or canals
1876	Public Health Act providing further measures against pollution
1935	Forest and Nature Conservation Act
1961	Establishment of a national authority for the management of nature conservation
1964	Water Act
1968	Laws on plant protection
1972	Public health measures
1976	Protection of the Human Environment Act
1977	National Council for Environment Protection and Nature Conservation established; National Authority for Environment Protection and Nature Conservation established
1979	Ratifies the Convention on Long-range Transboundary Air Pollution; Regulations on the management of the environment approved by the Council of Ministers.
1980	Institute of Environment Protection founded
1981	Declaration of five biosphere reserves: Hortobagy National Park, Kiskunsag National Park, Aggtelek Landscape Protection Area, Lake Ferto Landscape Protection Area and Pilis Landscape Protection Area
1982–86	Revision of regulations on nature conservation, water and air protection
1993	Decree on the Provisional Regulation of Environmental Impact Assessments
1995	Environment and privatization laws require reports on contaminated sites
1997	Kyoto target: 94

I

India

The Republic of India is a multiparty federal republic with two legislative houses, the Council of States and the House of the People. The capital is New Delhi. The population in 1997 was 968 million, at an average density of 306 persons per sq km. India abuts Pakistan, Bangladesh, Nepal and Kashmir. See Box 38 for the evolution of environmental law.

Box 38   India: evolution of environmental law

1873   Northern India Canal and Drainage Act
1897   Indian Fisheries Act
1901   Indian Ports Act
1905   Bengal Smoke Nuisance Act
1908   Koziranger National Park, Assam, established
1912   Bombay Smoke Nuisance Act
1917   Inland Stream Vessel Act; Mysore Destructive Insects and Pests
       Act
1919   Poison Act
1923   Indian Boilers Act
1927   Indian Forest Act
1935   Corbett National Park and Tadoba National Park established
1939   Motor Vehicles Act
1947   Mines and Minerals Act
1948   Factories (Pollution and Pesticides) Act
1953   Maharashtra Prevention of Water Pollution Act; Orissa River
       Pollution and Prevention Act
1954   Prevention of Food Adulteration Act
1956   River Boards Act
1958   Ancient Monuments and Archaeological Sites Act
1965   Gir Lion National Park established
1968   Insecticides Act
1969   Maharashtra Water Pollution Prevention Act
1972   National Committee on Environmental Planning and Coordina-
       tion to examine the environmental implications of major
       development projects, and to set guidelines for the protection
       of the environment; Silent Valley project abandoned to protect

---

Box 38 continued

ecological resources; Chipko Andolan Movement (tree-hugging movement) begins in Uttar Pradesh, as a protest against the cutting down of trees

1979 Social forestry program launched in Uttar Pradesh, the project being World Bank financed

1980 Department of Environment established; Forest Conservation Act

1981 Air Pollution Control Act

1984 Bhopal disaster: a catastrophic leak of methylisocyanate at a pesticide plant results in over 2000 deaths with thousands injured

1986 Introduction of EIA procedures; Environment Protection Act

1987 Pollution Control Act

1988 Technology impact statements introduced

1992 Sardar Sarova water projects initiated

1993 India decides not to seek further World Bank assistance for Sardar Sarova, due to disagreements over conditions including environmental conditions; however, the project would proceed; 100 000 people to be resettled.

1996 Life expectancy: 59.1 years for males, 60.3 years for females

1998 Access to safe piped water, 32.3 per cent; to wells, 32.2 per cent; and hand pumps, 30.0 per cent. Access to domestic electricity, 42.0 per cent

ICOMOS

See:
International Council for Monuments and Sites

Indonesia

The Republic of Indonesia is a unitary multiparty republic with two legislative houses, the House of People's Representatives and the People's Consultative Assembly. The capital is Jakarta. The population in 1997 was 200 million, at an average density of 104 persons per sq km. Indonesia lies in southeast Asia between the Indian and Pacific Oceans, north of Australia and west of Papua New Guinea. See Box 39 for the evolution of environmental law.

Box 39   Indonesia: evolution of environmental law

1921   Ujong-Kulong National Park; a nature reserve in 1921, becoming a national park in 1980

1978   Environmental policy guidelines endorsed by a General Session of the Consultative People's Assembly in order to: (1) safeguard natural resources vital to development; (2) promote EIA development projects, sectorally and regionally; (3) ensure the rehabilitation of impaired natural resources; and (4) secure an improvement in the living environment of low-income people

1982   Environmental Management Act, providing a legal basis for Indonesian environmental policy embracing natural resources, environmental management, conservation, pollution control, and EIA

1986   Regulations for EIA (AMDAL) introduced, providing a framework for comprehensive EIA in Indonesia

1987   EIA procedures established by all Indonesian ministries

1989   National clean waters programme inaugurated, a number of key river systems being targeted

1990   Water pollution control regulations; Environmental Impact Management Agency (BAPEDAL) created to develop and implement policies on pollution control, hazardous waste management and EIA

1993   Legislation requiring all companies to produce environmental audit reports on a five-year cycle, the only system worldwide of compulsory environmental audit

1994   World Bank finances a programme for the supply of clean and safe water and sanitation services for about 1.5 million low-income people in Indonesia

1997   Life expectancy: 63.0 years for males, 66.0 years for females

---

Indonesia Botanical Gardens

First used by the Dutch for the introduction of tropical plants, the gardens were officially converted in 1817 into a botanical garden, offering training in tropical botany. Much of the original rain forest has been preserved in its natural state, providing specimens for scientific study. The garden also has collections of palms, bamboos, cacti, orchids and ornamental trees.

Industry and Environment Centre, UNEP

A centre established by UNEP in 1975 to encourage the development and implementation of industrial policies, strategies, technologies and management practices that contribute to sustainable development and environment protection, reducing industrial pollution and risk. The centre has promoted environment protection through cleaner and safer industrial production and consumption, developing policies towards that end, and stimulated the exchange of information. The centre is based in Paris.

Injurious Affection

A term referring to the depreciation in the value of land caused by the adverse effects of public works through noise, vibration, smell, smoke, fumes, artificial lighting, overshadowing, loss of support, and restriction or loss of access. Injurious affection is usually associated with the carrying out of substantial public undertakings such as the construction of a freeway or an airport. Land surrounding an airport may well diminish in value because of noise resulting from aircraft. In some cases, injurious affection may result in compensation though usually only when the land is acquired for the project. However, under British legislation compensation is not so limited, being payable outside the actual acquisition area.

No compensation is payable to the community for injurious affection of community facilities. Nor do the law reformers suggest there should be. Indeed, it is hard to imagine how there could be compensation. The community must simply suffer the adverse affects of a road upon its facilities, including open space. The road, after all, is built because it serves the public interest. It will be important, therefore, to consider whether the community which suffers a degradation of its facilities (and especially open space) by the proximity of the road, nonetheless derives an equitable share of the benefits arising from the road.

Insecticide, Fungicide and Rodenticide Act, US

A federal measure, amended by the US Congress in 1978, which provides for the regulation by the EPA of pesticide substances; such substances include products to control insects, weeds and disease in agricultural production, disease vector control (for example, mosquitoes or rabid animals), and products used as hospital or home disinfectants and sterilants. The act directs the EPA to regulate such pesticide substances to ensure that they do not cause 'unreasonable adverse effects' on humans or the environment, requiring a balancing of risks against benefits in agriculture, public health and the economy. Every pesticide marketed in the United States must obtain premarket clearance and registration from the EPA; and pesticide residue tolerances (legally acceptable levels) or exemptions must be established for pesticides used on food or feed. In 1985, a major review of this legislation was initiated. Among the major issues were whether states should have the right to enforce standards for pesticide use that are tougher than the federal government's standards; whether the public should have access to confidential health and safety data filed by pesticide manufacturers; and whether the EPA should share pesticide data with foreign governments.

Inspector

Environmental legislation generally and pollution control legislation in particular provides for the appointment of suitably qualified individuals as inspectors. Their task is to supervise operations in the public and private sectors to ensure compliance with consent conditions, emission standards and best practice; to negotiate improvements in plant operations; to collect evidence leading to successful prosecutions; and to track down illegal operations. The role of the inspector is essentially front-line. Inspectors are backed by legal authority to enter industrial and commercial premises at any time, and often to enter domestic premises also, after notice. Obstruction of an inspector is an offence. Regular switching of inspectors becomes desirable.

Integrated Pollution Control (IPC)

Introduced initially into Britain under the Environmental Protection Act 1990, a procedure whereby all major emissions to land, air and water are considered simultaneously and not in isolation, avoiding frustrations, confusion, and situations in which one control measure for one medium adversely affects another. For example, an air pollution control measure may result in water pollution or excessive noise. Under this act, Her Majesty's Inspectorate of Pollution is able to recover the costs incurred in operating the IPC program. Several OECD countries have adopted IPC legislation. These include Denmark, Sweden, France, the Netherlands, the USA, Finland, Ireland, Italy and Japan. A somewhat broader scheme for integrated pollution prevention and control was adopted by the Council of the European Union in 1996 (Council Directive 96/61/EC).

Intergenerational Equity (Fairness Between Generations)

A concept that those living today should not compromise or restrict the opportunities open to future generations. It envisages a partnership among all the generations that will expect to thrive on the world's resources. It implies, at the very least, that each generation should hand over to the rising generation a world in as good an order as possible and with the full benefits of sustainable development. The World Commission on Environment and Development in *Our Common Future* stated that: 'Sustainable development is development that meets the needs of the present without compromising the ability of future generations to meet their own needs.' Problems arise with the application of the concept. Clearly, a treeless, barren planet, scorched with ultraviolet radiation and littered with radioactive wastes, would not meet the criteria. Yet, considering more likely outcomes, it is impracticable to envisage the circumstances of generations as yet unborn. One has only to ask whether anyone living in 1800 could predict the needs and aspirations of those living in 1900; and whether anyone living in 1900 could predict the needs and aspirations of those living in 2000.

Some have suggested that compensation funds should be set up which, with compound interest, would serve to compensate future generations for the ravages of the present. Apart from the risks to such funds which could be overwhelmed by inflation or simply forcibly acquired by the wrong people, such proposals cannot be morally supported. If the past is any guide, future generations will be substantially better off than those living at present. The future will inherit the present with all its progress in electronics and advanced technologies. To hand over a planet in fairly good order is all that is morally required from the present.

Intergenerational equity remains a noble concept which cannot be translated into useful and practical policies other than the pursuit of responsible management of resources to serve the interest of current generations. There is every reason to believe that problems with population growth, forestry, fisheries, biodiversity, global warming, the ozone layer and world food supplies will be resolved, while material progress continues to surge forward throughout many parts of the world.

See also:
Intragenerational Equity.

Intergovernmental Panel on Climate Change

See:
Kyoto Protocol.

International Airport, Hong Kong

The international airport at Kai Tak, located on the eastern fringe of Kowloon, has been replaced by a new international airport with two independent runways at Chek Lap Kok to the west of Hong Kong island. Land for the airport was formed by levelling the islands of Chek Lap Kok and Lam Chau, just off Lantau Island and by using excavated material from marine borrow areas. The entire program comprised ten interlinked infrastructure projects, with a completion year of 1997. Apart from the airport itself, these projects included 1669 ha of land reclamation, a harbor crossing and land tunnel, the longest road/rail suspension bridge in the world, a new town in Tung Chung, a 34 km airport railway and more than 30 km of expressway. The whole was known as the Airport Core Program, being one of the largest infrastructure programs in the world. Moving the airport from its original location provided relief to the nearby 350 000 residents affected by severe aircraft noise, and eased the congestion of air traffic.

The airport master plan study began in 1990, establishing a basic airport configuration. The configuration selected involved the dredging and disposal of more than 70 million cubic metres of marine mud and a requirement for over 150 million cubic metres of fill. An early decision was made to retain a sea channel between the airport island and the coast of North Lantau. This enabled the natural coastline west of Tung Chun to be largely preserved, allowing also for tidal flushing of a potential area to the east of Chek Lap Kok.

An early EIA study of construction impacts identified a number of significant effects. About 70 dwellings would be adversely affected by noise, the construction program commencing in 1992, on a 24-hour basis. The Hong Kong Executive Council granted exemption from the Noise Control Ordinances for the construction program. However, this exemption was subject to conditions, including provision for the installation of air conditioners in affected dwellings, allowing windows and doors to be closed. In addition, a temporary ten-metre earth berm was to be installed along the southern edge of the airport as a barrier to construction noise. Attention was to be given to noise minimization from the completed operational airport. Aircraft noise impacts were predicted for various assumed aircraft fleet mixes using Noise Exposure Forecast contours. It was concluded that by the year 2000, an acceptable level of noise would only be exceeded for a small number of dwellings at Sha Lo Wan on North Lantau, west of Tung Chung. These villagers were to be relocated, with all new noise-sensitive land uses being excluded from the airport vicinity.

Blasting, loading, transport and placement of fill material were the primary sources of dust. Concrete/asphalt plants were also a source of pollutants. In order to control the amount of dust, permanent monitoring stations were set up.

The destruction of the two islands along with their terrestrial and marine life, necessitated a number of compensatory conservation measures, among them the rescue, study and possible re-establishment of the rare Romer tree frog.

The excavation works required stripping the existing vegetation, and marine mud being disposed of by marine dumping. Potentially hazardous material and chemical wastes would require special measures . However, the EIA study confirmed that the airport island would have an insignificant effect on water quality, bulk and tidal regimes, subject to the preservation of a sea channel to assist tidal flushing some 200 metres wide.

Apart from incorporating environmental measures in construction projects, the Hong Kong government forged links with the community to provide quick responses to their problems. An Environmental Project Office was created to provide a continuous overview of environmental effects, and to coordinate and monitor remedial actions. The management of the airport development represented a further step in the implementation of EIA procedures, which became mandatory for all major public projects in 1997. The Hong Kong Environmental Impact Assessment Ordinance was enacted in January 1997, together with a Technical Memorandum on the EIA process.

The new international airport was officially opened in July 1998, by President Jiang Zemin.

Sources: Hong Kong Environment Protection Department (1992), *Environment Hong Kong 1992*, Government Printer, Hong Kong; A.M.M. Liu and L.Y. Ng 'Environmental issues in the new airport development in Hong Kong', paper presented to the Catalyst '95 Conference (July 1995), University of Canberra, Australia; Elvis W.K. Au (1998), 'Status and progress of environmental assessments in Hong Kong: facing the challenges in the 21st century', *Impact Assessment and Project Appraisal*, June 1998, vol. 16. no. 2, Beech Tree Publishing, Surrey, England.

International Commission for the Protection of the Rhine

An international commission created by the riparian countries in 1950 for the protection of the River Rhine against pollution. The commission includes representatives from France, Luxembourg (in connection with the Moselle), the Netherlands, Switzerland and Germany. The secretariat is based in Koblenz, Germany. Specifically, the responsibilities of the commission are to: determine the amount and nature of pollution in the river at various stages of its course and at various times of the year; identify the sources of pollution; compare the legislation of the member countries relating to water pollution control; collate national inventories of discharges and receive reports on monitoring results; prepare and submit recommendations to the governments concerned.

The commission set up a monitoring system for the waters of the Rhine; sampling is conducted at selected points in accordance with an established schedule and a laboratory testing program. The member countries also conduct monitoring and report to the commission.

The commission was given legal status by a convention signed by five countries in 1965. For some years, however, there was no international convention committing the riparian countries to take concerted action against water pollution. National legislation alone was relied upon. Nevertheless, the commission obtained much closer cooperation between the countries involved. Furthermore, the water supply authorities revealed a direct interest in the detection and prevention of dangerous contamination.

International Council for Monuments and Sites (ICOMOS)

Founded in 1965, an international NGO dedicated to the conservation and preservation of the world's historic monuments and sites. Its functions include advising UNESCO in respect of these matters and advising the World Heritage Committee on the nomination of new items to the World Heritage List. ICOMOS also seeks to establish international standards for the preservation, restoration and management of the cultural environment generally. An International Charter for the Conservation and Restoration of Monuments and sites was formally adopted in 1966, and used as a basis for ICOMOS charters in countries around the world.

International Labour Organization (ILO)

Established in 1919, an intergovernmental agency in which representatives of governments, employers and employees participate to improve occupational and working conditions. The ILO was recognized by the UN in 1946 as a specialized agency. Within the context of the working environment, the ILO has produced codes and guidance in respect of air pollution, noise and vibration, occupational cancer, chemical hazards and control of risks. It cooperates closely with the WHO.

World Employment is an annual report published by the ILO. The 1996–97 report stated that about one billion people worldwide, or about one-third of the global labour force, were either unemployed or underemployed in 1995. This compared with about 820 million in 1993 and 1994. The ILO warned that the growing numbers of the *working poor* would aggravate economic problems and social unrest.

The ILO argues that sustained economic growth is the best recipe for getting people back to work. The average level of unemployment in the EU during 1995 had been 11.3 per cent of the workforce, while unemployment in Central and Eastern Europe remained in double-digits. On the other hand, unemployment in the USA had been below 6 per cent for 26 straight months.

International Law

See:
Convention.

International Organization for Standardization (ISO)

Founded in Geneva, Switzerland, in 1946 a specialized international organization concerned with standardization in most technical and non-technical fields. Beyond the technical, ISO 9000 established international management quality standards. In 1994, ISO issued ISO 14000, a set of environmental management guidelines that can be adopted by virtually any organization in the world. For business, these systems provide a structured, cost-effective means of complying with environmental regulations, discharging 'due diligence' obligations, and of integrating economic and environmental performance. By the end of 1998, over 5400 companies had complied with ISO 14000 worldwide.

International Seabed Authority

An international body set up under the Convention on the Law of the Sea (Montego Bay convention) which came into force in 1994 after many years of debate. The authority is based in Kingston, Jamaica. Its function is to oversee and regulate the exploitation of the rich mineral resources of the oceans through a licensing system. The authority assesses and predicts the environmental impact of activities in the International Seabed Area; studies the effects of pollution; oversees exploration activities; develops rules and regulations for the conduct of seabed activities; approves plans of activities; and develops mechanisms for the enforcement of responsible behaviour.

See also:
Exclusive Economic Zone (EEZ).

International Tropical Timber Agreement (ITTA)

Set up in 1983, a trade agreement establishing a system of consultation and cooperation between consuming and producing countries. The agreement has the support of some 47 countries, representing about 95 per cent of the international trade in tropical timber. ITTA recognizes in its charter the importance of conservation and the principles of sustainable yield. In 1986, ITTA created an International Tropical Timber Organization (ITTO). ITTO has attempted to promote the sustainable management of tropical forests; in 1990, ITTO adopted a set of guidelines for sustainable tropical forest management and set the target of the year 2000 by which the entire tropical timber trade should come from sustainably managed forests. By 1994, perhaps no more than one per cent of tropical timber came from sustainably managed forests; further, the parties could not agree on the meaning of sustainable management. Clearly, incentives such as preferential entry to markets are needed to encourage good management. During a renegotiation of ITTA in 1993, the producer countries endorsed the putting of tropical forests under sustainable management by the year 2000, though with the qualification that the target be also applicable to timber from all forests, tropical, temperate and boreal.

International Union for the Conservation of Nature and Natural Resources (IUCN)

See:
World Conservation Union (WCU).

International Whaling Commission (IWC)

An international body formed in 1946 with the purpose of framing regulations for the conservation, development and optimum utilization of whale resources. It operates under the terms of the Convention for the Regulation of Whaling, and meets each year to review the condition of whale stocks. Its original membership of 14 nations has gradually increased to include a number of non-whaling nations. In 1982, in view of the virtual failure of the whale management programs, the IWC voted to discontinue commercial whaling worldwide, commencing in 1986. Some countries still persisted in some commercial whaling. In response, in 1994 the IWC agreed to create a vast oceanic sanctuary which would give whales permanent protection from commercial hunts. First proposed by France, the Southern Ocean Sanctuary covers an area more than five times the size of Australia. It embraces waters from Bass Strait to Antarctica and encircles the globe in a vast swathe. Japan and Russia objected to the sanctuary. The sanctuary is used by seven species of endangered whales.

Iceland left the IWC in 1992 to resume hunting minke whales. Norway stayed in the IWC, but resumed commercial whaling in 1993. Japan kills about 300 a year for research purposes. The 39 members of IWC continue, with these exceptions, to oppose commercial whaling, confirming a total ban in October 1997. Japan and Norway argue that the purpose of the IWC is to manage whaling, not to ban it. Opponents to whaling argue that it is better to ban it than to open the doors to the bloody and cruel excesses of the past.

Intragenerational Equity (Fairness Within Today's Society)

A concept of fairness between individuals and groups, within society, locally, regionally, nationally and globally. The concept of human rights and dignity was embodied in the UN Universal Declaration of Human Rights in 1948, and in a whole range of conventions and declarations since then. Such rights include equality before the law; protection against arbitrary arrest; the right to a fair trial; the right to own property; freedom of thought, conscience and religion; freedom of opinion and expression; freedom of peaceful assembly and association; the right to work; the right to equal pay for equal work; the right to form and join trade unions; the right to rest and leisure; the right to an adequate standard of living; and the right to education. These rights are compromised in all countries by reasons of birth, gender, race, property, class, caste, political division, territorial ambition, inequality of income, denial of rights, persecution, genocide, conquest, prejudice, bigotry, arrogance, maladministration and non-democratic forms of government. These factors work to the detriment of effective environmental management and sustainable development.

Despite enormous material progress the world at the social level remains substantially tribal and barbaric. Certainly, democratic forms of government have made substantial progress while a variety of dictatorships have collapsed. Society remains, however, relatively primitive; it is the area of least progress. Progress seems at times to come by chance, or through the actions of a small number of heroic people. People seem to find it easier to hate than to love, particularly in respect of people who look or sound different. Issues of race constantly intrude, and the author is reminded of his encounter with the Ku-Klux Klan in 1968. Although able to reach Mars, humanity remains at a low ebb in these matters of intragenerational equity.

See also:
Intergenerational Equity.

Israel

Israel is a multiparty republic with one legislative house, the Knesset. Located at the eastern end of the Mediterranean between Palestine in the south and the Lebanon in the north, the population in 1997 was 5.6 million, at an average density of 278 persons per sq km. See Box 40 for the evolution of environmental law.

Box 40   Israel: evolution of environmental law

1924	Technion-Israel Institute of Technology established
1925	Hebrew University of Jerusalem established
1948	UN partition of Palestine; Jewish state established
1952	Israel Atomic Energy Commission established
1955	Water Metering Act
1955–62	Water Drilling Control Acts
1957–61	Drainage and Flood Control Acts
1959	Water Measurement Act
1959–65	Water Act consolidated
1965	Planning and Building Act, establishing a comprehensive physical planning system
1970	Water Pollution Act
1972	Environmental Protection Service established
1977	A total of 125 million trees planted; Mount Carmel National Park created
1982	EIA requirements introduced: regulations define the type of project subject to EIA and set out the basic requirements
1992	EIA guidelines for quarries, industries, roads and other categories
1993	Review of EIA policy by the Technion-Israel Institute of Technology
1997	Life expectancy: 76.3 years for males; 80.2 years for females
1998	Israel has 3500 registered archaeological sites; Weizmann Institute of Science pursues solar research

---

Italy

Italy is a republic with two legislative houses, the Senate and the Chamber of Deputies. The population in 1997 was 58 million, at an average density of

Box 41   Italy: evolution of environmental law

1836   Gran Paradiso National Park established
1865   Water Supply and River Management Act
1902   Cultural Heritage Act
1922   Parks and Nature Reserves Act
1931   Fauna and Flora Act
1934   Air Pollution Act
1939   Coastal Protection Act; Cultural Heritage Act
1941   Waste Pollution Act
1942   Town and Country Planning Act
1961   Water Pollution Act
1966   Air Pollution Act
1971   Housing Act, to facilitate acquisition of sites suitable for subsidized housing
1973   Environmental Impact Assessment Act
1974   Toxic and Hazardous Substances Act
1976   Water Pollution Act; Seveso Dioxin Incident
1977   Hunting and Wildlife Protection Act
1979   Water Pollution Act
1980   Comprehensive national health and insurance services
1983   Air Pollution Act; Marine Pollution Act
1984   Parks and Nature Reserves Act; Toxic and Hazardous Substances Act
1985   Water Pollution Act; Stava Tailings Dam Disaster
1986   Ministry of the Environment created
1988   Decree requiring an EIA for certain public and private projects
1989   EIA legislation comes into force; EIA Commission created; introduction of public inquiries
1991   Nearly 100 per cent of dwellings have access to electricity, safe water supply and toilet facilities
1992   EIA requirements extended; legislation reviewed to ensure full implementation with EC Directive 85/337
1993   Life expectancy: 74.1 years for males; 80.5 years for females
1994   Investigation of major contraventions relating to pollution of the River Arno, which empties into the Gulf of Naples, involving raw sewage and untreated industrial wastes
1996   Presidential Decree extending the application of EIA in Italy as a whole
1997   Kyoto target: 92

192 persons per sq km. Italy lies between the Mediterranean and the Adriatic Sea, with the Alps to the north. See Box 41 for the evolution of environmental law.

J

Japan

Japan is a constitutional monarchy with a National Diet consisting of two legislative houses, the House of Councillors and the House of Representatives. The population in 1997 was 126 million, at an average density of 334 persons per sq km. The capital is Tokyo. Japan lies between the Sea of Japan and the Pacific Ocean, flanked to the west by Russia, Korea and China. See Box 42 for the evolution of environmental law.

Box 42   *Japan: evolution of environmental law*

1918	Wildlife Protection and Hunting Law
1934	Daisetsuzan National Park established
1936	Fuji-Hakone-Izu National Park established
1945	Destruction of 70 per cent of housing in 70 per cent of cities
1946–50	Agricultural reforms
1950	Housing Loan Corporation
1956	Japan joins UN and OECD
1957	Natural Parks Law
1962	Smoke Control Law
1965	Japan Environment Corporation established to finance pollution control projects
1967	Basic Law for Environmental Pollution Control
1970	Water Pollution Control Law; Soil Pollution Control Law; Waste Disposal and Public Cleansing Law
1971	Japan Environment Agency established; Offensive Odor Control Law; Agricultural Chemical Regulation Law
1972	Japanese contribution to the UN Conference on the Human Environment, Stockholm, with detailed accounts of mercury and cadmium poisoning in Japan; Air Pollution Control Law; Nature Conservation Law; EIA procedures for major public projects
1973	Pollution-related Health Damage Compensation Law; Chemical Substances Control Law; Nature Conservation Law and Natural Parks Law
1981	Housing and Urban Development Corporation established
1984	EIA procedures for general application adopted by Cabinet
1986	National survey of the natural environment (the Green Census); revision of Chemical Substances Control Law
1987	Comprehensive Resort Area Development Law; Amendment of Pollution-related Health Damage Compensation Law
1988	Protection of the Ozone Layer Law
1989	Water Pollution Control Law
1990	Nature Conservation Law and Natural Parks Law
1991	Wildlife Preservation Law; goal of seventh 5-year program 1991–95 to increase the percentage of population served by sewers to 55 per cent; Recycling Resources Law
1995	Life expectancy: 76.4 years for males; 82.8 years for females; Kobe earthquake
1997	Kyoto target: 94

K

Kavkazsky Nature Reserve

Established in 1924, a natural area set aside for scientific research at the western end of the Caucasus mountains, Russia. At low elevation, forests of oak and beech prevail while at high elevations, forests of fir and rhododendrum dominate. Wildlife includes brown bear, wild pig, lynx, red deer, chamois, wolf and bison. Research concentrates on the preservation of Caucasian flora and fauna.

Kew Gardens

Beginning in the late 1600s on the site of a former Royal estate, a botanical collection which is progressively enlarging. In 1841, the gardens were transferred to the nation, developing into an important botanical institution. In addition to a very large collection of plants, it has an important herbarium, a library, three museums and a laboratory. It is also a quarantine station. Kew maintains a record of all described higher plant species of the world, from the time of Linnaeus.

Korea (South)

The Republic of Korea is a unitary multiparty republic with one legislative house, the National Assembly. The population in 1997 was 46 million, at an average density of 460 persons per sq km. The capital is Seoul. It lies immediately south of North Korea and China. See Box 43 for the evolution of environmental law.

Kyoto Protocol

A protocol adopted by the international community in 1997 in an attempt to combat climate change by restricting the emissions of greenhouse gases, notably carbon dioxide. Box 44 traces the international steps leading to the Kyoto Protocol starting with the Villach Conference in 1985. Box 45 outlines the key elements of the Kyoto Protocol, while Box 46 summarizes the Kyoto Agreement in terms of emission targets.

Box 43   Korea, South: evolution of environmental law

1963   Pollution Prevention Act

1970   Saemol Undong (new community movement) initiated

1973   First 10-year national reforestation plan initiated

1976   First municipal sewage treatment plant constructed

1977   Environment Preservation Act; Marine Pollution Prevention Act

1978   Government institutes charter for nature conservation

1979   Environmental impact assessment (EIA) adopted as a regulatory mechanism

1980   Environmental Administration established; new constitution adopted guaranteeing the right to live in a clean and healthy environment; Korea Resource Recovery and Reutilization Corporation established

1981   Environment Preservation Act amended to introduce an emission charge system to enforce the measurement of emission standards; low-sulphur fuel oil policy for large cities, EIA process introduced

1986   Solid Waste Management Act; six regional offices of the Environment Administration established; Environment Preservation Act amended to extend the application of the EIA process to non-governmental projects

1987   Environmental Management Corporation establishes new emission standards for cars; introduction of unleaded petrol (gasoline); environmental education in schools strengthened

1990   Ministry of Environment established, replacing the Environment Administration; Basic Environmental Policy Act; Air Environment Preservation Act; Water Environment Preservation Act; Noise and Vibration Control Act; Hazardous Chemical Substance Control Act; Environment Pollution Damage Dispute Coordination Act, public hearings to be held in some cases

1991   Amendment of the Solid Waste Management Act and the Marine Pollution Prevention Act; Natural Environment Preservation Act; Central Environmental Disputes Coordination Commission established; Position of Ambassador for Environmental Affairs established; new deposit system for waste recovery and treatment

1992   Ministry of Foreign Affairs establishes the Science and Environment Office; ecomark introduced for consumer products

Box 43   continued

which are environmentally friendly; nationwide recycling programme
1994   Environmental Assessment Act
1997   Life expectancy: 69.0 years for males; 76.0 years for females

---

Box 44   *Approaches to the Kyoto Protocol*

Villach Conference on Climatic Change
Convened in October 1985, a conference of scientists from 29 countries held in Villach, Austria, at which scientific recognition was given to
the greenhouse effect.

World Conference on Climate and Development
An international conference organized by WMO, held in 1988 in Hamburg, Germany. The result was the Hamburg Manifesto on Climatic
Change, urging a 30 per cent reduction in the emission of carbon
dioxide by the year 2000, and 50 per cent by the year 2015, largely
through improved efficiency in the use of energy. The Second World
Conference on Climate and Development was held in Geneva, Switzerland, in 1990 to review progress.

Toronto Conference on the Changing Atmosphere
Convened in June 1988, a conference of scientists and policy-makers
from 48 countries held in Toronto, Canada, which gave much emphasis
to the greenhouse effect.

London Conference on Climatic Change
A conference convened in 1989 and attended by the representatives of
188 nations, to discuss the protection of the ozone layer and the
control of the greenhouse effect; the conference recognized the need
for a major reduction in the emission of carbon dioxide from the
burning of fossil fuels.

Hague Conference on the Environment
A summit of world leaders convened by the prime ministers of France,
Norway and the Netherlands, to consider ways to combat global
climate change arising from the greenhouse effect. In its Declaration of
the Hague Conference on the Environment 1989, the conference urged

Box 44   continued

the creation of a new institutional authority to devise means of combating global climatic change.

Intergovernmental Panel on Climate Change

A panel created by the WMO and UNEP to assess scientific information on climate change and its environmental and socioeconomic consequences, with the formulation of responses to such change. The panel released its first assessment report in 1990; the report was discussed at the 45th General Assembly of the UN, when the main findings were accepted. The panel predicted a rate of increase of global mean temperature during the next century of 0.3°C per decade, without remedial measures, with sea-level rises of between 3 and 10 cm per decade. By 2030, the global mean sea level might rise by 20 cm and might reach 65 cm by the end of 2100. The panel said its predictions were limited by: a lack of understanding of greenhouse gas sources and sinks; of clouds and oceans and how they influence climate change; and of polar ice-sheets and their impact on sea-level rises. Supplementary reports were published in 1992 and 1994. *Climate Change 1995* was the first full sequel to the original assessment. The new report concluded that many aspects of climate change were effectively irreversible and suggests a discernible human influence on global climate. Predictions of future temperature and sea-level rises were, however, modified (reduced a third in respect of global warming; and by a quarter in respect of sea-level rises).

UN Conference on Environment and Development, 1992

An international conference with representatives from some 167 countries held in Rio de Janeiro, Brazil, in 1992. The primary objective was to review progress since earlier conferences in 1972 and 1982 in safeguarding the human environment and promoting human welfare. One of the products of the conference was a Framework Convention on Climate Change. The aim was to protect the world's climate system most notably against the effects of greenhouse gases (principally carbon dioxide) and their warming influence. Initially, developed nations were expected to reduce their emissions of carbon dioxide and other greenhouse gases to 1990 levels.

International Conference on the Economics of Climate Change

A conference convened in June 1993 by the OECD and the International Energy Agency to help ensure that the UN Framework

Box 44   continued

Convention on Climate Change was based on sound economic rea-
soning, and to help OECD governments to consider practical options
and priorities for action. The conference was attended by about 250
economists and policy-makers.

Berlin Climate Conference

A conference of the world's environment ministers held in Berlin in
March 1995 to review progress towards achieving the objects of the
Framework Convention on Climate Change. The aim became to reduce emissions of carbon dioxide to 1990 levels by the year 2000.
Representatives from 150 countries attended, but there was little to
report in the way of solid achievement in respect of carbon taxes,
promotion of renewable energy sources, or the curtailing of actual
carbon dioxide emissions from transport or industry. The conference
received an initial report from the Intergovernmental Panel on Climate
Change.

The Geneva Talks, 1996

International discussions to review progress since the Berlin Climate
Conference, and to examine new evidence. Few countries could agree
on possible targets.

Kyoto Climate Change Convention

Held in Kyoto, Japan, in December 1997, a conference of 160 nations
which produced the Kyoto Convention, the first international treaty
relating to global warming, binding key nations to reductions in carbon
dioxide emissions to the atmosphere. The collective global target was
to cut greenhouse gas emissions by a little more than 5 per cent of the
1990 baseline, by the year 2012. This was a modest but attainable
target. However, Australia, Norway and Iceland were allowed to increase emissions over the same period, by 8 per cent in the case of
Australia. The talks began with the EU demanding cuts of 15 per cent
on 1990 levels, by the year 2012; although the US wanted stabilization
at 1990 levels by the year 2012. Australia wanted an increase of 18 per
cent over 1990 levels by 2010. The US introduced emissions trading
into the Protocol.

Buenos Aires Conference of the Parties

A follow-up meeting on the Kyoto Convention, held in Argentina in
November 1998, to review progress and make further decisions.

Box 44   continued

The conference received a fresh report from Britain's Hadley Cen-tre for Climate Change, based in Berkshire, predicting that:

- parts of the Amazon rain forest will turn into desert by 2050, threatening the world with an unstoppable greenhouse effect;
- land temperatures will increase by up to 6 degrees Celsius by the end of 2100;
- the number of people on the coast subject to flooding each year will increase from 5 million in 1998 to 100 million by 2050 and 200 million by 2080;
- another 30 million people will be hungry by 2050 because it will be too dry to grow crops in large parts of Africa;
- an additional 170 million people will live in countries with ex-treme water shortages;
- malaria will threaten much larger areas of the globe, including Europe, by the year 2050;
- the US prairies will be detrimentally affected; and
- global sea level will rise by 21 cm by 2050.

Other authorities such as the WWF warned that global warming could trigger an explosion of life-threatening infections in areas where they are not now present. These threats included not only malaria, but cholera, dengue fever, yellow fever and encephalitis.

It was confirmed that it will be the developing world that will produce the bulk of greenhouse gases by the year 2050, yet China and India refused to even discuss the matter. However, within an atmos-phere of doubt and uncertainty, the private sector emerged as an influential contributor to appropriate technical measures including DuPont, United Technologies, Enron and Royal Dutch Shell.

Box 45 Key elements of the Kyoto Protocol

- Developed (Annex 1) countries have collectively agreed to reduce greenhouse gas emissions by at least 5 per cent below
  1990 levels by 2008 to 2012.
- To achieve this collective target, individual nations were allocated differentiated targets, ranging from an 8 per cent reduction
  for the EU to a 10 per cent increase for Iceland from 1990 levels
  by 2008 to 2012. The USA and Japan have agreed to reduce
  greenhouse gases by 7 per cent and 6 per cent, respectively, over
  the same period. The target for Australia is an 8 per cent increase.
- Six greenhouse gases are covered by the protocol: carbon dioxide, methane, nitrous oxide, hydrofluorocarbons, perfluorocarbons
  and sulphur hexafluoride.
- Reductions in greenhouse emissions from sources and removal
  of carbon from sinks can be used to meet target commitments.
- Joint implementation, emissions trading and emissions banking
  can be used by the parties to meet their targets. Joint implementation projects may involve Annex 1 and non-Annex 1 countries.
- Some basic rules for emissions trading were established; further
  principles and guidelines are yet to be agreed.
- The Protocol recognizes that nations will need to implement
  policies and measures in accordance with their national circumstances if they are to meet their target commitments.
- The Protocol provides in principle for the establishment of
  bubble arrangements between any group of parties which choose
  to fulfil their commitments jointly.
- No agreement was reached of how to deal with non-compliance.
- The entry into force of the Protocol requires ratification by at
  least 55 parties to the Framework Convention on Climate Change;
  and such parties must represent at least 55 per cent of total
  Annex 1 carbon dioxide emissions in 1990.
- No agreement was reached on the future involvement of developing countries.

Box 46   *The Kyoto Agreement: Greenhouse Emission Targets between*
1990 and 2012, Annex 1 Countries

Australia	108
Austria	92
Belgium	92
Bulgaria	92
Canada	94
Croatia	95
Czech Republic	92
Denmark	92
Estonia	92
European Community	92
Finland	92
France	92
Germany	92
Greece	92
Hungary	94
Iceland	110
Ireland	92
Italy	92
Japan	94
Latvia	92
Liechtenstein	92
Lithuania	92
Luxembourg	92
Monaco	92
Netherlands	92
New Zealand	100
Norway	101
Poland	94
Portugal	92
Romania	92
Russian Federation	100
Slovakia	92
Slovenia	92
Spain	92
Sweden	92
Switzerland	92
Ukraine	100
United Kingdom of Great Britain and Northern Ireland	92
United States of America	93

L

Land and Environment Court, NSW

A court created in 1979 by the Land and Environment Court Act 1979, NSW, replacing the former Land and Valuation Court. It is a Superior Court of Record. The court comprises a Chief Judge and other judges, assessors and a registrar. The activities of the court are split into several divisions relating to environmental planning and appeals, local government appeals, land tenure valuation rating and compensation, environmental planning and protection, civil enforcement, environmental planning and protection summary enforcements, and enforcement appeals. The court has both civil and summary jurisdiction under planning and environment laws. The court has wide powers to make both interlocutory and final orders; grant injunctions to enforce rights and duties under the law; make declarations about rights and duties; and review the exercise of power given to persons and bodies. Some of the acts conferring jurisdiction include the Environmental Planning and Assessment Act, the Environment Protection Acts, the Heritage Act and the Local Government Act.

Land Compensation Act, 1973, UK

An act of the British Parliament which provides both for the granting of compensation for loss of value caused by the physical factors arising from the use of certain public works or land, and grants for insulation from noise. The principal works concerned are roads and aerodromes; while the physical factors are noise, vibration, smell, fumes, smoke and artificial lighting. The noise must arise from the use of the works and the source of the physical factors must be on or in the new or altered public works.

Thus, where a road is widened, the noise must arise from the traffic along the widened stretch of road; there is no compensation for the effects of increased traffic further down the road where no improvements have taken place. There is also no claim for the loss of view, for personal inconvenience, or the effect of increased traffic on unaltered roads. The loss of value is measured by the difference in value resulting from any new or increased physical factors arising from the use of the works, that is, the depressed effect on the market value of the property or the tenant's interest. The date of valuation is one year after the start of use. Noise or other physical factors during construction are separate matters for compensation.

The eight principles behind this legal measure were set out in the paper *Development and Compensation – Putting People First* (HMSO Cmnd. 5124) as follows:

(i)   Harmful impact on the immediate surroundings must be alleviated by comprehensive planning and remedial measures.

(ii)   Noisy and unattractive public developments must, by better planning, be separated from people and their homes.

(iii)   Damage to visual amenity by large-scale public works must be minimized by good pleasing design.

(iv)   Noise, smell and other forms of pollution must be reduced to a minimum at source – if it is practicable, eliminated.

(v)   Where, in spite of these efforts, damage still is done to individual amenities, reasonable compensation must be provided for those who suffer noise and other harmful effects.

(vi)   The processes of inquiry and decision on project, compulsory purchase and payment of compensation must be thorough but concentrated in time and must be conducted so as to minimize blight and the hardship this entails.

(vii)   No time must be lost in carrying through the new approach to design and planning, to remedial works and sound insulation, to acquisition and compensation.

(viii) People threatened by, or suffering from, the effects of public works must be told, in an understandable way, their rights and the help which is available to them.

In addition, the act is a measure which, taken in conjunction with the Noise Insulation Regulation, 1975, requires compensation in the form of insulation (and perhaps accompanying ventilation) once noise levels exceed 68 dB(A) measured one meter in front of the building façade; a standard which more or less approximates the results of surveys carried out to determine the level at which people are annoyed by noise.

Landscape Analysis – Factors to be Considered

Factors relevant to landscape analysis which may be applied systematically to environmental blocks or sub-areas of a total study area, with each factor rated on a scale from zero to ten and linked with a weighting system. Factors which may be considered include:

- slope;
- vegetation quality;
- vegetation extent;
- visual significance;
- flooding;

- mine subsidence;
- potentially erodible area;
- watershed;
- geology;
- natural features;
- fauna;
- weedbeds and mangroves;
- severity of inversion;
- mineral resources;
- salt spray;
- aspect, and
- wind exposure.

Landscape Evaluation, UK

An assessment of the quality of landscape for development planning and preliminary site selection purposes, as distinct from visual impact assessment of specific proposed developments. In the United Kingdom, landscape evaluation has been a long-established practice. The Town and Country Planning Act, 1947, the Countryside Act, 1967 (Scotland) and 1968 (England and Wales) made the conservation of natural beauty and amenity of the countryside a basic objective. The main approach used by the planning authorities to protect and manage the visual resources of the countryside has been the preparation of a county or regional landscape evaluation. Landscape evaluation has had the greatest influence and success in rural environments where development pressure is low, several alternative development areas are available, and the type of development is small scale. With increasing pressure in respect to large site-specific industrial developments, the traditional landscape evaluation can lose much of its effectiveness as a controlling element in planning. In such circumstances, comprehensive visual impact assessment during detailed project appraisal can be a significant factor in minimizing the adverse visual impacts of a project that may inevitably proceed.

Langkawi Declaration

See:
Commonwealth of Nations.

Laplandsky Nature Reserve

Established in 1930, a natural area set aside for research in the natural sciences in the western part of the Kola Peninsula, northwestern Russia. The reserve was established initially mainly to protect the natural habitat of the reindeer. It is a region of plains and low mountains, glaciated landforms, bogs, lakes and crystallized rocks of the Baltic Shield. Most of the park's vegetation is pine. Wildlife includes the beaver, elk, brown bear and wolverine, while birds include the golden eagle, osprey, grouse, and Siberian tits and jays. The reserve is used for scientific research on reindeer, fur-bearing animals and fish.

L'Enfant Plan for Washington, DC, 1974

The design and plans for the original City of Washington, District of Columbia, which were promulgated by President George Washington and recognized by the US Congress as the work of Pierre Charles L'Enfant. These plans were subsequently laid out by the Office of the Surveyor of the District of Columbia government according to the 'King Plats of the City of Washington in the District of Columbia, 1803'.

The city design focused on locating grand edifices on prominent sites; these sites were connected with broad avenues and a formal street and open space network which imposed a majestic sense of scale and order within the city. L'Enfant chose to locate the Capitol on Jenkins Hill, the most prominent site in the new city. The plan also chose a separate axial street with similar prominence for the President's Palace, known as the White House.

The L'Enfant Plan responded to the topographic and environmental conditions in the city by calling for 'a city within a garden'. This concept, subsequently termed 'city in a park', combines formal state squares, grand avenues, and natural parks to give a wide range of landscape opportunities within the city.

The original plan has for almost two centuries been embraced by individuals and organizations who have served as guardians of the plan, including presidents and senators. Senator James McMillan of Michigan is especially noted for the 1901 plan of the city which extended the original concept. The American Institute of Architects also contributed with their 'city beautiful movement' during the same era.

Licence

A statutory document, issued by an environmental agency under environmental legislation, permitting an individual or organization to discharge, emit, or deposit wastes into the environment, subject to a variety of restraints and conditions relating to pollution-control measures, monitoring, volumes, timing, nature and composition of the waste. Licences may often be varied, or cancelled, at any time, and are renewable annually. Breaches of licensing conditions or non-payment of fees may result in legal proceedings. In this way the emission of smoke, grit and dust, sulphur dioxide, nitrogen dioxide, carbon monoxide, lead and odors, for example, may be limited. Heights of stacks may be prescribed to promote the dilution of gases in the atmosphere. Ocean discharges at some distance may be required. Hence, licences may govern air pollutants, water pollutants, noise and landfills. Licences may prescribe programs for progressive improvements over time. Vehicle pollution may be controlled by design standards, and not by individual licensing. Noise standards may be set for aircraft by class.

Lifecycle Environmental Impact Assessment (LEIA)

Lifecycle EIA is a procedure for evaluating the environmental impacts of a product, process or activity throughout its whole lifecycle; a vertical exercise running from cradle to grave. The main purposes of LEIA are:
1. To assess the environmental effects of the getting and consumption of the raw materials and other inputs during the different lifecycle phases of a product, process or activity including the fate of all pollutants and residuals.
2. To assess the final disposal problem of any of the superseded product, process or activity.
3. To provide information useful for an aggregated EIA of products, processes and activities throughout the lifecycle.
4. To evaluate the environmental consequences of alternative processes and design concepts, permitting a comparison between products, processes and activities.

Each phase may be accorded a score on an environmental index, for example, for: natural resources, raw materials, land use; emissions to air, water and soil; noise; manufacturing procedures in relation to economy, energy, work and public safety; waste handling; recycling and ultimate disposal.

An LEIA extends beyond the boundaries of responsibility of the individual company or producer, backwards and forwards into matters entering the public domain. It goes beyond the realm of private ownership into the full social and resource implications of, say, car manufacture and ownership, including the ultimate disposal of car tyres, batteries and abandoned vehicles.

The principle could be applied as readily to household appliances, beverage containers, packaging materials, paints, plastics, steels, fuels, lubricants, detergents, cables, fast food, fertilizers, energy production and use, and major infrastructure developments.

It is distinct from project EIA which is much concerned with location, focusing on the lifecycle of individual projects rather than the lifecycle of infrastructure; its scope may be readily enlarged to embrace communication and transport systems.

The concept appears to have limited application so far, although some work by the Federation of Swedish Industries, the Swedish Environmental Research Institute and the Volvo Car Corporation has direct relevance.

Local Environmental Plan

Or local structural, statutory or town plan; a plan created and endorsed under national or state planning and environmental legislation. A local environmental plan may embrace the whole of a local elected council area, or part or parts of such an area. The development of a local plan may follow statutory guidelines prescribed by legislation, involve extensive discussions with the local population, and ultimately require endorsement at a national political level. A local plan must be consistent with any regional environmental plan, and conform with national directives and guidelines. The preparation of a plan will take place in stages, with exhibition and debate at each stage. Structure plan principles may be summarized as follows:

- ensure the efficient and convenient distribution of all land uses;
- provide a reasonable choice of residential accommodation in future urban development;
- avoid exclusionary zoning;
- designate land for the widest range of public facilities appropriate to the structure plan scale;
- provide an efficient and effective transportation system appropriate to the density and distribution of uses;
- prohibit development within permanently flood-liable areas;
- relate the future urban design and form to the drainage capabilities of the area to ensure acceptable limits on flooding;
- achieve a high degree of economic and social self-containment for the sector;

- relate surface development to existence of economically viable mineral resources, to avoid sterilization;
- relate surface development to areas of expected mine subsidence;
- ensure that the location of use zones does not contribute to pollution;
- ensure that the form and scale of urban development does not give rise to pollution of existing waterways and water bodies;
- prevent development in areas of high landscape value, and ensure a compatible range and intensity of use within areas of lesser landscape where some development may be allowed;
- the standard number of houses to the hectare fixed by the council;
- the amount of land to be provided as a public reserve out of the land to be subdivided;
- the provisions of any environmental planning instrument, including the use to which the land is proposed to be, or may be, put following the subdivision, in accordance with, or consistent with, that instrument; and
- whether any trees on the land should be preserved.

Locational Considerations

The location of a proposed development is often as important as the environment protection measures relating to the proposal itself. However, there are many factors determining or influencing the location of a development. The location of raw materials and markets, skilled labour and transport are strong influences. In some cases, tied to access to, say, coal seams or oil ports, there are few or perhaps no options. In some cases there is great flexibility. An optimal location must take into account many factors, including the environmental.

An optimum firm is a firm in which the costs of production per unit of output are at a minimum, having regard to the existing state of technical knowledge, managerial ability, competitive markets, financial facilities and communication skills. Expansion up to this size may be accompanied by falling average costs as a result of economies of scale; beyond this point costs begin to rise due to diseconomies. The optimum is not a fixed point but changes with every development. Also the optimum firm is not a simple concept; there is an optimum size for technical production, for finance, for marketing, and for risk. All these optima have to be reconciled as far as possible to the best advantage. For the multiproduct firm there is an optimal output for each of the firm's product lines. Whatever the settings, maximum profits are made when output has expanded to a point where marginal revenue equals marginal costs. Clearly, the minimization of costs and the maximization of returns is closely related to the choice of location, and movements in location as circumstances change.

See Box 47 for a summary of the factors influencing the optimal location of an enterprise.

Box 47   Enterprise: optimal location of

Physical locations considered the most efficient, in terms of profitability, having regard to capital, raw material, labour, industrial, transportation, marketing and social costs. Location is determined by a complex interaction of factors such as:

- access to markets for finished products, at home and overseas, meeting standards in relation to quality, safety, durability, composition, environmental standards, competitiveness, reliability, back-up service, guarantees and insurance;
- access to financial resources at competitive rates of interest and repayment terms, at home or overseas;
- access to raw materials or processed intermediate products at competitive prices, reliable in supply and quality;
- competitive transportation rates for inputs and outputs;
- access to skilled and unskilled labour, of both sexes, and the availability of full-time and part-time occupations;
- access to essential infrastructure services such as water, energy, rail, shipping, electricity, trucking, harbors, storage, communication systems and data;
- the prospects for future expansion and the long-term availability of essential inputs and markets;
- government policies, incentives, charges and taxes, and environmental protection measures and planning requirements; and
- government subsidies and support mechanisms, free services such as schools and hospitals, tax holidays and tax breaks, support for ailing and marginal industries, offers of government–private sector partnerships, or special financial assistance.

London Guidelines for the Exchange of Information on Chemicals in International Trade, Amended

In 1985, the outcome of the efforts of a UNEP working group, convened initially in Rome and then in London, to establish global guidelines for the safe handling and distribution of potentially hazardous chemicals. The London Guidelines were adopted by the UNEP Governing Council at its fourteenth session in 1987. After adoption, the London Guidelines replaced the earlier Provisional Notification Scheme. They set out a more elaborate set of provisions governing international notification of government action to ban or severely restrict chemicals and the provision of information regarding the export of such chemicals. UNEP envisaged then a more detailed set of guidelines and the possible need for an international convention on trade in chemicals.

In 1989, the UNEP Governing Council adopted the Amended London Guidelines for the Exchange of Information on Chemicals in International Trade. The Amended London Guidelines of 1989 made provision for 'prior informed consent' (PIC), a principle under which international shipment of a chemical that is banned or severely restricted in order to protect human health and the environment should not proceed without the agreement of the designated national authority in the importing country. The PIC procedure is a means for seeking the decision of an importing country on whether it wishes to accept future shipments of chemicals which have been banned or severely restricted. By incorporating the PIC procedure in the amended London Guidelines, importing countries have a tool for making decisions on acceptable risks in relation to hazardous chemicals.

The basic principle behind the PIC procedure, is the sovereign right of each state to consider the needs of its country, analyse risks and benefits from the use of chemicals, and decide on its own chemicals policy. The voluntary PIC policy covers both industrial chemicals and pesticides. UNEP and the FAO share operational responsibility through a joint program. UNEP continues to maintain its International Register of Potentially Toxic Chemicals. There has been much pressure for a legally binding PIC convention. This view was endorsed by the UN Commission on Sustainable Development in 1994.

UNEP convened a Meeting of the Expert Group on International Environmental Agreements and Trade in New York in 1995. Another step was taken in the development of an international legally binding instrument for the application of the PIC procedure. A convention was envisaged before 2000.

Lusaka Agreement on Cooperative Enforcement Operations Directed at Illegal Trade in Wild Fauna and Flora

An agreement signed in Lusaka, Zambia, in 1994 by six eastern and southern African states: Kenya, South Africa, Swaziland, Uganda, United Republic of Tanzania and Zambia. Lesotho and Mozambique also accepted the text, but were unable to attend the signing ceremony. This was the first regional agreement on enforcement measures to counter the trade in wildlife in Africa, and the first multilateral agreement of its kind to be signed by the new South African government. The objective of the agreement is to reduce and ultimately eliminate illegal trade in wild fauna and flora and to establish a permanent taskforce for this purpose. UNEP played a leading role in setting up the agreement. The groundwork for establishing the taskforce was undertaken at a Wildlife Law Enforcement Seminar held in Dar es Salaam, Tanzania, in 1995. Lesotho became the first country to accede to the Lusaka Agreement.

M

Malaysia

Malaysia is a federal constitutional monarchy with two legislative houses, the Senate and the House of Representatives. The capital is Kuala Lumpur. The population in 1997 was 22 million, at an average density of 66 persons per sq km. It encompasses the Malaysian Peninsula and North Borneo. See Box 48 for the evolution of environmental law.

Marine Mammal Protection Act, 1972, US

This act seeks to protect marine mammals such as whales, seals, polar bears and dolphins; it does not require them to be under threat. Some marine mammals are covered by both this act and the Endangered Species Act. The act provides for long-term management, research, conservation and recovery programs. It established a moratorium on the taking and importing of marine mammals and marine mammal products. The act is administered primarily by the Marine Mammal Commission, the National Oceanographic Administration and the Fish and Wildlife Service. The taking of marine mammals is today strictly controlled. Other federal laws for the protection of fish and wildlife include the Bald and Golden Eagle Protection Act, 1940; the National Wildlife Refuge System Administration Act, 1966; and the Marine Protection, Research, and Sanctuaries Act, 1972. The Mammal Act was amended in 1988.

Marine Protection, Research, and Sanctuaries Act, 1972 (MPRSA), US

An Act of the US Congress which established a permit system for the dumping of materials into the ocean, and for the transportation of materials to be dumped.

The EPA evaluates applications for permits to determine the need for the proposed dumping; the effect or likely effect of the dumping on human health and welfare (including economic, aesthetic and recreational values); the effect on marine ecosystems; the concentrations of materials dumped and the likely persistence of environmental effects; and alternative means of disposal.

Box 48   Malaysia: evolution of environmental law

1920	Waters Enactment
1929	Mining Enactment
1934	Mining Rules
1935	Forest Enactment
1949	Natural Resources Ordinance
1952	Poisons Ordinance; Merchant Shipping Ordinance; Sale of Food and Drugs Ordinance; Dangerous Drugs Ordinance
1953	Federation Port Rules; Irrigation Areas Ordinance
1954	Drainage Works Ordinance
1956	Medicine (Sales and Advertisement) Ordinance
1958	Explosives Ordinance; Road Traffic Ordinance
1960	Land Conservation Act
1965	National Land Code; Housing Development Act
1966	Continental Shelf Act
1968	Radioactive Substances Act
1969	Civil Aviation Act
1971	Malaria Eradication Act
1972	Petroleum Mining Act
1974	Environmental Quality Act; Geological Survey Act; Street, Buildings and Drainage Act; Aboriginal Peoples Act; Factories and Machinery Act; Pesticides Act
1975	Destruction of Disease-Bearing Insects Act; Municipal and Town Boards Act
1976	Protection of Wildlife Act 1976; Antiquities Act; Local Government Act; Town and Country Planning Act
1980	Malaysian Highway Authority Act; Pig Rearing Act
1984	Atomic Energy Licensing Act; Exclusive Economic Zone Act; National Forestry Act
1985	Fisheries Act
1988	EIA becomes mandatory; 19 categories of industry required to submit EIA reports
1991	331 major projects have now been subject to EIA
1991–95	Sixth Malaysia Plan
1997	Life expectancy: 70.0 years for males; 74.0 years for females
1998	Annual meeting of APEC, Kuala Lumpur, with 21 nations represented

The act authorizes the Secretary of Commerce to designate as marine sanctuaries those areas which he or she determines should be preserved or restored for their conservation, recreational, ecological or aesthetic values.

In 1977, the MPRSA was amended to prohibit the dumping of sewage sludge into ocean water after December 1981; industrial waste was also banned. Through the Surface Transportation Assistance Act, 1982, Congress further amended the MPRSA, placing a moratorium on the disposal of low-level radioactive waste into ocean water, save for research purposes. The MPRSA was reviewed and reauthorized in 1985.

Mekong River Commission

A commission established by an Agreement on Cooperation for the sustainable development of the Mekong River Basin that came into force in 1995; the parties to the agreement are the Kingdom of Cambodia, Lao People's Democratic Republic, Kingdom of Thailand and the Socialist Republic of Vietnam. The longest river in southeast Asia, the Mekong has its source in China's Qinghai province. It then passes through Laos, touching the frontier of Thailand, and then through Cambodia; in Vietnam the Mekong separates into four main branches and enters the South China Sea through a delta. The agreement between the four governments covers the lower Mekong River Basin. The Mekong River Commission consists of three permanent bodies: a council, a joint committee and a secretariat. The secretariat is located in Bangkok, Thailand. The function of the commission is to implement the principles of sustainable development enunciated by UNCED and the Rio Declaration on Environment and Development.

Meteorological Influences

The effect of a range of atmospheric characteristics on the dispersal of pollutants, including heat. In respect of air pollution, the concentration of pollutants at or near ground level is a balance between the amount emitted and the degree to which it is diluted and dispersed by the atmosphere, or removed from the atmosphere by gravitation or precipitation. In a modern, industrial society it is only the enormous dilution produced by the atmosphere which renders the situation at all tolerable; without turbulence, humans could not live in large communities.

The most important factor controlling the dispersal of pollution is turbulence. The intensity of turbulence depends on the following:
1.   wind strength at a standard height;

2.   profile of wind variation with height;
3.   variation of wind direction with height;
4.   profile of temperature variations with height;
5.   rate at which heat is exchanged between the atmosphere and the ground and outer space;
6.   nature of the earth's surface;
7.   cloud formation, rain, and so on.

Only in exceptional circumstances will high pollution levels be found when the wind is strong and possessing considerable turbulence. With low wind strengths and reduced turbulence pollution levels frequently increase, the most severe pollution occurs in non-turbulent conditions during an inversion when air temperature, instead of decreasing, increases with height.

On the other hand, if the potential temperature gradient is positive, a condition of equilibrium will be reached at which the plume ceases to rise and travels horizontally in an atmosphere of density equal to its own.

Vertical movement, whether upwards or downwards, is strongly inhibited and pollution remains near the level at which it was emitted or at the height to which it succeeded in penetrating. In these conditions an inversion is said to exist. This situation frequently arises on clear calm nights when the ground is cooled by outgoing radiation and the layer immediately above is colder than at higher levels. It also arises when a subsidence inversion occurs at a level well above the ground. In these conditions, plumes tend to follow a meandering path without change in height, a pattern called 'fanning'.

In a 'neutral' atmosphere, in which air temperature falls slightly with height, dispersion of pollution is usually good. Plumes tend to follow a roughly conical path, a pattern known as 'coning'.

Mexico

The United Mexican States is a federal republic with two legislative houses, the Senate and the Chamber of Deputies. The population in 1998 was 96 million, at a density of 127 persons per sq km. The capital is Mexico City. Mexico is a party to NAFTA. See Box 49 for the evolution of environmental law.

Mexico City Industrial Disaster, 1984

A fire and explosion at a natural-gas storage and distribution facility at San Juan Ixhuatepec, Mexico City, in November 1984, which resulted in several hundred deaths, many more injured, and 10 000 homeless; it was the worst

---

Box 49   Mexico: evolution of environmental law

1789   First waste-collection system in Mexico City

1824   Colonel Muzquiz promotes the hygiene of Mexico City and extends the waste collection system; fines introduced

1968   Mexico becomes one of 27 nations to organize the UN Conference on the Human Environment, 1972

1971   Mexico organizes the Latin American Regional Seminar on the problems of the Human Environment; Congress passes the first law against pollution

1972   Secretaria de Desarrollo Urbano y Ecologia established to address environmental problems

1973   Binational meetings on pollution of the North Border organized

1975   Mexico contributes to the Cocoyoc Declaration

1982   National Commission of Ecology established to coordinate the efforts of all agencies

1984   Mexico City Industrial Disaster

1988   General Law of Ecological Equilibrium and Environmental Protection; Environmental Impact Regulations

1992   The Commission for the Prevention and Control of Environmental Contamination in the Metropolitan Zone of the Valley of Mexico created

1994   Life expectancy: 66.5 years for males; 73.1 years for females

1996   Environmental Law of the Federal District and Regulations; Regulations of the Department of the Environment, Natural Resources and Fisheries

1997   Procedures for obtaining a single environmental licence through a single application; Annual Certificates of Operation

1998   Environmental Protection Specifications for the design and operation of electricity transmission and distribution substations that will be located in sensitive areas

---

industrial disaster in Mexican history. The disaster involved a private gas-bottling plant adjacent to the storage tanks of the government-owned oil corporation, PEMEX. The plant was situated in the very heart of a poor congested district, ignoring all environmental protection principles.

Such disasters are not inevitable, or the necessary price of progress. There are two important means for protecting the community from these major hazards. The first is through engineering controls such as better control systems, reduced inventories of hazardous materials, and better protection of vessels such as sand-mounting. The second is through planning controls such as the introduction of exclusion zones or buffer zones with restricted developments around such facilities. Such a dual policy will not preclude incident, but adequate engineering controls will reduce the likelihood of incident and the magnitude; while planning controls reduce the consequence to the public. These restrictions do ensure that large numbers of people are not affected. Progressive nations have been introducing these principles over some years.

See also:
Disasters.

Ministerial Conference on Pollution of the North Sea

A conference held in London, England, in November 1987 attended by representatives of the Nordic countries, the Netherlands, Germany and Britain to review growing concerns about pollution of the North Sea and the Skaggerak by nutrient salts. The Netherlands, Germany and Britain were responsible for the largest proportion of the discharges. The discharges of nutrient salts to the North Sea had doubled over the previous 30 years and the southern parts of the sea were now seriously threatened. The following aims were agreed at the conference: a 50 per cent reduction in the discharges of nutrients and persistent toxic substances by 1995; the dumping of hazardous waste material to end by 1989; the incineration of industrial waste to cease in 1994; more stringent standards to be introduced for discharges of waste by shipping and discharges of oily wastes from oil platforms; the use of the best available technology to minimize discharges of radioactive substances; and the promotion of more comprehensive research. Several of these steps agreed on for the North Sea and Skaggerak have since been extended to include the entire northeast Atlantic.

Monitoring

The measurement of environmental effects such as pollution streams, subsidence, noise, vibration, climatic variations, fauna and flora characteristics, surface- and groundwater changes. Monitoring results may then be analysed within a framework of statutory requirements and regulations, and as a guide in the formulation of policies. Monitoring may be conducted from platforms on stacks, at street level, or in the natural environment. Monitoring may be carried out by an environmental authority, or by a corporation undertaking self-regulation.

Montevideo Program

A program emerging from a meeting of senior government officials expert in environmental law held in Montevideo, Uruguay, in 1981. The meeting, organized by UNEP, was a direct outcome of UNEP Governing Council decisions to give urgent attention to the development of environmental law. Since the UN Conference on the Human Environment in 1972, many developing nations had experienced difficulties in this area. The Program for the Development and Periodic Review of Environmental Law (Montevideo Program) was subsequently approved by the UNEP Governing Council and integrated into the UN Environment Program.

The Montevideo Program identified three major subject areas for the development of guidelines, principles and agreements: marine pollution from land-based sources; protection of the stratospheric ozone layer; and the transport, handling and disposal of toxic and hazardous wastes. The program also identified eight other subject areas for action, together with agreed objectives and strategies for each area: international cooperation in environmental emergencies; coastal zone management; soil conservation; transboundary air pollution; international trade in potentially harmful chemicals; protection of rivers and other inland waters against pollution; legal and administrative mechanisms for the prevention and redress of pollution damage; and EIA.

Subsequently, notable international conventions were prepared and adopted in accordance with the program. These included the 1985 Vienna Convention for the Protection of the Ozone Layer and its 1987 Montreal Protocol, and the 1989 Basel Convention on Hazardous Wastes, as well as international guidelines in such areas as chemicals in international trade, marine pollution from land-based sources, and EIA.

In 1991, a review of the program was undertaken, formulating action during the decade to 2000. This phase culminated in the Draft Framework Convention on Climate Change and the Convention on Biological Diversity. The new program resulted in action in some 18 program areas.

In another area, the program has addressed illegal trade in wildlife in the Eastern and Southern African regions. The result was the negotiations of the Lusaka Agreement on Cooperative Enforcement Operations directed at Illegal Trade in Wild Fauna and Flora 1994. An intermediate review of programs was conducted in 1997.

Montreal Botanical Garden

Established in 1931, a garden with significant collections of commercially important plants, medicinal herbs, alpine plants, woodland plants, ferns, cacti and other succulents, begonias, orchids, aroids and bromeliads. Montreal is an important botanical research centre.

Mt. Laurel Decision, 1983, New Jersey, US

A decision by the New Jersey Supreme Court in 1983 in which disappointment was expressed in the current municipal planning and legal process which had failed to address the issue of affordable housing for the lower-income groups. The Court required forthwith positive efforts to produce affordable housing.

The decision obliged every municipality to provide for its own lower-income population, except where it was disproportionately large; and municipalities in growth areas to provide opportunities for prospective housing needs. The decision resulted in the abolition of the Division of State and Regional Planning, and the creation in 1983 of a State Planning Commission.

Multiple-Use Sustained-Yield Act, 1960, US

In effect an overriding policy statement of the US Congress for the management of national forests; national forests 'are established and shall be administered for outdoor recreation, range, timber, watershed, wildlife, and fish purposes'. The US Secretary of Agriculture was authorized to develop and administer the resources of the national forests for multiple use and sustained yield in respect to a wide range of products and services. Due consideration was to be given to the relative values of the various resources in particular areas. The concept of sustained yield involved the achievement and maintenance of a high-level annual or regular periodic output of the various renewable resources of land, without impairment of the productivity of that land.

N

Nairobi Declaration, 1982

The summarized outcome of an international environmental conference held in Nairobi, Kenya, marking the midpoint between the UN Conference on the Human Environment, 1972, and the UN Conference on Environment and Development, 1992. The Nairobi Conference was much smaller than the other two principal conferences, but was an opportunity to review progress since the 1972 Stockholm conference. Nairobi was classified as a conference of special character. Box 50 summarizes the outcome of Nairobi, the conference reaffirming the Stockholm Declaration on the Human Environment and the Action Plan.

National Ambient Air Quality Standards (NAAQS), US

US standards which define the maximum concentrations of certain air pollutants allowable in ambient air in order to protect public health and welfare. The EPA is required to set and periodically review these standards. Once NAAQS have been set by the EPA, individual state governments have the responsibility to determine how they can be met and maintained most efficiently at the local level. The main administrative mechanism used by state governments to characterize local air quality and define strategies to achieve national standards is the State Implementation Plan (SIP). Under the Clean Air Act, the EPA is required to approve, review and exercise surveillance over all SIPs.

Primary standards are aimed at the protection of public health; while secondary standards are concerned with the protection of welfare, amenity, materials, and crops. Initially standards were set for sulfur dioxide, particulate matter, carbon monoxide, nitrogen dioxide, and hydrocarbons. A national ambient air quality standard to protect the public health from exposure to lead particulates became effective in 1978. The new standard set an upper limit of 1.5 micrograms of lead per cubic meter of air based on a three-month average. The new limit was based on preventing children from experiencing blood levels exceeding 30 micrograms of lead per deciliter of blood. It has been argued that levels higher than this have been associated with an impairment of cell function. The attainment of this standard has been associated with a progressive reduction in lead in gasoline. From January 1986, the upper limit permitted became 0.10 gram lead per US gallon of gasoline.

Box 50   Nairobi Declaration, 1982

Declaration adopted by the session of a special character
The world community of States, assembled in Nairobi from 10 to 18
May 1982 to commemorate the tenth anniversary of the United Nations
Conference on the Human Environment, held in Stockholm, having reviewed the measures taken to implement the Declaration and Action
Plan adopted at that Conference, solemnly requests Governments and
peoples to build on the progress so far achieved, but expresses its
serious concern about the present state of the environment world-wide,
and recognizes the urgent necessity of intensifying the efforts at the
global, regional and national levels to protect and improve it.
1.   The Stockholm Conference was a powerful force in increasing
     public awareness and understanding of the fragility of the human
     environment. The years since then have witnessed significant
     progress in environmental sciences; education, information dis-
     semination and training have expanded considerably; in nearly all
     countries, environmental legislation has been adopted, and a
     significant number of countries have incorporated within their
     constitutions provisions for the protection of the environment.
     Apart from the United Nations Environment Programme, addi-
     tional governmental and non-governmental organizations have been
     established at all levels, and a number of important international
     agreements in respect of environmental cooperation have been
     concluded. The principles of the Stockholm Declaration are as
     valid today as they were in 1972. They provide a basic code of
     environmental conduct for the years to come.
2.   However, the Action Plan has only been partially implemented, and
     the results cannot be considered as satisfactory, due mainly to
     inadequate foresight and understanding of the long-term benefits
     of environmental protection, to inadequate coordination of ap-
     proaches and efforts, and to unavailability and inequitable distribution
     of resources. For these reasons, the Action Plan has not had
     sufficient impact on the international community as a whole. Some
     uncontrolled or unplanned activities of man have increasingly caused
     environmental deterioration. Deforestation, soil and water degra-
     dation and desertification are reaching alarming proportions, and
     seriously endanger the living conditions in large parts of the world.
     Diseases associated with adverse environmental conditions con-
     tinue to cause human misery. Changes in the atmosphere – such as
     those in the ozone layer, the increasing concentration of carbon
     dioxide, and acid rain – pollution of the seas and inland waters,

Box 50   continued

    careless use and disposal of hazardous substances and the extinction of animal and plant species constitute further grave threats to the human environment.

3.   During the last decade, new perceptions have emerged: the need for environmental management and assessment, the intimate and complex interrelationship between environment, development, population and resources and the strain on the environment generated, particularly in urban areas, by increasing population have become widely recognized. A comprehensive and regionally integrated approach that emphasizes this interrelationship can lead to environmentally sound and sustainable socio-economic development.

4.   Threats to the environment are aggravated by poverty as well as by wasteful consumption patterns: both can lead people to over-exploit their environment. The International Development Strategy for the Third United Nations Development Decade and the establishment of a new international economic order are thus among the major instruments in the global effort to reverse environmental degradation. Combinations of market and planning mechanisms can also favour sound development and rational environmental and resource management.

5.   The human environment would greatly benefit from an international atmosphere of peace and security, free from the threats of any war, especially nuclear war, and the waste of intellectual and natural resources on armaments, as well as from *apartheid*, racial segregation and all forms of discrimination, colonial and other forms of oppression and foreign domination.

6.   Many environmental problems transcend national boundaries and should, when appropriate, be resolved for the benefit of all through consultations amongst States and concerted international action. Thus, States should promote the progressive development of environmental law, including conventions and agreements, and expand cooperation in scientific research and environmental management.

7.   Environmental deficiencies generated by conditions of underdevelopment, including external factors beyond the control of the countries concerned, pose grave problems which can be combated by a more equitable distribution of technical and economic resources within and among States. Developed countries, and other countries in a position to do so, should assist developing countries, affected by environmental disruption in their domestic efforts to deal with their most serious environmental problems. Utilization of appropriate technologies, particularly from other developing

Box 50   continued

countries, could make economic and social progress compatible
with conservation of natural resources.

8.   Further efforts are needed to develop environmentally sound management and methods for the exploitation and utilization of natural
resources and to modernize traditional pastoral systems. Particular attention should be paid to the role of technical innovation in
promoting resource substitution, recycling and conservation. The
rapid depletion of traditional and conventional energy sources
poses new and demanding challenges for the effective management
and conservation of energy and the environment. Rational energy
planning among nations or groups of nations could be beneficial.
Measures such as the development of new and renewable sources
of energy will have a highly beneficial impact on the environment.

9.   Prevention of damage to the environment is preferable to the
burdensome and expensive repair of damage already done. Preventive action should include proper planning of all activities that
have an impact on the environment. It is also important to increase
public and political awareness of the importance of the environment through information, education and training. Responsible
individual behaviour and involvement are essential in furthering the
cause of the environment. Non-governmental organizations have a
particularly important and often inspirational role to play in this
sphere. All enterprises, including multinational corporations, should
take account of their environmental responsibilities when adopting
industrial production methods or technologies, or when exporting
them to other countries. Timely and adequate legislative action is
important in this regard.

10. The world community of States solemnly reaffirms its commitment to the Stockholm Declaration and Action Plan, as well as to
the further strengthening and expansion of national efforts and
international cooperation in the field of environmental protection.
It also reaffirms its support for strengthening the United Nations
Environment Programme as the major catalytic instrument for
global environmental cooperation, and calls for increased resources
to be made available, in particular through the Environment Fund,
to address the problems of the environment. It urges all Governments and peoples of the world to discharge their historical
responsibility, collectively and individually, to ensure that our small
planet is passed over to future generations in a condition which
guarantees a life in human dignity for all.

In 1979, the EPA announced an increase in the permitted level of ozone in the atmosphere from 0.08 ppm to 0.12 ppm. The states were required to meet this relaxed, though still exacting standard, initially by 1982. The petroleum and automotive industries considered this relaxation too small; environmentalists regarded it as too generous.

National Botanic Gardens of South Africa

Established in 1913, one of the world's largest botanical gardens, occupying a 552 ha site at Kirstenbosch, near Cape Town. The collection consists almost exclusively of plants native to southern Africa. One of the main objectives of the Gardens is to preserve endangered local plant species. In this, the Gardens are supported by regional gardens or reserves. These include the Karoo Botanic Gardens and the Edith Stephens Cape Flats Flora Reserve.

National Botanical Garden of Belgium

Originally founded in 1870, a garden now centred on an estate at Meise, the Domaine de Bouchot, on the outskirts of Brussels. Special attention is given to tropical plants of commercial value. The Palace of Plants is the largest greenhouse in the world.

National Environment Protection Council (NEPC) (Australia)

Established in 1995, an Australian ministerial council comprising representatives of the Commonwealth (Federal), State and Territory governments. The NEPC's role is to develop national environment protection measures to improve national outcomes related to environment protection. An initial review was conducted in relation to national ambient air quality standards. Under the federal legislation, draft policies must be made available for public comment for at least two months, with public comments taken into account in any final policy.

The creation of the NEPC required compatible legislation to be passed by all State, Territory and the Commonwealth parliaments. The NEPC is empowered on the basis of a two-third majority vote by its members to make national environment protection measures that automatically become law within each jurisdiction in Australia. The objective of the NEPC Act is to provide equivalent environment protection to all Australians wherever they may live and to ensure that markets are not distorted by environmental decisions. These national standards will progressively replace state-by-state standards, guidelines, goals and objectives that have been in use for many years. These national standards will join the existing national standards for the control of motor vehicle emissions. Environment measures thus join Australian Corporations Law in being applicable to all jurisdictions. Annual compliance reports from each jurisdiction to the NEPC will be tabled in each of the parliaments and made public. Each jurisdiction must develop adequate monitoring systems. The operation of the NEPC is governed by the National Environment Protection Council Act, 1994. See Box 51.

National Environmental Policy Act, 1969 (NEPA) US

An act of the US Congress the aims of which were to: declare a national policy which would encourage productive and enjoyable harmony between humans and their environment; promote efforts which would prevent or eliminate damage to the environment and biosphere and stimulate the health and welfare of màn; enrich the understanding of the ecological systems and natural resources important to the nation; require the preparation of environmental impact statements for major federal projects; and establish a Council on Environmental Quality.

The EPA has a unique responsibility in respect to the process. Under Section 309 of the Clean Air Act, the agency is required to review and comment in writing on the environmental impact of any matter proposed by another federal agency which would have a significant impact on the environment. Thus the agency has a mandate not only to police its own activities for compliance with NEPA, but must also carry out a quality control screening of environmental reviews prepared elsewhere in the federal government system.

In 1977, in an Environmental Message, the US President emphasized the importance of NEPA to the development of sound federal decisions and to public involvement in government. To improve the implementation of the act and, in particular, the use of environmental impact statements, he issued an Executive Order:

- authorizing the Council on Environmental Quality (CEQ) to issue regulations which would ensure the effectiveness of environmental impact statements while reducing unnecessary paperwork; and
- directing the Council to prescribe procedures to help resolve interagency conflicts regarding projects being reviewed under the act.

The Council's NEPA regulations were promulgated in November 1978, and became effective in July 1979.

Box 51   Australia: ambient air quality standards and goals

Column 1 Item	Column 2 Pollutant	Column 3 Averaging period	Column 4 Maximum concentration	Column 5 Goal within 10 years, maximum allowable excess
1	Carbon monoxide	8 hours	9.0 ppm	1 day a year
2	Nitrogen dioxide	1 hour	0.12 ppm	1 day a year
		1 year	0.03 ppm	none
3	Photochemical	1 hour	0.10 ppm	1 day a year
	oxidants (as ozone)	4 hours	0.08 ppm	1 day a year
4	Sulfur dioxide	1 hour	0.20 ppm	1 day a year
		1 day	0.08 ppm	1 day a year
		1 year	0.02 ppm	none
5	Lead	1 year	0.50 $\mu g/m^3$	none
6	Particles as PM_{10}	1 day	50 $\mu g/m^3$	5 days a year

Notes: For the purposes of this measure the following definitions shall apply:
1. Lead sampling must be carried out for a period of 24 hours at least every sixth day.
2. Measurement of lead must be carried out on Total Suspended Particles (TSP) or its equivalent.
3. In Column 3, the averaging periods are defined as follows:
   1 hour   clock hour average
   4 hours   rolling 4 hour average based on 1 hour averages
   8 hours   rolling 8 hour average based on 1 hour averages
   1 day   calendar day average
   1 year   calendar year average
4. In Column 5, the time periods are defined as follows:
   day   calendar day during which the associated standard is exceeded
   year   calendar year.
5. All averaging periods of 8 hours or less must be referenced by the end time of the averaging period. This determines the calendar day to which the averaging periods are assigned.
6. For the purposes of calculating and reporting 4 and 8 hour averages, the first rolling average in a calendar day ends at 1.00 am, and includes hours from the previous calendar day.
7. The concentrations in Column 4, are the arithmetic mean concentrations.

National Environmental Policy Regulations, 1979, US

Regulations introduced under the US National Environmental Policy Act to establish uniform procedures for the implementation of the act. The regulations had three principal aims: to reduce paperwork, reduce delays and produce better decisions in respect to the protection and enhancement of the quality of the human environment.

The regulations limited the length of an EIS to normally less than 150 pages, and for proposals of unusual scope or complexity to less than 300 pages. Plain language was advocated. A new scoping procedure was established to assist agencies in deciding what the central issues were in any instance. In 1983, the regulations were reviewed and strengthened.

National Forest

In the USA, any of the forest areas set aside nationally under federal supervision for the purpose of conserving water, timber, wildlife, fish and other renewable resources, while providing recreational areas for the public. The national forests are administered by the US Forest Service, created by federal legislation. The service is required to produce management plans for each of the national forest and national grassland management units, providing for the diversity of plant and animal communities. An extensive research program is maintained.

National Forest Management Act, 1976, US

An act which directed the US Secretary of Agriculture to develop a land and resource management plan for each administrative unit of the National Forest System by 1985; regulations were developed in 1979 to guide this effort, these being revised in 1982. Planning was to embrace such resources as recreation, fish and wildlife habitat, water, timber, range, wilderness and minerals. The plans for all 121 administrative units were published in 1985.

National Franchise Board for Environment Protection, Sweden

An agency responsible for hearing cases under the Swedish Environment Protection Act, 1969. Breaches of the act may lead to fines or a maximum of two years in prison. The Board also examines license applications for discharges to the environment under the act. The Board operates in a similar manner to a court of law.

National Heritage Memorial Fund, UK

A fund established by the British government under the National Heritage Act, 1980, for the purpose of assisting in the preservation of the national heritage through the provision of financial assistance for the acquisition, maintenance and preservation of land, buildings and objects of historical or other importance to the national heritage.

National Historic Preservation Act, 1966, US

An act authorizing the Secretary of the Interior to expand and maintain a national register of districts, sites, buildings, structures and objects of local, state and national significance and to grant funds for the purpose of undertaking comprehensive statewide historic surveys and preparing statewide plans.

National Legislation

See:
Environmental Law.

National Monument

In the USA, numerous areas, relics and historical remains preserved by Act of the US Congress or presidential proclamation. In 1906 President Theodore Roosevelt created the first national monument at Devils Tower in Wyoming. The jurisdiction of national monuments was unified in 1933 under the US National Park Service. See Box 52 for some US national monuments.

National Packaging Covenant, Australia

In 1997, the endorsement by the Australian and New Zealand Environment and Conservation Council (ANZECC) of a national agreement or covenant for the effective lifecycle management of packaging and paper products to reduce the strain on landfills and promote sustainable environmental benefits, with the promotion of kerbside recycling schemes. ANZECC has set a national target of reducing waste to landfill by 50 per cent by the year 2000, based on 1990 per capita levels.

Box 52   Some US national monuments

1978   Aniakchak National Monument and Preserve, Alaska
1929   Badlands National Monument, South Dakota
1931   Canyon de Chelly National Monument, Arizona
1918   Casa Grande Ruins National Monument, Arizona
1933   Cedar Breaks National Monument, Utah
1907   Chaco Culture National Historical Park
1890   Chickamauga and Chattanooga National Military Park, Georgia
       and Tennessee
1930   Colonial National Historical Park, Virginia
1911   Colorado National Monument, Colorado
1933   Death Valley National Monument, California/Nevada
1906   Devils Tower National Monument, Wyoming
1949   Effigy Mounds National Monument, Iowa
1935   Fort Jefferson National Monument
1948   Fort Sumter National Monument, South Carolina
1978   Gates of the Arctic National Park and Preserve, Alaska
1925   Glacier Bay National Park and Preserve, Alaska
1957   Golden Spike National Historic Site, Utah
1951   Grand Portage National Monument, Minnesota
1936   Homestead National Monument of America, Nebraska
1936   Joshua Tree National Monument, California
1978   Kobuk Valley National Park (Monument), Alaska
1978   Lake Clark National Park and Preserve, Alaska
1906   Mesa Verde National Park, Colorado
1906   Montezuma Castle National Monument, Arizona
1933   Mound State Monument, Alabama
1908   Natural Bridges National Monument, Utah
1909   Navajo National Monument, Arizona
1909   Oregon Caves National Monument
1937   Organ Pipe Cactus National Monument, Arizona
1906   Petrified Forest National Park, Arizona
1910   Rainbow Bridge National Monument, Utah
1939   Tuzigoot National Monument, Arizona
1933   White Sands National Monument, New Mexico

ANZECC endorsed National Packaging Guidelines in 1991, a National
Waste Minimization and Recycling Strategy and the National Kerbside Recycling Strategy in 1992. In 1997, ANZECC Ministers decided to endorse the

development of a National Packaging Covenant embracing all parts of the packaging chain. The covenant builds on previous strategies while taking into account the Intergovernment Agreement on the Environment and the National Strategy for Ecologically Sustainable Development. The covenant recognizes that a cooperative approach between industry and all spheres of government is essential to achieve a nationally consistent approach to the lifecycle management of packaging and paper including its recovery, utilization and ultimate disposal.

The covenant is based on the principle of 'product stewardship' which is the ethics of shared responsibility for the lifecycle of products including the environmental impact of the product through and including its ultimate disposal. It involves all participants in the supply chain: raw material suppliers, designers, packaging manufacturers, packaging users, retailers, consumers, all spheres of government, and collection agencies. All parties to the covenant agree to produce action plans for evaluating and improving environmental outcomes, and will work to develop best practice systems. Revenue received from a levy on producers and importers of paper and packaging is directed to funding recycling collection services, developing markets for recyclables or other beneficial activities. The level of levy needs to be adjusted from time to time. Ratepayers also pay a share of waste management costs.

National Park

A relatively large area of land set aside by legislation for its features of predominantly unspoiled natural landscape and its flora and fauna, permanently dedicated to public enjoyment, education and inspiration, being protected from all interference, other than essential management measures. In the USA, Yellowstone National Park was created in 1872, followed by Yosemite and Sequoia in 1890. In 1879, Australia established its first park, the Royal National Park; the Great Barrier Reef Marine Park was established in 1975. Canada's first park, Banff National Park, was established in 1885. In 1898, South Africa established the Kruger National Park. In 1934, Argentina created its first national park at Nahuel Huapi. In 1936, the Philippines established the Mount Appo National Park. In 1948, Mount Carmel National Park was created. In 1984, Taiwan established Kenting National Park. Hundreds of national parks and reserves have flourished in most of the 200 countries of the world. Marine parks have also been established. Box 53 summarizes some of the more significant parks.

Box 53   A selection of famous national parks

Addo Elephant National Park
Established in 1931, a national park in southern Cape Province, South Africa, lying in the Sundays River valley. The park is largely covered with dense, impenetrable, evergreen scrub and preserves a band of elephants, remnant of a great herd which was subject to an extermination program by landowners. The park is also the habitat of the hippopotamus, cape buffalo, antelope, black rhinoceros, and abundant birdlife and reptiles.

Amazonia National Park
Established in 1974, a national park comprising areas of submountainous forest with rock outcroppings along the sedimentary Amazon River Basin, with moderately undulating plains and meandering rivers. The park is characterized by a wide variety of flora. Trees include mangrove, rubber and palm. Fauna includes the armadillo, deer, tapir, weasel, dolphin and a great variety of monkeys.

Amboseli National Park
Originally established in 1948 as a game reserve in southern Kenya, East Africa. It comprises open plains, acacia woodland, lava-strewn thornbush country, swamp, marshland, the Amboseli Lake bed and the slopes of Oldoinyo Orok. A great variety of wildlife inhabits the park. Fauna includes the baboon, lion, cheetah, elephant, black rhinoceros, hippopotamus, Masai giraffe, buffalo, oryx, wildebeest, gerenuk, impala and gazelle.

Arusha National Park
Established in 1960 in Tanzania, a relatively small national park yet rich in fauna and flora. The area embraces mountain rain forest, acacia groves, grassland, swamps and moorland. Fauna includes the hippopotamus, elephant, black rhinoceros, giraffe, lion, leopard, buffalo, antelope and a variety of monkeys. Water birds and flamingo abound.

Awash National Park
Established in 1969 in Ethiopia, a national park embracing the semi-arid open plains of the Awash Valley at the foot of the Shewa escarpment and including Mount Fantale. The flora includes grassland, acacia, savannah and thorny thickets. The fauna includes the hippopotamus, leopard,

Box 53   continued

lion, cheetah, zebra, gazelle, antelope and crocodile. The park stands adjacent to the Awash West Game Reserve.

Banff National Park
Established in 1885, Canada's first national park located in Alberta, on the eastern slopes of the Rocky Mountains, embracing several large icefields and glacial lakes. It has been progressively enlarged over the years. The flora includes alpine meadows, while the fauna includes the bear, elk, deer, mouse, and wild sheep and goats. A special feature is the hot springs of Sulphur Mountain. The park is contiguous with Jasper National Park in Alberta and Yoho National Park in British Columbia, Canada.

Bavarian Forest National Park
Established in 1970 as a contribution to the European Conservation Year, the national park is located in southeastern Germany along the frontier with the Czech Republic. Tree-covered and mountainous, with the peaks Rachel and Lusen, the park is a refuge for the rarer kinds of wildlife.

Bialowieski National Park
Established in 1947 in Narododowy, Poland, a relatively small low-plains area, being the best preserved remnant of primeval European lowland forest with a range of vegetation. Some trees are hundreds of years old. The park is a breeding ground for the rare European bison.

Blue Mountains National Park
Located west of Sydney, NSW, Australia, a park which contains some of the most spectacular scenery in the country. The park embraces Glenbrook, Blackheath and the Grose Valley. The Blue Mountains are in fact the remnants of a vast sandstone plateau. The whole of the plateau and the flora of the gorges and valleys are densely vegetated. This includes the botanical marvel, the blue gum forest. In 1977, the NSW government extended the Blue Mountains National Park to the south, doubling its size, providing a huge easily accessible wilderness close to Sydney.

Boise National Forest
Established in 1908, a national forest in southwestern Idaho, USA. The main portion of the forest is steep and mountainous, descending into

Box 53   continued

the Boise River Valley. Following the discovery of gold in 1862 north of the Boise, numerous mining communities sprang up; many are now ghost towns. Recreation remains the basic land use of the park, offering fishing, hiking and hunting.

Border Ranges National Park

The core of the Border Ranges National Park, NSW, Australia, was laid down in 1983, after a decade of stormy debate on the question of logging. The boundaries were extended the following year to preserve major areas of rain forest, including Washpool and Nightcap. The Border Ranges lie to the north of NSW on the border with Queensland. With its rich volcanic soil, the park is clothed in luxuriant subtropical rain forest. Fauna includes swamp wallabies, potoroos, pademelons, tiger cats, possums, gliders, bandicoots, marsupial mice and echidnas. There is also an immense bird population.

Bwindi National Park

Located in Uganda, Africa, a park which embraces tangled jungle highlands, known in colonial times as the Impenetrable Forest. It is approached through the volcanic mountains of the Western Rift Valley. The park shelters some half of the remaining 600 or so mountain gorillas. The park attracts tourists from around the world.

Canaima National Park

Established in 1962, in Venezuela. It is a mountainous region with tropical rain forest, thickly wooded riverside areas, grassland savannah and open meadow. Fauna includes the jaguar, tiger, tapir, armadillo, opossum, numersou monkeys and many birds. A special feature is Salto Angel, the highest waterfall in the world.

Canyonland National Park

Established in 1964 in Utah, USA, a national park comprising wilderness with colorful rock formations at the confluence of the Colorado and Green Rivers. Both rivers have cut deep gorges through the sandstone in the area. The area has many mammals and birds, including a herd of endemic desert bighorn sheep.

Capital Reef National Park

Established as a national monument in 1937 and as a national park in 1971, in Utah, USA. It comprises a great buttressed cliff of colored

Box 53   continued

sandstone extending for 32 km along the western edge of Water Pocket Fold. The Freeman River and its tributaries cross the park through deep canyons. The vegetation is desertlike and sparse.

Cevennes National Park
Established in 1970, the park was created in southern France on the southeastern flank of the Massif Central. It is dominated by limestone plateaus, and forests covering more than half the park. Trees include evergreen oaks, chestnuts, common oaks, beeches, Scots pine and birches. There are some 1700 flowering plants, the most notable being wild daffodils, martagon lilies and lady's slipper orchids. The bird population includes golden eagles, peregrine falcons, hen harriers, eagle owls, stone curlews and little bustards. Animals include otters, badgers, foxes, martens, wild boar, and roe deer. The park also has a very substantial buffer zone.

Chobe National Park
Established in 1961 in Botswana, a national park comprising grassland, swamp, marsh and forest. Fauna includes the hippopotamus, white rhinoceros, elephant, lion, leopard, cheetah, hyena, buffalo, zebra, giraffe and many species of antelope. A special feature if a fossil lake bed.

Comoe National Park
Established in 1926, on the Ivory Coast, Africa, a national park embracing a series of ranges. The fauna includes the hippopotamus, elephant, lion, leopard, panther, hyena, and many varieties of antelope, baboons and monkeys. The flora comprises wooded Guinean savannah, sedge, bulrush and bombax.

Cradle Mountain–Lake St Clair National Park
Located in Tasmania, Australia, Cradle Mountain was first climbed by an Austrian, Gustav Weindorfer, in 1910. Eventually, a national park was declared largely through his efforts. Weindorfer constructed a forest home or chalet which has been restored. Cradle Mountain has an extraordinary range of wildlife. After dark, several species of nocturnal animals come to the doorways of cabins – the brushtail possums are the boldest, while native cats and tiger cats are more cautious, but all come inside to eat scraps.

Box 53   continued

Daisetsuzan National Park
Established in 1934, in Hokkaido, Japan, a national park embracing a volcanic range with many peaks, cliffs, gorges, lakes and waterfalls, with vast alpine meadows and virgin coniferous forests. Fauna includes the Asiatic black bear, northern pika, chipmunk and Japanese macaque. The park is the only habitat in Japan for the pika.

Dartmoor National Park
Established in 1951, a high plateau with granite hills, bogs and moorland located in the county of Devon, southwest England. The moorland is bleak and desolate, with heather the chief vegetation. Dartmoor was a Royal forest in Saxon times. In 1951 its wooded fringes were also designated a national park. Grazing supports wild ponies, sheep and cattle. It is the site of Dartmoor Prison.

Dinder National Park
Established in 1935, the park lies in the clayish flood plain of the Hahr River, in the Sudan. Vegetation in the park consists of thornbush savannah in the north and woodland in the south, with palm or gallery forests along the riverbanks. Wildlife includes the giraffe, hartebeest, reedbuck, antelope, bushbuck, waterbuck, kudu, gazelle, buffalo, lion and ostrich. The park lies almost 500 km from Khartoum. The Dinder River flows through Dinder National Park.

Ecrins National Park
Established in 1973, the second largest national park in France, located in the southeast Haute-Alpes. It encompasses alpine peaks as well as numerous lakes, *cirques* and gorges. Forests of larch cover the park. Fauna includes mountain hares and foxes, marmots and chamois. Birds are typically alpine and include golden eagles, partridges and ptarmigans. A substantial buffer zone has been developed.

Etosha National Park
Established in 1907, in Namibia, southwest Africa, a park of semi-arid plains which merge into the Etosha Pan, which is sometimes largely submerged. The park is one of the world's largest game resorts, with a considerable range of fauna and flora.

Box 53   continued

Everglades National Park
Established in 1934 in Florida, USA, a large flat region embracing most of Florida Bay, with many swamps, islands and extensive freshwater and saltwater areas. The flora comprises subtropical wilderness with open prairies, mangrove forests, palm trees, cypress and sawgrass marshes. Fauna includes manatees, crocodiles, alligators, turtles, panthers, raccoons, opossums, numerous snakes, and many kinds of bird. The Everglades is a refuge for many rare animals. Water levels in the park, however, are half of what they were 50 years ago, water having been diverted to growing population needs, such as drinking water. Water control systems have reduced the natural flow to the Everglades. Water management is now a central political issue.

Fiordland National Park
Established in 1952, in New Zealand, a rugged area on the southwestern coast of the South Island, including the Cameron, Hunter, Murchison, Stuart and Franklin mountains. The flora includes alpine meadow. There is a snow-covering on the higher slopes and subtropical rainforest on the lower slopes. The fauna includes mountain parrots (kea), owl parrots (kakapo), flightless rails, red deer and opossums.

Franklin–Lower Gordon Wild Rivers National Park
This Tasmanian national park was created and included in the World Heritage List, following the failure of the Tasmanian Hydroelectric Commission to establish hydroelectric plant on two major rivers, the Franklin and the Gordon. The park takes in the former Frenchman's Cap National Park and the Gordon River State Reserve. Frenchman's Cap is a huge plug of white quartzite rising to a height of almost 1500 m, with a sheer 300 m eastern face.

Galapagos National Park
Established in 1968, a national park administered by Ecuador with the assistance of the Charles Darwin Biological Station based at Santa Cruz island. The park is renowned for its unusual animal life and takes its name from its giant land tortoises. The island became internationally famous when visited by Charles Darwin, the English naturalist, in 1835; the unusual fauna contributed to the formation of his ideas on natural selection.

Box 53   continued

Gaspesian Provincial Park
Established in 1937 to protect the fast-diminishing herds of caribou as well as to preserve the natural beauty of the region, the park is located in eastern Quebec Province, Canada, near the mouth of the St. Lawrence River. The area is heavily wooded with many lakes and streams. Mt Jacques Cartier is the highest peak.

Gir Lion National Park
Established in 1965 in Gujarat, India, a somewhat hilly arid region, the last remaining natural habitat of the Asiatic lion, whose numbers in this sanctuary have increased to several hundreds. Other fauna includes the leopard, wild pig, spotted deer, four-horned antelope and chinkara. A central waterhole contains a few crocodiles.

Glacier National Park
Established in 1886, a national park in southeastern British Columbia, Canada, in the heart of the Selkirk Mountains. Snowcapped peaks such as Hermit, Cheops, Grizzly, Sifton, Grant, Avalanche and Sir Donald, flanked by immense ice fields and glaciers, present an impressive alpine panorama with canyons, rivers, waterfalls and flower-filled meadows.

Grampians National Park
Located 260 km to the west of Melbourne, Australia, the Grampians became Victoria's largest national park in 1984. The Grampians consist of towering sandstone peaks and ridges formed millions of years ago from great beds of sediments which were uplifted, tilted and eroded. The rich vegetation includes more than 800 plant species, varying from low heaths to red-gum woodland and tall eucalypt forest. Kangaroos, koalas, echidnas, possums and gliders are common. Over 200 bird species have been recorded.

Gran Paradiso National Park
Established in 1836, initially as a hunting zone, in northwest Italy, this is a national park with a typically alpine terrain and numerous glaciers. In 1856 it became the Royal Hunting Reserve of the Gran Paradiso. Fauna includes the ibex, ermine, weasel, hare and golden eagle. Scientific research work carried out in the park includes the study of soils and climatological problems. The Gran Paradiso is the highest mountain within Italy at over 4000 m. In 1860, John Cowell became the first person to reach the summit.

Box 53 continued

Grand Canyon National Park
Created in 1919, a national park embracing the Grand Canyon in northwestern Arizona, USA, noted for its fantastic shapes and colorations, awesome grandeur and beauty. The park was greatly extended in 1975. The depth of the Grand Canyon is due to the powerful cutting action of the Colorado River, and its great width is due to rain, wind and temperature, and the chemical erosion of soft rock.

Great Australian Bight Marine Park
A marine park, extending along the southern coast of Australia, with an area of 169 000 ha. The Park has Commonwealth (Federal) and South Australian components. The region is an important breeding ground for the Southern Right Whale. Management plans were still being developed in the year 2000.

Great Barrier Reef Marine Park
A marine park established in 1975 by the Australian government embracing substantial areas of the Great Barrier Reef which runs in an extended system along practically the whole east coast of Queensland. It is the largest assemblage of living corals and associated organisms in the world, covering an area of 350 000 sq km. It has evolved over the last 8000 years. The park is managed by the Great Barrier Reef Marine Park Authority, created with the park under the Great Barrier Reef Marine Park Act 1975. In 1991, the park was included in the World Heritage List. The reef is now fully protected against inappropriate activity, including oil exploration.

Great Basin National Park
Established in 1986, a scenic national park in eastern Nevada, USA, previously part of the Humboldt National Forest. It comprises part of Snake Mountain, reaching almost 4000 m at Wheeler Peak. A principal attraction of the park is the Lehman caves, a group of impressive limestone caverns.

Great Smoky Mountains National Park
Established in 1934, a national park in eastern Tennessee and western North Carolina seeking to preserve the last remaining sizeable area of southern primeval hardwood forest in the USA. It contains some of the highest peaks in the Appalachian Mountains. Important species of fauna in the park include black bears, white-tailed deer, foxes, bobcats,

Box 53   continued

raccoons, grouse and songbirds. The park was included in the World Heritage List in 1983.

Ise–Shima National Park
A national park on the Shima Peninsula, central Honshu, Japan. Its two main cities are Ise, famous for its Shinto shrines, and Toba, a seaport that guards the southern entrance to Ise Bay. The bay is renowned for its Mikimoto cultured pearl industry; the Toba area now produces most of Japan's cultured pearls.

Jasper National Park
Established in 1907, in western Alberta, Canada, to preserve a scenic mountainous area and its wildlife. It is located on the eastern slopes of the Rocky Mountains. The park includes the Athabasca Valley, the surrounding mountains, and part of the great Columbia icefield. Other attractions include waterfalls, lakes, canyons and hot springs. Wildlife includes the bear, elk, moose, caribou and cougar. Birds are abundant. Jasper is contiguous with Banff National Park in Alberta, and Yoho National Park in British Columbia. The flora includes pine, Douglas fir, spruce, alpine larch, aspen, paper birch, balsam, poplar and many flowering plants.

Kabalega National Park
Established in 1952, in Uganda, Africa, a hilly region bisected by the Victoria Nile, containing the Kabalega Falls. The flora comprises savannah, well-wooded in places, while the fauna includes the hippopotamus, elephant, black and white rhinoceros, buffalo, giraffe, lion, leopard and various species of antelope.

Kafue National Park
Established in 1950, in Zambia, Africa, a plateau area with Kalahari sand to the south. The flora comprises mixed forest, thicket, woodland and grass; while the fauna includes the black rhinoceros, hippopotamus, elephant, lion, buffalo, zebra, various species of antelope, and crocodile, with much birdlife.

Kakadu National Park
Established initially in 1975 in the Northern Territory, Australia, and then considerably enlarged. It is one of the most magnificent natural reserves in Australia, now included in its entirety in the World Herit-

Box 53   continued

age List. The topography ranges from tidal flats and flood plains to dramatic sandstone plateaus and escarpments. The wetlands are frequented by very large numbers of waterbirds. Kakadu contains more than 1000 aboriginal art sites. It is controversial because of the proximity of uranium deposits.

Kalahari Gemsbok National Park
Established in 1931, in South Africa, a national park located in the Kalahari Desert, extreme northern Cape Province, adjoining the Gemsbok National Park of Botswana. The park consists generally of reddish dunes with acacia growing in the river beds. Various shrubs provide forage for large herds of gemsbok (or oryx), wildebeest, springbok and some red hartebeest. Other wildlife includes lions, dogs, jackals, ostriches and numerous other birds. The two portions of park were established to protect migratory animals which cross the border between the two countries.

Katmai National Park
Established in 1918 in Alaska, USA, an area of dying volcanoes on the east coast of the Upper Alaska Peninsula in the Aleutian range. The park includes Katmai Volcano, Mount Denison and the Valley of Ten Thousand Smokes. By contrast, there are several glaciers and lakes. The flora comprises pine, spruce and fir and other sub-Arctic plants. The fauna includes the Alaskan brown bear, moose, wolf and many birds.

Kaziranga National Park
Established in 1908 as a game reserve and becoming a national park in 1974, it is located in Assam State, northeastern India. It lies between the Brahmaputra River and the Mikir Hills. Much of the park is marshland. Wildlife includes the Indian one-horned rhinoceros, tiger, leopard, elephant, wild pig, hog deer, swamp deer, buffalo, and pelican, stork and other waterfowl.

Kenting National Park
Established in 1984 in southern Taiwan, Republic of China, the park is located on the Hengchun peninsula with the Pacific coast to the east, Taiwan Strait to the west, and the Bashi channel to the south. The topography embraces coastal cliffs, coral reefs, sandstone peaks, karst terrain, limestone caves, shell sands, estuaries and lakes. The tropical flora ranges from coastal coral-reef plants and tropical coastal forests

Box 53   continued

to grassland, coastal bushes, marsh plants and low-altitude natural forest communities. Fauna diversity embraces many birds, reptiles, amphibians, and all kinds of insects.

Komoe National Park
Established in 1926 on the Ivory Coast, Africa, the park comprises series of mountain ranges. The flora includes Guinean savannah, sedge, bulrushes and bombax. The fauna includes the hippopotamus, elephant, lion, panther, hyena and many species of antelope.

Kruger National Park
A game sanctuary in northeastern Transvaal, South Africa, established in 1898. It is a gently undulating region of hills and doleritic dikes, with plains to the south. The flora includes grassy plains, park savannah, dry deciduous forest and thornbush, many flowering plants, and a wide variety of trees. Wildlife includes the elephant, hippopotamus, lion, leopard, cheetah, buffalo, rhinoceros, zebra, wildebeest, impala and numerous birds. It is one of the finest wildlife areas in the world.

Lake Clark National Park
Established initially in 1978 as Lake Clark National Monument, and renamed two years later, a national park and preserve in southern Alaska, USA, southwest of Anchorage. It has great biological diversity, with jagged peaks, granite spires, dozens of glaciers, hundreds of waterfalls, tundra plains and active volcanoes. Lake Clark provides the headwaters for the most important spawning ground for red salmon in North America. Wildlife includes caribou, sheep, brown and grizzly bears, bald eagles and peregrine falcons.

Lake District National Park
Established in 1951, a famous scenic region and national park in the county of Cumbria, northwest England. The many lakes include Windermere and Thirlmere and the highest English mountain, Scafell Pike, is found here.

Los Glacieres National Park
Established in 1937, the park is situated in Santa Cruz province, southwestern Argentina, in the Andes. It has forests and grassy plains in the east, and needlelike peaks, large glaciers and snowfields in the west. Wildlife includes chinchillas, pudu and guemal, condors and rheas.

Box 53 continued

Luangwa National Park
Established in 1972, along a stretch of the Luangwa River, northeastern Zambia, southern Africa. It occupies a wide area of alluvial flats. Vegetation in the park comprises woodland, savannah, thickets, grassland and riparian forest. The park's varied animal life comprises the ververt monkey, baboon, leopard, lion, elephant, zebra, black rhinoceros, hippopotamus, kudu, eland, buffalo, puku, wildebeest, wild dog, hyena, cheetah, giraffe and antelope. Birdlife includes storks, geese, cranes and bee-eaters. The river provides a habitat for the Nile crocodile.

Mammoth Cave National Park
Established in 1941 and located in Kentucky, USA. The park has an extensive system of limestone caverns. In 1972, a passage was discovered linking the Mammoth Cave and the Flint Ridge Cave system; the combined underground passages run for some 500 km. The caves contain unique geological formations such as the Pillars of Hercules and underground lakes and rivers. Various creatures have adapted to the dark environment, including cave crickets, blind fish and blind crayfish. Mummified Indian bodies have been found. Mammoth Cave has been included in the World Heritage List.

Manovo-Gounda-Saint Floris National Park
Established in 1933, located in the Central Africa Republic, in the upper basin of the Chari River, comprising wooded Sudanian savannah interspersed with marshy areas subject to seasonal flooding. The fauna includes the elephant, buffalo, antelope, giraffe, lion, hyena, cheetah, and many species of birds including the egret. The park is included in the World Heritage List.

Mesa Verde National Park
Established in 1906, a national park in southwestern Colorado, USA preserving notable prehistoric cliff dwellings. It contains hundreds of *pueblo* (Indian village) ruins up to 13 centuries old. The most striking remains are multistorey apartments built under overhanging cliffs. Cliff Palace, excavated in 1909, contains hundreds of rooms including circular ceremonial chambers. The park also has some very striking and rugged scenery. Deer are the most common large animals, with some bears and mountain lions.

Box 53   continued

Mount Appo National Park
Established in 1936, in the Philippines, a rugged region surrounding Mount Apo, a volcano, the highest peak in the nation. There are many waterfalls and medicinal hot springs. With diverse fauna and flora, the park is the only habitat of the monkey-eating eagle.

Mount Aspiring National Park
Established in 1964, a national park in the South Island of New Zealand, embracing a substantial area of the Southern Alps. The landscape is varied and complex, being the source of headwaters for seven rivers and featuring glaciers, rocky mountains, waterfalls and passes. Its forests are protected to control soil erosion. The park has scientific, wilderness, natural environment and development areas. Mount Aspiring is contiguous with Fiordland National Park, a rugged area with mountain peaks, many rivers and lakes. It is a refuge for the takahe and the kakapo.

Mount Carmel National Park
Established after 1948, in Israel, a national park embracing the Mount Carmel region near Haifa, overlooking the Plain of Esdraelon and the Mediterranean. It has diverse fauna and flora. There are many fine parks and woods on the slopes of the mountain. On the southwest slopes are caves where Stone Age human skeletons have been found. Mount Carmel has been sanctified since early times and is the site of a monastery.

Mount Cook National Park
Established in 1953, a national park in the South Island of New Zealand. Mount Cook, the highest point in New Zealand, is located within the park, dominating the valleys, glaciers and numerous surrounding peaks. More than a third of the park is covered by permanent snow and glacial ice. The flora includes beech, tussock, ribbonwood, alpine scrub, pine and others. Birdlife abounds.

Mount Rainier National Park
Established in 1899 in Washington, USA, to preserve the Cascade Range including Mount Rainier. The lower areas have dense forests while, during the warmer months, the park and mountain are covered with wild flowers that bloom progressively higher up the slopes. The fauna includes deer, elk, bears, mountain goats, raccoons and squirrels.

Box 53 continued

Mount Revelstoke National Park
Established in 1914 in British Columbia, Canada, a national park occupying the western slope of the Selkirk Mountains near the city of Revelstoke. The park affords a spectacular view of three mountains, Monashee, Selkirk and Purcell.

Mount Zebra National Park
Established in 1937, a national park in southwest Cape Province, South Africa. It is situated in the semi-arid Great Karroo region, west of Cradock. It was established to protect the endangered mountain zebra as well as other animals.

Nahuel Huapi National Park
Established in 1934, this was Argentina's first national park. The park and adjacent nature reserve include a region of dense forests, numerous lakes, rapid rivers, waterfalls, snow-clad peaks and glaciers. Its peaks include El Tronador and Mount Catredral. It embraces Lake Nahuel in the Andes.

Nairobi National Park
Established in 1948, a national park just south of Nairobi, the capital of Kenya. It consists partly of thick woods, partly of rolling plains and valleys, and partly of a wooded confluence of several rivers. Its flora is of a dry transitional savannah type. The fauna includes the lion, gazelle, black rhinoceros, giraffe, antelope and zebra, together with hundreds of species of birds.

Namid Desert/Naukluft National Park
Established in 1907, in Namibia, Africa, a park offering a wide range of landscapes including sand dunes, canyons, gorges, pools, waterfalls and the Naukluft Mountains. The flora includes true desert vegetation. The fauna includes the elephant, shrew, desert golden mole, jackal, bateared fox, hyena, leopard, cheetah, zebra, gemsbok, springbok and ostrich.

Odzala National Park
Established in 1940, in the Congo, Africa, a national park comprising a high plateau that is difficult to access. The flora includes humid tropical forest, changing to savannah in the south. The fauna includes the elephant, buffalo, antelope, ape, leopard, golden cat and bushpig. A few groups of Pygmies inhabit the park.

Box 53   continued

Olympic National Park
Established in 1938, in northeastern Washington, USA, a national park created to preserve the Olympic Mountains and their forests and wildlife. There are numerous glaciers and extensive rain forest. The ocean-shore portion contains scenic beaches, islets and points, with Indian reservations. The fauna includes deer, bears, cougars and rare Roosevelt elks. The park has been included in the World Heritage List.

Olympus National Park
Established in 1938 in Greece, a national park encompassing Mount Olympus. The flora is abundant with beech, pine and broad-leaved evergreens. The fauna includes the wild mountain goat, hare, wolf, fox, roe deer, golden eagle, partridge and hooded crow.

Padjelanta National Park
Established in 1962, in northwestern Sweden, the largest of the Swedish national parks and one of the largest parks in Europe. It contains several lakes, mountains, valleys and glaciers with a characteristic alpine flora. Among its fauna are the wolverine, Arctic fox and brown bear; its birdlife includes the golden eagle and merlin.

Pembrokeshire Coast National Park
Established in 1952, a Welsh national park with limestone and sandstone cliffs, sandy beaches, and deep river valleys, comprising four separate areas with Norman castles and many prehistoric remains. The flora includes beech and maple forests, while the fauna includes badgers, otters, grey seals, polecats, voles, squirrels, trout and salmon.

Rocky Mountains National Park
Established in 1915, a national park in north-central California, USA, containing numerous high peaks as well as broad valleys, gorges, alpine lakes and plunging streams. The flora comprises over 700 known species; the fauna includes the bighorn sheep, deer, mountain lion, and a rich variety of birds.

Rondane National Park
Established in 1962, this Norwegian national park embraces ten major peaks in a high alpine region. The flora is mainly sparse tundra; the fauna includes reindeer, roe deer, elk, Arctic fox, red fox, wolverine, lynx, lemming, marten and many birds including eagles, owls and hawks.

Box 53 continued

Ruwenzori National Park
Established in 1952, this national park in southwestern Uganda embraces rolling hills and many volcanic craters. The flora consists mainly of thickets of various types of small trees, including acacias and evergreens. The fauna includes the chimpanzee, leopard, lion, elephant, hippopotamus, water buffalo, antelope and many species of kingfisher.

Sequoia National Park
Established in 1890 in the Sierra Nevada of California, USA, to protect groves of large trees which are among the world's largest and oldest forms of life. The General Sherman Tree is the largest tree in the park, being some three to four thousand years old. The fauna in the park includes black bears, deer, foxes and squirrels.

Shenandoah National Park
Established in 1935, a national park in the Blue Ridge sections of the Appalachians, in northern Virginia, USA. Noted for its scenery, the park offers some of the widest views in the eastern states. The park is heavily forested with both hardwoods and conifers.

Snowdonia National Park
Established in 1952, a national park located in Wales, Britain. It is a wild mountain region extending southeastward from the Snowdon peaks to Cardigan Bay. It embraces a wide range of flora including maple and beech woodlands, while the fauna includes the otter, grey seal, polecat, pine marten, vole, squirrel, brown hare and numerous birds, among them the kingfisher, great crested grebe, whitethroat, golden plover, raven and red grouse. Snowdon peak is the highest in England and Wales.

South West National Park
This park occupies almost the entire southwest corner of Tasmania, Australia. It contains five major mountain ranges and more than fifty lakes, several river systems, vast tracts of button-grass plains, and forests of Antarctic beech. The southwest is one of the few temperate wilderness areas left anywhere in the world. The area achieved great publicity through the drowning of Lake Pedder for a hydroelectric scheme in 1972. The issue received national attention, although the cause was lost.

Box 53   continued

St Katherine Protectorate National Park
Established in 1998, a national park in the vicinity of Mount Sinai, Egypt, and the St Katherine Monastery. This historic area has been visited over time by Moses, Napoleon and Richard the Lionheart. St Katherine has been a place of pilgrimage for centuries. Apart from the usual national park problems, the park management is also concerned with the welfare of the indigenous people, comprising four tribes of Bedouin who owe their descent to people from South Romania brought over more than 1500 years ago as servants to the monastery. Improved sewage treatment is planned. Unlike other national parks there is little vegetation and surface water.

Tablas de Daniel National Park
Established in 1973, a nature reserve located about 30 km northeast of the city of Ciudad Real, south central Spain. It lies at the confluence of the Guiadiana and Ciguela rivers, with fresh and brackish waters supporting both migratory and resident waterfowl all-year-round.

Tadoba National Park
Established as a wildlife sanctuary in 1935, and later expanded, a national park in the Chandrapur district, western India, consisting of dense forests, interspersed with lakes and plains. The park has tiger, panther, leopard, jackal, bison, antelope, bear and crocodile.

Ujung-Kulong National Park
Set aside as a nature reserve in 1921, becoming a national park in 1980, a remote areas of low hills and plateaus, with lagoons and coastal dunes, on the island of Java, Indonesia. The park faces the Sunda Strait at the western tip of Java. It contains the last remaining low-relief forest in Java. Animals found there include the Javan tiger, the one-horned rhinoceros, gibbon, leaf-monkey, crocodile, sea turtle, green peafowl, barking deer and mouse deer.

Uluru (Ayers Rock–Mount Olga) National Park
Established in the Northern Territory, Australia, in 1977, the park is famous for Ayers Rock and the Olgas. Ayers Rock is a sandstone upcropping over 10 km in circumference. The vegetation is mainly semidesert including mallee, spinifex, acacia, desert oak and mulga; the fauna includes the kangaroo, wallaby, euro, dingo and bandicoot. There

Box 53 continued

are ancient aboriginal rock paintings. In 1988, the park was included in the World Heritage List.

Victoria Falls National Park
Established in 1931, a national park located within Zimbabwe, adjacent to the Livingstone Game Park in Zambia, both being centered on the spectacular Victoria Falls, about midway along the course of the Zambezi River, Africa. The parks abound with large and small game and offer recreational facilities.

Voyageurs National Park
Established in 1975, a national park in northern Minnesota, USA. It lies along the Canadian border, east of International Falls. The park comprises a network of streams and lakes. It sustains stands of fir, spruce, pine, aspen and birch. The park was named after mainly French-Canadian frontierspeople who were involved in fur trading in the area during the late eighteenth and early nineteenth centuries.

Wankie National Park
Established in 1930, Zimbabwe, Africa, a large national park encompassing a great expanse of Kalahari sands. The flora includes extensive forests of sand mopani. The fauna includes the hippopotamus, elephant, black rhinoceros, buffalo, giraffe, zebra, lion, leopard, cheetah, hyena, antelope, waterbuck, impala, steenbock, jackal, mongoose, baboon, monkey, crocodile and many birds.

Wood Buffalo National Park
Established in 1922 in Alberta and Northwest Territories, Canada, a large national park of open plain between Lake Athabasca and the Great Slave Lake, broken by bog and marsh and the Peace River. Fauna includes the buffalo, deer, elk, moose, caribou, bear, lynx, wolf, beaver, rabbit, squirrel, porcupine and many birds. The park is a refuge for the only remaining bison herds.

Yellowstone National Park
Established in 1872, the oldest national park in the USA, situated in northwest Wyoming, southern Montana and eastern Idaho. It consists mostly of broad volcanic plateaus, with mountain ranges and unusual geological features including fossil forests and eroded basalt lava flows. It has over 10 000 hot springs which find surface expression in a

Box 53   *continued*

variety of forms, including 3000 geysers. The Grand Canyon runs for 31 km through the park, with two majestic waterfalls. Most of the park is forested, mainly with pine. Animal life includes the buffalo, elk, bighorn sheep, deer, moose, black bear, grizzly bear and coyote. A scenic roadway connects Yellowstone with Grand Teton National Park. Yellowstone has been included in the World Heritage List.

Yosemite National Park
Established in 1890, a scenic mountainous national park in central California, USA. It embraces areas of the Sierra Nevada Range, the Yosemite Valley, and giant sequoia groves with trees thousands of years old. The flora of the park changes rapidly with elevation, trees ranging from conifers to lodgepole pine. Fauna includes deer, squirrels, chipmunks and black bears. Yosemite has been included in the World Heritage List.

Zion National Park
Established in 1919, in southwest Utah, USA, a national park of deep canyons and high cliffs. It was created to protect the Zion Canyon which contains much evidence of fossils and prehistoric cave dwellers. Wildlife includes deer, lions and more than 150 species of birds.

National Stream Quality Accounting Network (NASQAN), US

The US national water quality monitoring network operated by the US Geological Survey. The results over recent years appear to show that the nation's pollution control efforts are having a positive effect. However, since the network tends to emphasize chemical and physical variables, increasing attempts have been made to develop biological monitoring programs using aquatic organisms as a measure of environmental quality. One example of this type of monitoring is the Aquatic Life Survey, jointly designed and managed by the US EPA and the US Fish and Wildlife Service. The survey collects information on fish presence, productivity, habitat influences, usability and population trends.

National Trails System Act, 1968, US

Enacted by the US Congress in 1968, legislation to establish a national trails system. By 1979, 257 national recreational trails had been designated, including 21 trails for those using wheelchairs, and 13 trails for the use of blind people with directional and other signs in braille.

In 1979, the US President announced that the Forest Service would establish 145 new trails, reaching a goal of two trails for each forest system unit, and each federal land management agency would announce by January 1980 a goal for national trails on its lands. By December 1980, 75 new trails would be established on public lands other than national forests; the Secretary of the Interior would assist other agencies in surveying existing trails on federal lands to determine which can be made part of the national trails system; all agencies would encourage states, localities, Indian tribes and private landholders to designate trails; and legislation would be submitted to Congress to designate the 250 km Natchez Trace National Trail through Tennessee, Alabama and Mississippi.

National Trust

A British organization founded in 1895 and incorporated in the National Trust Act 1907 for the purpose of promoting the preservation of, and access to, buildings of historic and architectural interest and land of natural beauty. The trust was established partly through the efforts of Octavia Hill (1838–1912), the housing reformer. It serves England, Wales and Northern Ireland. The National Trust for Scotland was founded in 1931. By 1995, the National Trust owned 207 stately homes and about 270 000 ha of rolling hills and graceful gardens.

The first acquisition was cliff land at Dinas Oleu, overlooking Cardigan Bay in Wales, Others have included Bannockburn Monument, Chartwell, Cliveden, Culloden, parts of Hadrian's Wall, Hatfield Forest, Knole, Lyme Park, Penrhyn Castle, Petworth House, Powis Castle, Runnymede, Sudbury Hall and Wallington Hall. The two trusts are dependent financially on voluntary support in the form of donations, legacies, admission fees, the annual subscription of members, and some support from the Treasury.

National Wildlife Refuges, US

A national system of refuges and sanctuaries for wildlife developed at a federal and state level in the United States during the twentieth century, assisted by federal funds.

Reservation of federal land as national wildlife refuges was accomplished initially by executive orders of the President, the first refuge being Pelican Island off the east coast of Florida, established by Theodore Roosevelt in 1903. Many early bird sanctuaries, however, were created by the National Audubon society, a citizens' organization, to preserve egret rookeries in the south. The severe decline of waterfowl and shore birds (such as egrets, herons, ibises and pigeons) because of overshooting and drought, and diminishing populations of larger mammals (such as bison, bears, deer, moose, antelopes and beaver), evident during the first decades of the twentieth century, stimulated reservation of large federal units such as Malheur and Upper Klamath national wildlife refuges in Oregon, the Pribilof Islands reservation in Alaska, the National Bison Range in Montana and the Wichita Mountains wildlife refuge in Oklahoma. By 1929, there were 87 federal refuges in 24 states and the territories. By 1975, however, there were over 280 national wildlife refuges. Through the Wildlife Restoration Act 1937, states were given financial assistance in the acquisition and development of suitable lands for wildlife.

The growth of such a large and varied system of federal refuges, and the concurrent development of refuges and sanctuaries by the states and private organizations, is evidence of changed attitudes toward wildlife on the part of many American people. Since consumers seldom are dependent on game meat for food, hunting is regulated to preserve species for future generations. During the twentieth century there developed a large body of public opinion interested in wildlife for its own sake and as a source of personal enjoyment and scientific study.

National Zoological Park

Located in Washington, DC, a zoo created by the Smithsonian Institution by acts of Congress in 1889 and 1890, when a site in the wooded valley of Rock Creek was acquired. The zoo has developed one of the finest small mammal collections in the world and has collected rare animals, many presented by foreign embassies.

Natural Justice, Rules of

Procedures to be followed by any person or body charged with the duty of adjudicating upon disputes between parties, or conducting a public inquiry into a controversial issue, where a few or many parties and interests may be involved. The chief rules are to act fairly, in good faith, without bias, and in a judicial manner, thus giving each party the opportunity of adequately presenting that party's case while being able to contradict and correct arguments from other parties. All evidence and argument should be heard in public at the most convenient place for all; an adjudicator or commissioner should not meet parties in private, save in the most extreme circumstances, for example, when material of commercial sensitivity must be heard. The commissioner should be totally impartial without conflict of interest or any kind of compromise. Relevant documents should be available to all parties. Questions may be put to parties but usually only through the commissioner. Cross-examination in many public inquiries is allowed rarely and in special circumstances, to avoid the intimidation of residents by learned counsel. The timing of appearances may be adjusted to suit work and family considerations. Applications for adjournments must be carefully considered. In short, not only should justice be done, but it should be seen to be done. The principles of natural justice extend back to the statutory framework creating bodies of appeal and commissions of inquiry. The giving of public notice of a pending inquiry or hearing in appropriate places is important, as is the timing of events.

The public hearing has become a routine matter in the USA, Britain, Australia, New Zealand and in some other countries. In Britain, the public inquiry may be traced back to the early 1900s, turning initially on slum-clearance schemes. It is now a common means of handling appeals against decisions by local authorities to the Department of the Environment, relating to planning decisions, matters involving compulsory purchase, redevelopment schemes, highways, airports, planning schemes, port developments and major infrastructure.

In 1957, the Franks Commission was appointed by the British Lord Chancellor to study administrative tribunals and such procedures as the holding of a public inquiry. The committee declared that the work of administrative tribunals and of public inquiries should be characterized by openness, fairness and impartiality. Their report discussed these aims in great detail. The recommendations were largely accepted and resulted in the Tribunals and Enquiries Act of 1958.

See also:
Administrative Law.

Natural Resources Inventory

A study of the natural features of a community's environment; the product of such a study should be a series of maps showing the distribution of environmental features coupled with a written explanation of their importance for the community and its future land uses. The inventory should not be solely descriptive but include an interpretation of the data to show how and why it poses some limitation or opportunity for land use. For example, it is important to know where soils are likely to cause problems of erosion, leaky basements, or malfunctioning septic tanks.

Natural resources inventories should identify areas which pose:

- hazards to certain uses such as subsidence or landslide-prone areas;
- physical limitations which will make development more expensive or involve major environmental impacts such as soils which are unsuitable for use as disposal fields for septic tank effluent, or steeply sloped areas requiring major earth moving and vegetation removal;
- opportunities for certain kinds of uses such as a potential for high agricultural production;
- opportunities for multiple use of an area such as extraction of mineral deposits prior to use for residential or other purposes; and
- opportunities for the enjoyment of unique natural or scenic areas.

Nature and Monuments Conservation Act, 1974, Greenland

An act passed by the Danish Folketing in 1974 which provides for the conservation of nature, archaeological remains, and buildings, in the dependency of Greenland. Under this act, the whole of the northeastern part of Greenland has been classified as a national park.

As a hunting, nomadic people, Greenland's Eskimo population has existed for thousands of years in myriads of scattered, tiny communities. It was not until about 250 years ago that European colonization encouraged the population to congregate in rather large communities. About 1925, climatic changes caused havoc with the traditional industries of sealing, whaling and other forms of hunting. The seal was the first marine mammal of significance to evacuate Greenland waters. Fortunately the disappearance of the seal more or less coincided with an invasion of fish – chiefly cod – but this change meant a swing in the Greenlander's way of life from a subsistence economy to a money economy. These vital modifications in Greenlandic life further promoted the trend toward urban settlements, which was again encouraged by industrialization of the fishing industry after the Second World War.

The physical planning of development in Greenland began around 1950, master plans being prepared at that time for the four more important urban centers. Mining and oil recovery may bring new opportunities to the business community in Greenland, and these must be controlled.

Nature Conservancy, UK

Created by Royal Charter in 1949, a crown body under the supervision of a committee of the Privy Council, with the purpose of advising scientifically on conservation, operating nature reserves, and undertaking scientific research.

The program of national reserves includes areas in England, Scotland and Wales ranging in size up to approximately 16 000 ha and forming the best available examples of natural or seminatural habitats including arctic–alpine vegetation, bogs, woodlands (both deciduous and coniferous), ferns, grasslands, inland waters, dunes, salt marshes, expanses of shingle, sea cliffs and islands.

The majority of the reserves are open to public access but several are closed except to permit holders. Some are primarily selected as 'living museums' to conserve selected examples of natural communities of plants and animals or to serve as refuges for rarities. Others are partly or mainly used as open-air laboratories on which experiments are conducted into the effects of climate and drainage, or of different types of management treatment such as grazing, planting, fencing and control of burning. Comprehensive records are kept of the elements and changes in the animal life and vegetation and of the enrichment or impoverishment of soils.

The broad purpose of the Conservancy's nature reserves is to provide suitable and secure arrangements for long-term studies of the natural resources of Great Britain and to preserve for future generations the best possible range of examples of the natural vegetation and animal life. These official nature reserves are supplemented by a somewhat larger number of unofficial reserves managed by the Society for the Promotion of Nature Reserves, the Royal Society for the Protection of Birds, the National Trust, the National Trust for Scotland and various regional or country trusts, of which the Norfolk, Yorkshire and Lincolnshire Naturalists' trusts are leading examples. In addition, the conservancy has notified the local planning authorities of more than 1700 sites of special scientific interest, over which the Nature Conservancy must be consulted before permission for development is given. The membership of the Royal Society for the Protection of Birds is now over 330 000.

Nauru

Nauru is an island republic in the southwestern Pacific Ocean, with an area of 21 sq km and a population of little more than 10 000. It has one of the world's smallest parliaments. Nauru's economy has been almost exclusively based on the mining, processing and export of phosphate, the island being originally covered with beds of phosphate rock that were derived from rich deposits of

guano, the excrement of sea birds. The country's GDP had been the highest in
the Pacific, and among the highest worldwide. However, the phosphate deposits by the mid-1990s had been virtually exhausted, while the reclamation
of land for agricultural purposes had lagged behind. Nauru was left as a
moonscape after decades of mining. In 1993, Britain, Australia and New
Zealand agreed on a compensation package, payment being made over 20
years. The Nauru government committed itself to a rehabilitation program to
'recreate the Garden of Eden that was once Nauru'. Nauru subsequently
launched a law suit against Australia in the International Court of Justice at
The Hague, seeking massive additional compensation. Australia settled out of
court in 1993.

Netherlands

The Kingdom of the Netherlands is a constitutional monarchy with a parliament of two legislative houses. Population in 1997 was 15.6 million with a
density of 461 persons per sq km. Located in northwest Europe, the capital is
Amsterdam and The Hague the seat of government. See Box 54 for the
evolution of environmental law.

New Communities Program, US

The systematic development of new towns in the United States of America;
over 30 new towns have been constructed with a population range of 17 000
to 400 000. Following the First World War, four new towns were constructed:
Radburn, New Jersey; Greenhills, Ohio; Greendale, Wisconsin; and Greenbelt,
Maryland. Following the Second World War, construction proceeded on a
more ambitious scale. New cities, mostly in the range 50 000 to 100 000 have
included: Westlake, Valencia, Irvine, Mission Viejo, Laguna Niguel, Rancho
California, Rancho Bernardo, Rancho san Diego, Reston, Columbia, St.
Charles, Fort Lincoln, Audubon, Radisson, Roosevelt Island, Riverton,
Cananda, Flower Mound, San Antonio Ranch, The Woodlands, Clearlake,
Park Forest, Jonathan, Cedar-Riverside and Soul City. About half these towns
have had the support of the US federal government. On the whole, the towns
have remained largely residential in character unable to attract industry or
approach self-sufficiency. The program faltered in the recession of the 1970s
under the impact of rising interest rates.

See also:
New Towns Act, 1946, UK.

Box 54   Netherlands: evolution of environmental law

1918   Dutch Elm disease identified
1930   Hoge Veluwe National Park established
1966   Prevention of Pollution of Surface Water Act
1984   Netherlands government releases a plan to reduce industrial sulphur dioxide emissions by 70 per cent, nitrogen oxide emissions from motor vehicles by 30 per cent, and ammonia from agricultural fertilizers by 50 per cent, by the year 2000
1986   Environment Protection Act stipulating EIA procedures, scheduling works requiring EIA, and requiring post-project analysis
1989   The Hague Conference on the environment; National Environmental Policy Plan identifying objectives to be achieved by the years 2000 and 2010
1990   Report of an Evaluation Commission on the Environment Protection Act concludes that EIA procedures were working reasonably well
1991   Dutch Packaging Covenant
1992   Environmental Protection Act amendments: EIA to promote sustainable development
1993   Netherlands government to take potential consequences for the environment and sustainable development into consideration in national decision-making
1994   Environmental Management Act; Environmental Impact Assessment Decree
1995   Life expectancy: 76.4 years for males; 80.4 years for females
1997   Kyoto target: 92
1998   Strengthening of dikes on major rivers completed

New Source Performance Standards (NSPS)

New Source Performance Standards, in respect to new omission sources, including new coal-fired power plants, are standards set by the US federal government. They represent the best that is technically possible, taking costs, energy, health and welfare into account. The US EPA has adopted standards for over 60 categories of plant (such as cement, steel and glass plants) and equipment (such as incinerators, gas turbines and fluoride recycling units). Most of the plants existing at the time of the new requirements has since been reconstructed or replaced, thus having to meet the NSPS.

New Towns Act, 1946, UK

The legislative basis of a system of new towns in Britain; the aim was to achieve a measure of urban decentralization, relieving population pressures in the metropolitan areas which in turn would become revitalized. The new towns were to be self-contained, with the provision of local job opportunities; they were not intended simply to become dormitory towns only for commuters to sleep in. Social balance was also intended, at least in the sense of class balance in the community; the towns would, however, provide for different economic groups and social status.

The first generation of new towns around London were basically in the 50 000 to 100 000 population range; later second generation towns were in the 150 000 to 200 000 population range. The key to the structure of each town was the appointment of a development corporation, the board being appointed by the Environment Secretary. However, the central government has always maintained a strong role. The development corporations have been able to borrow from the UK Treasury for periods of 60 years at current interest rates. The corporations have also been able to buy land needed through a simplified form of compulsory purchase.

The British new towns, over thirty in all, include Bracknell, Harlow, Stevenage, Crawley, Hemel Hempstead, Hatfield, Welwyn Garden City, Telford, Basildon, Corby, Peterlee, Milton Keynes, Peterborough and Northampton. Self-containment has not always been achieved, and life in the new towns for some has been disappointing. A central problem has been the provision of basic infrastructure, such as hospitals, shopping centers in the suburbs, and institutions for higher education and training; some of these could not be provided while the population was relatively small. Life has not proved necessarily better than in the larger cities. However the achievement in the creation of so many new centers has been very great.

New Zealand

New Zealand is a constitutional monarchy with one legislative house. Population in 1997 was 3.6 million with a density of 13.5 persons per sq km. Located in the southeast Pacific, the capital is Wellington in the North Island. A member of the Australia and New Zealand Environment and Conservation Council (ANZECC). See Box 55 for the evolution of environmental law.

Box 55   *New Zealand: evolution of environmental law*

1874   Forest Act
1894   Tongariro National Park established, the first
1907   Animals Protection Act, to protect indigenous animal species
       and native birds
1941   Soil Conservation and Rivers Control Act; Soil Conservation
       and Rivers Control Council established
1952   Fiordland National Park established
1953   Mount Cook National Park established
1959   Antarctic Treaty signed
1964   Mount Aspiring National Park established
1967   Water and Soil Conservation Act
1972   Clean Air Act
1974   Commission for the Environment created; EIA procedures in-
       troduced by Cabinet
1977   Town and Country Planning Act
1981   Public Works Act
1985   *Rainbow Warrior*, flagship of Greenpeace, sunk in Auckland Har-
       bour by French terrorists acting for the French government
1986   Environment Act; Ministry for the Environment established; For-
       est Act; Parliamentary Commissioner for the Environment
       appointed
1987   Conservation Act; Department of Conservation set up; Clean
       Air Zone created in Christchurch; unleaded petrol introduced
1989   Tasman Conservation Accord to safeguard 52 areas of native
       forest throughout New Zealand
1990   Ozone Layer Protection Act
1991   Resource Management Act; Antarctica Protocol signed; conven-
       tion on the prohibition of fishing with long drift nets signed;
       additional tax on lead in petrol
1994   New Zealand industry required to reduce carbon dioxide emis-
       sions over three years, or face a carbon tax
1996   Life expectancy: 74.0 years for males; 80.0 years for females
1997   Kyoto target: 100
2000   Resource Management (Costs) Amendment Act: Resource Man-
       agement (Amendment) Act

Nigeria

The Federal Republic of Nigeria had a population in 1997 of 99 million at a density of 112 persons per sq km. Located in the Gulf of Guinea, west Africa, the capital is Abuja with Lagos as the major city. See Box 56 for the evolution of environmental law.

Box 56   Nigeria: evolution of environmental law

1969   The Petroleum Act restrains pollution

1976   Environmental Planning and Protection Division created within the Ministry of Industry, later transferred in 1979 to Ministry of Housing and Environment. River Basin Authorities created

1980   A federal housing program provides for the construction of low-cost housing for low- and middle-income workers in the state capitals and other large towns. The program seeks to combat the growth of shantytowns and slum districts generally. Health conditions are particularly poor in the suburbs of Greater Lagos and other large cities

1988   Federal Environmental Protection Agency Decree

1992   Environmental Impact Assessment Decree

1997   Public expenditure increases in respect of infrastructure, agriculture, water resources, rural development and urban sanitation

1998   Transfer of power to a civilian president

Noise Control Act, 1972, US

A measure aimed at 'the promotion of an environment for all Americans free from noise jeopardizing their health and welfare', the act authorizes a noise control program encompassing all federal activities and promotes assistance to all communities in the United States for the creation and improvement of noise abatement programs.

Until the 1960s, noise control was chiefly handled by state and local governments. In 1968, an Amendment to the Federal Aviation Act gave the Federal Aviation Agency authority to prescribe standards for measuring and controlling civil aircraft noise, including sonic boom. In 1970, an Amendment to the Clean Air Act authorized the establishment of an Office of Noise Abatement and Control within the US EPA. The Amendment also called for public hearings and a special report by the EPA to Congress. The result was the Noise Control Act, 1972.

Programs developed under the act have been a driving force behind all legislation, state and local, in the United States; a majority of the population is now covered by state legislation and regulations. The EPA has been responsible for programs in noise abatement known as ECHO (Each Community Helps Others); and for the preparation of Model Noise Control Ordinances in respect to different classes of noise. Many federal agencies now have noise control responsibilities; those undertaken by the EPA include:

- regulations on the operation of interstate motor and rail carriers;
- regulations on new products that are major sources of noise, including such controls as anti-tampering, warranty and useful life provisions;
- labeling of products that produce noise capable of adversely affecting public health or welfare or products that are marketed for their noise attenuation characteristics;
- providing technical assistance to state and local units of government desiring to develop and enforce noise abatement and control programs;
- public information dissemination to inform citizens of the hazards of noise to public health and welfare; and
- certification of low noise emission products.

North American Agreement on Environmental Cooperation (NAAEC)

An agreement reached in 1994 between Canada, the USA and Mexico to foster protection and improvement of the environment for the well-being of present and future generations; to promote sustainable development; to improve cooperation between the parties; to support the environmental goals and objectives of NAFTA; and promote economically efficient and effective environmental measures.

The NAAEC established a Commission for Environmental Cooperation with a secretariat and an advisory committee. It provides for a mechanism under which any NGO or person may report to the secretariat a party's apparent failure to effectively enforce the environmental law. A party may bring proceedings against another for persistently failing to effectively enforce its environmental laws. An action plan may be enforced to remedy the situation, or other measures adopted.

North American Free Trade Agreement (NAFTA)

An agreement concluded in 1994 between the USA, Canada and Mexico to form a free trade area; its aim is the phased abolition of tariffs, within a decade, on most goods traded between the three countries. NAFTA builds upon the pre-existing US–Canada Free Trade Agreement. The new agreement met with much hostility in the USA, being opposed by some sections of organized labor, environmentalists, consumer groups and political elements from right and left. It was argued that employers would seek to profit from lower wages and lower environmental standards in Mexico. Supporters of NAFTA argue that the provisions of the agreement are in harmony with the WTO and do not create new barriers to goods from other countries. Indeed, discussion has now ranged to a concept of a free trade area stretching from Alaska to Cape Horn, embracing 34 governments and 800 million consumers. Negotiations are due to be completed in 2005. Such an arrangement would have implications for other free trade groupings such as the Central American Common Market, the Andean Group and MERCOSUR.

Norway

The Kingdom of Norway is a constitutional monarchy with one legislative house. Population in 1997 was 4.4 million at a density of 13.6 persons per sq km. Located in northwest Europe with Sweden as her immediate neighbor, the capital is Oslo. The Prime Minister of Norway (Gro Harlem Brundtland) chaired the World Commission on Environment and Development. A member of the Nordic Council. See Box 57 for the evolution of environmental law.

NSW Council on Environmental Education

In 1999, the New South Wales government, Australia, created a Council on Environmental Education. The Council's main functions are set out in the Protection of the Environment Administration Amendment (Environmental Education) Act 1998. They are to advise the NSW government on key issues, trends and research requirements relating to environmental education, and to coordinate the preparation of statewide three-year plans for environmental education. The council is an independent body of 12 persons. It includes representatives from the Nature Conservation Council, the Australian Association for Environmental Education, the Local Government and Shires Association, peak industry and employer organizations, and a representative of the universities in New South Wales.

Box 57   Norway: evolution of environmental law

1957   Open-air Recreation Act
1959   Antarctic Treaty signed
1962   Rondane National Park established
1964   Salmon and Freshwater Fishing Act
1970   Nature Conservation Act; Nordic Council formed
1972   Ministry of Environment established
1973   Spitzbergen National Park established
1976   Product Control Act
1977   Watercourses Act
1978   Cultural Heritage Act
1981   Pollution Control Act; Wildlife Act
1983   Conservation of the natural environment in Svalbard
1985   Planning and Building Act, with EIA provisions
1986   Conservation of the natural environment in Jan Mayen
1987   Prime Minister Gro Harlem Brundtland presents the report of the World Commission on Environment and Development *Our Common Future* to the General Assembly of the UN
1988   Oslo Conference on sustainable development
1989   Amendment of the Pollution Control Act and the Planning and Building Act; restrictions on sale of detergents
1990   ECE conference on Action for a Common Future held in Bergen
1991   Introduction of a carbon dioxide tax applied to oil, natural gas and coal, accounting for about 60 per cent of carbon dioxide emissions, with the highest tax rate on gasoline (petrol)
1992   Amendment of the Salmon and Freshwater Fishing Act and Cultural Heritage Act; a plan for national parks presented to the Storting (parliament)
1994   Life expectancy: 74.9 years for males; 80.6 years for females
1997   Kyoto target: 101
1998   White Paper presented to the Storting on the Implementation of the Kyoto Protocol. Commission of experts appointed to devise a system of emission trading; Gro Harlem Brundtland heads the WHO
2000   Report of the Commission of Experts presented to the Ministry of the Environment

O

Occupational Health and Safety

An area of law concerned with the working environment of immediate concern to employers and workers. It is not strictly regarded as environmental law, though certain malpractices may present hazards to the public as well as operatives. Health and safety legislation embraces occupational diseases as well as physical hazards. Adequate measures involve careful planning, ventilation, lighting, safeguards, safety and emergency procedures, routine inspections, monitoring, records, personal protection by way of suitable clothing and masks, controlled atmospheres, medical and psychological supervision, workforce consultation, and health and safety rules built into enterprise and individual employment agreements.

Office of Environmental Protection, Switzerland

An agency created by the Swiss government in 1971. Article 2 of the Federal Council decree assigns to the office the following functions:
- drafting federal laws and orders concerning the protection of the natural environment and, in particular, the protection of waters, fishing, the preservation of clean air and noise control;
- enforcing such laws and orders where the cantons are not competent to do so under the federal constitution or the law;
- supervising the implementation of federal laws and orders by the cantons;
- cooperating with the federal and cantonal departments which deal with problems relating to the protection of the natural environment, and coordinating the work of these bodies in accordance with a uniform policy;
- taking emergency measures;
- publishing technical instructions and formulating principles and guidelines in agreement with the federal services concerned;
- advising federal services, cantons, municipalities and organizations on questions relating to the protection of the natural environment;
- informing the public on the need for and significance and organization of protection of the natural environment;
- assisting in the drafting and implementation of international agreements and conventions on the protection of the natural environment; and

234

• the enforcement of a 1997 regulation that heavy goods vehicles using Swiss roads be subject to an environmental tax calculated on the distance traveled.

Official Aid

Or foreign aid, a transfer internationally of funds either as grants or loans, goods, or services in the form of skills or technical training. Foreign aid as an instrument of national policy began in the eighteenth century and has continued ever since; often it embraced the transfer of arms and training, subsidies to allies, inducements to waverers, and then gradually involved economic objectives and humanitarian aims. Noteworthy, in 1947, was the European Recovery Program (known as the Marshall Plan). Later, the communist bloc countries and the Western powers competed for advantages among the developing nations. The USA traditionally furnished the most aid in absolute terms.

In recent years, multilateral programs have grown steadily, the major agency being the World Bank (International Bank for Reconstruction and Development) which began operations in 1946 as an independent agency of the UN. Several regional development banks also undertake lending in their respective areas: the Inter-American Development Bank, the African Development Bank, and the Asian Development Bank; the European Development Fund; the European Investment Bank and the Global Environment Facility. Grants are also awarded by such agencies as UNESCO, the WHO, and the FAO of the UN.

In 1970, the UN General Assembly recommended targets for the transfer of aid from the richer to poorer nations of a minimum net amount of one per cent of GDP by the year 1972 if possible, and not later than 1975. Of this, official aid should reach a minimum of 0.7 per cent of GDP. Since 1970, the official target for bilateral and multilateral funding of 0.7 per cent has been reaffirmed many times; for example, by the Brandt Commission; UNCED 1992; the UN Conference on Population and Development 1994; and the World Conference on Social Development 1995. Four industrial nations have met and sometimes exceeded this target. In 1975, official aid among the OECD nations stood at 0.32 per cent, falling to just over 0.3 per cent in 1993.

In 1995, the rich countries of the OECD donated a total of $59 billion in foreign aid to poor countries, about as much as the year before; allowing for inflation, this represented a decline in real terms. As a group, the OECD gave assistance still worth only 0.3 per cent of their combined GDP, the lowest ratio since the UN announced its target of 0.7 per cent in 1970. Of the total contributed, the US now gave $7.3 billion, or 12.4 per cent of the total. This compared with $14.5 by Japan, or 24.6 per cent.

Oil Pollution Act, 1990, US

An act which increases and extends civil and criminal liability limits for the clean-up of oil spilled from vessels; requires better planning and preparedness and measures to improve navigation safety; sets new standards for vessel constructions, crew licensing and staffing of vessels.

The act was a response to the *Exxon Valdez* disaster in Prince William Sound, Alaska. The act brought into operation the Oil Spill Liability Trust Fund. The fund derives revenues from an excise tax per barrel of oil received at US refineries and on other petroleum products. Claims may be made on the fund. Specified claimants can recover damages for injury or loss to natural resources and real or personal property. Thus the act imposes extensive financial responsibilities on the owners and operators of vessels, offshore facilities and deepwater ports. The act seeks to minimize and prevent oil pollution.

Oil Pollution Compensation and Insurance

The International Oil Pollution Compensation Fund (IOPC Fund) is a worldwide intergovernmental entity created by the IMO under two conventions, the Civil Liability Convention and the Fund Convention which came into force in 1975 and 1978, respectively. In 1995, some 91 nations were parties to the Civil Liability Convention and 66 nations were parties to the Fund Convention.

The Civil Liability Convention lays down the principle of strict liability for shipowners in respect of oil pollution damage and creates a system of compulsory liability insurance. The Fund Convention provides for compensating victims when compensation under the Civil Liability Fund proves inadequate. The IOPC Fund is administered by a secretariat located in London, UK. The conventions apply only to spills of *persistent* oil such as crude oil, fuel oil, heavy diesel oil and lubricating oil. Damage arising from non-persistent oil such as gasoline, light diesel oil and kerosine is excluded from the conventions. Non-persistent oils tend to evaporate quickly and do not require cleaning up. The conventions cover incidents therefore in which persistent oil has escaped or been discharged from a seagoing vessel actually carrying oil in bulk as cargo at the time of the spill, and within the territory or territorial sea of a nation which is a party to one or both conventions. Spills from tankers during ballast voyages, and spills from ships other than tankers are not covered.

Pollution damage include the costs of measures taken after an oil spill has occurred to prevent or minimize pollution damage, and includes clean-up operations on shore and at sea. Reasonable costs for the disposal of collected material are allowed. Claims for pure economic loss by victims are also admissible. Initial and annual contributions are payable by parties to the conventions; the level of contributions to the fund vary from year to year.

In 1994, the USA introduced Certificates of Financial Responsibility (COFR) to be carried by all oil tankers entering US waters. Their purpose is to provide insurance against the possibilities of environmental damage. This requirement springs from the US Oil Pollution Act of 1990, legislation introduced following the *Exxon Valdez* disaster.

See also:
Exxon Valdez Disaster.

OK Tedi Mine Operation, Papua New Guinea (PNG)

OK Tedi is a large copper and gold mine located in the remote Western Province of Papua New Guinea. The mine has been in operation since 1984 and is run by OK Tedi Mining Limited. Shareholders in OK Tedi are the Broken Hill Propriety Company Limited (BHP) (52 per cent), the government of Papua New Guinea (30 per cent) and Inmet Mining Corporation of Canada (18 per cent). The development phase of OK Tedi was long and costly, though it now makes a major contribution to the economy of the country. The biophysical environment is varied and subject to rapid changes; it is a difficult locality for people to live and work in. The area is subject to frequent volcanic activity, while the climate is equatorial.

The operation is based on a world-class copper–gold ore body that forms the core of Mt Fubiland in the central mountain range; the development program took over eight years and cost US$1.4 billion. Copper concentrate is sold under long-term contracts to smelters in Japan, Germany, Finland, South Korea and the Philippines. In 1991 an inaugural dividend was paid.

Most land in Papua New Guinea is owned in a complex and traditional system of private and clan ownership. Minerals and petroleum which lie underground are owned by the state, while forests and other resource above ground are owned by the clan. This leads to great legal complexities and disputes. Two groups of landowners have an interest in the OK Tedi mine; the first group are the landowners in the mine area itself, and the second are the landowners living further downstream from the mine along the banks of the OK Tedi and the Fly River.

Around the mine, the people receive lease and royalty payments, at set rates. Compensation payments are also made for special purposes. The lower OK Tedi–Fly River Development Trust was established in 1990, to spread benefits more widely.

PNG government environmental regulations are based on comprehensive studies of the effects of mine sediment on the waters and fish of the Fly River. The primary environmental control is a maximum limit on the mine's contribution to naturally high river sediment levels, known as the Acceptable Particulate Level (APL) of 940 mg/litre. Other controls cover changes in fish biomass, dissolved and particulate copper concentrations and river bed sedimentation. Monitoring is designed to provide warning of potential impacts on water and fish in river channels, floodplains, off-river water bodies and the Fly estuary.

An average of 60 million tonnes a year of ore residue and overburden is discharged into the OK Tedi River; about 40 million tonnes of this reaches the Fly River, which carries 88 million tonnes of natural sediments each year.

The management and disposal of tailings materials has presented significant problems. In 1983–84, after work on a dam to contain the tailings from the mine was well under way, the dam foundations collapsed due to landslip activity. Since that time, some 120 studies have been undertaken on waste retention schemes. These studies led BHP to the conclusion that, given the specific characteristics of the region, the stability and long-term safety of a tailings dam could not be assured. The search to limit impacts has continued, however.

The continued release of tailings has had some adverse effects. At the foot of the mountain range in which the mine is located, the river slows down and sediment is deposited on its bed and along its banks. At times of heavy rain, this causes flooding so some sediment is left as mud over gardens and around riverside trees, causing dieback. The main effect of this deposition may be seen along a 20 km stretch extending over an area of some 30 sq km. Compensation has been paid to villagers. See Box 58.

Open Cut Mining

A technique of mining employed when the coal is not far below the surface. The overlying earth and rock are mechanically stripped to expose the coal, which is then removed with or without blasting. A variant is opencast mining, where coal seams are mined near their outcrops, that is near the point at which coal appears at the surface. Open cut mining is also known as strip mining. In 1977, the US established the first uniform federal controls over strip mining, which had previously been a state matter. The legislation requires the restoration of stripped land so that it will serve the same or similar function as it did prior to mining. It gave farmers and ranchers the right to veto the mining of their land, even if they did not own the mineral rights,

---

Box 58   History of OK Tedi

1966   Geologists from the Kennecott Copper Corporation discover a major mineral deposit at Mt Fubiland

1975   Kennecott withdraw from the project. Negotiations begin between the PNG government and BHP

1976   Concession Agreement signed

1981   OK Tedi Mining Ltd (OTML) incorporated. Development of minesite infrastructure; treatment facilities for copper ore; and construction of a power station. Mining lease granted

1984   Production begins as an open cut operation; massive landslides destroy tailings dam; gold production commences

1987   BHP appointed managing shareholder in OTML; copper production commences

1989   PNG government establishes maximum sediment level from mining to the Fly River

1990   Lower OK Tedi/Fly River Development Trust formed

1991   Inaugural dividend paid

1993   Ownership restructure announced

1995   Since 1981, 1548 employees have received education and training; Ralph Nader campaigns against BHP. Villagers bring $4 billion damages claim against BHP in the Victorian Supreme Court. The plaintiffs claimed that the mine had destroyed their traditional way of life. Compensation offered by BHP of $110 million to villagers, payment of legal costs, and renewed attempt at tailings-waste control, perhaps totalling $500 million, ending the two-year court battle

1996   On 11 June, BHP and the solicitors for the plaintiffs Slater and Gordon confirmed an agreement to resolve the litigation concerning the OK Tedi Mine. The PNG government proposed an independent inquiry into a preferred option for a tailings disposal scheme

Sources: BHP publications and Press Releases; Slater and Gordon Press Releases; PNG government announcements; an article by Ralph Nader 27 February 1996 in *The Sydney Morning Herald*; Annual Report 1995 of the Lower OK Tedi/Fly River Development Trust; Geoff Clarke case studies.

---

while establishing a restoration fund. Box 59 summarizes the economic, social and environmental elements to be considered in the environmental impact assessment of a mining proposal.

Box 59   Open cut mining: economic, social and environmental elements to be considered

1.   The contribution to meeting energy demands, including export opportunities, that the mine might meet.
2.   The alternatives to the proposal by way of alternative sites, or alternative ways of meeting energy demands.
3.   The consistency of the proposal with national, regional or local planning instruments; the relationship with national parks, wilderness areas or nature reserves.
4.   The prospective life of the mine and the staging of operations.
5.   Coal handling, processing and stockpiling facilities.
6.   Rail loading facilities.
7.   Road loading facilities.
8.   Rail spur lines.
9.   Access roads.
10.   The industrial area of the site including bathhouse amenities, plant maintenance workshops, administrative buildings and ancillary facilities.
11.   The various water management structures, site haul roads, construction facilities and dragline erection area.
12.   The rehabilitation program.
13.   Landscaping and site perimeter screen planting.
14.   Vegetation and topsoil stripping; topsoil stockpiles.
15.   Overburden removal and dumping areas.
16.   Details of the coal preparation plant and stockpiles.
17.   Handling of tailings from the coal preparation plant.
18.   Water for the washery and for road dust suppression.
19.   Details of the sewerage treatment system.
20.   Heavy vehicles access and movement during the construction phase and the operational phases.
21.   The routes chosen for heavy vehicles.
22.   Project employment during the construction and operational phases; the housing of employees.
23.   The existing environment and its modification as a result of the intended mining operation.
24.   The arrangement for mine drainage and prevention of water pollution.
25.   Unwanted rock waste and backfilling.
26.   The effect of the mine on habitats, fishing, biodiversity and wildlife.

Box 59   *continued*

27.   Pollution consequences in terms of air, water and noise.
28.   The implications for aesthetics, amenity, ecology and health on nearby residential districts.
29.   The implications for local industry.
30.   Environmental management of the mine.
31.   Potential damage to or destruction of archaeological or historic sites.
32.   The implications for sacred and cultural sites.
33.   Facilities for monitoring and post-project analysis.
34.   The risks and hazards of a major industrial project.
35.   The implications for training.
36.   The implications for technology in a national context.
37.   The implications in respect of foreign investment.
38.   The implications in respect of trade and the balance of payments.
39.   The political implications of the project.
40.   The arrangements for continuing public involvement following the initial EIA.
41.   The proponent's contribution to local infrastructure development and social facilities; improved roads, underpasses and overpasses for people and farm animals.
42.   Electricity transmission lines, easements and access roads; prospective routes.
43.   Emergency services and responses.
44.   Annual report to the environmental, planning and energy agencies.
45.   Prospective future developments in the same district or region, which might suggest cumulative impacts.
46.   Arrangements for the acquisition of houses and properties which are likely to impede the progress of the mine or otherwise be adversely affected.
47.   Proposals by the government for mine bonding.

Organization for Economic Cooperation and Development (OECD)

An international body which came into being in 1961, succeeding the Organization for European Economic Cooperation (OEEC). The members of the OECD include Australia, Austria, Belgium, Canada, the Czech Republic,

Denmark, Finland, France, Germany, Greece, Hungary, Iceland, Ireland, Italy, Japan, Korea (South), Luxembourg, Mexico, the Netherlands, New Zealand, Norway, Poland, Portugal, Spain, Sweden, Switzerland, Turkey, the UK and the USA, being some 29 democratic countries with market economies. The OECD has as its primary aim the achievement of the highest sustainable level of economic growth in its member countries with the expansion of world trade on a multilateral basis.

In 1970, the governing council of the OECD created an environment committee to advise on patterns of growth and development which would be in harmony with protection of the world. This committee took a lead in promoting the polluter-pays principle. In 1974, a Declaration on Environment Policy was adopted. In 1985, the OECD extended the principles of EIA to development assistance projects and programs, in order to mitigate potentially adverse environmental effects. Since then, the OECD has also encouraged the use of economic instruments in environmental policy. Subsequent work has resulted in recommendations on the use of economic instruments as quoted in Box 60.

Box 60   *Recommendations of the Council on the use of Economic Instruments in Environmental Policy, January 1991*

Inter alia, Member countries should:
- make greater and more consistent use of economic instruments as a complement to, or a substitute for, other policy instruments such as regulations, taking into account national socioeconomic conditions;
- work towards improving the allocation and efficient use of natural and environmental resources by means of economic instruments so as to better reflect the social cost of using those resources;
- make efforts to reach further agreements at an international level on the use of environmental policy instruments with respect to solving regional and global environmental problems as well as ensuring sustainable development; and
- develop better modeling, forecasting and monitoring techniques to provide information on the environmental consequences of alternative policies and their economic effects.

P

Parker Windscale Inquiry, UK

In early 1978, a British judicial inquiry that reported on a proposed major expansion of the Windscale nuclear waste reprocessing plant which would convert uranium oxide waste into reusable uranium and plutonium. Windscale would thus open the way for greater adoption of plutonium using fast breeder reactors. The inquiry, conducted by Mr Justice Parker, heard all sides of the uranium debate. The anti-nuclear lobby argued that a large increase in plutonium output from reprocessing plants such as Windscale would be a threat to world peace. Mr Justice Parker concluded, however, that there was more likely to be a potentially dangerous proliferation of such plants around the world if Britain did not expand its facilities. The inquiry concluded that there was no sufficient reason to halt the proposed expansion.

In May 1978, the House of Commons endorsed the recommendations of the judicial inquiry that a major reprocessing plant should be built at Windscale. This vote was a rejection of the anti-proliferation policies of the US government announced by President Carter in 1977. The UK was now firmly committed to nuclear waste reprocessing, and a plutonium future. The new plant would take ten years to complete. The issue remains controversial to the present time.

Phosphate Cooperative Co. of Australia Ltd v. Environment Protection Authority

A case involving a decision of the Australian High Court, in which it was argued that economic considerations should be relevant when the Environment Protection Authority (EPA) of Victoria sets licensing conditions. The High Court found that the work of the EPA was the protection of the environment and that the economic consequences for the licensee and community were irrelevant. It was a majority decision by the High Court following an earlier judgment in the Victorian Supreme Court. The arguments of the High Court in the Phosphate case were valid only in relation to the licensing provisions in the Environment Protection Act 1970.

Source: Phosphate Cooperative Co. of Australia Ltd v. Environment Protection Authority (1976) 4 VPA 159; Phosphate Cooperative Co. of Australia Ltd. v. Environment Protection Authority (1978) 52 ALJR 148 at p. 149.

Pippard Committee on the Tidal Thames, 1961

In 1961, a committee chaired by Sutton Pippard reported to the Minister of Housing and Local Government (Mr Henry Brooke) on the effects of heated and other effluents on the condition of the tidal Thames, London, both as at present and in the context of future developments. The committee concluded that:

- There had been a fairly steady deterioration in the condition of the tidal river water since 1930–35, this deterioration becoming much more marked since the Second World War.
- The belt of worst pollution had been gradually extending both up-stream and downstream, and now stretched from Bermondsey to Thames Haven.
- The temperature of the water in the middle reaches had risen since 1920, heated effluents from power stations clearly playing an important part.
- The stretch between London Bridge and Gravesend was often offensive, the predominant source of pollution being the combined discharge of inadequately treated sewage effluent from the northern and southern outfall works; a drastic reduction in this pollution load would improve the river substantially.

The committee also noted the contribution of sulphite to the river from the Battersea and Bankside power stations where the flue gases were washed to remove sulphur.

Following the committee's report, measures were put in hand to clean up the Thames. By 1969, sand goby, flounder and smelt were being found on the screens at Fulham power station which was situated 16 km above London Bridge and 64 km from the sea. In 1985, a seal reached central London in search of fish. The Thames had not been cleaner for more than a century.

Planned Cities

See:
Brasilia; Burley Griffin Plan for Canberra; L'Enfant Plan for Washington, DC, 1974; New Communities Program, US; New Towns Act, 1946, UK.

Planning Commission, US

A planning agency created by a municipality or county, under a state enabling act, for the purposes of planning the area within the corporate limits possibly involving the preparation of a comprehensive plan for future development and the establishment of procedures for implementation; the commission acts in an advisory capacity to the government body and is the legal agency through which planning is carried out.

Hartford, Connecticut, established the first planning commission in the United States in 1907. Since then more than 2000 municipalities and counties have established planning commissions; commissions have also been established for metropolitan areas, regions and states. Planning tools such as zoning and subdivision regulations have become commonplace while programs now embrace matters of long-range as well as short-range concern.

Planning commissions usually consist of up to a dozen members appointed by the government body; the selected members consist of leaders of the community in business, real estate, industry, labor and the professions. Their success depends decisively on the selection of persons interested in the welfare of the community, never an easy task. Planning commissions today are concerned with a wide range of matters including:

- preparation of comprehensive plans, and transportation plans for expressways and parking projects;
- urban renewal and central business district improvement programs;
- public housing programs;
- capital improvement programs;
- control of urban sprawl;
- industrial parks;
- shopping centers and school sites;
- cluster subdivisions and planned unit developments to provide more common open space;
- purchase of easement rights and adoption of other methods to preserve scenic views;
- open space zoning and acquisition of lands for permanent open space; and
- improvement of living conditions in older neighborhoods.

Poland

The Republic of Poland is a unitary multiparty republic with two legislative houses, the Senate and the Diet. Poland has a population of 39 million, at a density of 320 persons per sq km. The capital is Warsaw. Box 61 sets out the environmental legislation introduced since the Second World War.

Box 61   *Poland: evolution of environmental law*

1953   Mining Law allowing the state to conduct all kinds of mining, with protection of the environment

1960   Mining Law amendment

1974   Water Law restricting the dumping of untreated water into rivers, with a deadline of 2000

1980   Environmental Protection Law, aiming to protect the surface of the earth, water and the marine environment, the atmosphere, fauna and flora, landscapes and urban and rural greenery

1989   Law creating the Ministry of Environmental Protection, Natural Resources and Forestry, setting goals for environment protection

1990   Law creating an environmental police enforcing environmental standards for emissions, imposing fines and closing some plants

1991   Law for the Protection of Nature, operates national parks and protects fauna and flora; Forests Law

1994   Landscaping Law; Toll Highways Law protecting nature, agricultural land, forests and national monuments

1997   Extensive Water Law amendments. Life expectancy: 68.3 years for males; 76.9 for females

---

Polluter-pays Principle and the Internationalization of Environmental Costs

Originally, a principle that equates the price charged for the use of environmental resources with the cost of damage inflicted on society by using them. The price charged may be levied directly on the process which generates pollution or as the purchase price of licenses which entitle the holder to generate specific quantities of pollutants. The polluter may find the charges greater than the cost of abating the pollution by pollution-control equipment or changes in the processes or fuels. The difficulty with this procedure is to decide the right price to charge, when the damage to society cannot be assessed in monetary terms in any realistic way. Further, it bestows the right to pollute on any scale; that is the right to continue to damage the health of members of the community in known and unknown ways over time. In addition, there is the inherent problem that the penalty paid may never reach the actual community affected or, if it does, may never be distributed in an equitable way. The effects of some pollutants, such as lead in children, can only be assessed with difficulty; to suggest compensation seems a most inappropriate response when prohibition is to hand. An overriding problem is the problem of attributing atmospheric pollutants to a particular firm when there are several similar plants in the neighborhood. The task of allocating charges to vehicles seems impracticable.

In a later version, a principle that asserts that the full cost of controlling pollution by whatever means to an adequate degree shall be undertaken by the polluter, preferably without public subsidy or tax concession. Hence the potential cost of pollution to society at large is translated into pollution-control costs which are internalized and reflected in the costs of production. Depending on the elasticity of demand, these cost increases may be transferred to the purchasing public. In many cases, the polluter-pays principle becomes a public-pays principle, though the public benefits from the measures taken. While all appropriate measures appear in the accountancy costs of polluters, the adverse environmental effects on the public are minimized or abated.

The polluter-pays principle was affirmed at the UN Conference on the Human Environment held in Stockholm in 1972, and by the OECD in the same year. The principle was reaffirmed by the OECD in 1985. Since then a hybrid philosophy has emerged stressing the need for overall statutory pollution-control regulation and the setting of ceilings augmented by economic instruments to encourage abatement activities beyond the requirements of regulations, to yield a market in pollution credits.

Pollution-control Strategies

Pollution-control measures have been adopted by all countries over the years, with varying degrees of effectiveness. Since 1972, many countries have created environment departments and agencies to manage the whole spectrum of air and water pollution, noise pollution, land contamination, solid and liquid waste disposal, marine pollution and protection of the environment generally. Environmental planning has become a strong feature in many advanced countries; while much more attention is given to the economic base of natural resources. The concept of 'sustainable development' is now referred to in much legislation, while traditional regulation by laws and regulations is now being increasingly supplemented by what are called 'economic instruments'. Above all, the principle of environmental impact assessment has been accepted in many countries. EIA allows a comprehensive view to be taken of all major developments, so that the full implications may be taking into account by the decision-makers, usually local, state or national governments. This is now widely practised in Europe, North America, and all Asian countries. See Box 62 for an outline of pollution-control strategy.

Box 62   Pollution-control strategy; a spectrum of measures to combat pollution both at source and subsequently

Measures include the following:
- The reduction or elimination of the discharge of residuals through emission standards which require changes in production technology, the adoption of gas cleaning, water treatment, or fuel modification.
- The adoption of correct stack heights.
- Waste minimization and the recycling of residuals recovered from domestic and industrial waste streams to the productive system.
- Noise-abatement measures and the control of radioactivity.
- Cleaner production through better housekeeping and management practices.
- The utilization of the assimilative capacity of the natural environment in respect of pollutants unavoidably discharged, in a manner unlikely to impair the environment to any significant extent.
- The minimization of the potential adverse effects of pollution through buffer zones and strategic siting.
- The careful management and siting of landfill sites; the discouragement of littering.
- The careful management and disposal of hazardous wastes.
- Measures to avoid the creation of contaminated sites.
- A system of fees and emission charges to discourage discharges.
- Demand-management of specific products in appropriate cases; product taxes.
- Continuous research into the effects of specific pollutants on human health and welfare, fauna and flora.
- Implementation of international agreements regarding protection of the ozone layer and the emission of greenhouse gases.
- The promotion of sustainable development.

Power Lines and Electromagnetic Radiation

Electromagnetic radiation is energy that is propagated through space or matter in the form of electromagnetic waves such as radio waves, visible light and gamma rays. Such radiation spans an enormous range of frequencies or wavelengths and there are many sources of such radiation, both natural and humanmade. In recent years, electromagnetic rays from power lines (overhead transmission lines) have been suspected of causing leukaemias. Suspicions were aroused when a 1979 Denver report first suggested that children living close to high-energy power lines were two or three times more likely than other children to develop cancer.

In October 1993, the *British Medical Journal* reported conflicting findings emerging from studies of the health effects of power lines. One report, from the Danish Cancer Society, examined 1707 cases of various types of cancer in children over a 20-year period. It found that the number of cases living within 45 metres of power lines was five times higher than would normally have been expected. On the other hand, a Finnish study of almost 135 000 children living within 500 metres of power lines, revealed little variation and reported no increased cancer risk. A report of the British National Radiological Protection Board of 1993 similarly found no strong biological evidence for a general link between electromagnetic radiation and cancer, but went on to say that some Scandinavian evidence suggested a possible link with childhood leukaemia.

In August 1993, the British Institution of Electrical Engineers, reporting on a two-year study also found no clear evidence to link exposure of electromagnetic radiation with cancer. That investigation analysed 245 separate earlier studies in the course of drawing a conclusion.

In June 1997, the *New England Journal of Medicine* published the results of yet another report concluding that children who live near high-voltage power lines do not have a greater risk of developing cancer than other young people. The report was based on an eight-year study coordinated by the National Cancer Institute and involved 1250 subjects in nine states. However, the report met with mixed reactions among health experts (*International Herald Tribune*, 4 July 1997). Some were not prepared to say that there was absolutely no risk.

Precautionary Principle

A principle adopted by UNCED (the Earth Summit) in 1992 that, in order to protect the environment, a precautionary approach should be widely applied. The Rio Declaration on Environment and Development (Principle 15), interprets the precautionary approach as meaning that where there are threats of serious or irreversible damage to the environment, lack of full scientific certainty should not be used as a reason for postponing cost-effective measures to prevent environmental degradation. Critics of this approach are concerned about large commitments of resources to deal with vaguely defined problems. It should be noted, however, that the reference to cost-effective measures implies a high degree of certainty about the nature of the problem.

The precautionary principle already had a long history. It first emerged in Germany in 1980 when it was considered by the European Council of Experts on Environmental Matters in relation to marine pollution. Within a few years, the principle appeared in a variety of documents and treaties, such as the Montreal Protocol on Substances that Deplete the Ozone Layer, 1988; the Bergen Ministerial Declaration on Sustainable Development, 1990; the Convention on the Protection of the Marine Environment of the Baltic Sea, 1992; and the UN Framework Convention on Climate Change and the UN Convention on Biodiversity, both 1992. Since then the concept has been incorporated in the Maastricht Treaty, 1993. There have been few guides as to interpretation.

The British White Paper on the Environment, 1992, stated:

> Where the state of our planet is at stake, the risks can be so high and the costs of corrective action so great, that prevention is better and cheaper than cure ... Where there are significant risks of damage to the environment, the Government will be prepared to take precautionary action to limit the use of potentially dangerous materials or the spread of potentially dangerous pollutants, even when scientific knowledge is not conclusive, if the balance of likely costs and benefits justifies it.

The Australian Intergovernmental Agreement on the Environment, 1992, offers this guidance:

> In the application of the precautionary principle, public and private decisions should be guided by: careful evaluation to avoid, wherever practicable, serious or irreversible damage to the environment; and by an assessment of the risk-weighted consequences.

Clearly there are several different interpretations of the principle and there are many different ideas concerning its application. It may be simply regarded as a reversal of the principle of the burden of proof, that proponents of developments must offer proof that the proposal will not be harmful to the environment, subject to conditions. In which case we are not far from today's public inquiry, now well established in many countries.

A central question today, following the Kyoto Protocol, is whether enormously expensive measures should be adopted now to constrain global warming, when the scientific evidence is not yet conclusive. The precautionary principle will now be tested to the limit.

Private Certification

An arrangement under some planning and environmental legislation to allow some professional associations to accredit and register private certifiers in respect of development, construction, compliance, occupation and subdivision certificates. Normally these functions are performed by local councils and some statutory bodies. Private practitioners operate with adequate insurance cover.

Private certification has been introduced in New South Wales, Australia, through amendments to the Environmental Planning and Assessment Act. In 1998, the Institution of Engineers Australia became the first professional association to gain approval to accredit practitioners as private certifiers. Certificates testify that designs, works, or proposals, comply with relevant standards and conditions, such as subdivision and building standards or codes. Certifiers may be audited.

Product Charges or Ecotaxes

Taxes on inputs to economic activities, or on products and services themselves, as a means of indirectly controlling environmental impacts. In some European countries, charges are levied on fuels according to their sulphur or carbon content, as an incentive to reduce emissions of sulphur dioxide or carbon dioxide.

Differential taxes may be applied to recycled paper to encourage the reuse of paper, conserve timber supplies, and reduce waste disposal and litter. Produce charges act as substitutes for emission/effluent charges; they alter the relative prices of products, so influencing consumers and purchasers.

Belgium has imposed ecotaxes on products since 1993, being applied to goods considered to be harmful to the environment. Ecotaxes are linked closely to existing indirect taxes and apply only to products consumed in Belgium. Product taxes in Belgium relate to all drink containers, disposable razors and cameras, industrial packaging, batteries, pesticides, pharmaceutical products and paper. The taxes are kept under review by a special commission, reporting to the federal government. The introduction of these taxes in Belgium proved to be much more complicated than the parliament anticipated. It was not easy to combine environmental objectives on the one hand, with the free movement of goods and services within the EU (of which Belgium is a member) on the other. This delayed the process of implementation; however the effect on industry was marked, with an energetic search for solutions.

Protective Covenant

Or restrictive covenant; a legal requirement attached to a deed or statement of ownership imposing duties and restrictions additional to normal municipal requirements. Subdivision regulations are designed to establish minimum requirements and are not necessarily those which might be the most desirable. Protective covenants enable subdividers, developers and purchasers to adopt a higher set of standards.

Covenants may simply strengthen the existing regulation or they may go much further in terms of type, size, quality and architectural design of dwellings; they may involve the setting up of an architectural committee. To be of uniform effectiveness, protective covenants should apply to the land and be binding on all property owners in the protected area.

Public Hearings and Inquiries, Procedures at

A spectrum of proceedings and principles that may be adopted in a public inquiry or hearing into environmental issues and development applications; these procedures may range from court-like procedures with evidence taken on oath and cross-examination permitted, to more informal procedures in which cross-examination is restricted or excluded and in which the normal rules of evidence are not applied. Submissions may be accepted verbally, the whole proceedings being recorded with the subsequent circulation of transcripts, or may be accepted in written form only (thus primary submissions, answers to questions, and closing addresses would all be in writing).

Rules guiding an inquiry should be circulated in advance to all likely participants. The following is an example of a procedure adopted for a public inquiry:

- The hearings connected with the inquiry will be conducted in public.
- The inquiry will be informal and not legalistic and persons making submissions may stand or sit as they please. Neither the legal rules of evidence nor formal court procedures will apply.
- Evidence will not be taken on oath.
- If a person relies upon the evidence of some other person, that other person may speak in support of the submission.
- Persons making an oral submission will not be subjected to cross-examination though she or he may be asked questions by the commissioner or a solicitor appointed to assist the inquiry.
- Similarly persons speaking in support of a submission will not be subjected to cross-examination.
- The submission will be recorded on a tape-recorder and a transcript will be typed. A copy of the transcript will be sent to the person making the submission.
- The inquiry appreciates that persons may wish to comment upon the written or oral submissions made by other parties. They may do so in

the course of their own oral evidence. Alternatively, any persons may lodge a further written submission within one month of any other person or body giving oral evidence to the inquiry.

Public Local Inquiry, UK

The long-established form of public environmental planning inquiry conducted in Britain under housing, development, energy and environmental legislation; many pieces of legislation allow for appeals to the central government or more specifically to the ministry involved against decisions of local authorities in respect to a wide range of matters. It is customary for a public local inquiry to be conducted by one or more of Her Majesty's Inspectors specially appointed for the conduct of inquiries. Objections are carefully heard in a non-intimidatory atmosphere, the inspector reporting to the minister on the findings, decision, or recommendations. In some instances, the inspector(s) will be assisted by technical assessors with expertise in the area under consideration.

The subjects of objection include power stations, transmission lines, highways, housing development, redevelopments schemes, slum-clearance schemes, smoke-control areas, zoning and rezoning, airports and airport extensions, industrial installations of many kinds, pipelines, storage facilities and docks.

Public Participation

The participation of members of the public in the deliberations leading to important environmental planning and development decisions; such participation requires an interested and educated contribution by individuals, groups and voluntary organizations utilizing opportunities provided in law for such contributions. There may of course be active demonstrations by members of the public outside of this framework in relation to such controversial issues as the mining, export and utilization of uranium; nuclear tests; rain forests and hydroelectric dams.

Public participation is a cornerstone of the National Environmental Policy Act, 1969, in the United States. Under the NEPA regulations, agencies are required to make 'diligent' efforts to involve the public in the various procedures and provide notice of hearings, public meetings, and the availability of environmental documents.

When an agency is considering a project whose anticipated effects are of national concern, public notices must include advertisement in the *Federal*

Register and direct written notice to national organizations reasonably expected to be interested in the matter.

An agency must arrange for public hearings or public meetings whenever: environmental controversy concerning the proposed actions exists; substantial interest in the holding of a hearing is expressed by members of the public; or there is a request for a hearing by another agency with jurisdiction over the action or project.

When a draft EIS is to be considered at a public hearing, the agency must make the statement available to the public at least 15 days in advance, together with any relevant supporting documents. Scoping provides an additional opportunity for public participation at an early stage of the decision-making process. The NEPA process has shown that not only can the public be heard, but will be listened to.

Administrative inquiries or hearings are one of the means adopted by governments to enable ministers to achieve public participation and to ensure that the rights of individuals are protected before decisions on certain matters are made. Normally such inquiries or hearings arise because of a general concern felt by the community on some issue, or as a result of a right to a hearing given by an Act of Parliament before a decision is made.

Public Policies, Components of

The segments of national domestic policies that impinge most sharply on the quality of life. These components and aims are;
- *Economic policy* To fully deploy the available factors of production (land, labor and capital) in such combinations and in such places as to produce the goods and services demanded by society at a minimum of cost. The result may be a mixed economy (an economy with substantial public and private sectors) with varying degrees of national planning. It may encompass a resources and energy policy.
- *Social policy* To modify the effects of economic policy, where necessary, to achieve equity, for example, a more equitable distribution of after-tax incomes, supportive services for those unable to participate in the economic process, satisfactory housing for low-income groups, education and fairness of opportunity for self-help and advancement, and a high and stable level of employment for all social groups.
- *Environment and conservation policy* To protect land and other resources (including the free goods of air and water) from degradation due to overuse and misuse. To some extent, environment policy supports economic and social policies insofar as it ensures self-sustaining

yields, or protects areas of natural beauty. It will interrelate with any resources and energy policy.

- *National settlement policy*   To combine and blend the three strands of economic, social and environment policies to achieve an acceptable national balance in population distribution; in effect to strike a balance between efficiency, equity and ecological considerations within a spatial context.

Public Trust Doctrine

A view that common property resources such as rivers, coastal beaches, clean air and wilderness areas, are held 'in trust' by government for the benefit and use of the public. It follows from this view that before a government ratifies a decision about the use of public lands or resources, it must be shown that some observable public benefit will ensue from the proposal which will outweigh the facilities lost to the public if the project goes head.

Q

Quality of Life

In current usage, a concept embracing a miscellany of desirable things not recognized, or not adequately recognized, in the marketplace. Some qualities of life of a community which cannot readily be valued or measured include such matters as civil liberties, compassion, justice, freedom and fair play. There are also such things as observance of law, health and education, clean air and water, recreation, wildlife and enjoyment of wilderness – desirable 'goods' which are partly or wholly outside the market economy. The morale of the nation is also relevant, the attitude to its history and achievements in literature and the arts, conduct in war, and contributions to international peace. The list does not end there, for the individual's life and its quality are strongly influenced by personal and family relationships, community relationships, personal safety, security of employment, job satisfaction, travelling time, housing conditions, working conditions, diet and general stress, qualities in respect to temper and temperament, and religious and social influences. However, current usage, while emphasizing a range of matters of crucial importance, shifts attention almost entirely from the determinants of the basic standard of living of development, production and productivity. Indeed, it has been fashionable in some circles to regard development as inimical to the quality of life rather than its supporting arch, and for developers to be regarded with disfavor. This view is as unbalanced as any earlier view that development was invariably 'progress', and progress was the sum of all good things.

R

Rain Forest

See:
Amazonian Rain Forest

Ranger Uranium Environmental Inquiry, Australia

A public inquiry set up by the Australian Federal government in 1975, under
the provisions of the Environment Protection (Impact of Proposals) Act,
1974–75. The presiding commissioner was Mr Justice Fox. The commission
was required by the Minister for Environment and Conservation to inquire
into the environmental aspects of: the formulation of proposals; the carrying
out of works and other projects; the negotiation, operation and enforcement
of agreements and arrangements; the making of or the participation in the
making of decisions and recommendations; and the incurring of expenditure
by or on behalf of the Australian government and the Australian Atomic
Energy Commission and other authorities for and in relation to the development by Ranger Uranium Mines Pty. Ltd. of uranium deposits in the Northern
Territory of Australia.

The first report of the inquiry was presented on 28 October 1976, dealing
with the generic issue of nuclear development and the basic question of
whether any uranium mining should be allowed to proceed anywhere in
Australia.

The second report was presented on 17 May 1977. This latter report dealt
in detail with the Ranger proposal itself. The Fox Commission sat, therefore,
for over two years, hearing evidence from the proponent, the Australian
Atomic Energy Commission, environmental organizations, overseas experts,
and the Aborigines of the Northern Territory. The commission heard a total of
303 witnesses, the evidence resulting in 13 525 pages of transcript and 419
exhibits.

The response of the Australian government was the acceptance of almost
all of the inquiry recommendations. Where the government decided on a
course of action different to that recommended, it did so on the basis of
achieving the same purchases and satisfying the same principles. The key
elements of the policy are that the Australian government retains its right to
be selective in choosing the countries to which uranium exports will be
permitted. In the case of non-nuclear weapon states, sales will be made only

to subscribers to the Non-Proliferation Treaty. Nuclear weapons countries receiving Australian uranium must not use it for explosive or military purposes.

Recycling

The return of discarded or waste materials to the productive system for utilization in the manufacture of goods, with a view to the conservation as far as practicable of non-renewable and scarce resources, contributing to sustainable development.

Recycling goes beyond the reuse of a product (such as glass milk bottles) and involves the return of salvaged materials (such as paper, metals, plastics, or broken glass) to an early manufacturing stage (pulping or melting). Some recycling has always been profitable in certain industries such as the return of steel scrap to the iron and steel industry, glass cullet to the glass industry, and aluminium drink cans to the aluminium industry. However, developments in the recent years have raised the levels of recycling in commercial and domestic premises through financial incentives to local councils and collection bodies. The principle of recycling has been extended in actual manufacturing processes, such as the recycling of water, heat and other inputs within the plant itself. Box 63 indicates the recycling rates and targets for members of the EU.

Among ways of promoting recycling, the 'Green Dot' system, has come into widespread use in Europe. Major operators pay a licence fee for the use of the on-pack Green Dot symbol which shows they are making a financial contribution to the management of packaging waste from households. Green Dot organizations administer the scheme, collecting funds and disbursing the revenues to promote recycling. The Green Dot countries include Austria, Belgium, France, Germany, Luxembourg, Portugal and Spain. Similar arrangements are in use in Finland, Norway and Sweden. The Green Dot system started in Germany.

Regional Environmental Plan

Between national environmental planning policies and the local environmental plan lies the regional environmental plan. Such a plan may incorporate several local structural plans, reflecting national policies and providing a framework for local council plans. The regional environmental plan is a complex structure embracing a whole spectrum of economic, social and environmental considerations. It is, however, the crucial connecting link be-

Box 63 European Union member states recycling rates and targets

Country	Recycling rates (%)				Recycling targets
	Glass (1996)	Rigid and flexible plastics (1995)	Aluminium cans (1996)	Steel cans (1996)	
Austria	n/a	22	50	47	70% glass, 60% paper/board, 50% metals, 20% plastics from 1996
Belgium	66	13	25	30	40% for each material in each region in each waste stream by 1997
Denmark	66	11	0	n/a	80% glass, 40% C/I PP, 50% C/I LDPE, 50% C/I EPS, 70% C/I HDPE by 1997
Finland	63	n/a	80	n/a	53% paper/board, 48% glass, 25% metals, 15% plastics by 2001
France	50	9	14	44	Range as in EC Directive
Germany	79	43	81	81	72% household glass, steel and aluminium, 64% household paper/board and plastics from 1995
Greece	39	n/a	35	17	not set yet
Ireland	46	2	20	n/a	25% *recovery* by 2001, and 55% glass recycling
Italy	53	7	37	n/a	>25% overall, >15% for each material by 2001
Netherlands	81	12	25	58	90% glass, 27% plastics, 80% metals, 85% paper/board by 2001
Portugal	43	1	17	n/a	25% *recovery*
Spain	35	6	17	19	>25% overall, >15% for each material by 2001
Sweden	72	9	91	54	90% al and pet bev containers, 70% glass and non-bev metals, 65% corrugated, 40% other paper/board and other plastics, by 2001
UK	22	7	31	16	>52% *overall recovery*, >15% recycling for each material by 2001

Source: National Environment Protection Council, Australia, 1999.

Box 64   Regional environmental plan: matters to be considered in its preparation

1. The boundaries of the area under consideration; the topography, geology, soils, meteorology, hydrology, catchments and other physical, biological and ecological characteristics.
2. The results of resource surveys (geology, soil, water resources, erosion, vegetation and fauna).
3. The pattern of settlement, growth and decline, agricultural, forestry and industrial activities.
4. The economics of the region.
5. The social structure of the region.
6. The environmental features of the region (sensitive and high-value areas, recreational opportunities, marsh and wetland areas, national parks, nature reserves, wildlife habitats, rare and endangered species, mangroves, coral, forests and bushland, amenity areas).
7. Relevant national, state and regional environmental and planning policies.
8. Local planning policies in relation to zoning, urban settlement, rural development, roads and communications, traffic control, utility corridors, alternative land uses, erosion control, protection of sensitive areas, local subdivision, local and regional infrastructure, future development options, population distribution, housing standards, land-use patterns, land-use constraints, environmental quality targets, floods, sewerage and drainage, provision of other services, agriculture, recreational and tourist activities, landscape.
9. Zones for industrial development; prospective sites for major developments linked with regional resources; protection of catchments; provision of drainage and sewerage systems with sewage treatment.
10. Evidence of pollution of air and water, salinization, eutrophication, noise and blasting, blue-green algae, sedimentation, erosion, abandoned quarries and industrial sites, destruction of landscape and natural assets.
11. Mitigation measures against pollution and damage to the environment in the public and private sectors; the minimization of waste discharges.
12. Evidence of cumulative environmental effects and countermeasures.

Box 64 continued

13. Restraints on future development of various categories.
14. Opportunities for future development in various categories.
15. Avoid sterilization of resources.
16. Promote an efficient transport system.
17. Monitor trends in all key areas.
18. Environmental quality targets and objectives.
19. Quality of life objectives and attainability.
20. Arrangements for the involvement of the public, government at all levels, the private sector and local and national organizations in future development plans and project decision-making.
21. Responsibility for the regional environment plan and its implementation involving possibly a regional authority.
22. Relevance to planning in contiguous areas.
23. Inter- and intragenerational equity.
23. Compliance with the precautionary principle and the polluter-pays principle.
24. Compliance with the principles of sustainable development.

tween local environment plans and the grander national design. It may be prepared by a government department, in consultation with local councils, or by a group of local councils acting in unison. The result is a large segment in the national plan, taking account of many local interests. As with all plans it needs to be revised at intervals of, say, five years. See Box 64 for matters to be considered in the preparation of a regional plan.

See also:
Local Environmental Plan.

Regional Seas Program, UNEP

A program organized by UNEP to protect the marine environment and its living resources against pollution and overexploitation through the development of conservation policies. By 1984, action plans had been developed for the protection and management of the marine environment in respect to ten regional seas. International and other regional conventions for the protection of the marine environment had been brought into effect, including the Convention for the Protection of Marine Pollution by Dumping from Ships and Aircraft (Oslo, 1972), the Convention on the Prevention of Pollution from

Ships (London, 1973), and the Convention on the Prevention of Pollution from Land-based Sources (Paris, 1974).

The regional seas examined have included the Baltic Sea, the North Sea, the Mediterranean Sea, the West African coastal waters, the Gulf of Mexico, the North American coastal waters (Atlantic, Pacific and Arctic), the South-West Atlantic (Brazil and Argentine Basins), South-East Pacific Coast (Ecuador, Peru, and Chile), the Indian Ocean, Australian and New Zealand coastal waters, the Persian Gulf and the Red Sea.

By 1999, the Regional Seas Program covered 13 regions worldwide with the participation of more than 140 states and territories. The program is supported by many conventions and protocols to prevent, reduce and control marine pollution.

The 1976 Barcelona Convention for the Protection of the Mediterranean Sea against Pollution was the first to be concluded. This was reinforced by the 1980 Athens Protocol for the Protection of the Mediterranean Sea against Pollution from Land-based Sources. In 1978, the Kuwait Regional Convention for Cooperation on the Protection of the Marine-environment from Pollution was concluded, followed by the 1990 Kuwait Protocol for the Protection of the Marine Environment. In 1981, the Lima Convention for the Protection of the Marine Environment and Coastal Area of the South-East Pacific was concluded, followed by the 1983 Quito Protocol. In 1992, the Bucharest Convention on the Protection of the Black Sea against Pollution was concluded, followed by the 1992 Bucharest Protocol. In 1992, the Helsinki Convention on the Protection of the Marine Environment of the Baltic Sea against Pollution was concluded.

Two global instruments also apply: the 1982 Convention on the Law of the Sea and the 1985 Montreal Guidelines for the Protection of the Marine Environment from Land-based Sources of Marine Pollution.

In 1993, a conference was held in Nairobi to assess the effectiveness of the Regional Seas Agreements. A comprehensive world conference was held in Washington, DC in 1995. A Global Program of Action at regional and national levels was adopted. See Box 65.

Box 65   UN Regional Seas Program

Mediterranean Action Plan
- Convention for the Protection of the Mediterranean Sea Against Pollution (Barcelona, 16 February 1976)
- Protocol for the Prevention of Pollution of the Mediterranean Sea by Dumping from Ships and Aircraft (Barcelona, 16 February 1976)

Box 65   continued

- Protocol concerning Co-operation in Combating Pollution of the Mediterranean Sea by Oil and Other Harmful Substances in Cases of Emergency (Barcelona, 16 February 1976)
- Protocol for the Protection of the Mediterranean Sea against Pollution from Land-based Sources (Athens, 17 May 1980)
- Protocol concerning Mediterranean Specially Protected Areas (Geneva, 3 April 1982)

Kuwait Action Plan

- Kuwait Regional Convention for the Co-operation on the Protection of the Marine Environment from Pollution (Kuwait, 23 April 1978)
- Protocol concerning Regional Co-operation in Combating Pollution by Oil and Other Harmful Substances in Cases of Emergency (Kuwait, 23 April 1978)

West and Central Africa Action Plan

- Convention for Co-operation in the Protection and Development of the Marine and Coastal Environment of the West and Central African Region (Abidjan, 23 March 1981)
- Protocol concerning Co-operation in Combating Pollution in Cases of Emergency (Abidjan, 23 March 1981)

South-East Pacific Action Plan

- Convention for the Protection of the Marine Environment and Coastal Area of the South-East Pacific (Lima, 12 November 1981)
- Agreement on Regional Co-operation in Combating Pollution of the South-East Pacific by Hydrocarbons or Other Harmful Substance in Cases of Emergency (Lima, 12 November 1981)
- Supplementary Protocol to the Agreement on Regional Co-operation in Combating Pollution of the South-East Pacific by Hydrocarbons or Other Harmful Substances (Quito, 22 July 1983)
- Protocol for the Protection of the South-East Pacific against Pollution from Land-based Sources (Quito, 22 July 1983)
- Protocol for the Conservation and Management of Protected Marine and Coastal Areas of the South-East Pacific (Paipa, 21 September 1989)
- Protocol for the Protection of the South-East Pacific against Radioactive Contamination (Paipa, 21 September 1989)

Box 65   continued

Red Sea and Gulf of Aden Action Plan
- Regional Convention for the Conservation of the Red Sea and Gulf of Aden Environment (Jeddah, 14 February 1982)
- Protocol concerning Regional Co-operation in Combating Pollution by Oil and Other Harmful Substances in Cases of Emergency (Jeddah, 14 February 1982)

Caribbean Action Plan
- Convention for the Protection and Development of the Marine Environment of the Wider Caribbean Region (Cartagena de Indias, 24 March 1983)
- Protocol Concerning Co-operation in Combating Oil Spills in the Wider Caribbean Region (Cartagena de Indias, 24 March 1983)
- Protocol Concerning Specially Protected Areas of Wildlife to the Convention for the Protection and Development of the Marine Environment of the Wider Caribbean Region (Kingston, 18 January 1990)

East African Action Plan
- Convention for the Protection, Management and Development of the Marine and Coastal Environment of the Eastern Africa Region (Nairobi, 21 June 1985)
- Protocol concerning Protected Areas and Wild Fauna and Flora in the Eastern African Region (Nairobi, 21 June 1985)
- Protocol concerning Co-operation in Combating Marine Pollution in Cases of Emergency in the Eastern African Region (Nairobi, 21 June 1985)

South Pacific Regional Environment Programme
- Convention for the Protection of the Natural Resources and Environment of the South Pacific Region (Noumea, 25 November 1986)
- Protocol concerning Co-operation in Combating Pollution Emergencies in the South Pacific Region.

A South Asian Regional Seas Programme is currently under preparation.

Regulatory Impact Analysis (RIA), US

An analysis which US federal agencies must perform on all new 'major' regulations to ensure that the potential benefits to society outweigh the potential costs of the proposed action; this requirement was introduced under the US President's Executive Order 12291 of 1980. Analyses are to be submitted to the Office of Management and Budget (OMB) for review. The measure applies to all proposed regulations likely to have an annual effect on the economy of $100 million or more; to result in a major increase in costs or prices for consumers, individual industries, federal, state, or local government agencies, or for geographic regions; or likely to have significant adverse effects on competition, employment, investment, productivity, innovation, or the ability of US-based enterprises to compete with foreign-based enterprises in domestic or export markets. Such benefit–cost calculations are still not the final determining factor in the making of regulations (for political considerations are not taken into account) but they have become an indispensable tool in the analysis of the likely effects of government regulations. See Box 66.

See also:
Benefit–Cost Analysis.

Resource Conservation and Recovery Act, 1976 (RCRA), US

An act with historical roots in the Solid Waste Disposal Act, 1965; its primary object was to promote and protect the public health and the environment; and to conserve valuable material and energy sources. These objectives were to be accomplished by providing technical and financial assistance to state and local governments and interstate agencies for the development of solid waste management plans; prohibiting future uncontrolled open dumping on land, and requiring the conversion of existing open dumps to controlled and managed nonhazardous facilities; regulating the treatment, storage, transportation and disposal of hazardous wastes which have adverse effects on public health and the environment; providing for the promulgation of guidelines for solid waste collection, transport, separation, recovery, and disposal practice and systems; and establishing a cooperative effort among the federal state and local governments and private enterprise in order to recover valuable materials and energy from solid waste.

The RCRA established the statutory framework for comprehensive federal and state regulation of hazardous wastes. The act required the identification and listing of hazardous wastes, taking into account such factors as toxicity, persistence and degradability in nature, the potential for accumulation in

Box 66   *Appraisal and evaluation methods applied to environmental*
          regulations in OECD countries

Australia	Benefit/cost analysis applied to bills and lower-level rules that may have significant business/cost impacts (applied at Commonwealth aand certain state levels)
Austria	Fiscal analysis recommended for bills
Canada	Benefit/cost analysis (with findings presented in a Regulatory Impact Analysis Statement) supplemented by Business Impact Test and Regulatory Cost Account Protocol
Denmark	General impact analysis required for new legal proposals which, *inter alia*, may require both an economic study and an EIA
European Union	Treaty on European Union (article 130 r. 3) requires that the costs and benefits of each proposed regulatory action be assessed
Finland	General impact analysis, distributional and fiscal analyses applied to bills and lower-level rules
Hungary	The Act on Environment prescribes detailed economic evaluations of proposed environmental regulations
Italy	'Cost–output analysis' used, with the main emphasis placed on fiscal costs
Japan	General impact analysis applied, as necessary, to permit rules and social regulations
Mexico	Cost–benefit and cost-effectiveness analyses applied to 'business-related' procedures and requirements
Netherlands	General impact analysis for bills and lower-level rules. Regulatory impact analyses of likely financial effects of new regulations on industry and trade. RIAs may also cover environmental impact assessments of proposed regulatory changes originating from non-environment ministries
New Zealand	Fiscal analysis/compliance cost assessment applied to draft laws originating from Cabinet.
Norway	Studies of economic impacts of proposed regulations, sometimes in the form of cost–benefit analyses. Also review undertaken of the effects of environmental policy instruments in relation to goal

Box 66   *continued*

	achievement, cost-effectiveness, distributional effects and effects on technological development
Portugal	Fiscal analysis of bills and lower-level rules; also environmental impact assessment of certain bills
Spain	Financial analysis of effect of regulatory proposals on public budget
Turkey	General impact analysis for bills and lower-level regulations
United Kingdom	Compliance Cost Assessment of new and amended regulations, focusing particularly on costs to business. A fuller cost–benefit analysis may be undertaken in certain cases
United States	Regulatory analysis has evolved from a relatively simple analysis of costs to a comprehensive benefit–cost analysis for actions subject to Executive Order 12866. In other contexts, EPA also carries out Regulatory Flexibility Analyses and more specific cost and cost–benefit analyses in accordance with the Clean Water and Clean Air Acts.

Sources: Environment Directorate (1996); OECD (1996), *An Overview of Regulatory Impact Analysis in OECD Countries*, Paris: OECD (1997), *Regulatory Quality and Public Sector Reform*, Paris.

tissue, and other characteristics. It directed promulgation of such standards for generators of hazardous waste as might be necessary to protect human health and the environment. These standards were to include requirements for record keeping, labels for containers, disclosure of chemical components, use of a manifest system, and reporting to the EPA. Similar standards were to be developed for transporters of hazardous wastes in cooperation with the US Department of Transportation.

The act also provided for the establishment of a permitting system to control the treatment, storage, and disposal of hazardous wastes, thus ensuring that all hazardous waste facilities would be operating under conditions specified in an RCRA permit. The act also directed the EPA to promulgate guidelines to assist states in the development of their own hazardous wastes programs; the EPA was also given a wide range of enforcement tools for ensuring compliance with the regulations. Regulations were promulgated in May 1980, and in January 1981 (amended in July 1982). There are now in effect detailed regulations governing every aspect of hazardous waste management.

In November 1984, the US President signed into law a bill reauthorizing and amending the Resource Conservation and Recovery Act. The new legislation broadened government restrictions on land disposal of hazardous waste and greatly increased the number of waste generators subject to EPA regulation. Other provisions significantly improved the quality of landfills and surface impoundments, and placed underground storage tanks under EPA regulation. By specified dates, the EPA had to decide whether it is safe to continue land disposal of a large variety of hazardous wastes. A failure to meet these deadlines meant that so-called 'hammer clauses' would go into effect prohibiting such disposal. The specified dates ranged from November 1986 to May 1990, for various categories of waste.

In addition to ruling on various types of land disposal, the EPA must promulgate regulations specifying methods of treatment capable of substantially reducing the toxicity of the waste or its likelihood of migration from a disposal unit or injection zone. Wastes which are so treated will be exempt from the ban on land disposal.

The 1984 RCRA requires that permits for hazardous waste facilities be renewed every ten years; land disposal permits, however, are subject to review every five years. Applications for permit renewal are subject to all the requirements that pertain to the issuance of new permits. The RCRA also specifies that these applications must reflect improvements in control and measurement technology that have occurred since the previous permit was issued. In certain cases, private citizens are authorized to bring legal action where past or present hazardous waste management practices pose an imminent danger. They can bring this action against companies, governmental entities, or individual citizens.

See also:
Comprehensive Environmental Response, Compensation, and Liability Act, 1980 (CERCLA), US ('Superfund').

Review of Environmental Factors

An approach adopted when the environmental impact of a proposal is readily shown to be minor; in such cases it is often sufficient for the applicant to submit a 'review of environmental factors' as a supplement to a development application. The review should describe: the nature of the proposal; the zoning and general nature of the environment affected; the safeguards designed for control of pollution and protection of the environment; the aspects of the proposal that may enhance the environment; the aspects of the proposal that may adversely affect the environment with reasons why they cannot be avoided.

Rhine

See:
International Commission for the Protection of the Rhine.

Right of Common Access, Nordic

In principle, a right of entry by the public which includes passage on foot over all types of land. However, growing crops or the right to privacy of a houseowner are by no means unprotected. As regards passage on foot over most land, the rights are similar to the Scottish ones, also of Norse origin, that make much of their countryside accessible, in contrast to the more restricted situation in England.

Care is taken in Swedish planning legislation to protect the Right of Common Access. This is particularly true of the current work on National Physical Planning, which calls upon municipalities to implement the general guidelines for physical planning that the Riksdag (parliament) laid down in 1972. One important criterion for the further protection of natural areas and for planning decisions in the municipalities is the wish to keep open such areas that are now open to everybody. This means that valuable areas will be protected by various planning restrictions to prevent land use – urban development, afforestation with dense plantations and so on – which is in conflict with free accessibility to the land.

One planning measure to ensure the accessibility of valuable land is the general ban on building within 100 meters of the shore. Similar regulations have been in operation in some coastal areas and around certain lakes for a long time.

Rio Declaration on Environment and Development

A declaration on environment and development adopted at the international conference on the human condition which met in Rio de Janeiro, Brazil, in 1992. Representatives from some 167 countries attended the conference. Apart from the Rio Declaration on Environment and Development, the conference adopted Agenda 21, a work program for the twenty-first century. It

Box 67   Rio Declaration on Environment and Development

Preamble
The United Nations Conference on Environment and Development:
- having met at Rio de Janeiro from 3 to 14 June 1992,
- reaffirming the Declaration of the United Nations Conference on the Human Environment, adopted at Stockholm on 16 June 1972, and seeking to build upon it,
- with the goal of establishing a new and equitable global partnership through the creation of new levels of cooperation among States, key sectors of societies and people,
- working towards international agreements which respect the interests of all and protect the integrity of the global environment and developmental system,
- recognizing the integral and interdependent nature of the Earth, our home,

Proclaims that:

Principle 1
Human beings are at the centre of concerns for sustainable development. They are entitled to a healthy and productive life in harmony with nature.

Principle 2
States have, in accordance with the Charter of the United Nations and the principles of international law, the sovereign right to exploit their own resources pursuant to their own environmental and developmental policies, and the responsibility to ensure that activities within their jurisdiction or control do not cause damage to the environment of other States or of areas beyond the limits of national jurisdiction.

Principle 3
The right to development must be fulfilled so as to equitably meet developmental and environmental needs of present and future generations.

Principle 4
In order to achieve sustainable development, environmental protection shall constitute an integral part of the development process and cannot be considered in isolation from it.

Box 67   continued

Principle 5
All States and all people shall cooperate in the essential task of eradicating poverty as an indispensable requirement for sustainable development, in order to decrease the disparities in standards of living and better meet the needs of the majority of the people of the world.

Principle 6
The special situation and needs of developing countries, particularly the least developed and those most environmentally vulnerable, shall be given special priority. International actions in the field of environment and developments should also address the interests and needs of all countries.

Principle 7
States shall cooperate in a spirit of global partnership to conserve, protect and restore the health and integrity of the Earth's ecosystem. In view of the different contributions to global environmental degradation, States have common but differentiated responsibilities. The developed countries acknowledge the responsibility that they bear in the international pursuit of sustainable development in view of the pressures their societies place on the global environment and of the technologies and financial resources they command.

Principle 8
To achieve sustainable development and a higher quality of life for all people, States should reduce and eliminate unsustainable patterns of production and consumption and promote appropriate demographic policies.

Principle 9
States should cooperate to strengthen endogenous capacity-building for sustainable development by improving scientific understanding through exchanges of scientific and technological knowledge, and by enhancing the development, adaptation, diffusion and transfer of technologies, including new and innovative technologies.

Principle 10
Environmental issues are best handled with the participation of all concerned citizens, at the relevant level. At the national level, each individual shall have appropriate access to information concerning

Box 67   continued

the environment that is held by public authorities, including information on hazardous materials and activities in their communities, and the opportunity to participate in decision-making processes. States shall facilitate and encourage public awareness and participation by making information widely available. Effective access to judicial and administrative proceedings, including redress and remedy, shall be provided.

Principle 11
States shall enact effective environmental legislation. Environmental standards, management objectives and priorities should reflect the environmental and developmental context to which they apply. Standards applied by some countries may be inappropriate and of unwarranted economic and social cost to other countries, in particular developing countries.

Principle 12
States should cooperate to promote a supportive and open international economic system that would lead to economic growth and sustainable development in all countries, to better address the problems of environmental degradation. Trade policy measures for environmental purposes should not constitute a means of arbitrary or unjustifiable discrimination or a disguised restriction on international trade. Unilateral actions to deal with environmental challenges outside the jurisdiction of the importing country should be avoided. Environmental measures addressing transboundary or global environmental problems should, as far as possible, be based on an international consensus.

Principle 13
States shall develop national law regarding liability and compensation for the victims of pollution and other environmental damage. States shall also cooperate in an expeditious and more determined manner to develop further international law regarding liability and compensation for adverse effects of environmental damage caused by activities within their jurisdiction or control to areas beyond their jurisdiction.

Principle 14
States should effectively cooperate to discourage or prevent the relocation and transfer to other States of any activities and substances that

Box 67 continued

cause severe environmental degradation or are found to be harmful to human health.

Principle 15
In order to protect the environment, the precautionary approach shall be widely applied by States according to their capabilities. Where there are threats of serious or irreversible damage, lack of full scientific certainty shall not be used as a reason for postponing cost-effective measures to prevent environmental degradation.

Principle 16
National authorities should endeavour to promote the internalization of environmental costs and the use of economic instruments, taking into account the approach that the polluter should, in principle, bear the cost of pollution, with due regard to the public interest and without distorting international trade and investment.

Principle 17
Environmental impact assessment, as a national instrument, shall be undertaken for proposed activities that are likely to have a significant adverse impact on the environment and are subject to a decision of a competent national authority.

Principle 18
States shall immediately notify other States of any natural disasters or other emergencies that are likely to produce sudden harmful effects on the environment of those States. Every effort shall be made by the international community to help States so afflicted.

Principle 19
States shall provide prior and timely notification and relevant information to potentially affected States on activities that may have a significant adverse transboundary environmental effect and shall consult with those States at an early stage and in good faith.

Principle 20
Women have a vital role in environmental management and development. Their full participation is therefore essential to achieve sustainable development.

Box 67   continued

Principle 21
The creativity, ideals and courage of the youth of the world should be mobilized to forge a global partnership in order to achieve sustainable development and ensure a better future for all.

Principle 22
Indigenous people and their communities, and other local communities, have a vital role in environmental management and development because of their knowledge and traditional practices. States should recognize and duly support their identity, culture and interests and enable their effective participation in the achievement of sustainable development.

Principle 23
The environment and natural resources of people under oppression, domination and occupation shall be protected.

Principle 24
Warfare is inherently destructive of sustainable development. States shall therefore respect international law providing protection for the environment in times of armed conflict and cooperate in its further development, as necessary.

Principle 25
Peace, development and environmental protection are interdependent and indivisible.

Principle 26
States shall resolve all their environmental disputes peacefully and by appropriate means in accordance with the Charter of the United Nations.

Principle 27
States and people shall cooperate in good faith and in a spirit of partnership in the fulfilment of the principles embodied in this Declaration and in the further development of international law in the field of sustainable development.

also recommended the creation of a UN Commission for Sustainable Development and initiated framework conventions on climate change and biological diversity. See Box 67 for the text of the Rio Declaration.

See also:
Box 86 for a summary of UN conferences on the human environment.

Road-pricing Schemes

The traditional response to traffic congestion has been the building of more and better roads; however, budgetary limitations and the ever-increasing demands for more roads as traffic increases has focused attention on demand management in general and road-pricing in particular.

The introduction of toll charges has served as both a cost-recovery technique and as a regulator of traffic, marginally discouraging use. The main objection to tolls has been the need for drivers to stop and pay the toll either by cash or pre-paid ticket, detracting from some of the benefits of faster routes and recreating a measure of traffic congestion. In response to this problem, electronic automatic charging systems have been developed in Denver, Colorado, USA; Cambridge, England; Singapore; and Bergen, Oslo and Trondheim, Norway.

The Colorado Toll Highway E–470 was opened in 1991; the system here enables cars to drive through at speed, the toll booth automatically charging a toll to the driver's credit card by picking up electronic signals from the ID card located in the vehicle. The system has the capacity to vary the toll according to the level of congestion, charging higher tolls during rush hours. Drivers may respond to this by using alternative routes or travelling at alternative times. Congestion at critical times is much reduced, with pollution reduced because of higher speeds. In addition, the government or road-operator raises revenue for road maintenance and further construction works. The main objection has been that the individual's movements are monitored, although this objection can be offset by separate toll booths for those who wish to pay cash.

Apart from the above, charges may be imposed on all private cars entering delineated central city areas. More cheaply perhaps, traffic congestion may be eased in the central business district by a combination of high parking charges and limited parking facilities, coupled with efficient public transport from the outer limits, achieving a balance of supply and demand through the medium of price. Traffic may also be excluded by a marked increase in pedestrian-only precincts. All such schemes need to be complemented by ample and inexpensive parking at the fringes of congested areas. In Britain, doubling the real price of gasoline (petrol) over the next decade has been recommended by the Royal Commission on Environmental Pollution, though this may not reduce urban congestion at critical times (*The Economist*, 22 June 1996).

Royal Commission into UK Nuclear Testing

A Royal Commission appointed by the Australian Commonwealth government in July 1984 to inquire into nuclear tests carried out, during the period 1952–63, by the UK government on the Monte Bello Islands, off the coast of Western Australia, and at two sites, Emu and Maralinga, in South Australia. The inquiry arose from suggestions that servicemen and Aboriginals had died as a result of exposure to radiation. After hearing evidence in the UK and Australia, the commission presented its report in November 1985. In a detailed study of 12 major bomb detonations, the report found that on several occasions tests were undertaken when weather conditions were unsuitable; the Monte Bello Islands were judged as an inappropriate test site because prevailing winds carried fallout across a wide area of the mainland. On the question of health risks to the Australian population, the report maintained that, although it found no positive evidence that the tests had caused deaths, 'it is probable that cancers which would not otherwise have occurred have been caused'. The UK government was called on to decontaminate the test areas.

Royal Commission on Environmental Pollution, UK

A commission set up in 1970 as a permanent or standing body to advise the British government as a whole in relation to environmental matters. The terms of reference have been: 'To advise on matters, both national and international, concerning the pollution of the environment; on the adequacy of research in this field; and the future possibilities of danger to the environment'. The Royal Commission was intended to serve as a general watchdog on pollution and environment protection.

A number of substantial reports have been published. In 1975, in its Fifth Report ('Air Pollution Control: An Integrated Approach'), the commission urged the creation of a central inspectorate to control all forms of pollution. It recommended also the creation of a diploma in pollution control; this would be awarded to engineers and scientists suitably qualified and experienced in all aspects of pollution control to meet the needs of policy-makers.

Royal Commission on the Great Barrier Reef, Australia

A commission set up by the Australian federal and Queenland State governments to examine the implications of oil drilling on the Great Barrier Reef. The Reef lies off the eastern Queensland coast of Australia and is widely regarded as the largest assemblage of living corals in the world. The commission concluded in 1975 that if petroleum drilling occurred, some spills ranging from small to substantial would occur. Two commissioners found there was a risk of uncertain magnitude to marine life and recommended that drilling should not be permitted in large areas of the Reef. The chairman (the remaining member of the commission) was not convinced that drilling could be conducted anywhere on the Reef unless more research provided some clear evidence that no harm would result.

Following the report of the Royal Commission, the Australian federal government decided that no further exploratory drilling would be permitted until research into the effects of oil on coral reefs had been undertaken. However, subsequently large areas of the Reef were proclaimed as a marine park under the control of a Great Barrier Reef Marine Park Authority, thus precluding oil drilling.

With the declaration in 1983 of five additional sections of the Great Barrier Reef Marine Park, some 98.5 per cent of the Great Barrier Reef became protected. The Great Barrier Reef Marine Park has an area of about 344 000 sq km, and is by far the largest marine park in the world.

Under section 38 of the Great Barrier Reef Marine Park Act, 1975, operations for the recovery of minerals including petroleum within the marine park are prohibited. The Great Barrier Reef Marine Park (Prohibition of Drilling for Petroleum) Regulations prohibited, from September 1983, the drilling for petroleum in any part of the Great Barrier Reef Region not included as part of the marine park.

Russia

The Russian Federation is a federal multiparty republic with a bicameral legislative body or Federal Assembly, comprising a Federation Council and a State Duma. The capital is Moscow. The population in 1997 was 147 million, at an average density of 8.6 persons per sq km. Russia extends from Western Europe to the Far East. In the west it abuts Poland and the Baltic States, Romania, the Slovak Republic, Belarus, Ukraine, Finland and Iran; and to the east Afghanistan, Turkistan, Mongolia, China, Korea and Japan. It is a communist economy in transition. See Box 68 for the evolution of environmental law.

Box 68   Russia: evolution of environmental law

1960   USSR Council of Ministers adopt proposals to conserve water resources and protect those resources against pollution

1970   Supreme Soviet adopts water management legislation

1972   Supreme Soviet adopts measures to improve nature conservation and promote the rational utilization of natural resources; issues an appeal to the nations of the world to combat pollution and protect the environment; approves decrees to protect the Volga and Ural Basins, the Black and Azov Seas, and Lake Baikal; US–USSR Joint Committee for Environment Protection established. USSR and East Germany do not attend the UN Conference on the Human Environment, held in Stockholm

1973   Convention signed to manage fishing in the Baltic Sea and The Belts

1975   The Supreme Soviet issues decrees for the protection of mineral wealth and the natural environment

1976   Guidelines issued for the development of the national economy, dealing in detail with measures to protect the environment, control pollution, and manage natural resources

1977   Amendment of the Constitution to promote the rational use of land and its mineral and water resources, protect fauna and flora, prevent pollution, and ensure sustainable development

1981   Adverse official report on the condition of Lake Baikal

1986   Disastrous explosion at the Chernobyl nuclear reactor in the Ukraine, spreading radioactivity widely over Europe

1992   Convention signed for the protection of the Baltic Sea

1993   Explosion at the Siberia Chemical Centre plant near Tomsk, releasing radioactive material into the atmosphere; the Ministry of Ecology and Natural Resources reports high levels of pollution affecting over 50 million people

1994   Following adverse reports on Lake Baikal, the Baikal pulp and paper mill is closed; Komi pipeline disaster

1996   Life expectancy: 58.3 years for males; 71.7 years for females

1997   Kyoto target: 100

S

Safe Drinking Water Act, 1974, US

An act which provides for the safety of drinking water supplies throughout the USA by establishing and enforcing national drinking water quality standards. Under the act, the EPA has the primary responsibility to establish national drinking water quality standards, and to supervise public water supply systems and other sources of drinking water. Regarding the enforcement of drinking water quality standards, a state can qualify for 'primary enforcement responsibility' if it adopts regulations at least equal to the federal regulations in protecting public health, and can provide adequate surveillance and enforcement procedures.

In 1984, the EPA recommended maximum contaminant levels (MCLs) for a group of nine chemical compounds that might cause health problems if found in drinking water at significant levels; these were volatile synthetic organic chemicals found in industrial solvents, degreasing agents and dry-cleaning fluids.

By 1985, most states and territories had accepted primary enforcement responsibility. Two classes of regulations have been introduced: primary regulations are concerned with the protection of public health, while secondary regulations are concerned with the taste, odor and appearance of drinking water.

Scoping, US

A significant innovation in the National Environmental Policy Act, 1969 (NEPA); when a federal agency determines that a proposed action requires the preparation of an EIS, it must take prompt action at the outset of its planning process to identify those issues that require full analysis, and separate them from less significant matters that do not require detailed study. This sifting out of issues is known as 'scoping'.

Further, the scoping process helps the agency identify any environmental review and consultation requirements imposed by laws other than NEPA and to allocate responsibilities among lead and cooperating agencies. Thus, where an EIS is required for a coal-fired power plant, the scoping process would afford the opportunity to coordinate the preconstruction environmental reviews required by the Clean Air Act, Clean Water Act, and other environmental laws into the overall EIS process. To ensure such coordination, affected federal, state and local agencies and interested members of the public must be invited to participate in this scoping process.

Selous Game Reserve

A game reserve in southeastern Tanzania, East Africa, the largest in the world, bestriding a complex of rivers. The vegetation is woodland with some of the finest virgin bush left in Africa. The reserve holds concentrations of big-tusked elephants, large-maned lions, buffalo, leopards, rhinoceros, zebra, antelopes, and numerous bird species. It has been included in the World Heritage List.

Sewage Treatment

The modification of sewage to make it more acceptable to the environment. Sewage treatment may be divided into four main stages:
1. *Primary treatment* The removal of suspended matter by physical and mechanical means, for example, screening, grinding, flocculation or sedimentation.
2. *Secondary treatment* The removal of finely suspended solids and colloidal matter, and the stabilization and oxidation of these substances and the dissolved organic matter by means of air and the activity of living organisms.
3. *Tertiary treatment* The attainment of higher effluent standards for many purposes.
4. *Sludge disposal* The disposal of the suspended matter removed.
A decision as to the stages of treatment to be adopted depends on what is to become of the final effluent. A town situated close to the sea may discharge its sewage without pre-treatment at a suitable distance out to sea; this approach is known as disposal by dilution. Where conditions are not satisfactory for this method of disposal, pre-treatment becomes necessary. With regard to inland towns, the final effluent which will be discharged into a watercourse undergoes at least two stages of treatment.

Sewage Treatment Plant Assessment

The factors to be taken into account in the EIA of a sewage treatment plant. A curious feature of such an assessment is that sewage treatment in itself is a major pollution-control instrument; in consequence an objective assessment

Box 69 Sewage treatment plant: economic, social and environmental elements to be considered

1. The contribution the sewage treatment plant would make to improving the environment of the community served, through the elimination of septic tank and other systems, and the protection of the effluent receiving waters.
2. Alternative sites for the proposal and alternative treatment systems.
3. The consistency of the proposal with national, regional or local planning instruments; the relationships to neighbouring residential or tourist areas.
4. The types of sewage and waste to be treated (domestic, industrial, hospital, agricultural).
5. The number of inhabitants to be served by the plant both now and in the future; arrangements for extension.
6. Quantity of sewage and wastes involved, cubic metres per day, per year, per season.
7. Characteristics of sewage and wastes to be treated.
8. Layout of the plant.
9. Final disposal of treatment effluent (for agriculture, to sea or river); chemical, physical and bacteriological characteristics of the treated effluent.
10. Sludge quantity and characteristics.
11. Method of sludge treatment and disposal (incineration, discharge into the ocean after stabilization, improving fertility of soils, providing compost for the horticultural industry, land rehabilitation, landfill).
12. The measures to maintain the reliability of the sewage treatment plant, so that plant bypasses which lead to raw sewage discharges are reduced to a minimum.
13. The measure to reduce overflows from the sewerage system resulting from illegal stormwater connections.
14. The arrangements for the separation of stormwater from the sewerage system, and the mode of disposal of stormwater.
15. The measures to reduce the emission of odors from the treatment and disposal activities; use of odor scrubbers.
16. The provision of additional sewerage services to reduce the pollution of waterways caused by runoff from on-site sewage disposal systems.
17. Measures which could be adopted for reducing the deleterious effects of urban runoff.

Box 69   continued

18. The possible impacts of measures on drinking water quality and recreational beaches.
19. The effects of the project on flora and fauna.
20. Proposals for landscaping and screening of plant.
21. The construction impacts should extensive construction of sewers be required.
22. In certain climates, the risks of mosquito breeding.
23. Measures to improve the quality of influents into the system, domestic, industrial and commercial.
24. Proposals for the monitoring of the entire system.
25. Proposals for the education of the public in environmentally sound practices.
26. Measures for the progressive improvement of plant performance and environmental management of the entire system over coming years.
27. The existing environment: physical site characteristics; climatological and meteorological conditions; geological and hydrological condition; present land use of site and surroundings; any other particular characteristics.
28. Enforcement procedures by management; the management structure.
29. Emergency services and responses.
30. Prospective future developments in the same locality which might suggest incompatibilities.
31. The political implications of the project.
32. The implications for aesthetics, amenity, ecology and health; nearby residential districts, schools, hospitals and so on.
33. The arrangements for continuing public involvement following the initial EIA.
34. Annual report to the environmental, planning and public works agencies.

takes place in a positive environment. This does not detract from the need for an EIA in order to achieve the best environmental outcome. See Box 69 for the economic, social and environmental elements to be considered in relation to a development consent.

Singapore

The Republic of Singapore at the southern tip of the Malaysian Peninsula, is a unitary multiparty republic with one legislative house. The population in 1997 was 3.0 million at a density of 4800 persons per sq km, one of the highest in the world. See Box 70 for the evolution of environmental law in this island state.

Box 70 Singapore: evolution of environmental law

1970 Anti-pollution unit established; Environmental Public Health Regulations; Keep Singapore Clean Campaign launched

1972 Ministry of the Environment formed; EIA procedures introduced; Clean Air Standards Regulations; sewerage program launched to cover the whole city, with six sewage treatment works

1973 Prohibitions on the use of open fires

1976 Trade Effluent Regulations; Sewage Treatment Plants Regulations; Drainage System Regulations

1977 Cleaning of river catchments

1986 Pollution Control Department formed, within the Ministry of the Environment; Poisons Rules issued

1988 Advisory Committee on Hazardous Substances and Toxic Wastes formed; Toxic Waste Regulations

1989 Building Control Regulations

1990 Annual Clean and Green Week launched; motor vehicle noise controls; Radiation regulations; Prevention of Pollution of the Sea Act

1991 Unleaded petrol introduced; CFCs regulated

1992 Green Plan launched to promote an environmentally conscious society; Environment Resource Centre created; catalytic converters required on cars; Waste Minimization Department formed; Green Labelling Scheme; Swimming Pool Regulations

1993 Radiation Regulations; Transport Regulations; Food Hygiene Regulations

2000 Singapore: a model Green City; all sewage treatment plants to be underground; all WHO and US EPA standards met; regular monitoring of ambient air, inland and coastal waters

---

Smoke Control Order

An order made under the British Clean Air Act, 1956, restricting smoke emissions within a prescribed area. The first smoke control order was made in the County of West Bromwich on 8 March 1957. Fuels authorized to be used within the area included anthracite, coke and other carbonized fuels, gas and electricity. A public inquiry into the proposed order became necessary following opposition by householders and the Coal Merchants' Association. The order was subsequently confirmed by the Minister for Housing and Local Government.

Social Impact Assessment (SIA)

An assessment of the impact on people and society of major development projects; SIA is often a weak point in EIAs. Social impacts may be defined as those changes in social relations between members of a community, society, or institution, resulting from external change. The changes in social relationships may lie in the areas of:
- the consequence of severance, both physical and psychological;
- general lifestyle;
- group relationships;
- cultural life (language, rituals, dress);
- attitudes and values;
- obligations to kin, marriage patterns, and visiting patterns;
- social tranquillity (disrupted, for example, by the arrival of a large all-male workforce); and
- relocation of large populations.

In the past, many proposed major projects and plans have not been assessed for social impacts; in consequence, adverse social impacts have not been ameliorated by appropriate measures adopted and prepared in advance. The results have been most notable in respect to hydroelectric dams where it has been necessary to relocate large populations into alien environments. The results have been social discontent, unhappiness, increased illness, and a loss of productivity resulting in loss of income. The closer proximity of different social groups with contrasting cultural characteristics may intensify the adverse effects.

Solid Waste Disposal Act, 1965, US

An act authorizing a research and development program with respect to solid waste disposal in the United States. It sprang from a recognition that continuing technological progress and improvement in the methods of manufacturing, packaging, and marketing of consumer products had resulted in an ever-mounting increase in, and a change in the characteristics of, the materials discarded by the purchasers of such products. In addition, increasing urbanization had presented many communities with serious financial, management, intergovernmental and technical problems in the disposal of solid wastes. Improper methods of disposal has resulted in scenic blights and created serious hazards to public health. A failure to salvage and reuse material had also resulted in unnecessary waste and depletion of natural resources.

The aim of the act was to initiate national research and development programs for new and improved methods of disposal, with provision for recovery and recycling. Technical and financial assistance was to be provided to state and local governments in the development of programs.

The law was reauthorized in 1970, a special report on the problems posed by hazardous wastes being requested. Following this report, the US Congress responded by enacting the Resource Conservation and Recovery Act, 1976. The RCRA established the statutory framework for comprehensive federal and state regulation of hazardous wastes. However, the act included provision for developing methods for the disposal of solid wastes which are environmentally sound and which conserve valuable resources. Federal grants have encouraged each state to develop its own solid waste management plan. In order to receive approval, each state plan must meet certain minimum requirements which emphasize the closing or upgrading of all open land dumps and a prohibition on the formation of new ones.

Under the RCRA amendments of 1984, EPA gained enforcement authority; the EPA is to step in if the states fail to meet deadlines for developing programs to ensure that their solid waste management facilities comply with the RCRA's existing and added criteria.

South Africa

The Republic of South Africa is a multiparty republic with two legislative houses, a National Council of Provinces and a National Assembly. Pretoria is the administrative capital and Cape Town the legislative one. The population in 1997 was 43 million, with an average density of 35 persons per sq km. Situated at the southern end of Africa, facing the Atlantic and Indian Oceans,

Box 71   *South Africa: evolution of environmental law*

1894   The first game reserve, the Pongola, established
1897   Establishment of the Hluhluwe and Umfolozi Game Reserves
1898   Sabie Game Reserve and Kruger National Park established
1926   National Parks Act
1931   Addo Elephant National Park, Kalahari Gemsbok National Park
        and Bontebok National Park established
1937   Mountain Zebra National Park established
1951   Merchant Shipping Act
1956   Water Act, to control the quantity of water used by industry
        and the quality of effluent; water pollution a criminal offence
1960   Decentralization plans introduced
1964   Golden Gate Highlands National Park established
1966   Aughrabies Falls National Park established
1967   Physical Planning and Utilization of Resources Act
1969   Soil Conservation Act
1970   Approval of sea-lanes for oil tankers
1971   Marine Pollution Act
1972   Creation of a Cabinet Committee on Environmental Conserva-
        tion; creation of a Department of Planning and Environment;
        creation of a South African Council for the Environment, previ-
        ously known as the South African Committee on Environmental
        Conservation
1974   Creation of the National Advisory Committee on Air Pollution;
        creation of a working group on noise disturbance; creation of
        the Council for the Habitat
1975   Creation of the National Committee for Nature Conservation,
        an interdepartmental body
1976   Creation of the South African Working Group on Environmen-
        tal Research which liaises with the South African National
        Committee for Oceanographic Research and the National Com-
        mittee for Environmental Sciences
1980   National plans to combat bilharzia (schistosomiasis); new meas-
        ures in bilharzia areas; improved water management; Atmospheric
        Pollution Prevention Act; City Council of Johannesburg first city
        with full-time noise control section
1985   Central Plan Guide Committees flourishing; 26 nature reserves
        in Natal, 17 in the Transvaal, 16 in the Cape Province, and five in
        the Orange Free State established. The combined area exceeds
        350 000 ha

Box 71   continued

1989   Environmental Conservation Act; EIA introduced; bilharzia remains a stubborn problem
1997   More than one million households given access to clean piped water since 1994; 332 000 houses built since 1994; improved access to health care and electricity

---

South Africa is bounded in the north by Namibia, Botswana, Zimbabwe and Mozambique. See Box 71 for the evolution of environmental law.

Space Law

That body of conventions, agreements, treaties, and regulations that governs international conduct in areas of space beyond the lower strata of the Earth's atmosphere. The concept was initiated by the USA before the UN in 1957; in 1959, a permanent Outer Space Committee was formed for the purpose of maintaining the UN Charter and other international law in space. The major powers recognized that it was not possible to extend sovereignty upwards into space, the upper atmosphere becoming a common property resource. In 1963, the Nuclear Test Ban Treaty was signed, followed by a prohibition of nuclear testing in space. In 1967, an Outer Space Treaty was ratified by the UN; this document was a landmark in the development of international space law.

Spain

The kingdom of Spain is a constitutional monarchy with two legislative houses, the Senate and the Congress of Deputies. The population in 1998 was 39 million, at a density of 202 persons per sq km. The capital is Madrid. Spain abuts Portugal and France. See Box 72 for the evolution of environmental law.

Special Use Corridors

Areas of land set aside for future use by public authorities and private enterprise in providing for such things as major roads, pipelines, transmission lines and other public utilities and for meeting regional open space requirements. Corridors also serve as physical and visual boundaries between or

---

Box 72   *Spain: evolution of environmental law*

1972   Air Quality Law
1973   Mining Law
1975   Adoption of EU Directive on Urban Solid Waste
1982   Royal Decree on Mining
1985   Water Law
1986   Royal Decree on Environmental Impact Evaluation; Toxic and
       Dangerous Wastes Law
1988   Coastal Zone Protection Law
1989   Conservation of Natural Spaces and Wild Flora and Fauna Law;
       Basic Plan for Nuclear Emergencies (PLABEN); prohibition of
       the hunting and fishing of endangered species; National Wetlands
       inventory; creation of National Commission for Nature Protec-
       tion; Ministry of Public Works Order on Titanium Waste and
       polychlorinated biphenyls
1994   Biotechnology Law
1997   Packaging and Waste Packaging Law; incineration of dangerous
       wastes decree
1998   Life expectancy: 74.9 for males; 81.8 for females

---

adjacent to existing and future urban areas. They are essentially long-term proposals to cater for demands arising from the expected population of the region and linkage requirements between cities and towns.

Provision for corridors is necessary because experience demonstrates that personal hardship and high social and economic costs result if land for future public purposes is not reserved early, and needs to be acquired later when the population density is much higher.

The size and location of the service corridors will depend upon the area demands of various known uses and likely future uses; in some cases they will need to be several kilometers wide and in others perhaps as little as 100 meters to allow for a limited number of linear service lines to pass through an urban area or along its boundary. They must also provide some flexibility and room for future unforeseen requirements.

Spot Zoning and Rezoning

Zoning which affects a particular property or a small group of adjoining properties, and is not necessarily related to the comprehensive environmental plan for the whole community. A spot zoning for a particular purpose may be good for the whole community; in other cases it may benefit or profit a particular owner. Generally, zoning and rezoning should take place within the framework of a comprehensive plan intended for the benefit of the whole community, but from time to time zonings and rezonings appear to be arbitrary or capricious. In New York in 1968, an appellate court dismissed a small area rezoning because it was not based on any underlying policy or comprehensive plan; the rezoning authority failed to show that the proposed amendment was 'for the benefit of the community as a whole, following a calm and deliberate consideration of the alternatives' (*Udell v. Haas* (1968) 21 NY 2d463).

Standards, Environmental

Standards of many kinds are universal. They include fundamental standards for weights and measures, potable water, foodstuffs, building construction, minerals, car design and emissions controls, safety requirements, traffic management, aircraft design, hospital equipment, household equipment, electrical wiring, drains and plumbing, fire precautions, street design, ship construction, dockside equipment, airport layout, telecommunications, radiation protection, and a range of others. In respect of environmental management, standards encompass ambient quality standards for air and water, emission standards, process standards, product standards, and international standards. See Box 73.

See also:
International Organization for Standardization (ISO).

Standing, Standing to Sue, *Locus Standi*

The right to be heard in court or other proceedings. The word 'standing' has emerged gradually during the twentieth century, coming into common use only from about 1950. The right to sue means *the right to institute legal proceedings against*. Legal standing is in many ways a reflection of social conscience, expanding with socially recognizable issues over time, slowly embracing the environment. The concept of standing has also expanded from the individual to the group, and now embraces challenges to government action. Even so, attempts by citizens and organizations to prevent or preclude environmental violations may often be frustrated. Courts tend to disallow actions which present formidable difficulties and cannot be resolved in simple financial terms.

Box 73   Environmental standards

Ambient quality standards
Environmental objectives in respect of the receiving environment; for example, the maximum concentration of sulphur dioxide in the atmosphere, the maximum concentration of nitrates in drinking water, or the maximum noise levels in residential districts.

Emission standards
The maximum allowable discharges of pollutants into the environment from fixed points; for example, the maximum emissions that may be discharged into the atmosphere from industrial stacks measured in weight per unit time or concentration; or the maximum biochemical oxygen demand (BOD) that may be discharged into water from a sewer or waste pipe.

Process standards
Standards that govern processes of production and diffuse sources of emission within industrial premises; for example, restrictions on the emission of fluorides from aluminium pot plants, or the specification of stages in effluent treatment.

Product standards
Standards specifying the characteristics of potentially polluting products; for example, detergents, fertilizers, chemicals, insecticides, fuels, motor vehicles, refrigerators, fire suppressants, lawn mowers, pneumatic drills, air conditioners, aircraft, paints and containers.

International standards
Environmental standards progressively introduced at an international level promoting satisfactory environmental management. For example, the International Organization for Standardization (ISO) issued in 1994 ISO 14000, a set of environmental management guidelines. Concurrently, the British Standards Institution issued BS 7750, also on environmental management systems; while the EU has issued an eco-management and audit regulation. Environmental audits are common to these standards. The WTO promotes the adoption of international environmental standards.

In respect of the environment, three cases greatly expanded standing to sue. Of note was Justice William O. Douglas's dissent in *Sierra Club v. Morton* (1972); *Japan Whaling Association v. American Cetacean Society* (1986); and *United States v. Students Challenging Regulatory Agency Procedures* (1973).

The right to standing tends to vary with the character and composition of the courts. Standing to sue has been refused in a number of cases. It will always be difficult, if not impossible, to gain standing for future generations. However in 1993, the Supreme Court of the Philippines granted standing to a group of children suing the government over decisions by the Philippines Department of the Environment and Natural Resources in relation to rain forest. The case *Oposa v. Factoran* became known as the Children's Case. The plaintiffs argued that they and future generations had a right to a healthy environment.

Statutory Instrument

A formal legal document which may take the character of an act of parliament or a regulation or order made thereunder by way of subordinate or delegated legislation. In the areas of environmental law, statutory instruments include not only major acts of parliament but important measures such as state environmental planning policies, regional environmental plans, and local environmental plans; measures creating individual national and marine parks, national monuments, and heritage items and relics; conservation orders; redevelopment schemes; development approvals and their conditions; curfews; protection of endangered species; protection of rain forest, marshland, peatland, coral, and coastal dunes; measures relating to environmental management, air, water, noise and land pollution; and measures for public participation, public inquiries and channels for appeals.

Stockholm Declaration

The Stockholm Declaration on the Human Environment was adopted on the final day of the world's first international conference on the human condition. This international gathering was held in Stockholm from 5–16 June 1972 (5 June became thereafter World Environment Day). Representatives from some 113 governments and agencies attended the conference. The result was an extensive work program for the future, a permanent headquarters in Nairobi, the creation of an environment fund, and the adoption of the Stockholm Declaration with its 26 principles. See Box 74.

Box 74   Stockholm Declaration on the Human Environment

The United Nations Conference on the Human Environment
Having met at Stockholm from 5 to 16 June 1972,
Having considered the need for a common outlook and for common principles to inspire and guide the peoples of the world in the preservation and enhancement of the human environment,

I
Proclaims that:
1. Man is both creature and moulder of his environment, which gives him physical sustenance and affords him the opportunity for intellectual, moral, social and spiritual growth. In the long and tortuous evolution of the human race on this planet a stage has been reached when, through the rapid acceleration of science and technology, man has acquired the power to transform his environment in countless ways on an unprecedented scale. Both aspects of man's environment, the natural and the man-made, are essential to his well-being and to the enjoyment of basic human rights – even the right to life itself.
2. The protection and improvement of the human environment is a major issue which affects the well-being of peoples and economic development throughout the world; it is the urgent desire of the people of the whole world and the duty of all Governments.
3. Man has constantly to sum up experience and go on discovering, inventing, creating and advancing. In our time, man's capability to transform his surroundings, if used wisely, can bring to all peoples the benefits of development and the opportunity to enhance the quality of life. Wrongly or heedlessly applied, the same power can do incalculable harm to human beings and the human environment. We see around us growing evidence of man-made harm in many regions of the earth: dangerous levels of pollution in water, air, earth and living beings; major and undesirable disturbances to the ecological balance of the biosphere; destruction and depletion of irreplaceable resources; and gross deficiencies harmful to the physical, mental and social health of man, in the man-made environment, particularly in the living and working environment.
4. In the developing countries most of the environmental problems are caused by under-development. Millions continue to live far below the minimum levels required for a decent human existence, deprived of adequate food and clothing, shelter and education,

Box 74   continued

health and sanitation. Therefore, the developing countries must direct their efforts to development, bearing in mind their priorities and the need to safeguard and improve the environment. For the same purpose, the industrialized countries should make efforts to reduce the gap between themselves and the developing countries. In the industrialized countries, environmental problems are generally related to industrialization and technological development.

5. The natural growth of population continuously presents problems on the preservation of the environment, and adequate policies and measures should be adopted, as appropriate, to face these problems. Of all things in the world, people are the most precious. It is the people that propel social progress, create social wealth, develop science and technology and, through their hard work, continuously transform the human environment. Along with social progress and the advance of production, science and technology, the capability of man to improve the environment increases with each passing day.

6. A point has been reached in history when we must shape our actions throughout the world with a more prudent care for their environmental consequences. Through ignorance or indifference we can do massive and irreversible harm to the earthly environment on which our life and well-being depend. Conversely, through fuller knowledge and wiser action, we can achieve for ourselves and our posterity a better life in an environment more in keeping with human needs and hopes. There are broad vistas for the enhancement of environmental quality and the creation of a good life. What is needed is an enthusiastic but calm state of mind and intense but orderly work. For the purpose of attaining freedom in the world of nature, man must use knowledge to build, in collaboration with nature, a better environment. To defend and improve the human environment for present and future generations has become an imperative goal for mankind – a goals to be pursued together with, and in harmony with, the established and fundamental goals of peace and of world-wide economic and social development.

7. To achieve this environmental goal will demand the acceptance of responsibility by citizens and communities and by enterprises and institutions at every level, all sharing equitably in common efforts. Individuals in all walks of life as well as organizations in many fields,

Box 74   continued

by their values and the sum of their actions, will shape the world environment of the future. Local and national governments will bear the greatest burden for large-scale environmental policy and action within their jurisdictions. International co-operation is also needed in order to raise resources to support the developing countries in carrying out their responsibilities in this field. A growing class of environmental problems, because they are regional or global in extent or because they affect the common international realm, will require extensive co-operation among nations and action by international organizations in the common interest. The Conference calls upon Governments and peoples to exert common efforts for the preservation and improvement of the human environment, for the benefit of all the people and for their posterity.

II   Principles
States the common conviction that:

Principle 1   Man has the fundamental right to freedom, equality and adequate conditions of life, in an environment of a quality that permits a life of dignity and well-being, and he bears a solemn responsibility to protect and improve the environment for present and future generations. In this respect, policies promoting or perpetuating *apartheid*, racial segregation, discrimination, colonial and other forms of oppression and foreign domination stand condemned and must be eliminated.

Principle 2   The natural resources of the earth including the air, water, land, flora and fauna and especially representative samples of natural ecosystems must be safeguarded for the benefit of present and future generations through careful planning or management, as appropriate.

Principle 3   The capacity of the earth to produce vital renewable resources must be maintained and, wherever practicable, restored or improved.

Principle 4   Man has a special responsibility to safeguard and wisely manage the heritage of wildlife and its habitats which are now gravely imperilled by a combination of adverse factors. Nature conservation including wildlife must therefore receive importance in planning for economic development.

Box 74   continued

Principle 5   The non-renewable resources of the earth must be employed in such a way as to guard against the danger of their future exhaustion and to ensure that benefits from such employment are shared by all mankind.

Principle 6   The discharge of toxic substances or of other substances and the release of heat, in such quantities or concentrations as to exceed the capacity of the environment to render them harmless, must be halted in order to ensure that serious or irreversible damage is not inflicted upon ecosystems. The just struggle of the peoples of all countries against pollution should be supported.

Principle 7   States shall take all possible steps to prevent pollution of the seas by substances that are liable to create hazards to human health, to harm living resources and marine life, to damage amenities or to interfere with other legitimate uses of the sea.

Principle 8   Economic and social development is essential for ensuring a favourable living and working environment for man and for creating conditions on earth that are necessary for the improvement of the quality of life.

Principle 9   Environmental deficiencies generated by the conditions of underdevelopment and natural disasters pose grave problems and can best be remedied by accelerated development through the transfer of substantial quantities of financial and technological assistance as a supplement to the domestic effort of the developing countries and such timely assistance as may be required.

Principle 10   For the developing countries, stability of prices and adequate earnings for primary commodities and raw material are essential to environmental management since economic factors as well as ecological processes must be taken into account.

Principle 11   The environmental policies of all States should enhance and not adversely affect the present or future development potential of developing countries, nor should they hamper the attainment of better living conditions for all, and appropriate steps should be taken by States and international organizations with a view to reaching agreement on meeting the possible national and international eco-

Box 74   continued

nomic consequences resulting from the application of environmental measures.

Principle 12   Resources should be made available to preserve and improve the environment, taking into account the circumstances and particular requirements of developing countries and any costs which may emanate from their incorporating environmental safeguards into their development planning and the need for making available to them, upon their request, additional international technical and financial assistance for this purpose.

Principle 13   In order to achieve a more rational management of resources and thus to improve the environment, States should adopt an integrated and co-ordinated approach to their development planning so as to ensure that development is compatible with the need to protect and improve the human environment for the benefit of their population.

Principle 14   Rational planning constitutes an essential tool for reconciling any conflict between the needs of development and the need to protect and improve the environment.

Principle 15   Planning must be applied to human settlements and urbanization with a view to avoiding adverse effects on the environment and obtaining maximum social, economic and environmental benefits for all. In this respect projects which are designed for colonialist and racist domination must be abandoned.

Principle 16   Demographic policies, which are without prejudice to basic human rights and which are deemed appropriate by Governments concerned, should be applied in those regions where the rate of population growth or excessive population concentrations are likely to have adverse effects on the environment or development, or where low population density may prevent improvement of the human environment and impede development.

Principle 17   Appropriate national institutions must be entrusted with the task of planning, managing or controlling the environmental resources of States with the view to enhancing environmental quality.

Box 74   continued

Principle 18   Science and technology, as part of their contribution to economic and social development, must be applied to the identification, avoidance and control of environmental risks and the solution of environmental problems and for the common good of mankind.

Principle 19   Education in environmental matters, for the younger generation as well as adults, giving due consideration to the under-privileged, is essential in order to broaden the basis for an enlightened opinion and responsible conduct by individuals, enterprises and com-munities in protecting and improving the environment in its full human dimension. It is also essential that mass media of communications avoid contributing to the deterioration of the environment, but, on the contrary, disseminate information of an educational nature, on the need to protect and improve the environment in order to enable man to develop in every respect.

Principle 20   Scientific research and development in the context of environmental problems, both national and multinational, must be pro-moted in all countries, especially the developing countries. In this connexion, the free flow of up-to-date scientific information and trans-fer of experience must be supported and assisted, to facilitate the solution of environmental problems; environmental technologies should be made available to developing countries on terms which would encourage their wide dissemination without constituting an economic burden on the developing countries.

Principle 21   States have, in accordance with the Charter of the United Nations and the principles of international law, the sovereign right to exploit their own resources pursuant to their own environmental policies, and the responsibility to ensure that activities within their jurisdiction or control do not cause damage to the environment of other States or of areas beyond the limits of national jurisdiction.

Principle 22   States shall co-operate to develop further the interna-tional law regarding liability and compensation for the victims of pollution and other environmental damage caused by activities within the juris-diction or control of such States to areas beyond their jurisdiction.

Principle 23   Without prejudice to such criteria as may be agreed upon by the international community, or to standards which will have

---

Box 74   continued

to be determined nationally, it will be essential in all cases to consider the systems of values prevailing in each country, and the extent of the applicability of standards which are valid for the most advanced countries but which may be inappropriate and of unwarranted social cost for the developing countries.

Principle 24   International matters concerning the protection and improvement of the environment should be handled in a co-operative spirit by all countries, big or small, on an equal footing. Co-operation through multilateral or bilateral arrangements or other appropriate means is essential to effectively control, prevent, reduce and eliminate adverse environmental effects resulting from activities conducted in all spheres, in such a way that due account is taken of the sovereignty and interests of all States.

Principle 25   States shall ensure that international organizations play a co-ordinated, efficient and dynamic role for the protection and improvement of the environment.

Principle 26   Man and his environment must be spared the effects of nuclear weapons and all other means of mass destruction. States must strive to reach prompt agreement, in the relevant international organs, on the elimination and complete destruction of such weapons.

Strict Liability

A legal situation in which proof of a contravention of law does not require evidence that the offence was deliberate or committed without due care; it is enough to prove that an offence occurred for a penalty to follow. The relevant legislation may allow certain lines of defence, or none. Under strict liability, the state of mind of the offender becomes irrelevant; ignorance or error of judgement cannot be conceded. It is enough to prove that food was contaminated, or that public health or safety was endangered for a conviction to be recorded. Evidence of a guilty mind or *mens rea* is not required. If despite all measures an explosion occurs, liability strictly applies whatever the explanation. The term 'strict liability' has superseded 'absolute liability' and 'liability without fault'.

Subdivision

Simply a division of land into parts for residential purposes; the basis of a housing estate. The term may be applied also to the subdivision of a building into individual ownerships, that is, strata titles. Subdivision regulations or controls define the standards for subdivision development; subdivision regulations and ordinances in many US cities have specified that new streets conform to the overall city plan and that new lots be properly laid out for building sites. Developers have been required to provide land for streets, playgrounds and school sites. The duties of developers have progressively increased over the years, and now embrace most and often all the requirements indicated in Box 75.

Most countries have adopted regulations requiring the approval of plans for new subdivisions before the owner or developer is allowed to proceed with construction. Such plans prescribe the layout of streets and open spaces, access for traffic and protection from through traffic, the location and types of utilities, houses, shopping centers and public buildings. As in the case of zoning, subdivision control gives effective direction to city growth only where it is combined with overall planning.

While developers tend to accept basic requirements readily enough, opposition arises when the requirements are perceived to be serving the needs of a larger community or other development, for example, when the roads are to be heavily paved or the water mains are of excessive size. Furthermore, excessive standards may tend to push the price per lot beyond the reach of the market which may lie in the lower-income brackets. See Box 75.

See also:
Zoning.

Sudan

The Republic of the Sudan is an Islamic military regime with one legislative house, the National Assembly. The capital is Khartoum. The population in 1997 was 33 million, with an average density of 13 persons per sq km. The Sudan abuts Egypt to the north, Chad to the west, Ethiopia to the east, and Uganda to the south. It borders the Red Sea to the northeast. See Box 76 for the evolution of environmental law.

Box 75   *Subdivisions: contemporary requirements for developers*

- Roads, paved or sealed.
- Suitable intersections with main roads.
- Curbing and guttering.
- Sidewalks.
- Parking strips.
- Turning circles.
- Drainage for stormwater.
- Street lighting.
- Street signs.
- Noise bunds.
- Buffer zones.
- Rights of way.
- Easements.
- Landscaping and tree planting; preservation of special characteristics.
- Playgrounds.
- Water mains.
- Fire hydrants.
- Water supply.
- Electric power.
- Open-space and parks.
- School-sites.
- Financial contribution towards nonland capital costs such as community facilities, or water supply or sewerage headworks.

Superfund

The US Comprehensive Environmental Response, Compensation, and Liability Act, 1980, created a Superfund to meet the costs of the clean-up of abandoned hazardous waste sites. The federal contribution to the Superfund was financed largely from a special tax imposed on feedstocks used by the petroleum refining and chemical manufacturing industries; the remainder from federal appropriations. Superfund was supplemented by 10 per cent matching grants from the states. Though some 600 companies pay Superfund taxes, some ten major petroleum and chemical companies meet about half the cost. The US EPA estimated that no more than 2500 sites out of 20 000 identified would need priority treatment, taking some ten years to complete

Box 76   Sudan, evolution of environmental law

1932   Forest Ordinance enacted to regulate forest tree utilization
       and preserve forest stands
1935   Dinder National Park established
1944   Government Commission examines accelerating soil erosion
       recommending solutions: known as the Soil Conservation Com-
       mittee. As a result, Rural Water Supplies and Soil Conservation
       Board created within the Ministry of Agriculture
1953   Attention focused on encroaching deserts
1954   Janglei investigation team report, the first environmental assess-
       ment investigation in the Sudan. The study involved many aspects,
       including water engineering, agriculture and livestock, and socio-
       economic considerations. Equatorial Nile Project completed
1971   Local People's Government Act causes ecological imbalance
1977   Desert Encroachment Control and Rehabilitation Program re-
       port, drawing further attention to desertification due to planned
       and unplanned pressures on fragile environments in the savan-
       nah belt of the Sudan
1980   Malaria, bilharzia, aquatic weeds and pesticides present serious
       problems
1984   Drought and famine conditions. Failure of the Sudan to become
       the breadbasket of the Arab World
1996   Life expectancy: 54.2 years for males; 56.1 years for females

the work. In 1986, the program was reauthorized with additional funds coming from a broader-based tax on corporate income, in addition to the taxes on
chemical and petroleum feedstocks with federal appropriations. Funds were
also provided for research into and development of new hazardous waste
disposal technologies. The program accelerated.

See also:
Comprehensive Environmental Response, Compensation, and Liability Act, 1980 (CERCLA), US

Surface Mining Control and Reclamation Act, 1977, US

A measure passed by the US Congress in 1977 establishing the first uniform
federal controls over surface or strip mining, which had previously been a
state matter.

Briefly, the law imposes requirements in five areas:

- Under *performance standards* operators are required to: restore stripped land to a condition capable of supporting the use that it was capable of supporting before mining; restore land to original contours; minimize disturbances to hydrologic balance; and permanently revegetate the stripped land.
- Under the *permitting* and *bonding* sections, operators must demonstrate their financial ability to conduct reclamation activities and purchase insurance covering personal injury and property damage.
- Under the *inspection* and *enforcement* provisions, one complete inspection every three months and one partial inspection every month, without advance notice to the operator, is required.
- Under the *citizen rights* section, public participation is allowed in nearly all phases of the law's implementation. This participation includes the right to be involved in administrative and judicial proceedings, to inspect surface mining activities, and to challenge any regulations in court.
- Under the *designation of unsuitable lands* provisions most surface mining is precluded if such operations: are not compatible with existing land-use plans; affect fragile or historic lands; affect renewable resources lands; or, affect *natural hazard* lands. Natural hazard lands include areas subject to landslides, cave-ins, severe wind or soil erosion, avalanches, or frequent flooding. Surface mining is now almost always precluded near national parks, wildlife refuge systems, and wilderness preservation systems.

Sustainable Development

In 1980, the World Conservation Strategy (WCS) was launched by the World Conservation Union (WCU), the UN Environment Program (UNEP), and the World Wide Fund for Nature (WWF). It demonstrated that development can only be sustained by conserving the living resources on which that development depends, and by the integration of development and conservation policies. It urged every country to prepare its own national conservation strategy, and many did. The chief successor to the WCS has been the document *Caring for the Earth: A Strategy for Sustainable Living* published by the same bodies in 1991. It included a wide range of recommendations for legal, institutional and administrative reform.

In 1987, the World Commission on Environment and Development (the Brundtland Commission) in its report to the Governing Council of UNEP, *Our Common Future*, defined sustainable development as: 'development that meets the needs of the present without compromising the ability of future generations to meet their own needs'. Sustainable development considers both the living and non-living resource base with regard for conservation and the advantages and disadvantages of alternative courses of action for future generations. It allows the use of depletable resources in an efficient manner

---

Box 77 Characteristics of sustainable development

- A shift from exclusive concern with raising the standard of living in materialistic terms to one of concern with the general quality of life such as health, education, equity and general social well-being.
- Increased emphasis on the value of natural, built and cultural environments; renewable and non-renewable resources.
- A concern with the long-term intergenerational aspects of developments, as well as the short and medium terms, with a view to fairer treatment of present and future generations.
- An increased emphasis on the needs of the least-advantaged in the community.
- Future generations should be compensated for unavoidable reductions in natural resources, where these are likely to be significant.
- Vast areas of wilderness, marine resources, the Arctic and the Antarctic, forests, coastlines, scenic areas, unique habitat, fauna and flora should be retained *en masse* for the potential use of future generations.
- The pursuit of alternative sources of energy.
- The progressive reduction of wastes, gaseous, solid, liquid, radioactive or sonic.
- The introduction of the user-pays principle where appropriate to regulate the use of natural assets and prevent the overuse and exploitation of natural assets.
- The concept of *environmental impact assessment* should be broadened to embrace more strongly health and social impact assessment, and over longer time-scales. Policies and programs should be embraced. Inquiries should embrace whole segments of the environment, and not simply be project-based.
- The philosophy of *sustainable development* involves further attitudinal changes by individuals, societies, governments and international associations.

with an eye to the substitution of other resources in due course. Sustainable development, the report argued, called for much more emphasis on conserving the natural resources base on which all development depends; and a greater regard for equity within society and between rich and poor nations, with a planning horizon that extends further than the present generations alive today. It requires an integration of economic, social and environmental considerations in decision-making at both government and corporation levels. See Box 77.

Sweden

The kingdom of Sweden is a constitutional monarchy and parliamentary state with one legislative house. The capital is Stockholm, the location of the UN Conference on the Human Environment in 1972. The population in 1997 was 8.9 million at a density of 21.6 persons per sq km. Sweden is a member of the Nordic Council with Norway, Denmark and Finland. See Box 78 for the evolution of environmental law.

Box 78   *Sweden: evolution of environmental law*

1909   Sarek National Park established
1962   Padjelanta National Park established
1964   Nature Conservancy Act superseding earlier laws in 1909 and
        1952
1967   Creation of National Environmental Protection Agency
1968   Environmental Advisory Committee appointed; Sulphur Con-
        tent in Fuel Oil Act
1969   Environment Protection Act; use of DDT stopped
1971   Marine Dumping Prohibition Act; aldrin and dieldrin banned;
        Nordic Council formed
1972   UN Conference on the Human Environment held in Stock-
        holm; the first day of the Conference, 6 June, named World
        Environment Day
1973   Products Hazardous to Health and the Environment Act
1975   Vehicle Scrapping Act
1976   Sulphur in Fuel Oil Act amended
1978   Environment Monitoring Program introduced
1979   Forest Conservation Act; Cleansing Act
1980   Rikstag vote to phase out nuclear power by the year 2010;
        Water Pollution from Vessels Act
1985   Chemical Products Act
1986   Building and Planning Act; Natural Resources Act; lead-free
        petrol introduced; Environmental Damage Act
1987   Hunting Act
1988   Phase-out plan for CFCs
1989   Catalytic converters compulsory for new cars
1990   EIA requirements extended
1992   EIA Regulations introduced: support for UNCED
1994   Environmental Code introduced by the Association of Swedish
        Industries to create better industrial environments
1995   Life expectancy: 67.8 years for males; 72.8 years for females
1996   Government Environmental Code Commission reports on sus-
        tainable development and standards for all Swedish industry
1997   Kyoto target: 92
1999   Sweden remains a leader in social welfare

T

Taiwan

The Republic of Taiwan is a multiparty republic with a National Assembly. Separated from mainland China, geographically and politically, the population in 1997 was 22 million, with a density of 598 persons per sq km. Taipei is the capital. See Box 79 for the evolution of environmental law.

Box 79   Taiwan: evolution of environmental law

1967   Taiwan government assigns air and water pollution control to the Taiwan Institute of Environmental Sanitation and the Taiwan Water Pollution Control Agency, respectively
1974   Water Pollution Control Act
1975   Water pollution control regulations promulgated for the Haintien River
1976   Water pollution control regulations announced for Taiwan as a whole
1979   Executive Yuan orders government departments to undertake EIAs in respect of proposed major projects to reconcile economic growth and development with social and environmental considerations
1980   Executive Yuan instructs the Taiwan Power Company to undertake EIAs in respect of all future nuclear power stations
1981   Atomic Energy Council establishes a radioactive waste unit
1982   Cultural Heritage Preservation Act; Environmental Protection Bureau established
1983   EIA procedures extended to major private sector projects
1984   Kenting National Park established
1985   National EIA program formulated; Yushan, Yangmingshan and Taroka National Parks established
1986   Protected areas for rare and endangered species; Hill Land Preservation Act; public demonstration against a proposed titanium dioxide plant at Lukang
1987   Environmental Protection Administration established to control pollution throughout Taiwan
1988   Basic Law of Environment Protection; aircraft noise control

---

Box 79 continued

1989 Wildlife Conservation Act; Toxic Chemicals Control Act; vehicle emission control

1991 Amendments to the Air Pollution and Noise Pollution Acts; paper recycling plan; all country and city administrations have their own environmental bureaux; Drinking Water Control Act; effluent standards

1992 Shei-Pa National Park established; sixth naphtha cracking plant endorsed after EIA; residents protest against fourth nuclear power station; 16 Environmental Acts now passed with 42 sets of regulations; Dispute Resolution Act; Air Pollution and Noise Control Acts

1993 Kinment Islands proposed as sixth national park

1994 Decision to build fourth nuclear power station; Coastal Protection Act. Life expectancy: 71.8 years for males; 77.7 years for females

1995 Wildlife Conservation Law; compliance with the Convention on International Trade in Endangered Species (CITES)

Taking Issue, US

An argument that may arise when zoning creates an excessive gap between the value of land for the use to which it is restricted and its value for more intensive development; an owner may claim the zoning is unconstitutional because it confiscates the increased value that might be realized if the land were put to its most profitable use. This is commonly called the 'taking issue'.

The argument is based on guarantees of the Fifth Amendment to the US Constitution and certain state constitutions, for example, Article 1, Section 10 of the Pennsylvania Constitution which states: 'nor shall private property be taken or applied to public use, without authority of law and without just compensation being first made or secured'. However, well-conceived and precise land-use regulations are generally upheld by the courts. It is in particular instances only that the courts have found that the cost of a particular land control was so burdensome on a landowner that it amounted to an illegal taking. Land-use controls should withstand a taking challenge where the owner of the land is left with a reasonable, profitable, use, even though it is substantially less than the most profitable use, and the restriction is necessary for the public welfare.

Tallest Chimney in the World

A record long held by the Canadian smelter at Trail, but when that closed down, the title was transferred to Mount Isa lead smelter, Mount Isa, Queensland, Australia. Mount Isa has been a considerable source of air pollution, notably sulphur dioxide from its copper and lead smelting operations. The prevailing wind at Mount Isa is a southerly, which carries the stack fumes over open country for most of the time. However, there are occasions when winds from other directions carry the waste gases over the town. The company introduced a closed loop system to monitor pollution in various parts of the town. This information is telemetered to a central computer where it is assessed along with meteorological information. At times, smelter production has been curtailed to keep concentrations at an acceptable level.

Initially, the mine was dependent on a 153 m stack serving the copper smelter. In 1975, the Air Pollution Council of Queensland resolved that the company should instal a 270 m stack (879 ft, or 1000 ft above ground level), twice the height of the copper smelter chimney. After a full year's operation, it was found that the ground-level concentration target was met. In 1977, the company announced the construction of the new stack, the highest chimney in the world with the greatest dispersal range. The new chimney was the latest multi-flue design, representing best practice.

Tanzania

The United Republic of Tanzania is a unitary multiparty republic with one legislative house, a National Assembly, the seat of government being Dar es Salaam. The population in 1997 was 29.5 million, at a density of 31.2 persons per sq km. Located on the east African coast facing the Indian Ocean, Tanzania is bordered by Malawi and Mozambique in the south; Zambia, Zaire, Burundi and Rwanda in the west; and Uganda and Kenya in the north. The main environmental diseases are malaria, sleeping sickness, schistosomiasis and onchocerciasis. Deficient nutrition remains a major problem. Tanzania was formed in 1964 by the merging of Tanganyika and Zanzibar. See Box 80 for the evolution of environmental law.

Thailand

The Kingdom of Thailand is a constitutional monarchy with two legislative houses, the Senate and the House of Representatives. The population in 1997 was 61 million, at a density of 118 persons per sq km. Located in southeast

Box 80   *Tanzania: evolution of environmental law*

1970   Fisheries Act
1974   Water Utilization (Control and Regulation) Act
1975   Rufiji Basin Development Authority Act; Standards Act
1978   Food (Control of Quality) Act
1979   Mining Act; Tanzania Industrial Research and Development Or-
        ganization Act; Tropical Pesticides Research Institute Act
1980   Tanzania Fisheries Research Institute Act; Tanzania Forest Re-
        search Institute Act
1981   Urban Water Supply Act
1983   National Environment Management Act, establishing a National
        Environment Management Council
1984   Tanzania Environment Society formed; National Land-Use Plan-
        ning Commission Act
1991   Directorate of Environment established

Asia, Thailand abuts Burma in the northwest, Cambodia in the east, and
Malaysia in the south. See Box 81 for the evolution of environmental law.

Thames, River

See:
Pippard Committee on the Tidal Thames, 1961.

Thermal Power Station Assessment

Electricity is pollution free at the point of use, displacing other forms of
energy which are undesirable in that they pollute the atmosphere. However,
the source of electricity generation and its distribution requires detailed assessment and analysis. A thermal power station may pollute the immediate
location, cause transboundary pollution, and will be a major source of greenhouse gases, a global problem. Coal, black or brown, is the prime culprit; oil
fuel comes next; and finally natural gas. The aim of an EIA is to establish the
need for a power station and having done so to define the essentials of a
power station that would minimize adverse environmental effects, near or far,
high or low. Box 82 seeks to define the economic, social and environmental
elements to be considered.

Box 81   Thailand: evolution of environmental law

1914	Local Government Act providing limited environmental protection in respect of public lands
1921	Wild Elephant Conservation Act
1941	Forestry Act
1960	Wild Animal Reservation and Protection Act
1961	National Parks Act
1962	Khao Yai National Park established; now an ASEAN Heritage Site
1964	National Reserved Forest Act
1967	Mineral Act with provisions for pollution control
1975	National Environmental Quality Act
1976–81	Fourth five-year development plan incorporating resource protection, rehabilitation strategies, water and soil conservation
1981	EIA introduced as a tool for environmental planning and management
1981–86	Fifth five-year national development plan incorporating an integrated approach to natural resource development and socioeconomic progress
1984	EIA reports to be prepared by consultant firms registered with the Office of the National Environment Board
1986–91	Sixth five-year national development plan recognizing that the depletion of the resource base could become a constraint to development
1989	Thailand's Natural Resource and Environmental Conservation Year
1991	Wildlife Conservation Act
1992	Thailand's Report to UNCED (the Rio Conference); National Environmental Quality Act, replacing the act of 1975; Wildlife Conservation Act
1992–96	Seventh five-year national development plan setting definite targets for improving environmental quality throughout the country and promoting sustainable development
1993	Catalytic converters required on all new cars; unleaded fuel introduced, national ambient air quality standards established
1994	Plans to increase national parks, nature reserves and recreational areas from 12.7 per cent of the country to 25 per cent, as provided for in the seventh national develop-

Box 81   *continued*

	ment plan; modification of the Pak Mun hydroelectric project
1997	Life expectancy: 67.0 years for males; 72.0 years for females

---

Box 82   *Thermal electricity generation: economic, social and environmental elements to be considered*

1. The contribution to a balanced system for the generation and supply of electricity to meet present and anticipated demand.
2. The alternatives to the proposal by way of alternative sites, alternative ways of generating electricity, or modifying the demand for electricity.
3. The consistency of the proposal with national, regional or local planning instruments; the relationship with national parks, wilderness areas or nature reserves.
4. The generating capacity of the proposed power station, the number and capacity of the individual generating sets.
5. The proposed fuel (oil, coal or gas) and its sources.
6. The mode of transportation of fuel to the site; the storage of the same.
7. The composition of the fuel to be used with particular reference to ash and sulphur content.
8. The types of steam generators and mode of combustion of the fuel.
9. The arrangements for dust arrestation and flue gas scrubbing.
10. The characteristics and composition of the final emissions to the atmosphere, with particular reference to greenhouse gases.
11. The number and heights of stacks; internal flue arrangement; efflux velocity and temperature.
12. Measures against downwash and downdraught, and adverse meteorological conditions.
13. Predictions for the dispersal of the final effluent into the atmosphere; local, regional, national and transboundary implications.
14. The ash disposal system, and dust suppression arrangements.
15. The disposal of exhausted scrubber reagents.
16. The cooling water system, either direct to a body of water or indirect via cooling towers.
17. The visual and humidity effects of cooling towers.

Box 82   *continued*

18. The potential effects of thermal discharges into water on fauna and flora, including coral and mangroves.
19. The environmental implications of construction by way of site preparation, road and railway construction and other supporting infrastructure.
20. The housing of the construction workforce.
21. The overall effects on the health of communities.
22. The risks and hazards of a major structure.
23. The implications for employment and local industry.
24. The implications for aesthetics, amenity and ecology at site and elsewhere; landscaping.
25. Electricity transmission lines, easements and access roads; prospective routes.
26. Housing for the permanent workforce.
27. The proponent's contribution to local infrastructure development and social facilities.
28. Facilities for monitoring and post-project analysis.
29. Potential damage to or destruction of archaeological or historic sites.
30. The implications for sacred and cultural sites.
31. The implications for training.
32. The implications for technology in a national context.
33. The implications in respect of foreign investment.
34. The implications in respect of trade and the balance of payments.
35. Emergency services and responses.
36. Environmental management of the power station.
37. Proposals for site rehabilitation at the end of the power station's useful economic life.
38. The political implications of the project.
39. The arrangements for continuing public involvement following the initial EIA.
40. Annual report to the environmental, planning and energy agencies.
41. Prospective future developments in the same district, or region, which might suggest cumulative impacts.

Times Beach, US

An example of the consequences of environmentally hazardous chemicals, in this case dioxin. In February 1983, the Reagan administration offered to buy out all 2400 residents of Times Beach, Missouri, after confirming that the town was too contaminated with the toxic compound dioxin to be safe for habitation. The dioxin levels had been found by the EPA to be 100 times what was considered safe.

Times Beach was one of at least 100 communities in Missouri where dioxin mixed with waste oils was sprayed on dirt roads in the 1970s to keep down dust.

See also:
Disasters.

Todd River Dam, Alice Springs, Northern Territory, Australia

The town of Alice Springs, at the centre of Australia, lies on the intermittent Todd River and the Stuart Highway, some 1650 km north of Adelaide and 1550 km south of Darwin. With a population of about 25 000, it is a centre of tourism. Tourists can visit nearby Ayers Rock, perhaps the world's largest sandstone monolith. The intermittent nature of the Todd River lends itself to dry boatraces, in which the boats are carried by runners.

However, at other times the Todd floods. It rises in the MacDonnell Ranges and flows southeast for 300 km passing through Heavitree Gap and Alice Springs, eventually disappearing into the Simpson Desert. To deal with the flood problem, at least in part, the Northern Territory government in 1983 proposed a dam, with a 30-metre retaining wall, to be built 6 km north of Alice Springs.

The dam proposal was bitterly opposed by Aborigines whose sacred sites would be lost. In consequence, a public inquiry was conducted by a former Royal Commissioner (Mr Wootten) into the matter to advise the Commonwealth (federal) government. In his report, Mr Wootten said:

> Aborigines can see no justice in their being asked to sacrifice their sacred sites, the only interest they are still accorded in their traditional land, to prevent infrequent damage to carpets and other property of white people who have chosen to build on flood-prone land, not to elevate their houses or commercial buildings to the small extent necessary to place them above flood level or otherwise flood proof them, or to buy buildings that are known to be subject to occasional flooding at prices that presumably reflected that.

Mr Wootten also concluded that the dam was highly uneconomic, and he was surprised that even after the experience of a 50-year flood in 1988, no comprehensive flood plain management study had been undertaken by the Northern Territory government. Mr Wootten emphasized that the land had profound significance for its traditional custodians, especially women, and involved a major 'dreaming' track. The dam would cause great anguish to many Aboriginal people, destroying race relations in Alice Springs and perhaps causing international outrage. Mr Wootten also concluded that the dam would not necessarily prevent flooding.

In May 1992, the Commonwealth (federal) government placed a ban on the dam under the Aboriginal and Torres Strait Islander Heritage Protection Act to save the sacred sites. It was the first time that the act had been so used to block a project. At the same time, the Northern Territory government was advised to apply for funds to complete a comprehensive flood management plan under the Federal Water Resources Assistance Programme.

The decision was bitterly opposed by the Northern Territory government, while central Australian Aboriginal women sang, danced and wept in gratitude. The traditional women custodians, members of the Arrernte people, visited the sacred dreaming sites which would have been destroyed.

Source: Conservation Commission, Northern Territory, *Australian Financial Review*, 18 May 1992.

Town and Country Amenities Act, 1974, UK

An act which imposes a duty upon local authorities to draw up proposals for the preservation and enhancement of defined urban conservation areas, and to submit such proposals to a public meeting. It introduced important new provisions for the basis of compensation when listed buildings are acquired compulsorily by a local authority for preservation. In addition, buildings could no longer be demolished in conservations areas without appropriate consents.

Town and Country Planning

In Britain, physical planning as it extends to the whole country; in the United States the usual term is 'city and regional planning'. Planning activities in Britain have included:
- schemes for the redistribution of industry and the building of new towns;

- slum clearance and development schemes;
- urban renewal;
- the creation of green belts to restrain the outward spread of towns and cities;
- the creation of national parks and the preservation of national monuments;
- the protection of heritage buildings;
- the provision of urban amenities in the countryside for the agricultural population;
- the preparation and approval of structure plans for county areas; and
- the preparation and approval of local plans for municipal or local authority areas.

Town and country planning is also referred to simply as town planning, physical planning, spatial planning, territorial, urban and regional, and environmental planning. See Box 83.

Town and Country Planning Act, 1932, UK

A British measure aimed at broadening the planning process by allowing local authorities (the local elected municipal councils) to prepare planning schemes for almost any kind of land. Comprehensive plans were to be drawn up within a three-year period and then approved by Parliament. A developer could, within this period, apply for planning permission under the clauses relating to 'interim development control'. By 1942, 73 per cent of England and 36 per cent of Wales were subject to 'interim development control'; but only 5 per cent of land in England and 1 per cent in Wales was under a fully operative scheme. At that time, there were 1400 planning authorities often linked through joint committees. The Second World War inflicted considerable damage on British towns, and new construction ceased. Postwar hopes surrounded the concepts of reconstruction, finding expression in the Town and Country Planning Act, 1947.

Town and Country Planning Act, 1947, UK

A British measure that embodied the principle that all development rights belonged to the nation; it created machinery for the comprehensive planning of all land in England and Wales (there was parallel legislation for Scotland). The system created in 1947 obliged planning authorities to draw up 'development plans', a combination of strategy and projection covering a period of twenty years. Development plans consisted of a written statement and a

Box 83   Objectives of town planning

- The pursuit of social improvement through changes in the physical infrastructure of urban centers, maximizing opportunities for personal choice and protecting the individual and family from the adverse actions of others.
- The orderly arrangement of the metropolitan area into residential, commercial, industrial, port and recreational areas, each part performing its function at least cost and with minimum conflict.
- The promotion of an efficient system of transportation and communication.
- The achievement of optimal standards in respect of infrastructure, lot sizes, building spaces and alignment, sunlight, open space and parks, parking facilities, fire and emergency facilities, road pavement, access and aesthetics.
- The promotion of a safe, clean and adequate public water supply, sewerage system, energy supply system, schools and other public services.
- The promotion of good-quality housing in a variety of types.
- The minimization of air pollution, water pollution, noise and vibration.
- The promotion of a satisfactory solid waste management system with recycling arrangements and well-located landfill sites.
- The progressive development of tree planting, landscaping, anti-litter programs, bicycle paths, nature walks, national and marine parks and reserves, community access to natural features, and recreational schemes.
- The identification, preservation and restoration of items of heritage value.
- The identification of natural resources with measures against the alienation of the most valuable of them.
- To achieve consistency between local plans and any metropolitan, regional, provincial, state, federal or national plans and relevant international conventions.
- To promote EIA.
- The provision of ample opportunities for public participation in the decision-making process, including participation in public inquiries.
- Finally, the promotion of economic prosperity and the good life for all.

number of maps. Between them, these expressed intentions for development and intentions for preservation in the different areas under the planning authority's control. Plans were to encompass urban and rural areas.

Plans became the responsibility of the local planning authorities, primarily the larger units of local government, the counties and county boroughs. These were drawn up by planning departments, professional and expert administrations which the authorities were obliged to employ. After approval by the planning authority, the plans were submitted to the minister in Whitehall (the central government) who could accept them, reject them, or require their modification. Development plans had to be revised every 5 years. Between 1947 and 1951, the central government department was the Ministry of Town and Country Planning; from 1951 to 1970 the Ministry of Housing and Local Government; and from 1970, the Department of the Environment.

Individuals and organizations were directly affected by the system in that they required 'planning permission' for any development, subject to a number of exemptions. For large projects, planning permission could be divided into two halves, 'outline' and 'detailed' permission, in order that architectural effort should not be wasted on detailed plans for a non-starter. Anyone who was refused planning permission by a local authority could appeal to the minister. This could be done by written representation, and could result in a public local inquiry. At such inquiries, an inspector from the ministry heard the case put by the developer and any objections to the development which other individuals or organizations might wish to put. The inspector would then report in writing to the minister who finally refused or allowed development. In the 1970s some 10 000 inquiries were held each year, with the inspector's recommendations being accepted in 95 per cent of cases.

See also:
Town and Country Planning Act, 1968, UK.

Town and Country Planning Act, 1968, UK

A British measure aimed at speeding up the planning process by a distinction between 'structure plans' which could be ordered and must be approved by central government, and local plans which do not need to go through the same process. A later document outlined seven functions for the structure plan:

1. Interpreting national and regional policies.
2. Establishing aims, policies and general proposals.
3. Providing framework for local plans.
4. Indicating action areas.

5. Providing guidance for development control.
6. Providing a basis for coordinating decisions.
7. Bringing the main planning issues before the minister and public.

The public was to be consulted on both structure and local plans, enlarging the area for public participation.

See also:
Town and Country Planning Act, 1947, UK.

Town and Country Planning Act, 1971, UK

An act which consolidated and reenacted most of the current planning legislation in Britain, including the Town and Country Planning Act, 1968 and the Civic Amenities Act. It was augmented by the Town and Country Planning (Amendment) Act, 1972.

Town and Development Act, 1952, UK

An act which made provision for the relief of congestion in large industrial towns in England and Wales by encouraging the transfer of population from these areas to places suitable for expansion where employment was available. Centers brought within the scope of the act included the already well-established towns in the south of England of Basingstoke, Andover and Haverhill.

Toxic Substances Control Act, 1976, US

A measure introduced by the US Congress to regulate environmentally hazardous chemicals. Under the act, the EPA was authorized to regulate the manufacture, distribution, use, or disposal of chemical substances. The agency was required to adopt rules requiring the testing of chemicals that presented a risk of injury, will be produced in substantial quantities, and could reasonably be expected to result in extensive human or environmental exposures. The cost for such testing would be borne by the manufacturers. Chemical substances specifically controlled under existing legislation (pesticides, tobacco, food, food additives, drugs, cosmetics, nuclear materials, firearms and ammunition) were not included in the act.

By November 1977, the administrator of the EPA was required to publish an inventory of existing chemicals. Any substance not on the inventory would then be considered a new chemical substance for which manufacturers must give 90-days notice of intent to manufacture. This procedure gave the administrator the opportunity to evaluate the hazard-causing potential of the new chemical substance or significant new use and control of its introduction into commerce if deemed harmful. The 1985 inventory comprised over 60 000 chemicals.

Polychlorinated biphenyls (PCBs) were the only chemical substances specifically mentioned in the act. The use, distribution, manufacture and processing of PCBs were prohibited after January 1978, except for enclosed uses or uses approved by the administrator. Manufacture was totally prohibited after January 1979. Since 'manufacture' was defined to include importation into the US, imports were also prohibited. Distribution was prohibited after July 1979, except for PCBs being recycled for use in a manner not prohibited by the act.

Trail Smelter Case, 1941

Trail is a city and metropolitan area in southeastern British Columbia, Canada. It lies along the Columbia River at the mouth of Trail Creek, adjacent to Rossland, in the Selkirk Mountains. It is just north of the US–Canada border and the state of Washington. Its economy has rested almost entirely on the mining and smelting of metals, especially silver, zinc and lead, and on the production of chemicals and fertilizers. Trail boasted the highest chimney in the world. The Tribunal appointed for the *Trail Smelter Arbitration* found that the smelter at Trail had caused damage in the United States (in the state of Washington) and was called upon to decide what indemnity should be paid for the damage. The Tribunal made two awards, though neither dealt with environmental damage.

The Tribunal held that no state had the 'right to use or permit the use of its territory in such a manner as to cause injury by fumes in or to the territory of another or the properties or persons thereof'. Compensation was given for some of the damage the US claimed to have suffered, and changes were made in the plant's operation to keep harmful emissions below an acceptable threshold.

Source: Trail Smelter Arbitration (Decision), 11 March 1941, 3 *UNRIAA* 1965 (1949).

Transfer of Development Rights (TDRs)

Tradable permits issued by US local governments increasingly being applied to land use in environmentally sensitive areas, redistributing development rights without much cost to government and without penalizing property owners. A TDR involves the transfer of the rights to develop a given piece of land to a second piece of land, the first piece of land losing development rights, and the second gaining development rights it did not have before. Usually in such a transfer, the second property owner pays the first for development rights at a price which reflects the value of the rights had that land been developed. This enables the local jurisdiction to freeze large areas of environmentally sensitive land for public purposes without the risk of giving ground for a *taking issue* under the US Constitution that might require payment from the public purse of *just compensation*. It also avoids much displeasure among farmers and other landowners, when land is zoned in such a way as to involve substantial losses. The transfer of purchased development rights to other areas requires local government approval, involving as it does development beyond the original environmental plan, but such transfers have a pragmatic value. The first owner makes nearly as much money by not developing as would have been made by developing, while the second landowner may undertake additional development which allows a recovery of the development costs. It avoids the need for government to compensate for the loss of development rights with public funds and ensures that zoning ordinances of a restrictive kind may be imposed without opposition. To government such a transfer is essentially a trade-off, to achieve the most desirable public outcome. The customary procedure is for local government to create certificates of development rights which are made available to landowners in the affected district. Landowners who purchase these certificates become entitled to increased densities and floor areas in designated areas.

The concept was pioneered by New York City in the 1970s, when developers were allowed to build extra storeys on one site, in exchange for preserving environmental amenities such as open space or heritage assets nearby. On Long Island, east of New York City, several local councils have created a system of TDRs to preserve the Pine Barrens, a 40 500 ha area that provides the region's water supply. Where new construction is forbidden, property owners have been issued with Pine Barrens Credits in compensation. The credits may be sold on an exchange or to a developer; they may be used to build more than would otherwise be allowed in approved nearby areas. Other states are developing TDR programs, although not all schemes have been successful.

Transport Plan

A compilation of policy statements, goals, standards, maps and action programs for guiding the future development of the various modes of transportation of municipality, county, or regions and its environs such as streets and highways, mass transit, railroads, air transportation, trucking and water transportation, and which includes a major thoroughfare plan.

The circulation element of the General Plan for the City of Los Angeles sets forth objectives, policies and programs to guide the location and development of the city's transportation facilities linking parts of Los Angeles with each other and other parts of the metropolitan area. It is recognized that the transportation network will significantly shape the development of the city and the region although the private automobile, modified to conform to required air quality standards, will continue to provide the principal means of transportation in the foreseeable future.

However, it is conceded that traffic congestion remains a serious problem during peak hours. Public transportation is provided primarily by buses, which compete with the automobile for space, offer limited routes and time schedules and attract insufficient revenues; public transit facilities remain inadequate and the non-driver has limited mobility. However, a rapid transit system is being developed to improve the situation and efforts are being made to meet the special needs of various communities.

The objective of the Los Angeles Transport Plan are stated as follows:

- To provide an integrated transportation system coordinated with land use which adequately accommodates the total travel needs of the community.
- To minimize the use of air-polluting motor vehicles.
- To improve the safety and efficiency of all transportation modes, particularly during peak travel periods, giving priority to public transportation.
- To achieve within an exclusive right-of-way a rapid transit system as an effective alternative to the private automobile for trips between centers and also between the regional core and outlying suburban areas.
- To locate, operate and maintain transportation facilities to be compatible with adjacent areas.
- To promote improved design and appearance of transportation facilities.
- To minimize conflict between vehicular and pedestrian traffic.
- To utilize the transportation system as a tool in developing planned land-use patterns so as to minimize detrimental effects upon urban life.
- To provide adequate local bus transportation throughout the metropolitan region, as a part of the integrated transportation system.
- To provide for the efficient movement of freight.
- To encourage the development of air rights over publicly owned rights-of-way in areas of high intensity where appropriate and consistent with public health, safety and welfare.

- To improve the city's highway and freeway system as a major component of the city's integrated transportation system.
- To encourage the use of bicycles as a viable means of transportation.

Transport Planning, Objectives of

The aims of transport planning as they have evolved during the twentieth century. They include the following:
- The reducing of the length of the journey to work.
- The reducing of journey time.
- The provision of reasonable access to opportunities within a region for the population of that region.
- Roads and public transportation should work in combination to handle the transport task of the region, rather than in competition.
- The improvement of the urban arterial road network to safely and efficiently carry all major traffic movement.
- The reducing of existing congestion on arterial roads.
- The reduction of through traffic on residential streets, especially truck traffic.
- The reduction of the conflicts caused by traffic passing through shopping centers.
- The improvement of accessibility to employment, shopping and recreation centers by private and public transportation.
- The enhancement of public transport operations to meet the needs of public transport users and reduce the demand for parking spaces in the city center.
- Provision for future traffic growth.
- The provision of routes for vehicles and tankers carrying inflammable, explosive, or hazardous loads, to avoid residential streets and densely populated districts.
- The progressive reduction of all heavy vehicle traffic through city, town and village centers.
- To coordinate the movement of road, rail, water and air public transport for the convenience of the public.
- To promote the safe movement of vehicles, and also promote the safety of passengers using public transport at all hours.
- To undertake research and the application of the results of research to improve the quality of roads.
- The achievement of cost-effectiveness in road provision and improvements.

Truck Routeing

The confinement of trucks and road tankers to a particular designated road system. Heavy trucks are excluded from residential districts and local roads, except for delivery or collection; heavy trucks can also be excluded from the centers of towns, villages and shopping areas. Separate haul roads are sometimes constructed for mines and quarries. The acceptance of truck routeing is becoming increasingly a condition of approval or consent for industrial developments such as oil refineries, gas terminals, waste disposal or processing plants, quarries, mines, sand extraction operations, logging, servicing of container terminals, enrichment plants and port traffic. The use of designated roads for heavy vehicle traffic is consistent with the concept of a functional road hierarchy. The public often regards heavy trucks as a major hazard and a source of discomfort. Heavy trucks are often involved in serious traffic accidents, and carry loads of flammable or explosive liquids and materials. They are a source of noise and vibration, and can psychologically overwhelm motorists and pedestrians. The enforcement of approved truck routes remains, however, a problem, particularly in the case of transport contractors.

See also:
Transport Planning, Objectives of.

Tumen Consultative Commission

Established by treaty in 1995, the five member countries are China, the Democratic People's Republic of Korea, Mongolia, the Republic of Korea and the Russian Federation. The commission overseas the UNDP-sponsored Tumen River Area Development Program, facilitating and promoting economic and environmental cooperation in the Tumen Region, northeast Asia.

Turkey

The Republic of Turkey is a multiparty republic with one legislative house, the Turkish Grand National Assembly. The capital is Ankara. The population in 1998 was 69 million, with an average density of 215 persons per sq km. Istanbul is the largest city. See Box 84 for the evolution of environmental law.

Box 84   *Turkey: evolution of environmental law*

1926   Waters Law
1930   Public Health Law
1937   Hunting Law
1943   Ports Law
1952   Food Laws
1956   Forests Law
1973   Antiquities Law
1974   Radiation, Health and Safety Law
1976   Water Pollution Law
1982   Environmental Law
1983   Conservation of Cultural and Natural Assets Law; National Parks Law; Bosporus Law
1985   Pollution Prevention Fund created; Construction Law
1986   Air Quality Control Law; noise control regulation
1988   Water pollution control regulation
1989   Creation of specially protected areas
1990   Coastal Law
1991   Household waste management regulation; solid waste control regulation
1993   Harmful chemicals and products regulation; municipal cleaning tax; environmental impact regulation; Wetlands Law; medical wastes regulation
1995   Incentives for private sector environmental investment; hazardous waste control regulation
1996   Life expectancy: 69.5 years for males; 74.4 years for females

U

United Kingdom (UK)

The United Kingdom of Great Britain and Northern Ireland is a constitutional monarchy with two legislative houses, the House of Commons and the House of Lords. The population in 1997 was 59 million at a density of 241 persons per sq km. The capital is London, but legislative functions are spread among London, Edinburgh, Cardiff and Belfast. The first of the industrial nations, Britain's experience of pollution and environmental degradation goes back to the seventeenth century. See Box 85 for the evolution of environmental law.

Box 85   UK: evolution of environmental law

1273   Use of coal prohibited in London as being 'prejudicial to health'
1306   Royal Proclamation prohibits use of sea-coal (coal by sea from Newcastle) in furnaces
1648   Londoners present petition to Parliament to prohibit importation of coal from Newcastle, because of its ill-effects
1661   John Evelyn presents his thesis on London smog to King Charles II
1798   Thomas Malthus's famous *Essay on the Principles of Population*
1817   Birmingham introduces first smoke-control measure
1848   Public Health Act prohibits black smoke
1863   Alkali Works Act to control industrial pollution from certain industries
1875   Public Health Act: the Great Charter
1903   Letchworth, the first garden city, established
1905   Lincoln: first use of chlorination to check typhoid epidemic
1906   Alkali Works Act, to extend the 1863 Act
1909   Town Planning Act
1922   Carr–Saunders Report on *The Population Problem*
1932   Town and Country Planning Act
1936   Public Health Act; Housing Act
1937   Food and Drugs Act
1940   Barlow Report on the geographical distribution of population
1942   Beveridge Report on Social Insurance; Uthwatt Report on Compensation and Betterment
1943   Abercrombie Plans for London

Box 85   continued

1945   Water Act; Distribution of Industry Act
1946   New Towns Act; new towns programme begins
1947   Town and Country Planning Act
1948   Rivers Boards Act
1949   National Parks Act; Nature Conservancy created
1951   Rivers (Prevention of Pollution) Act; Dartmoor National Park
       and Lake District National Park established
1952   Town Development Act; London smog disaster, 4000 dead
1954   Beaver Report on the London smog disaster
1956   Clean Air Act; first smoke-control order, West Bromwich
1957   Windscale nuclear reactor incident
1960   Clean Rivers Act; Noise Abatement Act; Radioactive Substances
       Act
1961   Pippard Report on pollution of the tidal Thames; River Thames
       clean-up begins; Holmepierrpont public inquiry, following which
       a development application for a 2000 MW power station was
       rejected
1962   Ratcliffe-on-Soar power station public inquiry
1964   Harbours Act
1965   National Environmental Research Council established
1966   Aberfan disaster; 144 dead, of which 116 were children
1967   Civic Amenities Act; *Torrey Canyon* oil spill
1968   Town and Country Planning Act; Clean Air Act
1970   Royal Commission on Environmental Pollution created; De-
       partment of Environment established
1971   Town and Country Planning Act; Oil Pollution Act; Roskill Com-
       mission reports on future London airport; International Institute
       of Environment and Development established
1972   Poisonous Waste Act; Local Government Act
1973   Land Compensation Act; Water Act; Nature Conservancy Council
       established
1974   Control of Pollution Act; Health and Safety at Work Act; Dump-
       ing at Sea Act
1975   Dobrey Report on the British development control system
1976   Greater London Development Plan
1978   Inner Urban Areas Act; Parker Windscale inquiry; Commission
       on energy and the environment
1980   Highways Act
1983   Conservation and development programme
1984   Survey of derelict land

Box 85 continued

1985 Britain adopts European Directive on EIA
1988 Town and Country Planning (Assessment of Environmental Effects) Regulations
1989 Electricity Act; London Conference on Climatic Change
1990 Town and Country Planning Act
1991 Environmental Protection Act; Planning and Compensation Act; guide to the environmental implications of government policies; integrated pollution-control introduced
1992 Town and Country Planning (Assessment of Environmental Effects) Regulations; Harbour Works (Assessment of Environmental Effects) Regulations; EIA guides published by Kent and Essex County Councils, the Passenger Transport Executive Group, and the Department of the Environment; British Report to UNCED.
1993 Clean Air Act; Radioactive Substances Act; BS 7750 on environmental management systems
1994 Environment Agency for England and Wales established; National Environmental Technology Centre created; Conservation (Natural Habitats) Regulations; Strategy on Sustainable Development
1996 Environment Agency took over responsibilities formerly exercised by the National Rivers Authority, the Inspectorate of Pollution, and local authority waste inspectors; Landfill Tax, imposing charges for material dumped into landfill sites; *Sea Empress* runs aground at the entrance to Milford Haven harbour, Wales, creating the worst oil spill since the *Torrey Canyon* in 1967; life expectancy: 74.4 years for males; 79.7 years for females
1997 Under the Kyoto Convention on Climate Change, Britain is committed to reduce its production of six greenhouse gases by 12.5 per cent of 1990 emissions by 2010; the Royal Commission on Environmental Pollution suggested dramatic increases in energy prices and significant improvements in the efficiencies of car engines
1998 Advisory Committee on Business and the Environment urges the British government to consider a levy on carbon dioxide emissions; energy taxes and emissions trading being considered

United Nations Commission on Sustainable Development

The concept of a Commission on Sustainable Development was first debated at UNCED in 1992 and proposed subsequently in Agenda 21. A decision to create the commission was taken by the UN in December 1992, with the commission beginning work in early 1993. Countries are invited to report regularly to the commission on their progress in the implementation of Agenda 21 and with respect to environmental management generally. The commission may make recommendations to the UN General Assembly and the UN agencies.

The commission comprises representatives from 53 countries; 13 from Africa, 11 from Asia, 10 from Latin America and the Caribbean, and 19 from East and West European states. In respect of funding, the commission must monitor the promised official development assistance of 0.7 per cent of GDP due from the developed nations. The commission must also review progress in respect of technology transfer. It must also receive and analyse input from NGOs and bodies outside the UN. The implementation of UN conventions must also be kept under review.

The commission meets annually for up to three weeks, addressing various topics within Agenda 21 such as health, human settlements and fresh water, toxic chemicals and hazardous waste, land, desertification, forests and biodiversity, atmosphere, oceans and sustainable development.

At the Earth Summit II Conference in 1997, five years after Earth Summit I held in Rio de Janeiro in 1992, the commission tendered a report warning world leaders that by 2025 humanity will face a global water crisis, caused by pollution and water overuse. This report contains the first UN warning about the risk of conflict caused by disputes over access to water. There were disputes involving more than 300 transboundary rivers, as well as many aquifers. Other outcomes were also disappointing, although the rate of growth of the world's population has eased. However, there were more than 450 million extra people on Earth than at the time of the Rio Conference. Further, the promised financial support from the richer countries had dwindled.

The UNCED Secretariat estimated that the average annual costs up to 2000 of implementing Agenda 21 in the developing countries would be over $600 billion, including about $125 billion on grant or concessional terms from the international community. These were order-of-magnitude estimates only, subject to actual programs. Official aid, promised at the UN Conference, would be the main source of this funding. Further sources of funding were to be the Global Environment Facility and the World Bank.

United Nations Compensation Commission

A UN body created following the adoption of Resolution 687 by the UN Security Council in 1990, following Iraq's invasion of Kuwait. For the first time, *environmental damage* was recognized as a basis for compensation. Resolution 687 provided for the establishment of a fund to pay compensation for claims. By Resolution 692 of 1991, the Security Council established a Compensation Commission to administer the fund. The commission comprises a governing council, a group of commissioners, and a secretariat. While created in the context of the Kuwait event, the new machinery creates a system with a potential for wider application and a growing development of international law in this area. In 1994, UNEP established a Working Group of Experts on Environmental Damage, Liability and Compensation. This presented options upon which the commission may address environmental claims.

United Nations Conferences on the Human Environment

Since the foundation of the United Nations, a whole range of international conferences turning on the central issues of human survival and well-being have been held in diverse locations. For the first time, the world has met to debate issues ranging from pollution control, environment protection, natural resources, population growth, social development, hazardous wastes, desertification, water resources, environmental law, global warming, the ozone layer, biodiversity, endangered species, nutrition and food supplies, marine pollution and regional seas. The search for solutions continues. Box 86 summarizes the most significant conferences held since the Second World War. Much environmental law, both national and international, has emerged from these conferences.

Box 86   UN conferences on the human environment

UN Conference on the Conservation and Utilization of Resources, 1949
Held at Lake Success, New York, a conference reviewing the world's critical shortages of minerals, fuel and energy, forest resources and food. Fears were expressed that many materials upon which the industrial world depended might become exhausted before the year 2000. Particular concern was expressed about supplies of copper, tin, zinc and lead.

Box 86   continued

UN Conference on the Human Environment, 1972

Held in Stockholm, a conference with representatives from some 113 governments and agencies. The purpose of the conference was to review environmental problems and provide guidelines to protect and improve the human environment. The conference achieved a Declaration on the Human Environment, agreement upon an extensive program of international activity, and the creation of a permanent secretariat in Nairobi, Kenya, to be known as the United Nations Environment Program (UNEP). A second environment conference was held in Nairobi in 1982, to review progress, and a third conference was held in Rio de Janeiro in 1992 on environment and development.

UN World Population Conference, 1974

A conference with representatives from 130 countries held in Bucharest, Romania. The purpose of this first world conference on population was to consider population policies and programs needed to promote human welfare and development. The principal achievement of the conference was a World Population Plan of Action and a number of related resolutions on matters such as the status of women, food production and the environment. Delegates from 132 countries attended a second World Population Conference held in Mexico City in 1984; a third conference was held in Cairo, Egypt, in 1994. This last conference sought means for modifying the growth rate of the world's population, which had reached 5.7 million people and might well reach 7.9 to 12 billion by the year 2050. The conference promoted the provision of contraceptive and family planning services, sex education and safe abortion, and sought a definite improvement in the status of women throughout the world.

UN Conference on Human Settlements, 1976

A conference held in Vancouver attended by representatives from 131 governments, concerned with the urgent problems of housing shortages, crises of urban and rural communities, the proper use of land, access to essential services such as clean and safe water, and public involvement in efforts to improve the living conditions of people throughout the world. The conference agreed on a Vancouver Declaration on Human Settlements and a Vancouver Plan of Action. The outcome was the establishment in Nairobi of a Centre for Human Settlements. A second UN Conference on Human Settlements (Habi-

Box 86 continued

tat II) was held in 1996, to review progress and set priorities for the next decade.

Habitat II, held in Istanbul, was warned that most cities in the developing world would face extreme water shortages by 2010 simply because they are not adequately prepared for the huge influx of people from the rural districts. The conference sought to address the urban ills of poverty, homelessness, social and environmental decay. The EU backed demands that housing be given the status of a human right, needing international financial help.

The conference listed Cairo, Lagos, Dhaka, Beijing, Calcutta and Sao Paulo among the developing cities having the greatest water problems. However, cities such as Houston, Los Angeles, Warsaw, Cardiff and Tel Aviv also face severe shortages. The water crisis had emerged not only because of a lack of rain in some regions, but also from the inability of governments to make the necessary investments in a timely manner to ensure that water is available to all cities. More than one billion people could not get clean and safe drinking water. About 100 million people worldwide, mostly women and children, were homeless and up to 600 million people poorly and unhealthily housed.

US Conference on Desertification, 1977

Held in Nairobi, the first worldwide effort to consider the problem of the advancing deserts. The outcome of the conference was a World Plan to Combat Desertification, which made little progress. Governments with desertification problems tend to have limited financial and human resources; insufficient financing has plagued the program. About one-fifth of the world's farmlands suffer from the effects of desertification. Later in 1994 a Convention to Combat Desertification was signed in Paris aimed at tackling the spread of deserts generally, giving fresh impetus to the program.

UN Water Conference, 1977

A conference held in Mar del Plata, Argentina, that attempted to focus the attention of policy-makers on the water needs of society up to the year 2000, the steps that could be taken to meet them, and the difficulties likely to be experienced by those who failed to make adequate provision. The conference noted that less than one-fifth of the world's population can get water simply by turning a tap; for the remaining four-fifths, the getting of water is part of the daily struggle for existence. The conference urged better water management at local,

Box 86   continued

regional and national levels. In 1992, a UN Conference on Water and the Environment was held in Dublin, Ireland, to review progress.

UN Conference on the Law of the Sea, 1974–82

A series of international discussions aimed at establishing a revised legal regime for the oceans and their resources, while maintaining the right of ships to free passage. An outcome was the creation of 200-mile EEZs for each country, where practicable, and the creation of an International Seabed Authority to administer the rules regarding the management of minerals and food supplies as yet unexploited, and the prevention of pollution and overexploitation. The conference ended with a Convention on the Law of the Sea (Montego Bay Convention).

UN Conference on New and Renewable Sources of Energy, 1981

Held in 1981, a UN conference on alternative sources of energy. It adopted a program of action for increased use of new and renewable sources of energy in a socially equitable, economical and technically viable, and environmentally sustainable manner. The plan particularly emphasized the need to consider the environmental aspects of programs for the exploration, development and utilization of new and renewable sources of energy.

UN Conference on Environment and Development, 1992

A conference with representatives from some 167 countries held in Rio de Janeiro; the purpose of this third international environment conference was to review progress since the earlier conferences in safeguarding the human environment and promoting human welfare. The results were: the Rio Declaration on Environment and Development; the adoption of Agenda 21 on environment and development (being a program for the twenty-first century); the creation of a Commission for Sustainable Development; the adoption of a Convention on Protecting Species and Habitats (the Convention on Biological Diversity); and the adoption of a Framework Convention on Climate Change. The secretary-general to the conference was Maurice F. Strong.

UN World Summit for Social Development, 1995

A conference held in Copenhagen, essentially as a follow-up conference to the UN World Summit for Children held in 1990. The achievements between the conferences have been outlined in *The State*

Box 86   continued

of the World's Children (UNICEF, 1995). Malnutrition has been reduced; poliomyelitis has been eradicated in much of the world; deaths from measles have been more than halved; and immunization levels have been maintained or increased. There has also been progress in preventing vitamin A and iodine deficiencies, and in providing safe water. As a result of these improvements 2.5 million fewer children would die in 1996 compared with 1990; and at least 750 000 fewer children would be disabled, blinded, crippled, or mentally retarded. But there was little progress to report in India, Pakistan and Bangladesh, or in sub-Saharan Africa, where there was a lack of resources to make improvements. Diarrhoea still killed about three million children a year, with pneumonia still the biggest single killer of children.

UN World Food Summit, 1996

The World Food Summit was held at the Rome headquarters of the FAO in November 1996, bringing together once again world leaders to discuss food security. At a similar conference in 1974, countries had pledged a goal of eradicating hunger within a decade. This did not happen. The FAO had estimated that in 1996 about 14 per cent of the world's population suffered from chronic malnutrition. More than 80 nations had been identified as low-income food-deficit countries (LIFDCs), more than half of them in sub-Saharan Africa. The world's population, expected to increase by 50 per cent by 2020, faced a declining per-person supply of tillable land and water. The record low cereal stocks added to the urgency of the summit.

The summit finalized a *Declaration on World Food Security* that identified the basic causes of the problem and the actions needed by governments. The summit's goal was to reduce the number of undernourished people to half their present numbers no later than 2015. Although reducing poverty was a major focus of the declaration, the future need for stable and expanding food supplies and effective emergency food assistance was also emphasized. A plan of action was adopted by the summit to achieve its objectives. No new international agency was to be created. The FAO Committee on World Food Security gained responsibility for monitoring the program.

United Nations Economic and Social Commission for Asia and the Pacific (ESCAP)

ESCAP was created by the Economic and Social Council of the UN in 1978 as a regional economic commission with a broad range of interests. As a priority, ESCAP initially investigated several environmental problems such as industrial pollution in the Asian area, determining various means of tackling these problems and estimating the costs of pollution control.

Since then, these activities have broadened considerably. In 1990, ESCAP produced a report on the state of the environment in Asia and the Pacific, resulting in a ministerial declaration on environmentally sound and sustainable development in the region.

Within this strategy, the alleviation of poverty was clearly a most urgent task with emphasis on basic necessities such as food, shelter, safe drinking water, fuel, sanitation, primary and preventive health care, and education. ESCAP has also strongly supported the principles of EIA coupled with public participation, urging the integration of environmental considerations into national economic policies. The views of ESCAP were strongly advanced at UNCED in 1992.

United Nations Environment Program (UNEP)

Created by the UN Conference on the Human Environment, 1972, UNEP was charged with implementing its recommendations and those of subsequent environmental conferences. Based in Nairobi, Kenya, UNEP is subject to a governing council. Its activities are supported by an environment fund, to which nations contribute. UNEP's environment assessment program, Earthwatch, has four closely-linked components: evaluation and review; research; monitoring; and exchange of information. Earthwatch contains such important and operational elements as the Global Environmental Monitoring System (GEMS), the International Referral System (INFOTERRA), and the International Register of Potentially Toxic Chemicals (IRTC). There has been much successful activity in the area of regional seas, resulting in several conventions; for example, the Barcelona Convention for the Protection of the Mediterranean Sea Against Pollution. UNEP has promoted the Vienna Convention for the Protection of the Ozone Layer, and the Basel Convention on the Control of Transboundary Movement of Hazardous Wastes and their Disposal. UNEP also provided support for two conventions on wildlife protection: the Convention on International Trade in Endangered Species of Wild Fauna and Flora (CITES) and the Convention on the Conservation of Migratory Species of Wild Animals (CMS). In 1978, UNEP established an

EIA division. Later, the Governing Council of UNEP adopted goals and principles for EIA, for adoption throughout the world. In 1982, the Governing Council adopted the Montevideo Program for the Development and Periodic Review of Environmental Law which has been a mainspring behind the development of more recent conventions and agreements.

In 1990, UNEP established the UNEP Collaborating Centre on Energy and Environment at the Riso National Laboratory, Denmark. Core funds come from UNEP, the Danish International Development Agency (DANIDA) and Riso National Laboratory. The centre cooperates with other bilateral and multilateral agencies. The mandate of the centre is to promote the incorporation of environmental considerations into energy policy and planning, especially in developing countries. The centre collaborates with institutions and experts worldwide and provides direct support to UNEP headquarters. The Riso National Laboratory is the largest research institution in Denmark, the main research areas being energy, environment and materials. It considers projects at the national, regional and global levels. UNEP's Collaborating Centre has focused on climate change, mitigation analysis, environmental and developmental economics, national and international policy instruments, energy efficiency and energy sector reform.

United States of America (USA)

A federal republic with 50 states and two legislative bodies, the Senate and the House of Representatives. The capital is Washington, DC. The population in 1997 was 268 million at a density of 28 persons per sq km. To the north lies Canada and to the south Mexico, comprising NAFTA. The USA belongs to OECD, APEC and NATO. See Box 87 for the evolution of environmental law.

United States Court System

See Box 88.

United States Emissions Trading Program

Introduced into the USA in the early 1980s, an attempt to introduce some free market principles into the use of environmental resources. The amount of pollution allowable from individual firms within a region or catchment is fixed by the US EPA, though the limits may be reduced progressively over

Box 87   USA: evolution of environmental law

1872   Creation of Yellowstone National Park
1890   Creation of Yosemite National Park
1899   Refuse Act
1908   State of the Union Message by President Theodore Roosevelt
       on the need for the conservation of natural resources
1935   Historic Sites, Buildings and Antiquities Act
1940   Bald and Golden Eagle Protection Act
1946   Start of Pittsburgh clean-up
1947   Los Angeles anti-smog programme launched; Federal Insecti-
       cide, Fungicide and Rodenticide Act
1948   Federal Water Pollution Control Act
1956   Water Pollution Control Act re-enacted as a permanent meas-
       ure. Fish and Wildlife Act
1962   *Silent Spring* published by Rachel Carson; White House conser-
       vation conference
1963   Federal Clean Air Act
1964   Wilderness Act; national wilderness preservation system
1965   Federal Water Quality Act; Solid Waste Disposal Act; Further
       Clean Air Act; Anadromous Fish Conservation Act
1966   EIA policy established; Clean Water Restoration Act; National
       Historic Preservation Act
1967   Federal Air Quality Act
1968   National Trails System Act; Wild and Scenic Rivers Act
1969   National Environmental Policy Act; Council on Environmental
       Quality appointed
1970   US Environmental Protection Agency (EPA) created. Environ-
       mental Quality Improvement Act; Water Quality Improvement
       Act; Clean Air Amendment Act; Mining and Minerals Policy Act;
       President's Message on the Environment
1972   Noise Control Act; Coastal Zone Management Act; Clean Wa-
       ter Act; Marine Mammal Protection Act
1973   Endangered Species Act
1974   Safe Drinking Water Act; Solar Energy Research, Development
       and Demonstration Act
1975   Energy Policy and Conservation Act
1976   Toxic Substances Control Act; Resource Conservation and Re-
       covery Act; Magnusan Fishery Conservation and Management
       Act; National Forest Management Act; Federal Land Policy and
       Management Act

Box 87 continued

1977 Environmental impact procedures strengthened; Clean Water Act; Clean Air Amendment Act; Surface Mining Control and Reclamation Act; Soil and Water Resources Conservation Act; President's environmental message

1978 Environmental impact assessment regulations promulgated; Renewable Resources Extension Act; Public Rangelands Improvement Act; Surface Mining Control and Reclamation Act; Cooperative Forestry Assistance Act; National Energy Conservation Policy Act; Solar Photovoltaic Research, Development and Demonstration Act; Uranium Mill Tailings Radiation Control Act; National Ocean Pollution Planning Act

1979 Introduction by the US EPA of the 'bubble concept' for the management of pollution

1980 Alaska National Interest Lands Conservation Act; Comprehensive Environmental Response, Compensation and Liability Act (Superfund); Wind Energy Systems Act; Low-level Radioactive Waste Policy Act; Act to Prevent Pollution from Ships

1982 Coastal Barrier Resources Act; Reclamation Reform Act; asbestos-in-schools rule: Nuclear Waste Policy Act

1983 Times Beach found too contaminated with dioxins for human habitation

1985 International Security and Development Act

1986 Emergency Planning and Community Right-to-Know Act

1987 Water Quality Act; Driftnet Impact Monitoring, Assessment and Control Act

1988 Ocean Dumping Ban Act

1989 First nationwide survey of more than 320 toxic chemicals released to air by industry; tanker *Exxon Valdez* goes aground in Alaska; North American Wetlands Conservation Act; Marine Pollution and Research and Control Act

1990 Clean Air Act to reduce substantially air emissions; California Air Resources Board introduces strictest vehicle-emission controls ever; Coastal Wetlands Planning, Protection and Restoration Act; Coastal Barrier Improvement Act; Oil Pollution Act; Food Security Act; Pollution Prevention Act; Antarctic Protection Act; Global Change Research Act; Food, Agriculture, Conservation and Trade Act; National Environmental Education Act

1991 US signs UN ECE convention on EIA in a transboundary context

Box 87   continued

1992   US Congress requires the analysis of the environmental effects of major US federal activities abroad; National Geologic Mapping Act
1993   California Desert Protection Act
1995   Life expectancy: 73.4 years for white males; 79.6 years for white females
1997   Regulatory Improvement Act; new ambient air quality standards; US Senate unanimously passes the Byrd–Hagel Resolution asking that the US not sign a protocol with legally binding emissions limitations unless developing countries agree to binding limitations within the same time frame
1998   US President announces a five-year multi-billion dollar package of tax incentives and research programs to reduce emissions and address climate change

time. At each stage, the region as a whole must meet the specified restrictions. Under a trading program, there is an incentive to achieve reductions in emissions below the legal requirements, enabling a firm to expand, or to sell the resultant credits to other firms needing them. Sulfur credits are traded on the Chicago Board of Trade (*Environment Reporter*, 28 August 1992).

In order to reduce acid rain in the USA and Canada, Title IV of the Clean Air Act Amendments of 1990 established the US Acid Rain Program. Title IV of the Act sets as its primary goal the reduction of annual sulfur dioxide (SO_2) emissions by ten million tons below 1980 levels. In other words, the program will cut SO_2 emissions by half. It will also substantially reduce nitrogen oxide (NO_x) emissions from electric utility plants.

To achieve these reductions, the scheme requires a two-phase tightening of the restrictions on fossil fuel-fired power plants. Phase 1 began in 1995 and affects 110 mostly coal-burning power stations located in 21 eastern and midwestern US states. Phase 2 begins in the year 2000, tightening the annual emission limits imposed on these larger plants, and also sets restrictions on smaller, cleaner plants, fired by coal, oil and gas. The act also calls for a two million ton reduction in NO_x emissions by the year 2000. Much of this will be achieved by coal-fired utility boilers that will be required to install low NO_x burner technologies and to meet new emission standards.

The market-based SO_2 allowance trading component of the Acid Rain Program allows utilities to adopt the most cost-effective strategies to reduce SO_2 emissions at units under their control. Affected utilities are also required to install systems that continuously monitor emissions of SO_2 and NO_x and

Box 88   US court system

In the United States, most environmental cases are litigated in the federal courts. The federal court system is established under provisions in the federal Constitution, and coexists with the system of state and local courts established under the constitutions and laws of each of the states. The federal court system is essentially a three-tiered system. Cases usually enter the system at the district court level, and appeals are usually first heard at the appellate or circuit court level. There are 94 federal districts courts, organized into federal circuits. There are 13 federal appeals courts in the United States. The US Supreme Court is the second and final appellate level. The nine justices of the Supreme Court, and all of the judges of the federal district and appellate courts, are appointed by the President, with life tenure, upon the advice and consent of the US Senate.

Cases arising under the environmental laws of the United States generally enter the judicial system at the district court level; however, appeals from decisions of administrative law judges may proceed directly to the courts of appeals. In addition, some specialized disputes between states over matters pertaining to water allocations can be brought directly to the Supreme Court. Although several specialized federal courts of appeals deal with specific types of controversies, there is no separate federal court for environmental matters.

The process of filing civil environmental cases in the federal court system is generally the same as for other types of civil actions. Complaints brought on behalf of the federal government to enforce federal environmental laws are filed by the attorney general or his/her designate. Any other person (regardless of citizenship) also may file a complaint alleging an environmental grievance. The plaintiff must allege that the matters complained of fall within the federal court's limited jurisdiction. The defendant named in the complaint may then file an answer admitting or denying the plaintiff's allegations. Through a process called 'discovery', each party may seek to obtain from the other party documentary and other information pertaining to the allegations, which the parties may then seek to use in support of their respective positions.

Over 90 per cent of all federal civil cases, including environmental cases, are settled by mutual agreement or otherwise disposed of without proceeding to a trial. If, however, a case proceeds to trial, then the trial can be held before a jury selected by the parties, or simply before the judge. At the trial, each side may present evidence, including

Box 88   continued

testimony by lay and expert witnesses, and each side has the opportunity to cross-examine the witnesses presented by the other side. Environmental trials often involve extensive testimony by expert witnesses on scientific or technical matters in dispute. After the presentation of the evidence, the judge instructs the jury (if the case has been tried before a jury). The jury decides questions of fact, and the judge rules on questions on law. If the case is not tried by a jury, the judge will decide all issues of fact and law. To prevail in environmental cases involving disputes over factual matters, the plaintiff must meet a 'preponderance of the evidence' standard; that is, the plaintiff must show that it is more probable than not that events occurred as the plaintiff alleges. In environmental challenges to federal agency decision-making, the plaintiff typically must demonstrate that the agency's decision was arbitrary, capricious or not in accordance with law.

Sanctions and relief in civil cases may include monetary penalties, awards of damages, and injunctive and declaratory relief. Using their injunctive powers, the courts in environmental cases may direct, for example, that pollution cease, that contaminated sites be cleaned up, or that environmental impacts be assessed before a project proceeds or, in some cases, litigations may settle on an agreement that a defendant will undertake projects beneficial to the environment.

Criminal cases under the federal environmental laws may be brought only by the government, via the attorney general or his/her designate. State attorneys general also initiate criminal environmental actions. A criminal investigation can lead to an arrest or indictment, followed by an arraignment, where the defendant must enter a plea of guilty, not guilty, or no contest. In environmental crime cases, as in all other criminal cases, the government must prove the defendant guilty beyond a reasonable doubt. Criminal sanctions in environmental cases, as in other types of criminal cases, may include fines and imprisonment.

other related pollutants to ensure compliance and give credibility to the trading component of the program. A variety of penalties apply for non-compliance with the program.

Allowance trading is the core of the EPA's Acid Rain Program. One allowance authorizes a unit within a utility to emit one ton of SO_2 during or following a given year. At the end of each year, a unit must hold an amount of allowances at least equal to its annual emissions. A plant that emits 5000 tons of SO_2 must hold at least 5000 allowances that are usable in that year.

Regardless of this, a plant must never exceed the limits under Title I of the act to protect human health. Allowances are fully marketable commodities. Once allocated or acquired, allowances may be sold, bought, traded or banked for use in future years.

Utilities can reduce emissions by adopting energy conservation measures, increasing reliance on renewable energy, reducing usage, employing pollution-control technologies, switching to lower-sulfur fuel, or adopting other alternative strategies. Allowances are allocated annually by the US EPA. The act effectively places a cap of 8.95 million tons on the whole geographical area. Allowances are also available from three EPA reserves, subject to a range of restrictions. New units are not allocated allowances. Instead, they have to purchase allowances from the market, or from the EPA auctions and direct sales from the reserves. The EPA maintains an Allowance Tracking System (ATS); every account has a unique identification number and every allowance a unique serial number. Appeals may be directed to the Environmental Appeals Board.

The Acid Rain Program represents a dramatic departure from traditional regulatory (command-and-control) methods, harnessing the incentives of the free market to reduce pollution.

In 1998, details of Phase 2 were announced, involving a reduction in sulfur emissions from 8.87 to 4.5 million tons by 2002. See Box 89.

United States Environmental Protection Agency (EPA), Duties of

See Box 90.

United States Legislative Branch: Environmental Responsibilities

See Box 91.

United States National Parks and Specially Protected Areas

See Box 92.

Box 89   Terminology in the US Air Emissions Trading Program

- *Emission reduction credit (ERC)*   A credit given by the US EPA in respect of a reduction of emission from a stationary source below the permit or regulatory level. The credit may be traded internally or externally involving other firms.
- *Netting*   Introduced in 1974, some ERCs may be transferred between plants within the same premises. A reduction of pollutants from certain sources may allow an increase of similar pollutants from new sources within the same plant, achieving the same overall targets.
- *Offsets*   Introduced in 1976, a rule that allows firms to enter non-attainment areas (that is, areas where ambient standards are not being met), providing they have acquired ERCs from sources in the same area, to offset the new emissions, perhaps by a factor greater than one.
- *Banking*   The saving of ERCs for future sale or use.
- *Bubbles*   The enclosing of complete works within imaginary bubbles, with aggregate limits for pollutants imposed on each bubble; trading in ERCs takes place within the bubble. Managers may impose severer limitations on emissions which can be reduced relatively inexpensively, in return for some relaxation on emissions more expensive to control.
- *State implementation plans (SIPs)*   Since 1970, plans prepared by individual US states to meet national ambient air quality standards. Annual SO_2 emissions have since declined significantly, being halved by the year 2000
- *Allowance*   The unit used in ERCs, an allowance authorizes a plant within a utility or industrial source to emit one ton of SO_2 during a given year. At the end of each year, a unit of plant must be credited with allowances at least equal to its annual emissions; that is, a unit that emits 5000 tons of SO_2 must hold at least 5000 allowances that are usable in that year. Allowances are fully marketable commodities that may be bought, sold, or banked. Trading is on the Chicago Board of Trade.
- *Continuous emission monitoring (CEM)*   Under the US Acid Rain Program, equipment that must be installed in all plant for the continuous monitoring of SO_2, NO_x and carbon dioxide, along with other basic data.

Box 90   *Duties of the US Environmental Protection Agency*

- To protect and enhance the environment to the fullest extent possible under the laws enacted by the US Congress.
- To mount an integrated, coordinated attack on environmental pollution in collaboration with state and local governments.
- The development of national programs and regulations for air pollution control; national standards for air quality; emission standards for stationary sources; emission standards for hazardous pollutants; the Acid Rain Program; the Emissions Trading Program; and field training.
- The study, identification and regulation of noise sources; and radiation protection programs.
- The development of national programs and regulations for water pollution control and water supply; water supply quality standards and effluent guidelines; and field training.
- Guidelines and standards for the land disposal of hazardous wastes; assistance in the operation of waste management facilities; the recovery of energy from solid waste; the administration of Superfund; and ocean dumping.
- The development of national strategies for the control of toxic substances; assessing the impact of new chemicals and chemicals with new uses.
- The control and regulation of pesticides; tolerance levels for pesticides in relation to food, fish and wildlife; and the investigation of pesticide accidents.
- Enforcement procedures in relation to control programs in air, water (including groundwater), toxic substances, solid waste management, radiation, and noise.
- The conduct of conferences, hearings and other legal proceedings.
- The conduct of national research programs.
- Environmental impact assessment under the National Environmental Policy Act, 1969.
- Advice to the US Council on Environmental Quality.

The agency was established in 1970, following the amalgamation of some 15 separate agencies. It has a staff of some 7000 people.

Box 91   US legislative branch: environmental responsibilities

The legislative branch of the US federal government consists of two democratically elected bodies, or chambers: the Senate, which is composed of 100 members, two elected at large from each state; and the House of Representatives, which consists of 435 members, elected from single-member districts of approximately equal population established by the state legislatures. The Commonwealth of Puerto Rico, the territories of Guam, the Virgin Islands, American Samoa and the District of Columbia are also represented by delegates in the House of Representatives who do not vote directly on legislation.

The two chambers, the Senate and the House of Representatives (the latter chamber is usually called simply 'the House), have generally equal functions in the making of laws, including environmental laws. Environmental proposals, like other laws, may be initiated by members of either chamber, by the executive branch, or by citizens, groups or associations through petition to their elected representatives. After being introduced by members of either chamber, such proposals, known as bills, are referred to specialized committees and subcommittees. For example, a bill may be referred to specific subcommittees concerned with marine matters, forestry, agriculture, water resources, toxic substances, wastes, energy, mining, public lands or other environmental issues.

Committees and their subcommittees, where most legislative work takes place, hold public hearings to receive written and spoken testimony on bills from other members, from representatives of the executive branch, persons with special interest or expertise and the public. The committees review the comments received, deliberate and make changes in the bills. When a committee has finished its consideration, it reports the bill to the chamber floor for further debate by the full membership of that chamber. Differences between bills originating in each chamber are usually resolved in formal conferences between the two chambers.

To become law, a bill must be approved by the majorities of both chambers. In addition, it must be signed by the President; or, if the bill is opposed by the executive branch, the President may veto the bill. If a bill is vetoed, it may still be enacted into law, but only if it is then approved by a two-thirds majority of each chamber. A bill can also become a law without the President's signature if Congress is in session and the President chooses not to veto it; if Congress is not in session the President may 'pocket' the bill and thus veto it without sending it back to the Congress.

Box 91 continued

The legislatures of the several states have also enacted a significant body of environmental legislation. In certain circumstances states have been delegated the authority to implement federal programs under state statutes.

Urban Impact Assessment

The principle of EIA often extends to major works such as shopping malls, car parks, office buildings, hotels, apartment blocks, major institutions, corporation headquarters, government buildings, restaurants, entertainment centers, cinemas, theaters, casinos, transport systems, music centers, art galleries, museums, stock exchanges, banking and financial centres. The factors to be considered before development consent is granted at local or state level are numerous and perhaps difficult to weigh and assess. Errors are likely to occur. See Box 93, which summarizes most of the factors to be considered and reported on, with a recommendation and the conditions to be imposed on any development.

Box 92   US national parks and specially protected areas

Areas that are specially protected in the United States range from terrestrial to coastal and open ocean sites. These areas have been designated by federal law to protect their unique characteristics and diversity of life.* Some of these specially protected areas have been designated and managed, with federal approval, by local and state governments and NGOs. These areas are enjoyed by millions of Americans annually.

National Park System

	Number of units	Area (million ha)
1970	282	11.8
1990	358	32.0

National Wildlife Refugees

	Number of units	Area (million ha)
1970	332	11.6
1990	477	35.6

National Wilderness Preservation System

	Area (million ha)
1970	4.2
1990	38.0

National Wild and Scenic River System

	River km
1970	1 389
1990	14 909

National Marine Sanctuaries

	Number	Area (ha)
1975	2	25 856
1990	9	1 335 040

National Estuarine Research Reserves

	Number	Area (ha)
1975	1	1 880
1990	18	103 978

Note: *The numbers given in this table are not strictly additive, because some of the wilderness areas, and some of the wild and scenic river corridors, are located within national parks and national wildlife refuges.

*Box 93   Urban impact assessment: matters for consideration under
          planning law*

In determining a development application, a consent authority should
take into consideration such of the following matters as are of relevance to the proposed development:

1. The general character of the proposed site and any possible
    alternative; the natural, urban, commercial or industrial history of
    the site.
2. The consistency of the proposed development with any relevant
    statutory instruments, planning policies, heritage orders or meas-
    ures under aboriginal legislation; and with any planning studies
    and recommendations under consideration.
3. The provisions of any government strategies or policies for the
    development or redevelopment of the central business district
    or urban area in question.
4. The results of any specific social, health, economic or ecological
    impact assessments.
5. The nature and character of the existing environment in the
    vicinity of the proposed development.
6. The commercial and economic basis of the proposal.
7. The character, location, siting, bulk, scale, shape, size, height, den-
    sity, design or external appearance of that development.
8. The size and shape of the land to which that development appli-
    cation relates, the siting of any building or works thereon and the
    area to be occupied by that development.
9. The relationship of that development to development on adjoin-
    ing land or on other land in the locality.
10. Whether the proposed means of entrance to and exit from that
    development and the land to which that development application
    relates are adequate.
11. Whether adequate provision has been made for the loading,
    unloading, manoeuvring and parking of vehicles within that devel-
    opment or on that land.
12. The amount of traffic likely to be generated by the development,
    particularly in relating to the capacity of the road system in the
    locality and further afield; repercussions throughout the entire
    metropolitan road system.
13. The effect of traffic to and from the development on the immedi-
    ate road system.

Box 93 continued

14. Whether additional public transport services are necessary to help serve the development; and whether they will be adequate.
15. Whether utility services generally are adequate for the development.
16. Whether adequate provision has been made for the landscaping of the land and the aesthetic treatment of the building.
17. The effect of the building on the meteorology of the district by way of blocking sunlight or casting shadows; or causing wind turbulence or wind tunneling.
18. The effect of the building on the general character of the area through being excessively dominating or high, significantly varying a generally accepted character; or creating ravines or reducing areas of relaxation in the city area.
19. The effect of the nature of employment offered on the nature and character of employment in the central business district or suburban centre; the implications for the employment and advancement of women.
20. Any multiplier effect such as support services that the development might induce.
21. The implications for the heritage values of the city or suburban centre.
22. The implications for public space generally in the area.
23. The implications for existing occupants in the vicinity in any aspect.
24. Whether the development adds status to the urban and city scene.
25. The implications of additional office space for the supply and demand situation generally.
26. The effect on suburban centres following a further concentration of services in the city centre.
27. The effects on air pollution.
28. The effects on noise levels.
29. The implications for garbage removal services.
30. The financial implications at local government level.

V

Vancouver Plan of Action

A product of Habitat (UN Conference on Human Settlements); the Vancouver Plan of Action urges all countries to establish as a matter of urgency a national policy on human settlements, embodying the desired distribution of population together with related economic and social activities over the national territory. A national policy for human settlements and the environment was regarded as an integral part of any national economic and social development policy.

While the plan envisaged the continuous improvement, renewal and rehabilitation of existing settlements, the process must respect the rights and aspirations of inhabitants, especially the least advantaged, and preserve the cultural and social values embodied in the existing fabric. The plan recognized that in the development of human settlements the quality of the environment must be preserved, pollution prevented by minimizing the generation of wastes, and unavoidable wastes effectively managed and whenever possible turned into a resource. Transportation policies should favor mass transportation, reduced congestion and reduced pollution by motor vehicles.

In respect to land, the plan declared that the management of land should be subject to public surveillance or control in the interest of the nation. The increased increment resulting from the rise in land values deriving from changes in the use of land, from public investment or decision, or due to the general growth of the community must be subject to appropriate 'recapture' by public bodies (that is, the community), unless the situation calls for other measures such as new patterns of ownership, or the general acquisition of land by public bodies. Past patterns of ownership rights should be transformed to match the changing needs of society and be collectively beneficial. The supply of usable land should be maintained by appropriate methods, including soil conservation, control of desertification and salination, prevention of pollution, and use of land capability analysis, and increased by long-term programs of land reclamation and preservation.

Venezuela

The Republic of Venezuela is a federal multiparty republic with two legislative houses, the Senate and the Chamber of Deputies. The capital is Caracas. The population in 1997 was 23 million, at an average density of 25 persons per sq km. Located on the northern coast of South America, Venezuela faces the Caribbean Sea. It abuts Colombia, Guyana and Brazil. See Box 94 for the evolution of environmental law.

Box 94   *Venezuela: evolution of environmental law*

1951   National Conservation Prize introduced
1959   National Parks Service created
1961   National Constitution revised
1976   Organic Law of the Environment; Environmental Impact Assessment Regulation; creation of the Ministry of the Environment and Natural Renewable Resources with 14 administrative zones
1980   Law for Penal Protection of the Environment; Law for Water Protection

---

Visual Pollution

Visual squalor in an environmental context including such items as:
- overhead wirescape;
- litter and unauthorized tipping;
- abandoned cars and large items of equipment;
- derelict factory premises and abandoned industrial equipment;
- unattractive hoardings and advertisements;
- overhead highways;
- parked cars along the length of residential roads;
- large commercial vehicles parked 'at home' in residential streets;
- unmaintained residential property;
- accumulation of bottles, garbage, and unwanted items on residential premises (in the yard or on the roof);
- squatter settlements; and
- some kinds of alternative lifestyles.

W

Washington Declaration

The outcome of an international conference held in Washington, DC in November 1995 concerned with the protection and preservation of the marine environment. The conference was concerned mainly with pollution from land-based sources such as sewage, persistent organic pollutants, radioactive substances, heavy metals, oils, nutrients, sediments, litter and destruction of habitats. Nations were requested, along with UN agencies, to prepare programs for the protection of the marine environment, the total program to be placed on the agenda of the UN Commission on Sustainable Development. The conference adopted a Global Program of Action for the Protection of the Marine Environment from Land-based Activities. See Box 95.

Water Act, 1973, UK

An act under which ten regional water authorities were established in Britain to take over and integrate the functions of several statutory bodies. In addition to enforcing of pollution control legislation, the duties of the new authorities were extended to include environmental and aesthetic considerations. Thus, in carrying out their functions they are to have regard to the preservation of natural beauty, the conservation of flora and fauna and features of scientific interest, and the protection of buildings of architectural value and public rights of way. The act recognizes the amenity and recreational value of water space and requires the authorities to provide, wherever practicable, for public access to, and utilization of, the amenity.

Water Pollution

Substances, bacteria or viruses present in such concentrations or numbers as to impair the quality of the water rendering it less suitable or unsuitable for its intended use and presenting a hazard to humans or to their environment. Pollution may be caused by:
1. Bacteria, viruses and other organisms that can cause disease, for example, cholera, typhoid fever and dysentery.
2. Inorganic salts that cannot be removed by any simple conventional treat-

---

Box 95   Washington Declaration on Protection of the Marine Environment from Land-based Activities

The representatives of Governments and the European Commission participating in the Conference held in Washington from 23 October to 3 November
1995,
Affirming the need and will to protect and preserve the marine environment for present and future generations,
Reaffirming the relevant provisions of chapters 17, 33 and 34 of Agenda
21 and the Rio Declaration on Environment and Development,
Recognizing the interdependence of human populations and the coastal
and marine environment, and the growing and serious threat from
land-based activities to both human health and well-being and the
integrity of coastal and marine ecosystems and biodiversity,
Further recognizing the importance of integrated coastal area management and the catchment-area-based approach as means of coordinating
programmes aimed at preventing marine degradation from land-based
activities with economic and social development programmes,
Also recognizing that the alleviation of poverty is an essential factor in
addressing the impacts of land-based activities on coastal and marine
areas,
Noting that there are major differences among the different regions of
the world and the States which they comprise in terms of environmental, economic and social conditions and level of development which will
lead to different judgements on priorities in addressing problems related to the degradation of the marine environment by land-based
activities,
Acknowledging the need to involve major groups in national, regional
and international activities to address degradation of the marine environment by land-based activities,
Strongly supporting the processes set forth in decisions 18/31 and 18/32
of the Governing Council of the United Nations Environment Programme for addressing at the global level the priority issues of persistent
organic pollutants and adequate treatment of waste water,
Having therefore adopted the Global Programme of Action for the
Protection of the Marine Environment from Land-based Activities,
*Hereby declare their commitment to protect and preserve the marine
environment from the impacts of land-based activities, and
Declare their intention to do so by:*
   1.   Setting as their common goal sustained and effective action to
        deal with all land-based impacts upon the marine environment,

Box 95   continued

specifically those resulting from sewage, persistent organic pollutants, radioactive substances, heavy metals, oils (hydrocarbons),
nutrients, sediment mobilization, litter, and physical alteration and
destruction of habitat;

2. Developing or reviewing national action programmes within a
few years on the basis of national priorities and strategies;

3. Taking forward action to implement these programmes in accordance with national capacities and priorities;

4. Cooperating to build capacities and mobilize resources for the
development and implementation of such programmes, in particular for developing countries, especially the least developed
countries, countries with economies in transition and small island
developing States (hereinafter referred to as 'countries in need of
assistance');

5. Taking immediate preventive and remedial action, wherever possible, using existing knowledge, resources, plans and processes;

6. Promoting access to cleaner technologies, knowledge and expertise to address land-based activities that degrade the marine
environment, in particular for countries in need of assistance;

7. Cooperating on a regional basis to coordinate efforts for maximum efficiency and to facilitate action at the national level,
including, where appropriate, becoming parties to and strengthening regional cooperative agreements and creating new
agreements where necessary;

8. Encouraging cooperative and collaborative action and partnerships, among governmental institutions and organizations,
communities, the private sector and non-governmental organizations which have relevant responsibilities and/or experience;

9. Encouraging and/or making available external financing, given that
funding from domestic sources and mechanisms for the implementation of the Global Programme of Action by countries in
need of assistance may be insufficient;

10. Promoting the full range of available management tools and
financing options in implementing national or regional programmes
of action, including innovative managerial and financial techniques,
while recognizing the differences between countries in need of
assistance and developed States;

11. Urging national and international institutions and the private
sector, bilateral donors and multilateral funding agencies to accord priority to projects within national and regional programmes

Box 95   continued

to implement the Global Programme of Action and encouraging the Global Environment Facility to support these projects;

12. Calling upon the United Nations Environment Programme, the United Nations Development Programme, the World Bank, the regional development banks, as well as the agencies within the United Nations system to ensure that their programmes support (through, *inter alia*, financial cooperation, capacity-building and institutional-strengthening mechanisms) the regional structures in place for the protection of the marine environment;

13. According priority to implementation of the Global Programme of Action within the United Nations system, as well as in other global and regional institutions and organizations with responsibilities and capabilities for addressing marine degradation from land-based activities, and specifically:
    a. Securing formal endorsement of those parts of the Global Programme of Action that are relevant to such institutions and organizations and incorporating the relevant provisions into their work programmes;
    b. Establishing a clearing-house mechanism to provide decision makers in all States with direct access to relevant sources of information, practical experience and scientific and technical expertise and to facilitate effective scientific, technical and financial cooperation as well as capacity-building; and
    c. Providing for periodic intergovernmental review of the Global Programme of Action, taking into account regular assessments of the state of the marine environment;

14. Promoting action to deal with the consequences of sea-based activities, such as shipping, offshore activities and ocean dumping, which require national and/or regional actions on land, including establishing adequate reception and recycling facilities;

15. Giving priority to the treatment and management of waste water and industrial effluents, as part of the overall management of water resources, especially through the installation of environmentally and economically appropriate sewage systems, including studying mechanisms to channel additional resources for this purpose expeditiously to countries in need of assistance;

16. Requesting the Executive Director of the United Nations Environment Programme, in close partnership with the World Health Organization, the United Nations Centre for Human Settlements (Habitat), the United Nations Development Programme and other

Box 95   continued

> relevant organizations, to prepare proposals for a plan to address the global nature of the problem of inadequate management and treatment of waste water and its consequences for human health and the environment, and to promote the transfer of appropriate and affordable technology drawn from the best available techniques;
>
> 17. Acting to develop, in accordance with the provisions of the Global Programme of Action, a global, legally binding instrument for the reduction and/or elimination of emissions, discharges and, where appropriate the elimination of the manufacture and use of the persistent organic pollutants identified in decision 18/32 of the Governing Council of the United Nations Environment Programme. The nature of the obligations undertaken must be developed recognizing the special circumstances of countries in need of assistance. Particular attention should be devoted to the potential need for the continued use of certain persistent organic pollutants to safeguard human health, sustain food production and to alleviate poverty in the absence of alternatives and the difficulty of acquiring substitutes and transferring of technology for the development and/or production of those substitutes; and
>
> 18. Elaborating the steps relating to institutional follow-up, including the clearing-house mechanism, in a resolution of the United Nations General Assembly at its fifty-first session, and in that regard, States should coordinate with the United Nations Environment Programme, as secretariat of the Global Programme of Action, and other relevant agencies within the United Nations system in the development of the resolution and include it on the agenda of the Commission on Sustainable Development at its inter-sessional meeting in February 1996 and its session in April 1996.
>
> Washington, DC,
> 1 November 1995

ment process, making the water less suitable for drinking, for irrigation and for many industries.

3. Plant nutrients such as potato, phosphates and nitrates which, while largely inorganic salt, have the added effect of increasing weed growth, promoting algal blooms and producing, by photosynthesis, organic matter which may settle to the bottom of a lake.

4. Oily materials that may be inimical to fish life, cause unsightliness, screen the river surface from the air thus reducing re-oxygenation, accumulate in troublesome quantities, or have a high oxygen demand.
5. Specific toxic agents, ranging from metal salts to complex synthetic chemicals.
6. Waste heat that may render the river less suitable for certain purposes.
7. Silt that may enter a river in large quantities causing changes in the character of the river bed.
8. Radioactive substances.

Water Pollution Control Amendment Act, 1972, US

An act of Congress amending earlier US water pollution measures. The effects of these 1972 amendments were far-reaching, effectively rewriting the 1956 act and the subsequent amending and augmenting legislation. The objective of the new act was to restore and maintain the chemical, physical and biological integrity of the nation's waters. It reaffirmed the primary responsibilities and rights of the states to prevent, reduce, and eliminate pollution; and to plan the development and use of land and water resources. The federal agencies were to cooperate with state and local agencies to develop comprehensive solutions to prevent, reduce and eliminate pollution, in concert with programs for managing water resources.

The legislation set out a number of policies and goals, namely that: the discharges of pollutants into navigable waters be eliminated by 1985; wherever attainable, interim goals for water quality to provide for the protection and propagation of fish, shellfish and wildlife, and for recreational purposes in and on the water be achieved by July 1983; the discharge of toxic pollutants in toxic amounts be prohibited; federal financial assistance be provided for the construction of publicly-owned waste treatment works; area-wide waste treatment management processes be developed to ensure adequate control of the sources of pollution in each state; and a major research and demonstration effort be mounted to develop technologies necessary to eliminate the discharge of pollutants into navigable waters and the oceans.

See:
Clean Water Amendment Act, 1981, US; Federal Water Pollution Control Act, 1956, US.

Water Quality Act, 1965, US

An act to improve water quality approved unanimously by the US Congress in 1965. The act established the Federal Water Pollution Control Administration under a commissioner. While the legislation set up the new administration within the Department of Health, Education and Welfare, a presidential reorganization order transferred the new administration to the Department of the Interior on 10 May 1966.

A key provision of the act provided for the establishment of water quality standards. The states were given the option of setting water quality standards by 30 June 1967, for interstate waters within their borders. These standards had to 'enhance the quality' of waters and be accompanied by a plan of implementation, including enforcement, of the proposed criteria. As a first step, states were given a deadline of October 1966 to give notice to the Secretary of the Interior that they were willing to set their own standards. All 50 states, the District of Columbia, the Territories of Guam and the Virgin Islands and the Commonwealth of Puerto Rico did so and most of the states held the required public hearings to give interested groups an opportunity to comment on what uses of water should be provided for and what the required water quality should be for these uses.

The standards and implementation plans submitted by the states were subject to approval by the Secretary of the Interior. In order to receive approval, the standards had to be consistent with the objective of enhancing the quality of these interstate waters for such purposes as public water supplies, fish and wildlife, recreation, agriculture, industry and other legitimate uses. If a state failed to adopt appropriate water quality standards, the Secretary of the Interior could, after consulting the representatives of federal departments, the states, municipalities, industries and other affected parties, prepare suitable water quality regulations for the interstate waters in the state concerned.

See also:
Federal Water Pollution Control Act, 1956, US; Water Pollution Control Amendment Act, 1972, US.

Water Quality Improvement Act, 1970, US

An act of the US Congress passed in 1970 which required, *inter alia*, that a complete investigation and study of all methods of financing the cost of water pollution control be undertaken and submitted to Congress. Responsibility for water pollution control was transferred forthwith from the Department of the Interior to the new EPA. In addition, the state governments became the final arbiters in the establishment of water quality standards, the EPA simply acting as adviser. This was a retrograde step, in the opinion of many.

See also:
Clean Water Amendment Act, 1981, US.

Wetlands

Areas that are inundated by surface- or groundwater with a frequency sufficient to support vegetative or aquatic life that requires saturated or seasonally saturated soil conditions for growth and reproduction. Wetlands may be swamps, marshes, fens or bogs, depending on soil wetness and type of vegetation. Wetlands may be located in uplands, along flood plains, around lake margins, in glaciated depressions and in estuarine tidal marshes. Wetlands perform important hydrologic functions; they also provide important habitat for wildlife. The US Clean Waters Act regulate dredging and filling in tidal and freshwater wetlands.

Whales

See:
International Whaling Commission.

WHO

See:
World Health Organization.

Wild and Scenic Rivers Act, 1968, US

A US measure for the protection of wild and scenic rivers; the idea was to create a national system of designated rivers, restored as necessary to a condition suitable for fishing and swimming. However, implementation of the act lagged somewhat. By 1979, only 27 river segments (some 2200 miles or 3500 km) were components of the national system. In that year, the US President directed that:

all federal agencies shall act to avoid or mitigate adverse effects on rivers identified as candidates for designation by the Heritage Conservation and Recreation Service; all federal land management agencies shall assess whether rivers located on their lands are suitable for inclusion in the wild and scenic rivers system, and take appropriate action; the Secretaries of Agriculture and the Interior shall jointly revise their guidelines for evaluating wild and scenic rivers and shorten the time for studying rivers for designation.

In addition to these initiatives, the President affirmed his support for the designation of four river segments named in his previous Environmental Message, and added four new segments. The eight segments were: Gunnison River, Colorado; Encampment River, Colorado; Priest River, Idaho; Illinois River, Oregon; Bruneau River, Idaho; Dolores River, Colorado; Upper Mississippi River, Minnesota; and the Salmon River, Idaho. By 1985, the national wild and scenic rivers system embraced 7000 miles or 11 200 km of river.

Williamsburg Restoration, US

A striking example of a heritage conservation program is the restoration of Williamsburg, the capital of colonial Virginia, to much of its early eighteenth century appearance. From 1699 until 1780, when the capital was moved to Richmond, Williamsburg was the political, social and cultural center of the entire colony. Virginia was at that time the largest and most populous of the original British colonies. Its prosperity was largely dependent on the growth and sale of tobacco and the institution of slavery. It was also the center of protest against British authority. Acquisition and renovation has continued since 1926. The work has been carried on by a non-profit organization, dedicated to the theme 'that the future may learn from the past'.

The first major edifice to be restored was the Wren Building at the College of William and Mary, the second oldest college in the United States. The design of the building is thought to have originated with Sir Christopher Wren, the English architect. The 68 ha historic area contains today more than 80 original eighteenth-century structures, many other buildings that have been reconstructed after extensive archaeological and documentary research, and a hundred gardens and greens. The larger buildings, in addition to the college, include the Governor's Palace, the Capital building which housed the Assembly, the Bruton Parish Church, the Courthouse of 1770, the public gaol, the magazine and guardhouse. The principal street, Duke of Gloucester Street, was described by President Franklin D. Roosevelt as 'the most historic avenue in all America'.

In 1977, a heritage conservation program was introduced by the Secretary of the Interior, and a national register of historic places established. In 1979, the US President foreshadowed the establishment of a more comprehensive federal program to identify and protect significant natural areas as well as historic places with a new register of natural areas to supplement the original register. Federal agencies, state and local governments, Indian tribes and citizens would be encouraged to identify potential heritage areas.

Wind Rose

A diagram indicating the frequency and strengths of winds in a definite locality for a given period of years. It is conventional to consider the wind direction as the direction from which the wind blows, for example, a north-east wind will carry pollutants to the southwest of the source.

Winds

Ordered horizontal air motions; known as advection. Vertical motions are called convection, while turbulence describes the chaotic motion of air in all directions.

Works Approval

Planning and environmental legislation, involving the issue of licences and approvals, often requires the prior approval of the proposed works. The methods to be used, the proposed works, and the techniques of pollution control or avoidance, are thus to be approved in advance of the actual construction and the issue of licences. In significant cases, the requirements of prior approval may be superseded by EIA, a much more substantial procedure. See Box 96.

World Bank Group

An agency of the United Nations, the World Bank comprises the International Bank for Reconstruction and Development (IBRD) and its affiliates, the International Development Association (IDA), the International Finance Corporation (IFC) and the Multilateral Investment Guarantee Agency (MIGA). The common objective of these bodies, known collectively as the World Bank, has been to help to raise the standards of living in developing countries, channeling resources from the richer to the poorer nations. The Bank

---

Box 96 *Works approval applications: information to be supplied by proponent*

- If required, a Review of Environmental Factors; an Environmental Effects Statement; or an Environmental Impact Statement.
- Evidence that all other necessary approvals have been applied for, or obtained, such as the landowner's consent, the local council's approval and licences required under soil conservation, mining, contaminated land, water, rivers and waterways, hazardous waste, land use, and noise legislation.
- A description of the proposed installation, modification, replacement or alteration; the raw materials and the fuels to be used; and likely waste products, with tonnages.
- A detailed description of proposed pollution-control techniques and methods with ultimate disposal arrangements for wastes and sludges.
- Heights and designs of stacks and details of outfalls or irrigation systems.
- Results of dispersion modeling wherever appropriate.
- An assessment of cumulative effects.
- Proposed methods of monitoring and recording.
- A locality and site plan, drawn to scale, with facilities, existing and proposed, indicated and other premises and dwellings.
- A topographic or contour map of the area.
- Details of transportation requirements to and from the site.
- The consistency of the proposal with local, regional and national plans and policies for environmental planning and management.
- Estimated dates of commencement and completion of each phase or stage of the proposed works.
- Additional information as may be required by clean air, clean water, noise control, hazardous waste, solid waste, toxic emissions, building and drainage legislation, odor control, insecticides, and local government legislation.

It should be noted that applicants may employ any manner of equipment, technique, or management to meet the requirements of the planning and environmental authorities.

---

was established in 1945. In 1970, the Bank created an Office of Environmental and Health Affairs, but with limited resources. Since 1979, investment and assistance began to extend to afforestation and reforestation, soil conservation, flood mitigation and control, range management, wildlife protection, and abatement of air and water pollution. However, in more recent years, the Bank has been accused of failing in its original role of reducing poverty and of disregarding in whole or part the environmental effects of major development projects. It has, it is claimed, financed roads for settlers who devastated the Amazon rain forest and financed dams that forced many thousands to be resettled in less satisfactory circumstances. Since 1991, there has been much more attention to these problems; several projects have been modified as a result of environmental assessment. In 1992, the Bank published its three-volume sourcebook on EIA.

In June, 1997, the World Bank issued its Green Top 10 Plan, a list of proposed actions to address the world's most pressing environmental problems. The plan pointed out that worldwide energy-related subsidies, amounting to $800 billion annually, rarely benefited the poor and inevitably harmed the environment. Carbon dioxide emissions had increased by nearly 25 per cent since the Rio Earth Conference in 1992, and 1.3 million people continued to be adversely affected by polluted air.

Among the proposed actions were the global phaseout of leaded gasoline (petrol) and a reduction in the manufacture and use of CFCs. The plan also encouraged the trading of greenhouse emissions, enabling countries which fail to reach their targets to buy pollution credits from countries that have achieved more than their allotted targets. This enables countries to exceed their targets agreed to internationally, by incurring a financial penalty.

In 1998, the Bank revised its Operational Policy on Environmental Assessment. The policy requires that all Bank investment policies be screened for their potential environmental effects and that the EIA process be built into the Bank's project cycle, as an integral part of project design and implementation.

The Bank has undertaken two reviews of the effectiveness of EIAs, in 1992 and 1995, applying lessons to EIA procedures. The general outcome was to move upstream in the planning process, addressing programs and policies, as well as individual projects, and addressing sectoral and regional concerns. In other words strategic environmental assessment is becoming more the norm.

World Charter for Nature, 1982

A Charter for Nature adopted by the UN General Assembly, Resolution 37/7, 1982. The charter proclaims a range of objectives and policies to be pursued by nations, agencies, corporations and individuals. The charter supports the principles of sustainable activity. See Box 97.

Box 97   *World Charter for Nature, 1982*

(UN General Assembly Resolution 37/7)
The General Assembly,
Reaffirming the fundamental purposes of the United Nations, in particular the maintenance of international peace and security, the development of friendly relations among nations and the achievement of international cooperation in solving international problems of an economic, social, cultural, technical, intellectual or humanitarian character,
Aware that:
a.   Mankind is a part of nature and life depends on the uninterrupted functioning of natural systems which ensure the supply of energy and nutrients,
b.   Civilization is rooted in nature, which has shaped human culture and influenced all artistic and scientific achievements, and living in harmony with nature gives man the best opportunities for the development of his creativity, and for rest and recreation,
Convinced that:
a.   Every form of life is unique, warranting respect regardless of its worth to man, and, to accord other organisms such recognition, man must be guided by a moral code of action,
b.   Man can alter nature and exhaust natural resources by his action or its consequences and, therefore, must fully recognize the urgency of maintaining the stability and quality of nature and of conserving natural resources,
Persuaded that:
a.   Lasting benefits from nature depend upon the maintenance of essential ecological processes and life support systems, and upon the diversity of life forms, which are jeopardized through excessive exploitation and habitat destruction by man,
b.   The degradation of natural systems owing to excessive consumption and misuse of natural resources, as well as to failure to establish an appropriate economic order among peoples and among States, leads to the breakdown of the economic, social and political framework of civilization,
c.   Competition for scarce resources creates conflicts, whereas the conservation of nature and natural resources contributes to justice and the maintenance of peace and cannot be achieved until mankind learns to live in peace and to forsake war and armaments,
Reaffirming that man must acquire the knowledge to maintain and enhance his ability to use natural resources in a manner which ensures

Box 97   continued

the preservation of the species and ecosystems for the benefit of present and future generations,
Firmly convinced of the need for appropriate measures, at the national and international, individual and collective, and private and public levels, to protect nature and promote international co-operation in this field,
Adopts, to these ends, the present World Charter for Nature, which proclaims the following principle of conservation by which all human conduct affecting nature is to be guided and judged.

I.   General principles
1.   Nature shall be respected and its essential processes shall not be impaired.
2.   The genetic viability of the earth shall not be compromised; the population levels of all life forms, wild and domesticated, must be at least sufficient for their survival, and to this end necessary habitat shall be safeguarded.
3.   All areas of the earth, both land and sea, shall be subject to these principles of conservation; special protection shall be given to unique areas, to representative samples of all the different types of ecosystems and to the habitat of rare or endangered species.
4.   Ecosystems and organisms, as well as the land, marine and atmospheric resources that are utilized by man, shall be managed to achieve and maintain optimum sustainable productivity, but not in such a way as to endanger the integrity of those other ecosystems or species with which they coexist.
5.   Nature shall be secured against degradation caused by warfare or other hostile activities.

II.   Functions
6.   In the decision-making process it shall be recognized that man's needs can be met only by ensuring the proper functioning of natural systems and by respecting the principles set forth in the present Charter.
7.   In the planning and implementation of social and economic development activities, due account shall be taken of the fact that the conservation of nature is an integral part of those activities.
8.   In formulating long-term plans for economic development, population growth and the improvement of standards of living, due account shall be taken of the long-term capacity of natural systems to ensure the subsistence and settlement of the populations

Box 97 continued

concerned, recognizing that this capacity may be enhanced through science and technology.

9. The allocation of areas of the earth to various uses shall be planned and due account shall be taken of the physical constraints, the biological productivity and diversity and the natural beauty of the areas concerned.

10. Natural resources shall not be wasted, but used with a restraint appropriate to the principles set forth in the present Charter, in accordance with the following rules:
    a. Living resources shall not be utilized in excess of their natural capacity for regeneration;
    b. The productivity of soils shall be maintained or enhanced through measures which safeguard their long-term fertility and the process of organic decomposition, and prevent erosion and all other forms of degradation;
    c. Resources, including water, which are not consumed as they are used shall be reused or recycled;
    d. Non-renewable resources which are consumed as they are used shall be exploited with restraint, taking into account their abundance, the rational possibilities of converting them for consumption, and the compatibility of their exploitation with the functioning of natural systems.

11. Activities which might have an impact on nature shall be controlled, and the best available technologies that minimize significant risks to nature or other adverse effects shall be used; in particular:
    a. Activities which are likely to cause irreversible damage to nature shall be avoided;
    b. Activities which are likely to pose a significant risk to nature shall be preceded by an exhaustive examination; their proponents shall demonstrate that expected benefits outweigh potential damage to nature, and where potential adverse effects are not fully understood, the activities should not proceed;
    c. Activities which may disturb nature shall be preceded by assessment of their consequences, and environmental impact studies of development projects shall be conducted sufficiently in advance, and if they are to be undertaken, such activities shall be planned and carried out so as to minimize potential adverse effects;

Box 97   *continued*

    d. Agriculture, grazing, forestry and fisheries practices shall be adapted to the natural characteristics and constraints of given areas;

    e. Areas degraded by human activities shall be rehabilitated for purposes in accord with their natural potential and compatible with the well-being of affected populations.

12. Discharge of pollutants into natural systems shall be avoided and:

    a. Where this is not feasible, such pollutants shall be treated at the source, using the best practicable means available;

    b. Special precautions shall be taken to prevent discharge of radioactive or toxic wastes.

13. Measures intended to prevent, control or limit natural disasters, infestations and diseases shall be specifically directed to the causes of these scourges and shall avoid averse side-effects on nature.

III. Implementation

14. The principles set forth in the present Charter shall be reflected in the law and practice of each State, as well as at the international level.

15. Knowledge of nature shall be broadly disseminated by all possible means, particularly by ecological education as an integral part of general education.

16. All planning shall include, among its essential elements, the formulation of strategies for the conservation of nature, the establishment of inventories of ecosystems and assessments of the effects on nature of proposed policies and activities; all of these elements shall be disclosed to the public by appropriate means in time to permit effective consultation and participation.

17. Funds, programmes and administrative structures necessary to achieve the objective of the conservation of nature shall be provided.

18. Constant efforts shall be made to increase knowledge of nature by scientific research and to disseminate such knowledge unimpeded by restrictions of any kind.

19. The status of natural processes, ecosystems and species shall be closely monitored to enable early detection of degradation or threat, ensure timely intervention and facilitate the evaluation of conservation policies and methods.

Box 97   continued

20. Military activities damaging to nature shall be avoided.
21. States and, to the extent they are able, other public authorities, international organizations, individuals, groups and corporations shall:
    a. Co-operate in the task of conserving nature through common activities and other relevant actions, including information exchange and consultations;
    b. Establish standards for products and other manufacturing processes that may have adverse effects on nature, as well as agreed methodologies for assessing these effects;
    c. Implement the applicable international legal provisions for the conservation of nature and the protection of the environment;
    d. Ensure that activities within their jurisdictions or control do not cause damage to the natural systems located within other States or in the areas beyond the limits of national jurisdiction;
    e. Safeguard and conserve nature in areas beyond national jurisdiction.
22. Taking fully into account the sovereignty of States over their natural resources, each State shall give effect to the provisions of the present Charter through its competent organs and in co-operation with other States.
23. All persons, in accordance with their national legislation, shall have the opportunity to participate, individually or with others, in the formulation of decisions of direct concern to their environment, and shall have access to means of redress when their environment has suffered damage or degradation.
24. Each person has a duty to act in accordance with the provisions of the present Charter, acting individually, in association with others or through participation in the political process, each person shall strive to ensure that the objectives and requirements of the present Charter are met.

World Commission on Environment and Development (Brundtland Commission)

A commission created by the UN General Assembly in 1983 for the purpose of examining potential conflicts between environmental protection and economic growth. The 21 members of the commission were drawn from a range of nations with widely different economic, political and cultural backgrounds. The commission was chaired by Gro Harlem Brundtland, then Prime Minister of Norway. The commission held a large number of meetings, traveling widely. Its report, *Our Common Future*, was published in 1987. Box 98 reproduces the Tokyo Declaration of the commission as it completed its task.

Box 98   Tokyo Declaration of the World Commission on Environment and Development, 1987

At the close of its final meeting, in Tokyo, the Commission issued the following as the Tokyo Declaration, dated 27 February 1987:
The World Commission on Environment and Development was constituted in 1984 as an independent body by the United Nations General Assembly and set out to:
a.   re-examine the critical issues of environment and development, and formulate innovative, concrete, and realistic action proposals to deal with them;
b.   strengthen international co-operation on environment and development, and assess and propose new forms of co-operation that can break out of existing patterns and influence policies and events in the direction of needed change; and
c.   raise the level of understanding and commitment to action on the part of individuals, voluntary organizations, business, institutes, and governments.
    As we come in Tokyo to the end of our task, we remain convinced that it is possible to build a future that is prosperous, just, and secure.
    But realizing this possibility depends on all countries adopting the objective of sustainable development as the overriding goal and test of national policy and international co-operation. Such development can be defined simply as an approach to progress which meets the needs of the present without compromising the ability of future generations to meet their own needs. A successful transition to a sustainable development through the year 2000 and beyond requires

Box 98 continued

a massive shift in societal objectives. It also requires the concerted and vigorous pursuit of a number of strategic imperatives.

The World Commission on Environment and Development now calls upon all the nations of the World, both jointly and individually, to integrate sustainable development into their goals and to adopt the following principles to guide their policy actions.

1. *Revive growth* Poverty is a major source of environmental degradation which not only affects a large number of people in developing countries but also undermines the sustainable development of the entire community of nations – both developing and industrialized. Economic growth must be stimulated, particularly in developing countries, while enhancing the environmental resource base. The industrialized countries can, and must contribute to reviving world economic growth. There must be urgent international action to resolve the debt crisis; a substantial increase in the flows of development finance; and stabilization of the foreign exchange earnings of low-income commodity exporters.

2. *Change the quality of growth* Revived growth must be of a new kind in which sustainability, equity, social justice, and security are firmly embedded as major social goals. A safe, environmentally sound energy pathway is an indispensable component of this. Education, communication, and international co-operation can all help to achieve those goals. Development planners should take account in their reckoning of national wealth not only of standard economic indicators, but also of the state of the stock of natural resources. Better income distribution, reduced vulnerability to natural disasters and technological risks, improved health preservation of cultural heritage – all contribute to raising the quality of that growth.

3. *Conserve and enhance the resource base* Sustainability requires the conservation of environmental resources such as clean air, water, forests, and soils; maintaining genetic diversity; and using energy, water and raw materials efficiently. Improvements in the efficiency of production must be accelerated to reduce per capita consumption of natural resources and encourage a shift to non-polluting products and technologies. All countries are called upon to prevent environmental pollution by rigorously enforcing environmental regulations, promoting low-waste technologies, and anticipating the impact of new products, technologies and wastes.

Box 98   continued

4. *Ensure a sustainable level of population*   Population policies should be formulated and integrated with other economic and social development programmes – education, health care, and the expansion of the livelihood base of the poor. Increased access to family planning services is itself a form of social development that allows couples, and women in particular, the right to self-determination.

5. *Reorient technology and manage risks*   Technology creates risks, but it offers the means to manage them. The capacity for technological innovation needs to be greatly enhanced in developing countries. The orientation of technology development in all countries must also be changed to pay greater regard to environmental factors. National and international institutional mechanisms are needed to assess potential impacts of new technologies before they are widely used. Similar arrangements are required for major interventions in natural systems, such as river diversion or forest clearance. Liability for damages from unintended consequences must be strengthened and enforced. Greater public participation and free access to relevant information should be promoted in decision-making processes touching on environment and development issues.

6. *Integrate environment and economics in decision-making*   Environmental and economic goals can and must be made mutually reinforcing. Sustainability requires the enforcement of wider responsibilities for the impacts of policy decisions. Those making such policy decisions must be responsible for the impact of those decisions upon the environmental resource capital of their nations. They must focus on the sources of environmental damage rather than the symptoms. The ability to anticipate and prevent environmental damage will require that the ecological dimensions of policy be considered at the same time as the economic, trade, energy, agricultural, and other dimensions. They must be considered on the same agendas and in the same national and international institutions.

7. *Reform international economic relations*   Long-term sustainable growth will require far-reaching changes to produce trade, capital, and technology flows that are more equitable and better synchronized to environmental imperatives. Fundamental improvements in market access, technology transfer, and international finance are necessary to help developing countries widen their

> *Box 98 continued*
>
> opportunities by diversifying their economic and trade bases and building their self-reliance.
>
> 8. *Strengthen international co-operation* The introduction of an environmental dimension injects an additional element of urgency and mutual self-interest, since a failure to address the interaction between resource degradation and rising poverty will spill over and become a global ecological problem. Higher priorities must be assigned to environmental monitoring, assessment, research and development, and resource management in all fields of international development. This requires a high level of commitment by all countries to the satisfactory working of multilateral institutions; to the making and observance of international rules in fields such as trade and investment; and to constructive dialogue on the many issues where national interests do not immediately coincide but require negotiation to be reconciled. It requires also a recognition of the essential importance of international peace and security. New dimensions of multilateralism are essential to sustainable human progress.
>
> The Commission is convinced that if we can make solid progress towards meeting these principles in the balance of this century, the next century can offer a more secure, more prosperous, more equitable, and more hopeful future for the whole human family.

World Conservation Union (WCU)

Known previously as the International Union for the Conservation of Nature and Natural Resources (IUCN), the WCU is a voluntary international body whose main objective is promoting the perpetuation of wild nature and natural resources throughout the world. Formed in 1948, the body has its headquarters in Gland, Switzerland. Its membership comprises nations, government agencies, private bodies, and international organizations. With UNEP and WWF, the WCU participated in the preparation of a World Conservation Strategy, as a framework for sustainable development. This strategy was released in 1980. In 1991, its successor was launched under the title *Caring for the Earth: A Strategy for Sustainable Living*. It includes a wide range of recommendations for legal, institutional and administrative reform.

World Employment

An annual report published by the ILO. The 1996–97 report stated that about one billion people worldwide, or about one-third of the global labour force, were either unemployed or underemployed in 1995. This compared with about 820 million in 1993 and 1994. The ILO warned that the growing numbers of the 'working poor' would aggravate economic problems and social unrest. The UN agency argues that sustained economic growth was the best recipe for getting people back to work. The average unemployment in the EU during 1995 had been 11.3 per cent of the workforce; while unemployment in Central and Eastern Europe remained in double-digits. On the other hand, unemployment in the US had been below 6 per cent for 26 straight months. The report also said that there was no hard evidence to back up theories that technological change was displacing people; and there was no hard evidence that high levels of unemployment were inevitable.

World Environment Day

The fifth of June each year was adopted by the United Nations Conference on the Human Environment, 1972, to mark the beginning of the First Conference and as a means of focusing attention on national and world environment problems.

World Health Organization (WHO)

An agency of the UN, WHO came into being in 1948. Based in Geneva, WHO absorbed the health activities of the UN Relief and Rehabilitation Administration which had assisted the health departments of many countries with both advice and practical aid, the Paris office of epidemic intelligence, and the health organizations of the former League of Nations.

WHO became the sole international health organization. It operates with a high degree of autonomy, though directed and guided by the World Health Assembly which meets annually. The work of WHO encompasses the control of communicable diseases; water supply and waste disposal; air and water pollution; standards for biological and chemical substances; nutrition; food hygiene, and food standards; occupational health; the effects of radiation; psychosocial influences; carcinogenic risks; and environmental health impact assessment.

Health has been defined by WHO as 'a state of complete physical, mental and social well-being and not merely the absence of disease or infirmity'.

However, most assessments of health still rely upon morbidity and mortality statistics, such as infant- and child-mortality rates and the average life expectancy in various countries.

Smallpox (variola), until 1977 one of the world's most dreaded plagues, has been declared eradicated. Routine smallpox vaccination has been discontinued in most countries. The battles against such diseases as malaria, typhoid, typhus, schistosomiasis (bilharziasis) and yellow fever, continue.

In May, 1997, WHO published the results of an assessment of 12 toxic organic pollutants conducted by the International Program on Chemical Safety. The report found sufficient evidence to warrant international action to reduce or eliminate the discharge of the following chemicals: polychlorinated biphenyls (PCBs), dioxins, furans, aldrin, dieldrin, dichlorodiphenyltrichloroethane (DDT), endrin, chlordane, hexachlorobenzene (HCB), mirex, toxaphene and heptachlor, being substances which can be transported long distances from their sources by air and water.

In 1998, WHO entered a phase of restructuring with greater emphasis on such issues as chronic non-communicable diseases, urban environmental health problems, rising rates of cancer, cardiovascular diseases, mental illness, and the promotion of national health insurance systems. The task of reforming the WHO has fallen to Dr Gro Harlem Brundtland, former prime minister of Norway and chair of the World Commission on Environment and Development.

World Heritage List

A list created by the Convention for the Protection of the World Cultural and Natural Heritage (the Paris Convention) and administered by UNESCO. The convention came into force in 1975. The list includes properties of great cultural significance and geographic areas of outstanding universal value. To be included a nation must nominate the property or location to a World Heritage Committee consisting of 21 nations, elected from those nations who are parties to the convention. The executive body of the World Heritage Committee is the World Heritage Bureau. Well over 300 places and sites now appear on the World Heritage List. They include the Pyramids of Egypt, the Grand Canyon of the United States, the Taj Mahal of India, Westminster Abbey in London, Sagarmatha National Park (which embraces Mount Everest) in Nepal, the Great Wall of China, and the Great Barrier Reef of Australia.

World Trade Organization (WTO)

A body created by the Uruguay Round of the General Agreement of Tariffs and Trade (GATT) to give expression to and coordinate the application of that agreement. The WTO came into operation in 1995. More than 110 governments embracing over 80 per cent of the world's trade are members of WTO. Environmentalists have argued that further trade liberalization encourages economic growth and so damages the environment, further limiting the use of environmental protection measures. WTO committees have devoted much attention to the interaction of growing world trade and the environment.

World Wide Fund for Nature (WWF)

Formerly the World Wildlife Fund, a worldwide voluntary conservation organization with headquarters in Gland, Switzerland. While covering the major environmental issues, WWF runs its own practical, scientific research, and conservation projects in the field. WWF seeks to preserve genetic species and ecosystem diversity; to promote sustainable development; to minimize pollution and the overuse of resources and energy; and to reverse the accelerating degradation of the planet's natural environment.

In 1998, the WWF, the New Economics Foundation and the World Conservation Monitoring Centre at Cambridge, England, published the *Living Planet Report*, comparing the impact human activities were having on the global environment with the impact they had in 1960. The report stated that since 1960, the use of freshwater had doubled, causing a decline in freshwater habitats. Carbon dioxide emissions had also doubled; consumption of wood and paper had increased by two-thirds; and the consumption of sea fish had more than doubled. Most fish stocks were either fully exploited or declining, and few forests were being exploited sustainably. Consumption and population levels had continued to increase.

Z

Zoning

The most common development control; conventional zoning operates to reserve certain areas for specific land uses. The zoning ordinance generally divides the community into districts, and specifies for each the permitted uses, height and bulk of structures, minimum lot sizes, and dimensions and density of development. Many refinements to conventional zoning ordinances have been employed to protect environmental characteristics. Some of these are flexible zoning, environmental protection districts, performance standards, development zones and holding zones.

Traditionally, zoning is a technical or physical approach to the segregation of incompatible activities, such as housing and industry; it has certainly been effective in preventing generally the worst aspects of mixed development in new areas. However, it can achieve little in the short term to solve problems in existing areas. Zoning controls future development or redevelopment, while activities already established are granted 'existing use' rights which ensure continuity and even some limited expansion. The success of zoning depends upon the regulations being strictly applied, and rezoning applications being agreed to or refused only after full inquiry by a higher level of government. Many examples exist where slack administration, or simple non-enforcement, has allowed residential development to spring up in 'industrial zones' and around airports and large factories; further, green belts and buffer zones tend to have limited lives and to be slowly whittled away. There is also the problem where the large corporation selects its preferred site and seeks approval to construct a facility; if the proposal is of great economic and social value, the zonings are then swiftly adapted to the new situation. Planning then becomes reactive, responding as best it can to situations outside of its control.

Zoning has some profound implications, for in separating homes from workplaces a transportation problem emerges involving many in the lower-income categories. Zoning has also proved somewhat inflexible in its categories, for once they are written down in schedules they are found not to be suitable for specific cases. One solution suggested has been the introduction of performance standards, instead of zones; access to certain locations would thus depend on meeting criteria relating to aesthetics, noise, pollution, traffic, parking and other standards; however, such a concept is difficult to administer because of the scientific or subjective nature of the criteria. Zoning remains the preferred approach in North America and Europe. It has been applied in the area of national physical planning or macro-scale planning, to confine certain industries to certain areas and to protect major resources such as clay, sand, gravel, limestone, hard-rock and coal.

Zoning Ordinances, US

Laws passed by municipalities relating to the zoning of land. In the United States, these ordinances are made by municipalities without, in most cases, the endorsement of a higher level of government, though subject to challenge in the courts.

The zoning ordinance is the principle legal regulator of urban design; it specifies the uses to which property may be legally put and the intensity of development allowed, stated usually in terms of floor area. A zoning plan may often specify off-street parking requirements or off-street truck loading facilities as a ratio of floor area.

Zoning designations in the United States have become more and more elaborate, with numerous subclassifications to encompass complex variations and combinations. However, zoning ordinances are negative in the sense that they can protect the individual owner and the public from ill-suited developments but they cannot plan school locations, traffic movements, or create beauty, order and amenity. Further zoning ordinances are a parochial exercise, in the hands of local administrations and may not be linked with any community plan; indeed, they are often adopted in the absence of a city or town plan.

Generally, zoning ordinances or regulations contain:

- A text which lists the types of zones which may be used, and the regulations which may be imposed in each zone; these must be uniform throughout the zone. The text usually makes provision for the granting of dimensional variances, conditional use permits, and for nonconforming use of land and structures. Procedures for the granting of any zoning change are set out.
- A map showing the boundaries of the zoned area and the boundaries of each zone.
- Requirements in respect to the filling or excavation of land, the removal of natural resources, the use of watercourses and flood-prone land; the size, width, height, bulk and location of structures and buildings; setback lines; minimum or maximum areas or percentages of areas, courts, yards, or other open spaces which are left unoccupied, and minimum distances between buildings or other structures; floor area to ground area ratios; intersections, interchanges and transportation arteries.
- Requirements in respect to historical and conservation districts.

SHORT BIBLIOGRAPHY

Bates, G. (ed.) (1997), *Butterworths Environmental Management and Law Dictionary*, Butterworths, Sydney, Australia.

Encyclopaedia Britannica (1999), *Britannica Book of the Year*, Encyclopaedia Britannica Inc., Chicago, USA.

Gilpin, A. (1986), *Environmental Planning: A Condensed Encyclopedia*, Noyes Publications, New Jersey, USA.

Gilpin, A. (1995), *Environmental Impact Assessment: Cutting Edge for the Twenty-first Century*, Cambridge University Press, Cambridge, UK.

Gilpin, A. (1996), *Dictionary of Environment and Sustainable Development*, John Wiley & Sons, Chichester, UK.

Gilpin, A. (1999), *Environmental Economics: A Critical Overview*, John Wiley & Sons, Chichester, UK.

Kormondy, E.J. (ed.) (1989), *International Handbook of Pollution Control*, Greenwood Press, New York, USA.

Lin, S. (ed.) (1995), *UNEP's New Way Forward: Environmental Law and Sustainable Development*, UNEP, Nairobi, Kenya.

Robinson, N.A. (ed.) (1997), *Comparative Environmental Law and Regulation*, Oceana, New York, USA.

Shea, E.E. (1995), *Introduction to US Environmental Laws*, Oceana, New York, USA.

United Nations Environment Program (1996), *Handbook of Environmental Law*, UNEP, Nairobi, Kenya.

United Nations Environment Program (1997), *Register of International Treaties and Other Agreements in the Field of the Environment*, UNEP, Nairobi, Kenya.

White House (1992), *United States of America National Report to the UN Conference on Environment and Development 1992*, White House, Washington, DC, USA.